If You Have a Lemon, Make Lemonade

If You Have a Lemon,

Make Lemonade

WARREN HINCKLE

W. W. NORTON & COMPANY
New York • London

Printed in the United States of America
Library of Congress Catalog Card Number: 72-79525
Portions of this book have appeared in *Esquire* and *The Atlantic Monthly*.

First published as a Norton paperback 1990

Library of Congress Cataloging-in-Publication Data

Hinckle, Warren.
  If you have a lemon, make lemonade / Warren Hinckle.
      p.   cm.

    1. Hinckle, Warren.   2. Journalists—Unites States—Biography.
I. Title.
PN4874.H49A3   1990
070'.92—dc20
[B]   89-77172

ISBN 0-393-30636-4

W. W. Norton & Company, Inc., 500 Fifth Avenue, New York, N.Y. 10110
W. W. Norton & Company Ltd., 37 Great Russell Street, London WC1B 3NU

1 2 3 4 5 6 7 8 9 10

To Denise,

who put up with all this

But now bear with my foolishness for a moment.
I want to tell you, as I have promised I would,
how such events have taken place in me.
I know it to be a matter of no importance.
But I put myself forward only that I
may be of help to you. If you derive any profit,
I shall be consoled for my forwardness; if you do not,
I shall simply have displayed my foolishness.

—St. Bernard of Clairvaux (1091-1153)

ACKNOWLEDGMENTS:

Art Finger-Finley suggested the title, taken from the Gossage; Max and Anne Geismar goosed me into finally writing this book; Liadain O'Donovan typed the wretched mess until she wisely fled to Ireland for the duration, and Denise Hinckle took over that unenviable chore; my sister Vampira did early interviews with some of the victims herein; Cyrilly Abels was without peer as agent and counsel during the long and often frantic gestation period; June Oppen Degnan read it in takes, and told me what to take out; Peter Collier, in Berkeley, and Susan Cowley, in New York, got their fingers smudgy from plowing through the messy ms and flyspecking it for me; Decca Mitford saved me months of agony by making available her private account of the *Ramparts'* Coup D'Etat, which I have cowardly quoted in its entirety to get myself off the hook; G. M. Feigen spent many hours with me recalling the life and great times of our late friend Howard Gossage, and I know the process was painful for him; Cookie Picetti financed portions of this writing through the miracles of cash flow in his bar; Bill Turner provided important documents and memories of the Garrison investigation; if John Dodds, my editor, hadn't finally locked me up in an East German hotel in the garment district, this would still be a work in progress—the book is only two years overdue as it is, and Dodds has been so long-suffering as to be saintlike, were he not such a devil.

CONTENTS

Prologue: THE TUNNEL AT THE END OF THE LIGHT   ix

1. CATHOLIC DIRTY TRICKS   1

2. THE DRINKING PRESS   19

3. THE CULT OF THE CONVERT   35

4. LEAPING OVER THE WALL   53

5. RADICAL SLICK   89

6. GIVE US THIS DAY OUR PARANOIA   197

7. THE RELICS OF ST. CHE   269

8. CURTAINS FOR THE SIXTIES   337

Epilogue: ONE BLUSH FOR THE SEVENTIES   361

INDEX   365

Prologue:

THE TUNNEL AT THE END OF THE LIGHT

BEWARE the caption writers of the sixties. They lump it all as a decade of protest and malcontent, which it of course was. But to sloganize the whole slurs the very parts that make it understandable. The beginnings of the domestic wars of the sixties were considerably different from the end—as different in their way as the twenties from the fifties, goldfish swallowers from Joseph McCarthy followers.

In the beginning, we all believed. We believed in many things, but mostly in America. If the decade must be summarized, it could be said that the youth of America, who had so recently studied it in civics classes, tested the system—and it flunked.

It was the peculiar nature of my initiation into the disappointments of the decade that, for me, the bloom was first to come off the rose of the Catholic Church. But the early sixties were, for the most part, a study in progressive disillusion. Almost everyone started off believing in something —moral persuasion, civil disobedience, education, gradual progress, voting rights, effective new laws, good will among men—but those beliefs all ended as rumpled illusions.

It is not oversimplifying the history of this country to suggest that the system had really never been tested before the sixties. The past great debates in American politics, such as they have been, took place within the framework of what is fashionably called the "consensus"—a figment of political theory similar to, but far frailer than, the social contract, and as difficult to locate as the Garden of Eden—which was the

ix

textbook basis of liberal democracy: The idea was that interest groups are supposed to trade off issues, like haggling housewives at a garage sale. But in the nineteen-sixties two moral issues arose, tornadoes through the dust bowl of theory, that proved to be beyond the capacity of the atrophied "consensus" to cope with: the demand for racial equality, and the war in Vietnam. It is fair to observe that perhaps nobody on either side of these battles knew the system couldn't handle the problems; probably, everyone was surprised.

The protest movement of the early sixties was permeated by the overall sense of good feeling that one was helping one's fellows (or, subconsciously, one's lessers). It thrived on the optimism which is the blood plasma of liberalism—confront evil authorities and evil laws, show the people the wrong, and with adequate political pressure and education, the right law will be passed to correct the evil.

If that summary of the ethic of the early sixties sounds patronizing, it is not meant to be; that is simply the way we thought then. It is now easily forgotten that the beginnings of the New Left were as liberal and innocent of the ways of power as Doris Day is presumed to be of the ways of sodomy. Even the feared Students for a Democratic Society crawled from under a liberal rock. Tom Hayden's 1962 Port Huron manifesto launching SDS reads today more like Eisenhower's farewell address than a revolutionary tract; it even warns against the military-industrial complex and calls for a program to abolish poverty.

As late as 1964, when myopic television coverage of the Free Speech Movement was giving adult viewers the erroneous idea that four and ten letter words were coming from the mouths of babes on campus, SDS was still hanging in there with the system, opting to go at least "part of the way with LBJ" against the Hun, Barry Goldwater.

In 1964 *Ramparts* ran an election cover, which we thought daring at the time, portraying Goldwater as a rattlesnake. But Lyndon Johnson had barely got his automatic root beer machine and triple TV screen installed in the oval office than he turned and, viperlike, bit us all sorely in the collective liberal ass. The cynicism and despair in the democratic process that began to hang over the land like a tule fog were only partly of LBJ's immediate doing. They were the residue of lessons I had learned while banging about the country for several years as a domestic war correspondent:

That John Kennedy's, then Lyndon Johnson's much ballyhooed civil rights legislation amounted to a ton of horse feathers; that legislation without enforcement was Camelot without Merlin; that electing a peace President could get you a bigger war; that people in power would use the most reasonable arguments for the necessity of order and stability to maintain the most inequitable imbalance in a status quo of which they owned a piece, or hankered to. . . .

While we whites in our fashion were learning these and other lessons, the blacks had already suffered the results. And at a point, somewhere after Selma and before Watts, a curious bump was reached in the roller coaster politics of the sixties. Just as it appeared that many white activists were psychologically and politically prepared to join with more radical blacks in revolutionary approaches to political change—there was suddenly no more room left at the inn. While white students had been learning the hard way that there was little difference between the ways of power in Birmingham and Berkeley, the more oppressed black militants had abandoned the civil rights desk entirely to the likes of the NAACP.

The early sixties "We Shall Overcome" thing of black and white together was but nostalgia after Watts. There was considerable confusion and bleeding of hearts among white liberals by the ensuing period of "Thanks, but no thanks" to Whitey. The roots of that tension are deep, and were apparent earlier in SNCC, when black men began to take reasonable umbrage at well-meaning and well-stacked white coeds from Columbia and Brandeis who came South to help their movement by running their act. This black and white trauma occurred at a time when activist whites were undergoing the now popular phenomenon of being radicalized, and it is anyone's guess what would have happened next had not Lyndon Johnson, the *deus ex machina* of the Pedernales, intervened to reprogram white activists by escalating the war in Vietnam from a tea dance to a Wagnerian opera.

Along with a lot of Vietnamese over there, LBJ managed to kill off civil disobedience here. (That on the face of it is not something which the *National Review* might wish to cheer, as the idea of civil disobedience entailed an acceptance of the legitimacy of the institutions which the civilly disobedient were seeking by their example to change.) Sacrificial arrest made sense only as long as the people getting arrested thought the system could eventually effect the redress of their grievances; by mid-decade, it had become apparent to most that there just wasn't any give left in the old girl's girdle. It was a twice-told story, seemingly new to America, of the failure of the orderly process giving rise to the disorderly.

Catholic radicals such as Dan Berrigan were up front in the pack in the ensuing great race underground during the later sixties, and the accompanying shift from passive confrontation to active attack on the institutions of society. Catholicism, in many cases, seemed to speed up the metabolism of radicalism. Such a chemical-political reaction occurred at *Ramparts*. In 1964 we were still printing the cautious counseling of Thomas Merton in praise of the methods of Gandhi; hardly two years later the editors were burning their draft cards on the cover. Catholics, as radicals, tend to get a little hairy once they go through the unsettling discovery, as it happened at *Ramparts*, that Holy Mother the Church had been lying to them all those years; that leaves just about everything else up for grabs; if the Church was a perversion of its promise, there was no reason to believe the government could be anything but worse. Another factor tending to make politicized Catholics such wild men is that Catholics generally come from unsophisticated political and intellectual backgrounds. They thus are not tied down by any of the super-cautious respect for institutions, or dogmatic or dialectical considerations that so often hidebound more traditionally reared liberals and leftists of the variety inhabiting the Eastern seaboard. The speed and style of such a crude metamorphosis proved more upsetting to traditional leftists than even to rightists, and thus *Ramparts* came to be viewed with alarm from both directions.

That, with a little help from hindsight, is the larger, gloomier context, so as to guard against nostalgia, of the stories I have now to tell of the glory years of the sixties. They begin when black was still a paint color and the word in popular usage was "Negro." Those years now seem as distant in time and kind as Watts from Edwardian England. After 1968, radical politics went to the bomb and *Ramparts* went bust.

But before that, considerable madness went down. Among other unnatural phenomena of money, religion and politics to be described in these pages, the New York *Times* sent an investigative reporter to San Francisco to determine whether it was Moscow or Peking gold that was filling *Ramparts'* coffers, and the Minutemen offered to help unmask the real killer of John F. Kennedy. The record of these events is filled equally with errors and victories. However it does account for some basic changes in the style and content of American journalism in the sixties, which gave the government a little deserved consternation while at the same time occasioning hemorrhages of outrage on the American left, old and new.

If there is any single motif to the stories in this volume —which are so much a chronicle of the bizarre and the unexpected, the improvident and the perverse—it is that they are instructive of that principle of life enunciated by my friend, the late Howard Gossage: "If you have a lemon, make lemonade."

Many such lessons were learned, and it is best to begin somewhere near the beginning, which was with the Church of Rome in San Francisco.

1.

Catholic Dirty Tricks

THERE is something to be said for the disadvantages of Catholic education, at least as it was in San Francisco of the logy, foggy fifties. For one thing, in grammar school I learned about ransoming pagan babies. We had to save our dimes to ransom the poor unbaptized creatures of China. To facilitate the financial aspect of this spiritual transaction, we purchased savings certificates—watermarked in the fuzzy purple of the nuns' hectograph machine and resembling somewhat Blue Chip Stamps—which were popularly known as "Pagan Baby Stamps." When we had accumulated sufficient markers, we were assured that a yellow pagan baby of our choice would receive a Catholic baptism. We also got to name it, with a saint's name, of course. It cost five dollars to ransom a boy, and three dollars for a girl. The good Sisters explained that girls came cheaper, since the Chinese routinely drowned girls at birth, like baby kittens, because there were so many of them. This led to considerable discussion about the relative value of boys and girls, and provoked a compromise, arranged by the nuns, which was widely considered a bargain: for ten dollars we could ransom one boy and two girls.

The Catholic umbrella under which I grew up shaded a vacuum-sealed, middle-class and unflinchingly white ghetto. We all went to Catholic schools and our parents paid their dues and regularly received the sacraments, as did we kids, but it was more routine than a leap of faith. The Church seemed everywhere, Authority incarnate, yet it didn't really connect. It was authority largely without terror. The Church I

1

knew was not the Church of Savonarola, nor of James Joyce—it was too settled and comfortable to summon the fire and brimstone for Stephen Dedalus-type retreats. The priests who weren't stuck in the confessional box on Saturdays put on Pendleton sport shirts and went off to play golf at the Irish Catholic Olympic Club. Our confessors did scare us a little by warning we could lose our minds and maybe even our hair if we touched ourselves, but suggested that if we pulled hard on an ear it would dispel temptation. Naturally we tugged our ears, but otherwise the operating principle was to accept everything the Church taught while paying as little attention to it as possible. Thus we went to Mass on Sundays and sinned on Mondays and went to confession on Saturdays so we could receive Communion on Sunday and be in a state of grace to sin again on Monday.

I came to accept the Church for the tinsel, lazy, corrupt and at the same time appealing thing that it was. During those gray and quiet years, the Church was like some pervasive closed system dominating an endless science fiction novel, wherein it seemed the fate of the mutinous among us to do continuous, dubious battle against it; there was great fun in the rum of rebellion, and we fought on in the not unpleasant expectation of losing. Changing the Church was no more real than changing the ocean.

This background ill prepared me for the liberal Catholic reformers with whom I became involved in the early sixties. I was astonished to find that there were Catholics abroad who actually thought that unyielding institution was going to improve itself and thereby improve the world. Most of the reformers I encountered had not endured sixteen years of Catholic education as I had, but had escaped to prep schools and secular colleges far removed from the bad breath and pimples of the workaday Church.

I found it difficult to believe that these earnest people were attempting to make a blushing bride of that fine old whore, the Church. While these reformers were shocked to discover how materialistic the Vatican really was, I had learned in grammar school that profitable moneychanging was the natural condition of the priestly calling. Our pastor used to stand in front of the altar during collections at Christmas Mass and exhort the faithful to "make it a green Christmas." The reformers were freshly aglow with the illuminating theological proposition that the Church was as much human as divine; I knew that was the truth back in the third grade the first time I heard a nun fart.

I later watched the priests cream these well-meaning liberals: Lions 14, Christians 0. The odds were lopsided from the start. Just as the tougher, peasant Stalin made a better revolutionary than the more bourgeois and intellectual bolsheviks, these starry-eyed Catholic reformers with their idealized view of the Church were no match for the crafty and possessive priest-Pachucos who gave out karate chops instead of blessings. Most of the young priests who rushed to the aid of the reformers were likewise clobbered and have long since left the Church, along with a goodly percentage of the reformers. They succeeded in vulgarizing the Mass and making some other niggling reforms, and then drifted off to various new enthusiasms—anglicism, agnosticism, even astrology —leaving confusion in their wake, like little kids taking apart some gigantic radio set to improve the reception, then tiring of the project but not knowing how to put the set back together. These thwarted reformers then became bitter at the Church for doing what came naturally to preserve the monolith. The difference in my expectations of the Church of Rome and that of many of the liberal intellectual Catholics of the early sixties was that of sixteen years in Catholic schools, which were susceptible to all the analogies of *Stalag 17*.

CATHOLIC REFORM SCHOOL

My Catholic education taught me never to trust a priest —under or over 30. They became quite vicious if one threatened their sense of authority or in any way profaned their pride, which I was constantly doing. Here they had given up their lives in the service of God, got up at five every morning to say Mass, and wore lousy black gabardine slacks that itched, and had tossed their sex lives in the wastebasket and, goddamnit, they expected the laymen-serfs to click their heels and pay proper respect.

My four years in Catholic high school were a boot camp in guerrilla warfare against overweening authority. I served my sentence at Riordan High School, a newish cement-walled institution that served as sort of a respectable Catholic reform school for the children of lower-middle-class San Francisco Italian and Irish families and was otherwise distinguished by having been named after an Archbishop who had been killed by a train.

The student body was a monstrous assembly of truants who enjoyed committing battery on the men who had consecrated their bodies to God. The unenviable title of the worst of our bad lot was generally considered a tossup between myself and another student who had the unpleasant habit upon boarding a streetcar of unzipping his pants and urinating in the fare box. In the World War II epics popular at the time, John Wayne always painted tiny Japanese suns on the fuselage of his plane each time he bagged a Zero. Similarly, the lads at Riordan maintained a running box score on how many religious we were able to send down in flames.

Our teachers were the Brothers of Mary, an uninspired religious order whose ranks held the usual number of failed hedonists and sexual malcontents. The brothers, who preferred double-breasted black business suits to the more traditional clerical robes, were on the spectrum of religious vocation between the dull gray of the consecrated eunuch and the purple glory of the priesthood. In addition to the vows of poverty, chastity and obedience, they took an additional vow, that of special devotion to the Blessed Virgin Mary, an inamorata they referred to with some intimacy as the "BVM." The order was like a religious displaced persons camp for grade four and lower civil servants.

The all-male Riordan student body was warned about the physical dangers of public high schools, not the least of which was the hazard of bloody Kotex that shameless Protestant and Jewish girls were said to drop carelessly on dark stairways. Our contact with the outside world was largely limited to mandatory special pleading to the Lord to free Cardinal

Mindszenty from an atheistic holding cell in Hungary, and reading about contemporary events in the brown pages of a jejune publication called the *Junior Catholic Messenger*, which featured front-page photos of the eminent Catholic junior Senator from Wisconsin, Joseph McCarthy, buzzing about the Senate subway doing God's work in Washington.

Catholic high school proved an excellent place to learn the nature of bureaucracy and the fine art of bamboozling. I gained access to the school sherry supply and discovered the wonderful world of banquets and cocktail parties, the entrance to which could be gained by creating sundry committees, letterheads and other artifacts of eleemosynary hoodwinkery. I and my childhood buddy, a kindred musketeer named Gerry Davalos, got happily drunk every Saturday afternoon excepting Advent and Lent by putting on our good suits and walking into strange wedding receptions in the Catholic catering halls of the Sunset District, where we pretended that we were the groom's relations to the bride's people, and vice versa.

While thus being educated, I discovered that I was a print junky. I made the school newspaper my personal fiefdom to indulge my insatiable craving for the joys of printing plants—clunking linotypes spitting out words of metal, Ludlow machines creating veritable milky ways of headlines in type fat and thin, hissing stereotype machines, ill-mannered printers cursing instructively. For me, no secrets of science or metaphysics were comparable to that miraculous process whereby words were transported from your head through a typewriter to a typesetter into metal artfully arranged, which produced a printed page. If there was a heaven, it had to have a composing room. The printing plant over which I first lusted was a squat green building on the wrong side of Market Street called the Garrett Press, which produced shoppers and dreary house organs. (I began putting out newspapers there when I was thirteen and was still at it nearly two decades later at *Ramparts*, which, to keep me amused, published two newspapers, one of them a daily.)

I had found my place in the sun in this dark, dingy printing

plant which I thought of as King Solomon's Mines. I would
stand bent over the makeup forms for hours on end, drunk
with the ordeal. I became ecstatic when, in violation of all
union rules, I was allowed to handle a piece of hot type. The
hours I spent in the company of printers came to exceed those
in the classroom, and gave me quite a different view of the
universe than that afforded by the Brothers of Mary. I spent
my spare time and money on pilgrimages to the out-of-town
newspaper stands, which were located between skid row and
the red light district. I would step obliviously over the bodies
of winos and dodge around hookers to reach the delicious
racks of stale newspapers, and come away burdened with as
many copies as my money could buy of the New York *Daily
News*, the defunct Los Angeles *Daily News* and its also dead-
and-gone successor, *The Mirror*; at the time I had a crush on
tabloids.

Often at night I traveled to Mecca, which was the rundown
sports department of the San Francisco *Examiner*, where a
kindly, drunken old Hearst deskman would let me stand
around and drool over the teletype machines. My traveling
companion in these excursions was my high school sports
editor, a burly football player named Jim Clifford, who had
the reasonably balanced view of our journalistic calling that it
came somewhere after football and girls. One evening as we
stood watching the teletypes pound and ring in the news a
slight incident occurred that was illustrative of where my head
was at this point in young manhood. A copyboy dumped off
several copies of the advance "bulldog" news section of the
Sunday paper, printed early to be trucked off to the boonies
and filled with undated features about trout fishing in Alaska
and publicity stills of aspiring Swedish starlets with their titties
showing.

"Jez-zus, look at that!" Clifford said, staring at a large
front-page photograph of a girl with a cleavage as deep as the
Grand Canyon. But all I noticed was the unusual red headlines in a typeface the conservatively madeup *Examiner* normally reserved for world wars.

"Wow, that's really something," I replied to the salivating

Clifford. "That's beautiful! Can you imagine running 60 point Cheltenham italic in red ink?"

Clifford gave me a very strange look, and all the way home on the streetcar that night he read the sports section in silence, occasionally glancing up to stare at me as if I were some sort of nut.

The Brothers of Mary were so delighted to be rid of my person that they made me the valedictorian, a gesture they had cause to regret when I delivered an X-rated speech. I took at least one of them over the wall with me. He was a beanstalk-tall and scarecrow-thin friar with a mordant sense of Christianity, one Brother Nunes, a high-speed talker with a clapped-out sinus that occasioned his voice to come out his nose with the pitch and whine of a jet engine. Brother Nunes was constantly taking hits off a Vicks Inhaler, a habit he claimed I drove him to by my didos on the school paper, which he had the unwelcome detail of moderating. He described himself as hounded by the furies of Irish Catholic teenage journalists *manqués*. My co-conspirator in driving the good Brother to burn his black gabardines was Dan O'Neill—who in the sixties became the *enfant terrible* cartoonist at the San Francisco *Chronicle*, the creator of the comic strip Odd Bodkins, syndicated in some 300 papers while he was still in his early twenties. He was fired at the peak of his popularity for outrageously inserting Morse code obscenities and recruiting messages for the Irish Republican Army in his strip, and thereafter went underground in Belfast, where he drew propaganda comic strips for the IRA. After letting the two of us loose in the world, Brother Nunes quit.

EYEBALL TO EYEBALL WITH THE JESUITS

At various times during the checkered decade past I have been called licentious, a profligate, an adventurer, a sensationalist, a wastrel, a capitalist guerrilla, a boozer, a corpo rate wrecker, a degenerate, a wheeler-dealer, and a pirate, among other things.

There exist sufficient grounds for most of those appellations that they could be regarded as faint praise unto the truth, which is that all I am now or may be considered to be I owe to the Jesuits.

Jesuit college education was a continuing Congress of Wonders, at times approaching the delirium of a mushroom sect. One professor spoke confidentially of undertaking scientific experiments in support of the little-known theory of Justinian that homosexuality was the cause of earthquakes. Theology units were earned by becoming versed in the finer points of religious etiquette, such as if one's gums were bleeding one could swallow the blood and still receive Communion without breaking one's fast, but if one cut one's finger one could not suck it, finger blood apparently being of a different theological type than gum blood. The instruction concerning women seemed peculiar even in that insensitive time of the mid-1950's—women were worthy to receive Communion on their tongues, but no other part of their anatomy could come into contact with the Host; the rules were different for men. If a woman lay dying and for some ungodly reason had to be annointed on the mouth, her lipstick must be first wiped off or else the sacrament of Extreme Unction, like vaccination under the wrong conditions, might not take.

Seniors were required to take a Last Chance course in the Catholic dos and do nots about sex; when, on occasion, a married student, as none others could dare to speak on the subject for fear of scandal, would raise a practical objection to the explicit instructions, such as how could a priest know what gives with sexual foreplay, the answer would invariably come, in the manner of the Jesuits, in another question: Did a doctor have to endure cancer in order to treat it?

Sex seemed to be the only exception to the general principle of plasticity characteristic of the Jesuit approach to moral and religious absolutes. Their Hard Line on carnality led them, historically, to some extremes, such as removing the stairs to Madame de Pompadour's apartment so as to render more difficult the entrance of Louis XV to her bedchamber, for which, among other peccadillos, they were kicked out of court.

In addition to such mandatory instructions in theology, the Jesuits insisted that their students at the University of San Francisco, locally known by the call letters USF, learn about "the warped logic of Lenin." This study came under the academic category of political science, and everyone was required to take Poli Sci 140: "The Philosophy, Dynamics and Tactics of International Communism." The text for the course was J. Edgar Hoover's *Masters of Deceit*, and the FBI Director was said to be kindly disposed toward the Jesuit Fathers for unloading so many thousands of copies right there in the USF bookstore.

The ringmaster of Political Science 140 was Raymond T. Feeley, S.J., a bulldog-faced padre known as the "waterfront priest" for his activities in the 1930's on the labor-strife-torn San Francisco docks in the cause of anti-communism and responsible Catholic unionism, a phrase some of Fr. Feeley's critics translated as meaning pro-management.

Fr. Feeley was a tough man, said to have single-handedly tossed several Reds into the chill waters of San Francisco Bay. He stared a good deal when in the classroom, constantly peering up and down the rows of wooden chairs as if he expected to find a red herring underneath. He called the attendance role in a way that made you feel you should answer "Not Guilty" instead of "Present." We took notes from a scratchy recording of the "confession" of Whittaker Chambers. Our guest professors included an exiled Russian Jesuit named Urusov and the visiting Irish Catholic heads of the intelligence units called "Red Squads" in metropolitan police departments.

Fr. Feeley's lectures ran red with the blood of bolshevik history. He established a peculiar sense of authority by never referring to the great figures in Russian history by their common political names, reverting instead to their original Russian names, enunciating each syllable as if it were one count in an indictment:

Not Stalin, but *Jos-if Vis-sar-iono-vich Dju-gash-vi-li.*
Not Lenin, but *Vla-dim-ir Ill-ich Ul-yan-ov.*

Those four Ivory Tower years were therefore spent in a sort of Charlie Chaplin waltz, learning what I was forced to learn to stay in the place, then unlearning it from the original sources. Those academic activities I carried on in my spare time, most waking hours being devoted to playing with the school newspaper, the *Foghorn*, and its necessary corollary of engaging in guerrilla warfare against the Jesuits. I had but one eye so I was excused from the fangs of the Reserve Officers Training Corps known otherwise as ROTC. (My left eye had been blanked out in an automobile accident when I was eight.)

I, nevertheless, received plenty of military training in actual combat with the Jesuits.

When you are on the offensive against them the Jesuits work man to man rather than employing a zone defense. The Jesuit assigned to do me in was the Rev. Francis A. Moore, the Dean of Students, a tall, sun-tanned, cobra-eyed Jesuit with the stock smile of a hired assassin.

Moore did not like me, possibly because of an unfortunate incident in Corvallis, Oregon, in 1957 when I threw up all over him. I was drunk as only a college freshman can get, wandering aimlessly in the bowels of a basketball stadium, when two sportsmen from the rival college asked if I wanted some creme de menthe; I thought that was terrific of them and slugged the green substance down, which turned out to be liquid hand soap. This inconvenienced a number of USF rooters shortly after, when I staggered into the crowded stands and became violently ill. One of the unfortunate few within range was the Dean of Students, who I doubt ever forgave me that vile cascade of green slime and vomit down his black back. He threw the book at me for the putative crime of being drunk and disgraceful in a public rooting place.

That was the first—but the only one that stuck—in a relentless string of prosecutions and entrapments, the others of which I somehow escaped in the cliffhanger tradition of "Daredevils of the Red Circle"—a stubborn pin left standing in a 24-hour Jesuit bowling alley. I survived attempted firings, suspensions and expulsions, and those failing or being preempted, Jesuit threats and attempts to use the lend-lease power of the civil authorities for the prosecution of various offenses to the commonweal such as arson. An impartial observer of this extended combat once likened the relationship between the Dean of Students and me as that of Cardinal Richelieu to D'Artagnan—but if the truth be told we were both more Lady de Winter.

The Dean especially held against me the matter of the Jesuit President's niece, a flower of Irish Catholic girlhood whom I dated during my stormy career as Casey Crime Photographer at USF, which courtship Fr. Moore apparently assumed made it more difficult to whip me at the pillory lest she get upset; he was outraged, wrongly considering it a high card of knavery on my part, refusing to accept the relationship for the coincidence of honest affection that it was. His loathing rose to a new boiling point on the occasion, in the midst of an especially dull news week, when my friend Brennan Newsom and I burned down a wooden guard house protecting the entrance to the campus—all so I would have something to headline in the *Foghorn*, which I then edited.

I produced an inflammatory front-page editorial denouncing the arsonist as having no respect for private property and called upon the Dean of Students to get off his ordained duff, find the maniac responsible, and "root this evil from our midst." I recommended expulsion for the guilty party. The Dean knew, by intuition and stool pigeons, that I had done it, but he had no proof, the San Francisco Police arson inspectors only added fuel to his slow burn when, at his suggestion, they asked me my whereabouts at the time of the crime, and I replied that I had spent the night with the President's niece.

At the age of 18 I fell into the practice, having somewhere read that Gogol used to write in taverns, of working in bars, a habit of industry that I have maintained with religious consistency since. There is little in the job description of an editor that cannot be accomplished in a good saloon. Such tasks as reading, thinking, editing, interviewing, writing, laying out pages, conferring with colleagues, and general plotting and inventing lend themselves to the calming environment of a proper pub, particularly as opposed to the busy work, artificiality, social climbing and general beadledom of an office. You can be telephoned at a bar if people must, but the very distance from an office discourages trivia; and, as you are escaping the tyranny of your own institution, you can tell the bartender to say that you have left; a professional bartender is an infinitely more effective liar than the most efficient secretary. I have consequently maintained offices for the necessary evils that they encompass but have gone to them as infrequently as possible; over the years I have been the more productive, if in some dry minds the more notorious, for it.

The Jesuits recklessly struck down a technical improvement I had ordered—the installation of a telephone extension from the university switchboard to a bar I frequented some ten blocks distant. I retaliated by sawing up Fr. Moore's favorite table, a round rostrum of golden wood at which he sat in kangaroo court judgment of truant students, fashioning from the remains a horseshoe-shaped copy desk for the *Foghorn* office. I was indignant that these black pimpernels of the Pope would deign to be holier than thou about my right to drink. I vowed to spill as much Jesuit liquor as was humanly possible, and launched a blitzkrieg against temperance by a series of soirees, conferences and dinners on campus to which I invited important citizens of the town whose favor the Jesuits curried, so the Fathers could not but acquiesce in the serving of drinks. The result each time was that the staff of the student paper got thoroughly swacked. Such activities led to my becoming known, in an analogy not always used in a completely complimentary sense, as the Elsa Maxwell of USF.

The grandest party of all was hosted at Jesuit expense when I turned the *Foghorn* into a daily newspaper. It was a surprise party for the Jesuits, as they did not know it was happening. I had laid cunning plans to make the paper a daily, keeping them strictly to myself, as does a prisoner on Devil's Island an escape plan. This was a politic thing to do as even those minority Jesuits favorably disposed to me considered me a young Dr. Strangelove of journalism.

So I secretly wrote an inch-thick white paper explaining the new daily publishing schedule in which, in the sacred tradition of white papers, I rationalized the increased work load as actually less work for everyone. For security, I had that classified document printed and bound at Stanford University Press and sent the bill to the Jesuits. I distributed it after dark to a clandestine gathering of the newspaper staff a week before D (daily) Day, all reporters pledging not to let it fall into any Jesuit hands. I wrote a press release —"New Era of Journalism at USF; *Foghorn* Becomes First Catholic College Daily Newspaper in U.S."—and handed it to the university publicity man with exact instructions on how to distribute it to the news media. Carl Nolte, the flack, was a former *Foghorn* man so I thought I could trust him. But he turned out a journalistic Judas and sent the press release to the Dean for approval.

The morning the first edition was secretly scheduled to go to press I called Nolte to see if the announcement had gone out on time. The flack admitted that he had shown it to Fr. Moore, and that Fr. Moore had ripped it up. "He said you're not going daily," Nolte said. "He said you didn't get permission, and he's not going to let you do it, anyway." I began screaming in the general direction of the receiver, banging it on the table with such fury that the instrument broke in half and further communication was thereby ended, so I never did get to tell Nolte what I thought.

When I could walk again, I went directly to the nearest bar and composed a telegram announcing the daily publication of the *Foghorn*, which I sent to every newspaper in the state. I then sent out another telegram to various judges and city officials, prominent alumni, former *Foghorn* editors, and a goodly number of San Francisco reporters who would cross the Sahara itself for a free drink, inviting them all to a grand party that night to celebrate the *Foghorn* becoming a daily newspaper. I also invited many congressmen and senators in Washington, who of course would not come, but I knew someone on their staff would draft a routine telegram of congratulations. I told every Jesuit with whom I was on speaking terms to come to a party, neglecting to say what for.

Fr. Moore walked belatedly into the campus banquet hall that night and found it as packed as a Breughel people-scape with drunken newspapermen, students, Jesuits, San Fran-

cisco politicians and fat cat alumni, all raising toasts and sing-
ing hosannas to the grand event of the *Foghorn* becoming a
daily. Six girls wearing white tee-shirts with *"DAILY
FOGHORN"* emblazoned across the front—and otherwise
skimpily costumed in the tradition of the old *Paris Herald
Tribune* newsgirls—were dancing through the crowd dis-
tributing copies fresh off the press of the next morning's
edition of the *Foghorn*, with red headlines across the top of the
front page: "CITY'S FOURTH DAILY IS BORN."

I walked up to Fr. Moore and handed him two telegrams of
congratulations—from Vice President Richard Nixon and
Senator John F. Kennedy. He looked pale and I suggested he
break his fast and have a drink.

The next day the San Francisco newspapers all carried
editorials congratulating the University of San Francisco on
its great journalistic leap forward. It was a great victory for the
doctrine of *fait accompli*.

Once an exhausted student journalist, his eyes smallpox red
from lack of sleep, his grade point average dropping below
the freezing point, asked me a question about newspaper
frequency. He wanted to know why—as USF offered no journalism courses and gave no academic credit or relief for long
unpaid volunteer hours spent working on the newspaper
—just why did I want to go daily when everyone was already
half dead from the ball-busting effort of producing a weekly?

I understood at that moment why General Patton slapped
the crying soldier. I restrained my reply to a single decibel
answer: "Why? You fool, I'll tell you why. Because it's more
fun!"

It seems that I am possessed at times of an ungovernable
tendency to increase the pace and frequency of things. This
has to do with many activities in life, including mischief, and,
of course, publishing. I have made of quarterlies, monthlies;
of monthlies, biweeklies; and of weeklies, dailies. I once, in an
emergency, put out my college yearbook in six weeks, start to
finish, as the editor of record had fallen into a fearful lethargy
and had done nothing all year save hold meetings, finally

resigning and hiding himself in a closet; I found that to be a cheering crisis and volunteered to produce it in the six weeks before school ended.

The mechanics of the metamorphosis of the *Foghorn* from weekly into daily were outlandishly simple: the weekly newspaper was six standard garbage-can-liner-sized pages; I divided that whole into several parts—tabloid-sized pages suitable for emptying a small vacuum cleaner bag. The daily was therefore actually no more than the same substance as the weekly, yet by certain manipulations of format and frequency and saying it was so, it was now a daily. (Years later, when I told Howard Gossage this, he pointed out that I had without realizing it hit upon one of his fundamental principles: "Never mistake the thing promoted for the thing itself.")

This particular daily was supposed to come out three times a week—sometimes it came out four times, sometimes twice, occasionally once. I defended the semantics involved by citing that bible of the newspaper industry, *Editor and Publisher*, which luckily listed 14 colleges as having daily newspapers that came out three times weekly—but that was largely a dodge. I have never been too impressed by the arbitrary cycles of publication frequency, which by and large have a deleterious effect on content. In the five years I edited *Ramparts*, there was only one year when we actually published twelve times in twelve months. I often held an edition to get an important story so that by the time the April issue was ready to come out it would be nearly May, so we would "lose" April. I was forever writing notices to our subscribers from "the little man who runs our computer," informing them that their subscriptions would be extended as we had just "lost" another month. This practice gained *Ramparts* some important stories it would otherwise have lost but drove librarians to frenzy; they were always writing to ask where was April, and I would write back and say never to worry, that April was May, a simple enough metaphysic that they often failed to comprehend. (The entire dating game on magazines is a phony, anyway. If you subscribe to *Esquire*, it will come in the mail in the beginning of May but be dated June. That insanity is largely to accommodate illiterate newsstand dealers, who have become accustomed over the years to throwing away anything with an honest date; a May magazine in May is considered "stale.")

The strange thing called the *Daily Foghorn* was a monster frog in a small pond, causing distraction and disruption to those things the Jesuits held dear. Their nice Catholic college paper was transformed into a freak of Hearst proportions: "Sunday A.M." Extras, weekday "5 A.M." Extras, banner headlines in type suitable for the sinking of the Titanic, vitriolic front-page opinions, special editions, magazine supplements, exclusives in red ink, incessant and bitchy editorial crusades.

Jesuits picking up their campus paper read such headlines as "Virginia City Priest Assaults 47-Year-Old Woman Polio Victim"... "ROTC General Attempts to Strangle Student"... "Dorothy Day Asks: Who Baptized Capitalism?" The school newspaper paid scant attention to the school, its pages filled with Herblock cartoons and AP stories such as "Napoleon Memoirs Sold." (The *Foghorn* needed an AP wire as it did a jackhammer, but I installed one, to Jesuit dismay, as I have always had a fondness for teletypes—the kind that some men have for ladies' shoes or subway turnstiles.)

I assigned myself to cover the 1960 Winter Olympics in Squaw Valley, where I had a ball telegraphing front-page stories night press rate collect and otherwise ran the newspaper for two weeks via long distance telephone and telegraph from the bar at a ski lodge.

One Hallowe'en I stole the entire press run of the S.F. State College newspaper, thereby inspiring Fr. Moore to attempt to have grand theft charges brought against me. The Administration constantly tried to cut off the *Foghorn*'s funds so as to bring this roller coaster to a halt, and I was forever staying up nights drafting financial reports and revised budgets to stymie their attempts at sabotage. Near graduation, the Dean of Students sent me a bill for some $13,000, which he claimed was the *Foghorn* deficit, which I must personally pay before receiving my grades.

I had to get the famous barrister Jake Ehrlich to threaten the Society of Jesus with a lawsuit before I could get my transcript.

The *Daily Foghorn* had a short life. As soon as I left, the Jesuits busted it in rank back to a weekly.

2.

The Drinking Press

IN 1960 daily journalism was still a competitive enterprise in San Francisco. The *Chronicle* and the *Examiner* were slugging it out for the city's breakfast table readership and a good time was being had by all of us gladiators in the possession of a press pass. The perfume of blood was about us: The *Chronicle* was besting the *Examiner*'s time-immemorial circulation lead. The brainy *Chronicle* had traditionally been the weaker sister to the brawny Hearst *Examiner*. The *Chronicle*'s appellation of brainy stemmed from the years that editor Paul Smith used the daily to practice being a boy wonder before going off to Gotham in the fifties to save *Collier's*, where he ended up going down with the ship. Smith had also contributed to the *Chronicle*'s reputation of being a liberal newspaper. Yet its liberalism was, as is most liberalism, schizophrenic. While the paper's Republican ownership consistently endorsed GOP candidates for almost every office save dogcatcher (that position not being elective in San Francisco), the reporters, many of them refugees from the Eastern Establishment who would suffer anything short of hemophilia to live in San Francisco, were allowed relative freedom to attempt to write the other side in the news columns.

The *Examiner*, on the other hand, was paranoid. Still coasting on circulation gains achieved during Hearst's promotion of what became the Spanish-American War, the paper generally read like the house organ of the fallout-shelter industry. There were other telling differences, the women's pages of the two dailies providing perhaps the sharpest contrast. The *Examiner*'s women's pages ran helpful household hints, bulletins about parish bingo games (illegal but then sacrosanct in San Francisco), and formal photographs of Irish Catholic virgins in pageboy haircuts and junior prom décolletages who were about to commit the sacrament of matrimony. The *Chronicle*'s were filled with Paris and New York fashions, lengthy descriptions of the vacation plans of publisher Charles de Young Theriot's friends and neighbors, and sycophantic reports on the high jinks of San Francisco society, which was almost entirely Protestant and Jewish. The fact that a man presided over the *Chronicle*'s women's section was slightly more than the monumental manifestation of male chauvinism it would appear. City-room legend had it that the chain-linkage of male women's-page editors had originated some time back after Jane Maggard, one of the last female women's editors, printed a society news headline in the first Sunday edition after VJ-Day that read: THE BACHELORS ARE BACK WITH THEIR WONDERFUL BALLS! (The *Chronicle*'s women's section has recently been liberated and is run by women again, but the section's name has been changed to just plain "People.")

An interesting myth has grown up that San Francisco is an "open" town. The truth is now more in the opposite direction. The city officialdom has reacted with Teutonic grimness to the heralded flourishing of free life-styles within the city limits. The cops busted the beatniks, hassled the hippies, and lately are harassing the topless clubs out of business. In these enterprises they were egged on by the *Examiner*, which was the paper read by the long-dominant Irish Catholics whose stucco single-family dwellings anchored down the sand dunes; everybody on the block where I grew up, except for one family rumored to be Unitarian, took the *Examiner*. That paper's last days of glory were in the fifties, when it applauded the city authorities for prosecuting Allen Ginsberg's dirty poem, "Howl," and for mopping up North Beach with the unsavory beatniks who were making the town an unsafe place for sailors to get laid.

The *Examiner*'s slow-motion fall from circulation grace was due in part to the fact that a good percentage of its long-standing Irish readership had died and been buried. The *Chronicle*, by virtue of its comparative sophistication and sheer deviltry, gradually became the San Francisco paper read by the burgeoning, freeform suburbs. More specifically, it was due to the P. T. Barnumship of *Chronicle* editor Scott Newhall, a crusading journalist with a magnificent sense of the bizarre, with whom I was to become friends for reasons other than the fact that he had only one leg and I had only one eye.

One of Scott Newhall's most valuable columnists was "Count Marco," a lad whom Newhall had perversely enthroned on the women's page, amidst considerable ballyhoo about his royal blood, to provide a daily dose of male chauvinism; the Count gave the ladies bitchy advice on how to dress and undress, even unto connubial instructions on the ladylike way to climb into the bathtub with one's submerged husband watching—that column was headlined: HOW TO AVOID LOOKING LIKE A TORN BLIMP AS YOU ENTER THE TUB. This sort of copy had occasioned outcries of lust and horror among the Jesuits, and, while a vice-busting college editor, I had tracked down the sticky truth that the Count was really an itinerant hairdresser named Henry Spinelli, and I exposed him as phony royalty and a degenerate cur in the Catholic yellow pages of the *Foghorn*. This occasioned some minor embarrassment at the *Chronicle* and whoops of glee at the rival media.

When I applied for a job at the *Chronicle* some months thereafter, that act of perfidy hung about me like a leper's bell. The city editor, Abe Mellinkoff, usually did the hiring, but he sent me on to Newhall's office for further X-ray examination of my head. Newhall was still a little pissed, but more puzzled; he asked what manner of demon nerve had brought me to darken the *Chronicle*'s doorway after what I had done to it. I couldn't think of a good reason, so I said just what came into my head: It had been a good story; I didn't hear him denying it; hell, he should be proud of me for exposing the *Chronicle* so artfully; he would have done the same thing if he'd been in my place . . . and, besides, if I were him I'd rather have a journalistic menace like me working for the *Chronicle* than for the opposition. Newhall smiled a buccaneer's smile, and said he would think about it; I was hired the next day.

Westbrook Pegler, Sr., once likened the Hearst newspaper policies he helped formulate to "a screaming woman running down the street with her throat cut." Newhall ran the *Chronicle* somewhat along the lines of that logical imperative, only he substituted entertainment and the outrageous for the merely sensational. It wasn't that the *Chronicle* completely disregarded facts—despite its pizzaz there was more news in it than in most duller papers; but Newhall's operating assumption was that, since most readers got the news from television or other journals, they wanted something different to read over their Wheaties. He filled the *Chronicle* with the comments, social notes, and opinions of more than twenty signed columnists. Newhall bought syndicated columns the way independent television stations buy up reruns of the *Beverly Hillbillies* and *Star Trek*. But the syndicated types were only a minor act in a daily Disneyland of local features that included "Count Marco" and a Dear Abby-type column for pet owners, where one could write in confidence to ask the name of a good dog psychiatrist.

Much of the news that Newhall used to plug the remaining open space between the ads was of his own invention. The *Chronicle*'s front page was busy for a week with exclusive stories of a Southern California man's efforts to start a society to clothe "naked animals." Newhall once dispatched the *Chronicle*'s Art Hoppe to Africa to do a series of front-page articles on the efforts of some putative Zambian astronauts to launch a space rocket powered by a giant rubber band. Scott kept one-upping himself with fascinating story ideas about the Dark Continent. He sent George Draper, an urbane reporter with a drawl that defied description as either Border-Southern or Colonial British, to the Zanzibar area to attempt to purchase a slave girl in the thriving Mohammedan market. Newhall's plan was for Draper to contrive somehow to bring his body servant to New York and dramatically free the faithful creature in the plaza of the United Nations. The plot aborted when George reached Djibouti and ran out of money.

One of Newhall's grandest schemes backfired mightily. In

June, 1960, the *Chronicle* started publishing a heavily promoted front-page series called "The Last Man on Earth,"
consisting of dispatches from the middle of nowhere by the
paper's hunting and fishing columnist, a mild-mannered man
named Bud Boyd. Boyd, his wife, and three children had
been left in the rugged High Sierras with only the clothes on
their backs, an ax, rope, twine, salt, and a pocketknife apiece
(plus a rifle to be used only in direst emergency), to see if they
could survive. The declared purpose of this expedition was to
determine whether "a man of the 20th century [could] survive
if civilization were suddenly wiped out" by a nuclear
holocaust. To make official the experiment, the *Chronicle*
brought in Rear Admiral A. G. Cook, head of the San Francisco disaster office, and then State Attorney General Stanley
Mosk, to attest to the fact that the Boyds had indeed set out for
the wilds.

Nobody thought to ask how Boyd's dramatic stories of daily
survival were getting back to civilization and in type—nobody,
that is, but Ed Montgomery, an *Examiner* newshound of the
old *Front Page* tradition. Smelling a rat, Montgomery back-
packed into the Sierras, sniffing Boyd's trail. His commitment
to investigative journalism was such that, upon coming on two
human turds near a cold campsite that Montgomery deduced
(from other evidence) had been Boyd's, he scooped them up
to take to the nearest town for scientific evaluation. Shortly
thereafter Montgomery elatedly phoned his city desk to report that traces of canned corn had been discovered in the
stools of the "last man on earth." His scoop proved bigger still
when he traced Boyd's trail to his home just outside San
Francisco, where the last man was comfortably grinding out
the suspenseful tales of his fight for survival that were appearing daily under huge headlines in the *Chronicle*. Montgomery
sat down at his typewriter. The next morning the *Chronicle*
appeared with a banner-headlined account of the last man's
narrow escape from a killer bear, and the *Examiner* appeared
with an identically bannered exposé of the last man as a fraud
who was sending dispatches from the wilderness of his living
room.

Newhall then did just about the only thing a nervy person

can do under such circumstances: Ignoring the angry crowds, rumored to have been recruited by the *Examiner*, that milled in front of the *Chronicle* building, and paying no attention to the hoots and hollers of commentators throughout the country, he continued to run Boyd's articles as if nothing untoward had occurred. A week after the truth was out, the series ended with the downcast admission by the last man on earth that the wilderness had defeated him and that he was retreating to civilization. Newhall told everyone who asked that he had planned it that way all along.

Except for this brief foray into scatologic deduction, Montgomery stuck to the more traditional journalistic field of Red-baiting. A large man with a bulky hearing aid strapped to one ear and an ever-present ball-point pen clipped to his shirt pocket, he wore sincere gray and dark-blue suits and a brown hat that appeared to have been left behind in a Chicago pressroom when everyone rushed out to cover the Lindbergh kidnapping. Montgomery feasted on the good red meat of subversives and radicals. He had pipelines into police intelligence units around the country and friends in high places among the compulsive newspaper clippers at the House Un-American Activities Committee, and would on occasion journey to Washington, D.C., to testify before that body on matters of peril to the nation.

If Montgomery was left in a slough of despond when, at the end of the fifties, the Red peril slunk off, he became a young man in love on the first day of spring when the sixties brought to the Bay Area first the Black Panthers and later the basement infernal-machine shops of left-wing bombers.

On occasion Ed's preoccupations led him to a good story. It was Montgomery who in 1971 found Black Panther leader Huey Newton padded down on the shores of Oakland's Lake Merritt in a luxury penthouse that afforded a fabulous view of the slums wherein his people dwelled.

I viewed Montgomery's journalistic tribalism with a bemused historical detachment and found him a pleasant enough fellow to have an occasional drink with while exchanging newspaper gossip and nonpolitical stories about city politics. This practice I continued during the years I was editing *Ramparts*, since the New Left politics of the magazine had no effect on my drinking habits and I continued to frequent my favorite right-wing bars. This horrified my New Left friends and acquaintances. They thought it was bad enough that I drank in the company of cops, let alone with Ed Montgomery, whom they considered a Hearst monster with the blood of innocent leftists still dripping from his fangs.

One day I was standing in Cookie Picetti's Kearny Street bar, bending elbows with the usual clientele of off-duty police inspectors, bail bondsmen, on-duty postmen, and the like, when Montgomery walked in. He pulled me aside and warned me to be wary of the dangerous company I was keeping at *Ramparts*. "A lot of those people are on the lists," he said. Montgomery was particularly wary of Bob Scheer, a bearded Berkeleyite and national New Left leader who was a coeditor and a close friend of mine. I began telling Ed that Scheer was completely harmless and wouldn't hurt a fly, that he preferred eating in Northern Chinese restaurants to attending cell meetings, and that his most subversive indulgence that I had knowledge of was soaking in the bathtub for hours while reading the want ads to compare the prices of used Saabs. Then I noticed that the Hearst reporter was looking at me with the same strange gaze I got from Scheer whenever I tried to explain to him that Montgomery was really an all-right guy but just a little hung up on the bloodlust of the fifties. I shrugged, thanked Ed for the warning, and told Cookie to set up a round for all the cops in the house.

The only committed person, revolutionary or conservative, I've known who had a sense of humor about such matters was Eldridge Cleaver. I once took him into Cookie's. He loved the place. He especially got a kick out of drinking in a joint that had a sign on the wall that read THANK GOD FOR THE TAC SQUAD (short for Tactical Squad, an infamous flying squadron of San Francisco police who chased and clubbed political protesters with observably greater zeal than they showed in pursuit of burglars). Cleaver said that people at *Ramparts* wondered why

I drank only in right-wing bars but were afraid to ask. I asked Cleaver if he had ever heard of a good left-wing bar, and, that issue settled, we had another beer. But I digress.

NO NIGGERS CAN DIE AFTER
11 P.M., 9 P.M. ON SATURDAYS

Ed Montgomery's menagerie of menaces notwithstanding, the *Chronicle*'s Disneyland brand of journalism won the circulation war. My own modest contribution to that victory came from Oakland, where I was counting broken noses. The Oakland police beat was the Siberia of San Francisco journalism. Tough city editors sent tender young reporters there to age a bit in the barrel of degeneracy that was the Oakland press room. Oakland duty meant nothing interesting to do, nowhere to go, no stories to cover, and no by-lines. Even worse, in the Ivy League mentality of the *Chronicle* editorial staff, it meant having to be around the gang of bindle stiffs and drunks who inhabited the Oakland press room, which was said to be one of the last of the rotten boroughs of American journalism.

It was all of that, and I found it a lovely place. The press room, number 107, was on the ground floor of the Oakland City Hall, a stubby building of cookie-mold architecture and WPA esthetics, atop which was grafted an ornate tower suggestive of some design rejected by medieval guildsmen as insufficient to reflect the grandeur of God. The back door of 107 opened onto the carbon monoxide of the police garage. At the rear of the garage a rattling elevator led up to the higher-level evidence room, where partly consumed bottles of impounded liquor were often available to the press. Another floor up was the rabbit-warren jail.

Green leather couches of the style fashionable around the time of Freud's visit to America hugged the grimy press room walls. A wooden telephone box of the Dillinger era stood against one wall, a monument to those bygone times when competition was in flower and ace reporters required confidential communication with the city desk. Across one side of the old telephone box someone had scribbled four lines from a play by the sixteenth-century English dramatist John Heywood:

> *Let the world slide,*
> *Let the world go;*
> *A fig for care,*
> *And a fig for woe!*

The inhabitants of the press room were of a breed defying classification within the standard levels of purgatory and hell. The baby of the police beat, Bob Popp, had been on the job a mere fifteen years, which was what ex-cons of my acquaintance would refer to as Ping-Pong time compared to the length of the tours of duty of the elders. The king of the press room was Augy Sairanen, the bureau chief of the *Chronicle*'s one-man (Augy) Oakland bureau. The title was not without authority.

Augy had been covering politics in Oakland almost since the time of Jack London, and he was infinitely wise in the worldly ways of that poor-boy city. A friendly man of Shakespearean loquacity, with a frame sufficiently large to carry his stomach around, he wore yellow shirts and spectacular bow ties and seemed always to have a cigarette dangling from his mouth. His bright blue eyes twinkled from a round face that was not so much flushed as a constant, cheery, Valentine's Day pink. Every morning Augy went over the *Chronicle* like a jeweler looking for dust in a Swiss watch. He was searching for some error in fact or interpretation in the news stories he had dictated to *Chronicle* rewritemen the day before, and he knew, the way he knew that rivers run downhill, that he would find something wrong. When he found the inevitable mistake, he would snap up the hot line to the *Chronicle* city desk across the Bay. If the perceived error was inconsequential, Augy would start to bellow as if the editor on the other end of the phone had just run over his daughter. If, however, he had found a real blunder, he would begin with mock courtesy, inquiring into the weather and the health of friends and relations, proceed to some ambiguous compliments about the quality of the newspaper that morning, and then suddenly unleash his terrible thunderbolt at that day's stupidity, its manifest conse-

quences of embarrassment, libel suits, and community contempt. He would normally conclude the conversation by
banging down the receiver and then deliver a spirited oration
about the miscreant ancestry of the man he had just hung up
on. That accomplished, Augy would go off to lunch or some
civic function to collect all the dirt about Oakland that the
Chronicle would never see fit to print.

Augy decided when the time of day had arrived to send out
for a bottle of whiskey, preferably one hundred-proof Yellowstone bourbon, which was ritually consumed before the
shrine of the water cooler in straight shots from tiny paper
cups, to be chased by a slug of water drunk from the same cup,
as Augy did not approve of waste. Augy was generally credited with having conceived the most important and most consistent activity in the press room—the laborious unfolding,
sheet by sheet, of the many editions of all the daily newspapers
and the subsequent process of meticulously laying them flat in
great white piles on the otherwise unused desks. Augy would
judge when a pile was sufficient to be securely tied with string
and stacked on the floor with its fellows. This enterprise took
precedence over everything save sleeping and the occasional
gathering of news—and for good reason. A local hero had
arranged to sell the flat sheets to wholesale florists, who used
them to wrap flowers, and the proceeds went into a fund for
the purchase of drinking alcohol.

The acknowledged chaplain of the press room was Ed
Dougery, a charming rogue of a *Chronicle* reporter who was
said to be Roman Catholic and to have once attended Mass
with Monty Woolley. Dougery's position as moral arbiter was
based on the firm ground that, the most adventurous among
us, he was peculiarly fit to judge when the limits of press room
propriety had been exceeded, since this would have entailed
the offender's having done something that Dougery himself
would not have done. The other crime reporters were characters out of a discarded chapter of *Catch 22*. The *Examiner's*
daytime watch over urban crime was manned by Walter Crowley, a somewhat cranky man with a shock of white hair who
seemed to spend half his time calling home to see if his wife
had snuck out and gone shopping on him. That newspaper's

night watch was maintained by George Erickson, a lumbering Swede who represented the best that was Oakland about the Oakland police beat. Known variously as George, "Swede," and "Eric," he wore green shirts and creased brown gabardine slacks as if they were a uniform. Every afternoon he arrived at the press room carrying the same lunch: a large tin of pickled herring and a half-dozen bottles of potent home brew, which he had bottled in the used ginger ale bottles he was always collecting from the cops, who not infrequently dropped in for a taste.

George was the most efficient among us at flattening newspapers. The Swede would start in on the day's stack of papers as soon as he had hung up his coat. Flattening them at an even pace, frequently wetting his thumb to get better traction on the newsprint, he continued for approximately three hours straight, stopping only to answer the telephone or the call of nature or to toss down a slug of bourbon with his colleagues. When on occasion I or some other guardian of the public's right to know desired to leave the press room premises for an evening, protocol had it that we would clear with George, who was always the anchor man, then purchase a pint of Old Yellowstone, have one or two sips with him, then leave the bottle with him and go off about our mischief, checking in periodically during the night by telephone in the unlikely event that any news had occurred, in which case George would give the details so we could call the story to our city desk from wherever we might be in the province of dalliance.

After he had unfolded sufficient papers to ensure a leg up on the whiskey fund, George would settle himself at a desk and eat his pickled herring, which was always wrapped in heavy wax paper and transported in a large cookie tin that had yellow and red roses painted on the outside, and begin sipping at his home brew, poured carefully so as not to disturb the sediment at the bottom. He drank from a glass as big around as his hand. While thus sipping, he would begin the laborious process of reading the final edition of the Oakland *Tribune*, a newspaper so bereft of content that it normally required more time to read the comics than the remainder of the paper. But the procedure was for George more ritual than reading: After two to three hours of going through the *Tribune*, line by line, sip after sip, he laid his head down on the desk to nap. He was not disturbed except in the event of a story. When George's shift was over, at around 2 A.M., the early man on the *Tribune* police beat would gently shake him, and George invariably would snap up his head with a snort and demand to know whether anything had "happened" while he'd been taking a nap. Other reporters took to the couches to sleep; not the Swede. He considered it somehow a violation of duty to do anything but sit there at a desk reading and re-reading the newspaper until the home brew did its job. This was his routine of almost twenty years' standing.

Often, in subsequent years, standing at a bar in some over-sophisticated town of great distance from Oakland, I would think of the Swede, know precisely what he would be doing at that moment, and raise my glass to him in a silent salute to continuity and solidity in a universe of otherwise constant flux and change.

At that time my own Irish Catholic credentials as a white racist in good standing were in order. But my first murder stories taught me that the criteria for what was a news story, and what was not, were other than what I had imagined.

I was quick to learn the full spectrum of the color code for the reporting of murders and other fatalities in Oakland in those days of the New Frontier. Whether a homicide would be reported at all depended largely upon the neighborhood in which it was committed. Ghetto murders, being regarded as natural black events, were rarely considered newsworthy. White trash murders stood a poor to even chance of getting into the paper, the imaginatively instrumented murder being favored over the merely routine.

The unwritten guidelines for reporting fatal automobile accidents were more complicated, the rough rule of thumb being: No niggers after 11 P.M. on weekdays, 9 P.M. on Saturdays (as the Sunday paper went to press early). Fatal highway accidents were reported without regard to the color of the deceased until these home edition deadlines: To get a late story in the final editions required making changes, and by tradition only white traffic deaths were considered worth submitting. The exception to this rule was in the area of quantity: If two black persons died in a late evening auto crash, that event had a fair chance of making the news columns. Three dead was considered a safe number by everyone except those reporters who were known to be viciously anti-Negro. Most of us, of course, considered ourselves neutral or objective in that regard. Yet none of us questioned the professional proposition that the loss of a white life had more news value than the loss of a black life.

Sitting watertight in our press room, we crime reporters were surrounded by the ghetto, spying out upon what was happening like journalistic Captain Nemos, the telephone our periscope, night after night searching that sea of poverty and degradation for the impossible: a black crime of interest to white readers.

A FREEWAY IN A PARK

In 1963 the municipality of Oakland built a splendid *Palais de Justice*, and the press room was moved—lock, stock, and flattened newspapers—into a ninth-floor air-conditioned suite of rooms with a grand view of the ghetto. The police beat was never the same again. Although many of its most engaging eccentrics remained on the job, they were fish out of water in that shiny and hairless environment, typical of those "professional" press rooms in civic headquarters across the land, which are staffed by pipe-smoking graduates of journalism schools who have all the spirit of junior executives in a breakfast cereal factory.

I fled back across the Bay to the *Chronicle* city room, where Newhall drafted me into the front lines in what proved to be the last great battle of the *opéra bouffe* journalistic wars of San Francisco, as the feuding managements of the *Examiner* and *Chronicle* kissed and merged not long thereafter.

The field of battle was Golden Gate Park, through which the State Division of Highways wanted to plant a six-lane freeway. The engineers had it all together: They would dig a giant ditch fifty-feet deep through a corner of the park, build the freeway, and then replant the park over it. The only visible intrusions on the park's replanted state of nature would be exhaust pipes from the tunnel that would stick up in discreet places among the trees.

If you expect that such a proposal might be viewed with alarm, you do not know San Francisco. The city leadership, including the labor unions, Chamber of Commerce, and of course the *Examiner*, were all for it. The freeway would move cars and make jobs, and Golden Gate Park had once been a sand dune, anyway. The *Chronicle* went all-out on the attack, and I found myself in the somewhat professionally compromising position of both writing stories about the monster freeway and serving as the co-chairman of an independent "Citizens' Committee to Save Golden Gate Park." As the committee's work gradually took up most of my city room time, I had few moments to spare for the lesser details of newsgathering.

This was possible as I got along well enough with city editor Abe Mellinkoff, a conservative Brooks Brothers Democrat who was said to be a bit of a tyrant, although I never found him so. He taught me the rules of the game, and let me out of the office on a reasonably long leash, and I returned the favor by coming up with off-beat stories, such as that of a former slave from Alabama who emigrated to California, became rich in the pinball machine business, and then legally adopted the children of his former master.

However, the assistant city editor, an acerbic chap named Carl Latham, did not take so well to my meanderings, as I discovered one morning when I had to take off for a few hours to speak at a press conference of the Save-the-Park Committee, and said he should send a reporter to cover it.

"We're short-handed today," Latham said. "You're going to be there anyway; you cover it."

I told the day city editor that it was impossible for me to cover the press conference, I was *giving* the press conference.

He would have no such lame excuses for not working. "Crap," he said. "You know what you're going to say. Don't tell me you're afraid of misquoting yourself."

One does not escape taxes or death or win arguments with the city desk. So I put on my two hats and went to the press conference. I made a little speech and introduced some expert witnesses to tell of the horrors the freeway would bring, and then I stepped aside to dutifully take notes for my newspaper on what they said. The *Examiner* reporter came up and asked, with genuine incredulity, just what the hell I was doing. "Covering the story," I said. "What the hell do you think I'm doing?" And that was precisely the way the *Examiner* reported it the next day.

The freeway battle ended in a blaze of ambiguity. It had been difficult all along, reading the newspapers, to tell whether it was day or night: Freeway Ditch to Bring Giant Sandstorm, the *Chronicle* suggested; Freeway Plan Means a Little Bigger Park, a Hearst headline declared. Even more befuddling was the coverage of a climactic antifreeway rally in the park the day before the city supervisors were scheduled to vote to accept or reject the highway. Somewhat apocalyptically, I pounded out front-page articles in the *Chronicle* announcing that 100,000 people would turn up to protest the concrete snake; worse, I believed my own propaganda, and then effected the tragic overstatement of ordering chemical toilets installed in the park to convenience the expected throng. Malvina Reynolds wrote a song for the occasion which later achieved some prominence in rad-lib LP circles as "The Cement Octopus," and as gatherings of the masses go it was a pleasant, halfway splendid affair, marred only by the approach of a low-flying helicopter late in the afternoon. The *Examiner*, in an unexpected burst of Hearst martial excess, had hired an airship to overfly the rally site at an hour when the crowd had dwindled, and take an aerial photograph. PARKWAY PROTEST FIZZLES said the *Examiner* the next day, with the proof of an aerial photo showing a few antlike stragglers in an otherwise empty field. THE GREAT PARK RALLY, said the *Chronicle*, its proof a large photo of a mass of humanity jammed together like New Year's Eve on Times

Square, which had been angled and cropped to give just that impression.

The San Francisco Board of Supervisors, who seemed almost as confused as the city's newspaper readers, defeated the freeway by one vote, 6 to 5, in favor of the *Chronicle*.

I took a six-month leave of absence from the *Chronicle* in the fall of 1964 on temporary assignment to turn *Ramparts* into an intellectual Catholic monthly. The leave stretched into a year, and then two years, and I have yet to get back.

3.

The Cult of the Convert

MY baptism into the world of intellectual Catholicism was in the unlikely Jordan of Edward Keating's living room on a dulcet autumn evening in 1961.

Edward Keating was the founder and publisher of *Ramparts*. He was also an unusually candid person. I learned three things about him within three minutes of meeting him. He was a convert. He had diabetes. He was rich.

He didn't look like a millionaire to me, but then I had never met one before. His shoes were black FBI issue, his socks had clocks in them. His pants bagged at the bottom as if there were several dozen marbles in the cuffs. His shiny herringbone suit was pudgy with stuffed shoulders. His rumpled black tie dangled cheerlessly from his narrow starched collar. His face was round and wrinkleless, his black hair combed straight back Robert McNamara style, his eyes piercing and eager. He was short, with short fingers the girth of link sausages. He was a lawyer but he didn't practice. Instead, he was starting a literary quarterly to improve the quality of intellectual life in his adopted Church.

Ed Keating and I immediately discovered we shared a common antipathy for the Jesuits. He had taught English at the Jesuit University of Santa Clara, where the black robes canned him for flunking a dumb football player. That was

35

when he got the idea of starting a magazine. He remembered one Sunday morning after church listening to some chatter on the radio about the dearth of Catholic intellectuals in the United States. He resolved then and there to do something about it. The something was *Ramparts*.

Keating thought *Ramparts* a terrifically symbolic name because it could mean either defending the Church from the ramparts against secular attack, or Catholic intellectuals striking forth at the world with their ideas, from the ramparts. He said that the name had a built-in advertising bonus: "Just think, every time the national anthem is played at a football or baseball game, we'll get a free plug!"

The man responsible for bringing us together was yet another convert, Harry Stiehl, a frail poet of singular talent who was to be *Ramparts'* first editor. Harry had endured a strange childhood in Mexico and the West Indies, suffered through the University of Texas, picked up advanced degrees in English at Berkeley, written a critical biography of Hart Crane, and then found his emotional and artistic calling in Catholicism, to which he experienced a whopping traumatic conversion, and proceeded to immerse himself in a book-length poem about St. Teresa of Avila. I met Harry when he was teaching at USF, sort of between poems, and he and I had worked together on some oddball projects at the Blackfriars of the West, a cultural shop run by the Dominican Fathers to whom I had volunteered a hand as a rude gesture to the Jesuits. When Stiehl met Keating and found that he was rich and was starting a magazine, he suggested Keating hire me to help launch it—which, as Keating was to say, sometime later, "was a shitty thing to do to a fellow convert."

I was then a 21-year-old partner in a yearling public relations business, which did not last out its first year. I started the company upon getting out of college, and soon had occasion to reconsider the wisdom of that decision. The firm's accounts were mostly San Francisco cultural and do-good societies, which were living nightmares of dealing with grand dames and social dragon ladies who religiously cheated on paying their bills. The one amusing thing I accomplished was to turn an abandoned PG&E powerhouse into a fabulous baroque nightclub, Station J, with mirrored walls three stories high, green velvet everywhere and a twenty-six piece symphony orchestra for dancing—but that went bust when the two young men who owned it poured the cash receipts into doomed real estate speculations and telephone-equipped Rolls Royces. My firm's one straight client was P & O Orient Lines, but they dropped us when they were sued for a considerable sum of money after an old steam calliope I had hired to parade loudly around the Bay Area in honor of the *S.S. Canberra*'s docking in San Francisco had unwisely driven through the egg-capital city of Petaluma, freaking tens of thousands of chickens in the hatcheries to dash themselves to death against the walls to escape the calliope's loathsome melodies. The firm was, on balance, a disaster of Marx Brothers proportions; our only employee was my fifteen-year-old sister, nicknamed Vampira, who came in after school and whose main duties were to go out for ice and fend off process servers.

I naturally lied to Keating about all this, and he hired me to help him build *Ramparts* out of whole cloth.

The first order of business was a command performance invitation to Keating's home, where the new breed of Catholic intellectuals he was staking his stud fee on would be in attendance. "There might even be a swinging nun there," he said.

Keating lived in Atherton, which is to California's suburbs what Forest Lawn is to its cemeteries. It is near Stanford University but fenced in from the flatlands of blacks and poorer whites surrounding it, and prominent among its prominent residents is Shirley Temple Black (against whom Keating later tilted in an unsuccessful attempt at a seat in Congress).

The Keating house was a white, two-story, semi-colonial edifice, which was blanketed with at least a million perfect fall leaves. The living room was jammed. There was music but no one danced. I could make out the high crown of a Redemptorist nun in the crowd and was told that there were other nuns present but "out of uniform." Off-duty priests were in as plentiful supply as day-old bread, and two priests in uniform casually took off their Roman collars in a harmless kind of religious striptease. A bad joke about the Albigensian heresy was making the rounds; however, the main topic of conversation among the assembled Catholic intellectuals was football; it was a measure of their liberation that the group's sentiment was for the Southern Methodists rather than Notre Dame.

It was a strange crowd: breathless girls from the Newman Club in drip-dry dresses, predatory-looking lawyers and accountants, Keating's red-blazered prosperous neighbors, and some Episcopalian people from the Stanford Humanities Department who had come to witness a gathering of liberated Catholics.

Keating's friends came in two varieties: Catholics who did something else for a living, and Catholics whose religious and professional vocations were intertwined. Among the latter was Jim Colaianni, a chipper but shabby-looking fellow who was later to become one of the first managing editors of *Ramparts,* on the basis of his being a theological Eagle Scout. Colaianni described himself as a "lay theologian." He had just completed several years of advanced study in theology, a calling which had prompted him to give up a comfortable law career in New Jersey and adapt himself and his large family to starvation wages while he wrestled with that Empress science, as Martin Luther called it. Now he knew more theology than many priests and was about to take up his duties teaching religion at a nearby Catholic parish. The crafty old-fashioned pastor Colaianni worked for eventually broke his lay theologian's rice bowl, and Keating quite decently made him the managing editor because he had nowhere to go and as many children as Keating.

The heaviest of the Catholic professionals in attendance was newsman John O'Connor, city editor of *The Monitor*, the San Francisco Catholic weekly newspaper; he was to local Catholic liberals on a scale of heroes somewhere between Clark Kent and Jack Armstrong. He was handsome, intelligent, articulate, and progressive; he didn't have too many children and he had an attractive wife, and he knew how to escape the mess and humiliation of kissing the bishop's ring without making a scene of it. But his liberal popularity was without power, and he had to go to the Archbishop to get the key to the men's room.

O'Connor's fate was typical of the good, trusting liberal who was out to responsibly reform the crudities of power in the Church and ends up being screwed by the priests, a familiar syndrome of modern Catholicism. He fought losing battles within the Augean stables of the conservative San Francisco archdiocese for several years, and then made great Catholic waves by moving to Delaware to launch a superliberal Catholic weekly around the time of the cresting of the flood of reform fervor in the American Church. After several years of progressive publishing he lost his head to a hatchet squadron of priests and conservative laymen combined, and then went off to write the usual bitter book about his experience.

The precocious liberal Catholicism of the early sixties had some of the peculiar qualities of the panty raid. Gatherings to discuss such then unorthodox projects as folk masses were permeated with a robust feeling of conspiracy, a conspiracy at times stained by smugness that other Catholics were not as liberated as thou. Like a panty raid, there was a good deal of talk about sex, but not much getting into it; although the conversation was usually frank and knowledgeable about the sexual straightjacket of Irish Catholicism, most liberal Catholics of my acquaintance at that time maintained an orthodoxy about intercourse, not to mention fellatio. The intellectual freedom of many Catholics was often ironically coincident with the number and frequency of their issue. Among such examples Ed Keating was in the running for king of the mountain—at the time he had four, or five, children, a count difficult to finalize without asking because there were so many pictures of his kids around the house it looked as if he had a dozen, and he was always talking about having more—even during those not infrequent periods of gestation when his wife, as he put it, had "one in the oven."

But remember this was 1961, before the great Ecumenical Council. Pope John was still just another fat Italian in the Vatican and Lenny Bruce was being persecuted by the cops for making the same jokes about the crucifixion that some priests would be cracking a few years later. A measure of the basic orthodoxy of the time is that one of the most controversial essays *Ramparts* published during its Catholic years was "The Case For Contraception"—which had to be written by an Anglican. At that it required considerable soul-searching on Keating's part before he could bring himself to publish it.

A similar Catholic orthodoxy as to literary matters, or at least as to sex in literature, was suggested by a climactic conversation which heated up that autumn evening. It began with the spectacular entrance of Keating's wife, Helen, who floated gracefully down the stairs in a flouncy white dress of a conservatively fashionable Cinderella style. She was attractive and well composed, showing no strain either from her numerous children or from her afternoon volunteer work at the cooperative black nursery school in the nearby ghetto of East Palo Alto. Since Helen was to be the fiction editor of *Ramparts*, the talk turned to fiction. A great debate somehow began over the rather precious subject of J. D. Salinger. The setting was vaguely Inquisitional: Helen sat on the rug surrounded by her great flowing skirt, half-circled by neighbors in red blazers. They all listened attentively as Keating, suddenly a fiery prosecutor, denounced Salinger for moral turpitude.

Keating expressed similar opinions about the degeneracy of writers such as Tennessee Williams and Henry Miller: corruption, moral decay, the erosion of the classic values of Western Civilization, et cetera, ad infinitum. His special contempt for Salinger seemed to have something to do with the fact that he had found his oldest son reading a paperback book by the man.

At one point Keating made the hyperbolic assertion, which he later retracted, that if he were President he would put J. D. Salinger in jail! I asked why. "Because he's dirty," Ed said. I barely recalled something in *The Catcher in the Rye* about Holden Caulfield in the back seat unhooking a girl's bra but was otherwise at a loss to understand, and unleashed a more impassioned defense of Salinger than I normally would have felt impelled to make of a voguish writer whose mortal sin was his Ivy League slickness.

Our Salinger polemics gave Keating an idea for what he

called a "bomb." That was his favorite synonym for a hot story. The "bomb" which exploded in the first issue of *Ramparts* was the idea of a symposium on J. D. Salinger: me on the affirmative, Keating and a friend on the negative. The friend was Robert O. Bowen, a Catholic novelist who had written an obscure World War II epic called *The Weight of the Cross*. Keating felt a comradeship for Bowen because they both had been tossed out of their teaching jobs at the University of Santa Clara around the same time. Bowen was reputed to have been axed for being too embarrassing a right-wing *mensch* for even the Jesuits. Keating nevertheless made Bowen an associate editor of *Ramparts*. "We are a literary magazine. Politics should not interfere with literature," he said.

LAUNDRY LIST PRINTING

Edward Keating fired me via registered mail on January 25, 1962.

He later told inquiring interviewers that he canned me because I wanted him to promote his Catholic quarterly by going to cocktail parties with an actress named Rita Gam. I never had the pleasure of knowing Miss Gam, although the name alone sounds worth the acquaintance. The fact was that Keating and I argued over every conceivable aspect of the first issue from J. D. Salinger to the typefaces.

I would have cheerfully sacrificed J. D. Salinger to get my choice for the printer. I wanted Lawton Kennedy, an atavistic and splendidly efficient throwback to a better century. Lawton ran his presses on the bygone principles of printing as both an art and a craft. He shuddered at the thought of the trees that were chopped down to produce paper for printing *schlock*. With typical salty stubbornness he cursed the proposition that elegant printing had been doomed to the Smithsonian by the industrial revolution; he mastered the new machines, transplanting a craftsman's heart into the robot soul of modern production. For over sixty years he has produced from his family printing establishment in San Francisco, now run with his son Alfred, books and quarterlies that appear to be handcrafted by monks but come off the same presses as the income tax forms. Lawton specializes in books of Western Americana; although he never graduated from grammar school he is deferred to as a scholar in that field by the historians whose work he prints. Many years of working on publishing projects with Lawton afforded me an education in good taste, which had only incidentally to do with typefaces.

I couldn't imagine a quarterly of quality being printed by anyone but this renaissance man, but Keating was suspicious. He didn't seem to like Lawton's establishment, which resembled more the Huntington Library than it did a printing plant. Keating became particularly impatient when Lawton declined to enter into competitive bidding with other printers, explaining that he never matched apples to oranges. He instead volunteered to devise several differently priced formats for Keating's inspection. Keating became more impatient. Lawton suggested that Keating simply tell him what he could afford to spend, and he would then tell Keating if he could print the magazine for that sum or cheaper. If not, he would refer Keating to what he called "one of those laundry list printers." Keating interrupted: He simply must know things such as how much more money color would cost. Lawton looked up from behind the ornate desk in his book-lined, Pickwickian office where a telephone looked absolutely out of place. "Well, Mr. Keating," he replied, "it's the old story of the monkey pissing into the cash register—it all runs into money."

There were other contretemps. At one point I got Keating to ask Charles McCabe, Esquire, to contribute an essay on some of the more savory absurdities of Irish Catholicism. McCabe, Esq., is the full name of a crustily civilized Anglophile columnist for the San Francisco *Chronicle*. A newsman of numerous tours of duty who carries the scars of his Jesuit upbringing like pockmarks of honor, McCabe is the local Timon of Athens. He began his career by attacking sports, for which he had a healthy but too reverent dislike, and then graduated to attacking the human race itself. His prose style is that of a *New Statesman* leader writer beset by Irish remorse. He is one of the more literate daily essayists in the

country. Keating sent McCabe's article back with a note telling
him he should learn how to write.

The maiden issue of *Ramparts* appeared in May of 1962. It
carried a statement of editorial policy written by the publisher: "*Ramparts* presents creative works which, besides possessing literary excellence, possess the Christian vision of
man, his world, his God."

True to his threat, Keating published the symposium on J.
D. Salinger, complete with my essay in defense of the man,
which may have suffered from an incomplete awareness of his
transgressions—a list Robert Bowen, Associate Editor of
Ramparts, was not remiss in supplying, punctuated with anti-
Semitic slurs. Bowen wrote that Salinger was not only anti-
Catholic but, worse, was "pro-Jewish and pro-Negro." As
proof of Salinger's anti-Catholicism he cited an incident in
Catcher in the Rye where "Ackely, the Catholic, picks pimples
on other people's beds." In addition, Salinger was
subversive—"vehemently anti-Army and even anti-America,"
and a camp follower of "the sick line transmitted by Mort
Sahl" and other "cosmopolitan think people." Salinger was
supported in his insidious causes by the Anti-Defamation
League and "other Jewish pressure groups." Among his
causes? That of "Negro chauvinism."

The cover of the first issue of *Ramparts* depicted a scabrous
white rook emerging out of a glow-sock-red background. I
showed it to Lawton Kennedy. He squinted, and said: "Laundry list printing."

Ed Keating hired me back on November 17, 1962.

I never had asked him why he fired me, so I didn't ask why
he wanted to hire me again. I wanted the money, and I just
played dumb, like Twiggy when she said she thought
Hiroshima was a Japanese boutique on Madison Avenue; I
said yes, I would meet him for lunch on my day off.

I was then doing a relatively honest day's work as a reporter
for the San Francisco *Chronicle*, to which I had fled as to high
land from the waters of creditors and unhappy matrons flood-
ing my public relations business. While it was fun working for

the *Chronicle*, a reporter who wished to drink freely without
owing his soul to the company store, let alone eat red meat,
needed a job on the side to supplement the tokens paid out as
wages; one colleague wrote publicity blurbs for a nightclub,
another sold his essence to an experimental sperm bank at $25
a pop, but both sounded like hard work to me. So when Harry
Stiehl walked into the city room with a white flag and a
message from Keating offering greens for flacking part-time
for *Ramparts*, I figured it a steal.

Little did I know, as the voice-over says in anti-V.D. commercials, that when I drove down the Bayshore Freeway to
break bread with Keating I was starting off on a real-life
yellow brick road.

VADE RETRO ME, SATANAS

The reconciliation luncheon was in the surprise setting of
Caesar's Palace, a grandiose spit and plaster temple to mam-
mon that rose like a San Marco created by a McDonald's
hamburger architect in the dust off the main road between
Palo Alto and San Jose. The place was decorated in Las Vegas
vinyl and catered to crew-cut junior executives who worked
for IBM or Hewlett-Packard and had bad skin and worse
taste. Caesar's Palace was owned, with some complications, by
Doris Day; it later crumbled into bankruptcy, which I suppose
made it an appropriate place for a *Ramparts'* summit conference.

We were seated around a golden table which had the appearance of a modernistic plastic beach sandal of Italian manufacture turned upside down, one of several hundred identi-
cal tables, most of them empty, in a cavernous room deep
within Caesar's Palace; the cavern was called either the Lion's
Retreat or Nero's Cave, memory failing me on that and other
fine points of our environment except for the waitresses who
were Playboy rejects dressed up as Christian slave girls in
costumes with necklines as low as a Bob Hope dirty joke.

Keating said he had chosen this out-of-the-way place to
meet "to escape the Catholic environment."

Ramparts had published three issues, rich with a preciousness that is difficult to convey outside the reaches of Black Humor, and heavy with weird esoteric references to the decadent and the royalist in Catholic literature. There was tin art by Canadian Jesuits, tirades against homosexuality and pornography, unflattering references to the Dominican nuns who called themselves "The Servants of Relief for Incurable Cancer," impassioned appreciations of baroque writers of non-Euclidean and aristocratic bent, expensively-printed pages stained with the extravagant juices of poet-converts.

It should again be recalled that this was still the very early sixties. The subsequent radical awakening in American Catholicism has been so deep and pervasive that contemporary leftward developments have almost lost the ability to shock. The spectacle of nuns caught up in bomb plots still makes headlines, but no longer raises many eyebrows. The heroes of the new Catholicism are evangelical guerrilla fighters such as Dan and Phil Berrigan, and *Ramparts* in its later Catholic years would propose the brothers Berrigan for commemorative stamps and sainthood alike.

But in the beginning, the *Ramparts* hero was . . . Wyndham Lewis!

Wyndham Lewis may be obscure to some, but he was everything that the original *Ramparts* deemed holy: witty, elitist, classical, pro-Catholic, anti-Einstein, anti-Nietzsche, pro-Aristotle, anti-realist, anti-Bergson and his neo-Catholic foolishness about Life Forces, anti-Sartre, and a staunch defender and promoter of the Aristocracy of Art.

Lewis had to live a long time to be successfully anti so many things: He began spitting classical venom in 1907, and published, as late as 1956, the year before his death, a rather remarkable novel called *The Red Priest*, in which an Anglican priest attempts to bring about a reconciliation between Christianity and the brute reality of Atheistic Marxism and is murdered on an Arctic ice cap for his trouble. Lewis was a ranking satirist, novelist and artist of that long inning of early-twentieth-century English letters which Ford Madox Ford referred to with admiration as "the haughty and proud generation." He was a friend of T. S. Eliot and foe of James Joyce.

(*Ramparts* noted with approval that Lewis was critical of "the indiscriminate biological yes at the end of *Ulysses*.") *Ramparts* could barely find things nice enough to say about Lewis; his only failure was that he did not convert to Catholicism, although he was sufficiently pro-Catholic to please everybody to the right of the Pope.

One rarely hears of anyone converting *to* Catholicism these days, the process having taken the opposite direction; however, *Ramparts*' special heroes were the latter-day literary-type converts: Gerard Manley Hopkins, the Jesuit nature poet; the glib, dreadful G. K. Chesterton; Frederick B. (Baron) Corvo, of *Hadrian VII* fame; Ronald Firbank, the novelist of precious tinsel phrases, and Aubrey Beardsley, he of the wonderful decadence. Even Oscar Wilde made the list, having done the right thing before dying by signing his soul over to the Church. While the English convert-heritage tended toward the baroque, the American side of *Ramparts*' conversion column included several first-rate poets, all converts, with whom Harry Stiehl was in frequent correspondence: Allen Tate, Robert Lowell, and Brother Antoninus. Both Tate and Antoninus published in the quarterly.

This cult of the convert dominated the early *Ramparts*. As Harry Stiehl, a convert too, once observed, converts to Catholicism, and not only those of a literary bent, tend toward the "extravagant and extreme."

The original *Ramparts* was sufficiently Anglophile to make it out a strange Catholic version of the *New York Review of Books*. Harry provided the smoother part of the literary product; Keating for his part provided the gristle of involuted Catholic puritanism, particularly in the evangelical-sexual criticism of American literature. Having disposed of J. D. Salinger, Keating in the next edition took off after Tennessee Williams with a cat-o'-nine-tails. Keating called Williams a "decadent writer," attacked him for "glorifying" sexual perversions, and being pro-"abnormalities," and adjudicated that *Cat on a Hot Tin Roof* "attempts to cast a soft glow on homosexuality."

The pages of *Ramparts* were sprinkled with phrases such as *Vade retro me, Satanas; l'homme moyen sensuel*, and other untranslated slogans of the type that Orwell used to cite as examples of the unnecessary. The authors' biographies in italic type at the end of articles always told how many children the writer had, unless he was a priest.

Keating asked me what I thought of the magazine.

I answered, employing a device I learned from the Jesuits, with another question. I asked how it was selling.

It wasn't selling. The most optimistic guess was that the circulation had cracked the 1,000-copy barrier, and was hovering in the area of 1,100 subscribers, give or take free samples to the clergy. But Keating announced that he had a circulation "bomb" in the works: A symposium on Jesuit education, on one side laymen who would dare to be critical, and on the other side, in Christian fairness, the Jesuits defending themselves.

Keating presented his editorial plan eloquently. A meaningful dialogue. Respect on both sides. Breaking the barriers of silence. Laymen and priests together hashing out the problems. A crisis in American Catholic higher education. Generations of cretins and dummies graduating from Catholic colleges. The Jesuits, the great teaching order, with their twenty-six colleges and universities in the United States, having to take the lion's share of the credit and the blame for the state of the Catholic mind in America. An airing of the problem. Progress toward its resolution. Controversy. Headlines.

I said, grossly, it would never work.

Keating looked across the table at me as if he were a commander in Naval Intelligence and I had just suggested we would not be able to break the Japanese code. He demanded to know why it wouldn't work.

I said a convert wouldn't understand, and burst into analogies about snakes, tarantulas, hyenas, rats, poachers, and double-crossers—all relating to the character and temperament of the men enrolled for life as God's soldiers in the Society of Jesus.

Keating gave me instant absolution for my misguided excess. He said if I felt so strongly about the Jesuits that I, too, should write an article for the symposium—which was going to happen just as he said; never I mind about the rest.

"The Jesuits," said the convert-publisher, as we walked toward the plastic door of the luncheon cave, "are going to be the breakthrough that *Ramparts* has been waiting for."

"FROM NOW ON, IT'S NO MORE MR. NICE GUY"

God knows that I had entertained occasional thoughts about repaying the Jesuits—in the way one daydreams about blowing up post offices or kicking stray dogs. But for the most part I considered myself well rid of them and was satisfied to leave matters with the waves of the *Foghorn* debt lapping knee-high about their hiked-up black gabardines.

However, duty called, and I responded with what I suppose was a vengeance. I delivered to Keating a lengthy screed titled "The Saintly Narcissism of the Society of Jesus." It said, among other things, that the Jesuits, in the manner of General Motors calling in a defective Chevrolet, recalled their college Ethics textbook in 1945 to hurriedly revise the section on "Just Warfare" to make it morally permissible to use atomic bombs on civilian populations—as the United States had recently done at Hiroshima.

Keating refused to print it.

"You're too rough on them," he said. "We've got to be reasonable in our criticism. You can't describe the Jesuits as Rome's caterpillars! I'm seeking a dialogue. I need their cooperation. Why, I've got firm commitments from ten of the most important Jesuits in the country to write in response in the next issue. They want me to submit the laymen's manuscripts to them in advance—I'd never dare show them what you wrote."

Keating was possessed by a vision of priests and laymen together thrashing out their problems in the pages of his magazine, like blacks and whites at an NAACP encounter session of the mid-fifties. I tried to tell him that once the Jesuits got their manicured hands on those manuscripts he would be finished. They would never aid and abet any criticism, however mild, of themselves—they were just sucking him in, saying they would cooperate so they could sandbag him. Keating would hear none of this. "I have their word," he said.

Keating replaced my article with one by another USF man, whose literary credits included the authorship of an accounting textbook, and who was eager to defend his Alma Mater. He began: "Catholic education typified by the Jesuit institutions has a unique claim to intellectuality...." Keating himself wrote the lead essay; he said that Jesuit colleges had spread themselves too thin in such areas as science and business administration, and that they could make a real "worthy contribution" by concentrating more on what they were especially good at, like philosophy and theology. Another contributor was Keating's good friend Robert Bowen, who complained that the Jesuits hadn't paid him enough money when he worked for them, and hadn't let him into the faculty "club." A full-page announcement at the end of the symposium said that the "Jesuit view" of these meaty criticisms would appear in the next issue of *Ramparts*.

I had pleaded unsuccessfully with Keating to throw Bowen's essay in the trash along with mine, as I had used the facilities of the *Chronicle* to do some digging on Keating's ultramontane buddy, and feared that what I had rooted up was the top of the soil. Bowen had written a book, *The Truth About Communism*, published by a small mail-order publisher in Alabama that specialized in hard-to-get items like leather-bound copies of the *Protocols of Zion*. He had lately been teaching at the University of Dallas, a small uptight Catholic college which shared the politics of its namesake city; there he published what he termed "a patriotic little magazine" called the *Dallas Review*. The *Dallas Review* printed its credo on the first page over Bowen's initials:

"Our editorial policy is best stated in the words of the American patriot and warrior Edwin A. Walker: 'Fear God and nobody else.' "

Giving a self-declared member of the General Walker fan club a job as an editor of *Ramparts,* I analogized to the pub-

lisher, was like giving Quasimodo a salesman's job with Avon
Calling. But Keating, who was stubborn on principle, refused
to budge on what he considered the principled issue of Robert
Bowen.

Keating tossed an advance copy of the Jesuit issue at me as if
it were a plastique.

"Now go get some headlines for this," he said.

I dutifully culled each article for colorful phrases to take out
of context and sent a summary to the newsmagazines. To my
surprise, *Time* decided to do a story; in those days, any criticism of the Catholic Church by Catholics was still in the man-
bites-dog category. A reporter went to interview Keating, who
became overnight a man walking among swans. "This is the
big breakthrough," he said. "This is it." He kept calling me,
asking when the *Time* piece would appear.

It never did. I finally asked the *Time* bureau chief in San
Francisco what was happening; he said the story had been
killed because they had found out *Ramparts* was a right-wing
magazine peopled with cranks and even had a Bircher as an
editor.

I smelled the Jesuits at work. I was impressed. Here was this
piddling attempt at criticism, but they had mobilized as if the
Jewish Defense League had threatened to circumcise the
Black Pope in St. Peter's Square.

I laughed. "I'll bet you got that from the Jesuits," I said.

"Yeah—how'd you know? They sent over a shitpot of information, including a whole file on this guy Bowen that
clinched it," said the *Time* man.

I almost sprained my finger dialing Keating. "Oh, my God,"
he said. He kept repeating, "Oh, my God." He must have said
that as many times as I said, "I told you so."

The next day, Keating fired Robert Bowen.

Once the Jesuits had blacked out Keating's press, they
would not answer his earnest phone calls seeking the
bargained-for Jesuit manuscripts, which never arrived. The
holy beating these holy men gave Ed Keating was to prove
pivotal in the leftward development of *Ramparts*. It soured the
yogurt of his healthy and optimistic view of the Catholic

Church, and began the process of disillusionment that was to turn Keating from a respectfully orthodox convert to a brazen anticleric who would make jokes in public and even in the presence of nuns about "taking a bite out of the Pope's ass." The whole thing would be turned around, and the ramparts of *Ramparts* used for attacking the Church, rather than defending it as Keating first intended.

I could see this metamorphosis at work when I visited Keating a week after the Jesuit ambush. His skin tone was purple; his lips white; his hands trembled. His voice sounded as if he were undergoing the stress of leaving the earth's gravity. I have never seen another human being so angry. I didn't have to ask; he told me that the Jesuits had backed out on their solemn promise to respond in the next issue. He was writing a statement which he said must run in the front of the magazine to let *Ramparts'* readers know about this act of perfidy. He had been made an editorial cuckold to scheming and faithless Jesuits. He had made a solemn vow, under pain of death, that the Jesuits—no, the entire Catholic Church —would pay dearly for this.

"From now on," Keating said, "it's no more Mr. Nice Guy."

4.

Leaping Over the Wall

PHIL HARRIS used to sing a song about a man being chased through the forest by a bear. The man hadn't been to church in a long time and had forgotten how to say his prayers, so when he climbed a tree with the bear in hot pursuit he yelled up to the Heavens, "Oh, Lord, if you can't help me, for goodness sake don't you help that bear!"

More often than not, as I learned what the Catholic Church was about during the sixties, I found that it was helping the bear. I was puzzled to find the Church so consistently on the wrong side of social issues instead of on the side on which a cursory reading of the gospel would place it. If there is, in fact, such a thing as a Catholic social conscience, I fear it was defined best by the late Archbishop James Gibbons, of Baltimore, who once said that if "social convulsions" forced him to abandon his regular posture of "masterly inactivity," he would say "to the troubled waters, 'Peace, be still,' " rather than join in the convulsion.

As it was stories like these that drove *Ramparts* up and over the wall, some specifics are in order.

The happening that first put the paper into its troublemaking orbit on the national scene was its left-tackle role in the great religious scrimmage of 1964 over the Broadway staging of Rolf Hochhuth's Pope-baiting play, *The Deputy*.

53

Like many pivotal events in *Ramparts'* history, it came about
because I was somewhere I shouldn't have been because of an
inordinate thirst. One day at the *Chronicle* I was sneaking out
for a drink by tiptoeing through the composing room when I
passed a woman slaving over a hot makeup stone. She was
Judy Stone, a *Chronicle* copy editor revered by her fellows and
compatriots for being the sister of I. F. Stone, the journalist-
pamphleteer. Judy stopped me to ask what magazine I
thought she should sell a scoop she had lucked into just the
week before while winding up her vacation in Europe—an
exclusive interview with Hochhuth, the young German
dramatist whose play about the silence of Pope Pius XII while
six million Jews were killed had occasioned fisticuffs throughout Europe, and was headed for Broadway with storm signals
flying.

Judy said she realized *Ramparts* could not possibly run the
interview since it then came out quarterly and the interview
must appear when *The Deputy* opened in New York, just a few
weeks hence. So what did I think about offering it to *Look*,
which came out every two weeks and paid well and . . . I
tenderly withdrew the rough draft of the interview from her
hand as if it were a sliver in the royal behind of the Queen of
England and told her never to mind, that Keating would pay
almost as much as *Look*, that I would rip apart the *Ramparts'*
issue going to press to make room for her story, that Keating
was so rich he would buy *Look* from Gardiner Cowles if need
be just to get her story, that this *belonged* in *Ramparts*!

I had no idea how I would make good on my promise to get
her story out in time; but in such circumstances I trust in the
god of ingenuity to find a way. I simply knew that *Ramparts*
must have that story the way one knows he has a toothache or
has to go to the toilet.

I told Keating of my find, which occasioned a wondrous
transformation in him. A horseless paladin, he was suddenly
in the saddle; *Ramparts* had a good cause to ride. Keating's
office became stacked with the literature of revisionist
Catholic historians on the groveling posture of most German
Catholic bishops toward Hitler; he pored over these books
with the violent effect of cold water over hot rocks, steaming

vociferously in anger or agony when he would come across yet another unspeakable fact about the Pope.

There was a good deal a Catholic could get upset about in the story of Pius XII and the Jews. It is the story of a Church that could remain passive in the face of genocide. It is all the more disturbing in the perspective of the 2,000-year history of Christian anti-Semitism. The Catholic Crusades, which engaged in the slaughter of Jews in the eleventh and twelfth centuries, were led by Papal knights. In Germany in 1942 and 1943, SS men were goose-stepping regularly to the communion rail, and the Catholic Church was receiving substantial financial stipends from the Reich; the Vatican's concordat with Hitler remained undisturbed, and the Pope remained silent behind his crucifix. Historian Guenther Lewy quoted Pius's reply to a Vatican official who asked him why he did not condemn the Nazis as Jew killers: "Dear friend, do not forget that millions of Catholics serve in the German armies. Shall I bring them into conflicts of conscience?"

Hochhuth's play centered on the struggle of a fictional Jesuit to get Pius XII to condemn publicly the Nazi extermination of the Jews: At the play's end the Jesuit, unsuccessful, puts on a yellow star and goes off to join the Jews in the shower lines at Auschwitz. The proposition that Pius XII just might be something of an anti-Semitic bastard belongs to that class of propositions that most people, and not only Catholics, don't particularly wish to think about. Hochhuth told Judy Stone that he wrote the play because "atrocities are timeless." But recent atrocities would seem to be more timeless, or controversial, because *The Deputy* came to be widely regarded as the most controversial play of the century; in Paris, the audience climbed onto the stage and beat up the actors.

The welcoming committee in America had all the trappings of a lynch mob. Frank Conniff, a Catholic nut in the Hearst bucket of bolts, wrote several hysterical columns in the New York *Journal-American*, lumping *The Deputy* along with the recent assassination of John F. Kennedy as examples of virulent acts of anti-Catholicism. Conniff said the play was a "hate breeding tract" that was "calculated to sow mistrust and misunderstanding among New Yorkers in a manner that would

bring joy to the dark heart of Adolf Hitler." The Jesuits joined
in the mudslinging; *America*, the Jesuit weekly, attacked
Hochhuth as pro-Nazi and anti-Semitic, and suggested that
the New York Police Department—an organization as top-
heavily Catholic as the Swiss Guard—might look for fire code
violations in the theater where *The Deputy* was to be staged, a
tactic that had been employed in the Puritan past to harass or
close down undesirable theatricals. (The Jesuits had their own
bone to pick with Hochhuth; although he made the fictional
hero of his play a member of the Society of Jesus, Hochhuth
laced his dialogue with embarrassing bits of Jesuit financial
history—such as the charge that the Jesuits made money
selling mercury to both sides in World War II, amid other
fisco-criminological activities.)

The Jesuits and the Hearst press were the candy confetti
atop a hasty pudding of venom baking at high temperatures.
If it had been up to New York's religious grand dukes to settle
the fate of the young German Protestant playwright, he would
have faced the variety of justice administrated by a kangaroo
court of New York cab drivers to the hapless idiot who runs
out of gas on the Triboro Bridge approach at high rush time.
Among the groups making menacing noises about *The Deputy*
were the very unlikely bedfellows of George Lincoln
Rockwell's American Nazi Party and B'nai B'rith. I talked
Keating into sending me to New York to scout the war zone.

Encased in bulletproof glass and illuminated by soft lights, a
life-sized figure of Pope Pius XII, real down to the hairs in his
nose, sat on a replica of the Papal throne in the vestibule of St.
Patrick's Cathedral. It belonged in a Rosicrucian temple.
Christ done in ivory did not merit such display in most
Catholic churches. Cardinal Spellman was said to have had a
special devotion to the late Pope, who gave the American his
own Vatican radio program when he was but a young and
struggling ecclesiastic. This statue was closer to Druidism than
devotionalism, and the thousands of New York Catholics who
shuffled in to genuflect before this obscene, shiny wax Pontiff
gave measure to the depth of feeling for the Pope and against
the punk German playwright who would vilify him.

New York Catholics had been priest-whipped into a frenzy unequaled since Eleanor Roosevelt came out against federal aid to Catholic schools. The faithful milled about on street corners, after Sunday Mass; the Catholic War Veterans oiled their souvenirs; Holy Name societies vowed vengeance against the Germans; pressure was being brought on Mayor Bob Wagner to bar the play from New York on the grounds that it would cause a religious riot.

One somehow expects more in the way of the exercise of moral conscience from the Catholic Church than, say, General Motors, likewise the Protestants than the Pentagon, and more so organized Judaism than the Ford Foundation. One should not. My rudest instruction in New York was in a venality common to all organized religions; I knew my Church was capable of taking a dive, but I presumed, in the tradition of the grass being greener, that other religions would be more principled. I learned a few things.

The pressure on New York's Catholic Mayor was brought mostly by Jews, and that mostly at Catholic request. It was an impressive example of the hard-nosed ecumenism that maintained the balance of religious power in New York. The aim was to allow no waves—so that the leaders of each faith could float undisturbed on their comfortable sacramental inner tubes. The missionary age was long over. No faith was out to reap converts from the others' faithful; it was now a simple but vital matter of holding, and enjoying, the gains of pomp and power. Interfaith cooperation in New York was like the Mafia enforcing law and order so the various families could enjoy peace and domestic tranquility in their own territories.

One of the operating rules of the interfaith axis was "You do my dirt and I'll do yours." Thus the serious rejoinders to Hochhuth's charges against the Pope were handled by the Jews, which was the reason for the surprising defense of Pius XII by B'nai B'rith. The National Catholic Welfare Conference—the Catholic lobby and propaganda apparatus in Washington, D.C.—got itself a Jew, an executive of the Anti-Defamation League, to write the white paper in defense of the Pope. (The *Jewish Spectator* denounced that white paper as a "plant," and noted that the author, a certain Dr. Lichten, had neglected to point out that his roster of defense witnesses for the Pope was riddled with what it termed "renegade Jews"—meaning Jews who had embraced Catholicism.)

The Catholic-Jewish footsie-playing did not wholly exclude the Protestants, who pitched in to try and keep *The Deputy* off the telly. The Catholic-Jewish axis, represented in the instance by the National Council of Catholic Men and the American Jewish Committee, was joined by the Protestants under cover of the National Council of Churches, and all three organizations summoned executives of the three television networks to a secret luncheon a week before *The Deputy* was to open. In the name of "intergroup relations," they tried to talk the networks out of televising the play's opening night. The networks refused. Failing that, New York's religious leaders, exercising a dignity, as the late H. L. Mencken used to say, somewhere between chiropractors and spiritualists, let word leak down from their high Arctic camps to the faithful in Brooklyn and Queens that God's will should be done. There were great stirrings among such bands of religious cowboys as the Catholic Veterans of Foreign Wars and the Jewish War Veterans, who geared up to march on the play's opening and defend the Pope's honor by stumping in protest alongside Rockwell's Nazi neo-Storm Troopers, defending Hitler's honor.

It was, all in all, an extraordinary religious roughhouse that had the makings of an evangelical riot, with the Lord's shepherds seemingly doing their worst to make such an event predestined.

Herman Shumlin, the producer of *The Deputy*, was waiting dinner in the kitchen of Dinty Moore's, where he was one of the select Broadway nabobs permitted the honor of dining with the pots and pans.

Shumlin was both a man of the theater and a theatrical man: tall, thin, bespectacled, of Shakespearean mannerisms, he drank his soup as if he were on stage in the banquet scene from *Macbeth*. His full powers were given to the expression of his personal anguish, which was considerable, over that nasty question raised by *The Deputy*: "How?"

How did it happen that six million people died in such satanic fashion with no one of stature doing anything, saying anything, in Europe or in America? The silence of the Vatican about the Nazi death factories was also the silence of the White House. The producer was dismayed that Hochhuth, at 33, could have written such a play. "He was but a child when these horrible events occurred. . . . Why, he doesn't even know what a Jew looks like. . . . He has a stereotype of them as short men with eyeglasses. . . . None of these young Germans knew Jews. . . . There just weren't many left around for them to get to know."

Shumlin indicated a desire to kick himself around Dinty Moore's kitchen table over the fact—inconceivable to him in retrospect—that he, like so many others, did not know, until far too late, what was going on at the end of the line of those Nazi "deportation" trains which carried Jews off every day with the routine of Westchester commuters. But there were people who did know—and said nothing. Hochhuth's heavy play was cobbled down with evidence—excerpts from German and Allied archives, memoirs and correspondence of World War II diplomats, and the rooting and sifting of historians—which documented that the Allied leaders knew, as did the Vatican, what was going on inside Germany many years before world opinion was alerted by the abominable discoveries of the soldiers who kicked open the Auschwitz ovens. After reading the play, Shumlin spent weeks in the New York *Times* library reading through every paper published from 1940 until the end of the war in Europe. He was looking for clues to the crime of the century, but he found few. That did not make him feel any less guilty. "What little I did find in the newspapers—and I must have read those stories at the time they were published, too—should have forced me then to ask: 'What is really going on in Auschwitz?' But I didn't ask. Nobody asked."

The Broadway producer had sniffed the glue of that heady history of cynicism, cowardliness, expediency and simple anti-Semitism behind the horror of the silent execution of six million Jews; his was the dreamy sorrow of a man high on tragedy; his Ciceronian inflections were marred with station breaks of hesitation—the hesitation of a Jew who had read the documents of the unwritten history of the Christian belligerents in World War II and didn't want to come to grips with the unavoidable conclusions.

Conclusions were redundant; the facts were sorry enough, and they tumbled off the producer's tongue like peas off his fork:

. . . Ignorance was an obscenely lame excuse; no one in an Allied government with access to intelligence information believed the "deportation" stories after 1942, and Auschwitz was still working overtime in 1944. . . . The most the governments of England and the United States did was to put the continuing extermination of Jews on their list of things to be punished; a legalistic equation: the more Jews dead by the end of the war, the more punishment for the Germans. . . . The British did nothing; to have acted would have somehow affected or compromised their grand plan for Palestine and the oil of the Arab Middle East. . . . the American government said nothing because, among other tactical reasons, Roosevelt wanted to keep the British happy . . . what was it Ben Hecht called Roosevelt? "The humanitarian who snubbed a massacre." The Americans and English both had placed obstacles in the paths of Jews attempting to emigrate out of Germany from 1938 on, until it was too late. . . . And what of the leadership of American Jewry? Surely they had to know more than the few reports of executions that surfaced: There were BBC radio broadcasts by Thomas Mann in 1942, and bulletins issued by the Jewish Telegraph Agency in London in 1943 and 1944, which should have alerted all the world to the atrocities—but did not, because no one took up the cry. . . . Why were the leaders of the American Jews silent? Was it because they simply didn't believe such horror? Because they feared more pogroms? Because they feared at that moment a high profile for Jews in America? Because assimilation was more important to them than their identity as Jews? . . . Was their fear of anti-Semitism such that they believed what Joseph Kennedy, then Ambassador to England, told some important American Jews: that it would hurt the "war effort" if they protested the German exterminations, as world opin-

ion would then think that a "Jewish war" was going on? . . . Or
were they made secret promises that all was being done behind the scenes that was possible, only to find nothing was
done. . . .

Shumlin threw up his hands, repeating, "Six million, six
million," over and over, as if the very act of saying it over and
over could make some sense of how it had been allowed to
happen.

I found it impossible to comprehend what it meant to kill
and mutilate six million people. My only frame of reference
was what it had been like when forty-seven people died. I once
covered a plane crash in the hills east of San Francisco. Forty-
seven people got aboard a plane in Reno and no one got off
the easy way; an inconsiderate nut who wanted to kill himself
shot the pilot and the co-pilot, so everyone else on the plane
had to die with him. The bodies were spread over acres; it was
a hot day and you could smell the site long before you could
see it. The FAA investigators gave out little yellow identification tags to reporters and anyone else who had any need to
walk through the carnage; tags were also put on the little bits
and pieces of what had been people, spread all over the
hillside like broken Tinker Toys. There was nothing left that
was big enough for priests or ambulances to deal with; it was
all a matter for the bureaucrats of disaster to piece together.
All I could imagine was the type of bureaucrats the Nazis must
have had for all those people to have died with the relentless
grinding of millions of pencils being sharpened.

When the ovens were at last emptied, reasonable men got
together and punished some of the bureaucrats who pushed
through the requisitions. Before that, reasonable men apparently could do nothing.

Since nothing is done in the name of unreason, the worst
horrors are done in the name of reason. The "reasonable"
arguments for the Vietnam war are sufficiently recent as not
to require restatement. When it finally becomes apparent that
what has been accepted as reasonable is actually unreasonable, it is all too often too late: The Jews are all dead; Vietnam is
a brown-out, its population this side of a basket case. It reminded me of the title of the etching by Goya: "The Dream of

Reason Breeds Monsters."

The questions raised by *The Deputy* prompt one to question
the very nature of such reasonableness. This was but the first
of many quite outrageous facts of recent history into which I
have stumbled, a reporter looking for nothing more than a
story or a drink. My reaction of journalistic outrage has led
others, in turn, to be outraged—often at me. And this has led
in turn to the style of unreasonable journalism of which I have
been often accused, and stand happily guilty. I decided that,
what the hell, it should be the job of the press—at least some of
the press—to be unreasonable most of the time.

Being unreasonable means being mean and persistent
about the truth. It means more than merely telling the truth; it
means screaming like hell. Schopenhauer once wrote, in a
negative commentary on the press, that "the object of journalism is to make events go as far as possible." I would take
that in the affirmative—that should be the object of journalism.

There were two gospels told in Dinty Moore's kitchen that
evening. The Old Testament of misguided (to put the most
favorable adjective to it) Christian resignation at the annihila-
tion of six million Jews. The New Testament of the conspiracy
of the representatives of the victims, joined by the co-
religionists of those at least passively responsible, who would
together compound the crime of silence by enforcing further
silence. The whole lot of them—Jewish and Christian leaders
alike—seemed like a caricature chorus of Jewish mothers
saying it was not nice to talk about six million dead, and now
that they were gone what was the good in inquiring if anyone
could, or should, have done anything to try and save them? It
would only make trouble.

I told Shumlin not to worry: *Ramparts* would help him stave
off that prehensile conspiracy of knaves and ecclesiastics.
That was Little Beaver telling Red Ryder, "Don't worry, those
Indians circling on the war path out there won't really attack,"
as *Ramparts* had about as much influence in New York at that
time as a leg amputee feeling in his little toe.

The liberal wing of the Catholic press has never been what

one might describe as lionhearted. Journals such as the good gray *Commonweal* and the defunct artsy-crafty *Jubilee* reacted to the Catholic-Jewish *Deputy* juggernaut with proper editorials about the right to be heard, and sticks and stones breaking your bones, and similar latter-day latitudinarian sentiments. The Catholic diocesan weeklies, with few exceptions, called for Hochhuth's entrails to be removed and dried in the sun along with other beef jerky of the devil.

Editorializing in defense of the play seemed futile, and I decided that the only thing *Ramparts* could do to cripple the ecumenical conspiracy against Shumlin's play was to invent another ecumenical conspiracy—this one on the side of *The Deputy*.

I rang up Keating in Menlo Park and told him we were forming a committee! As much as I hate serving on committees, I love to organize them—if only for the joy of designing yet another letterhead. But, as I told a protesting Keating, there was no time for letterheads in this cause; the play was scheduled to open, or be derailed, in five days. Keating came to New York like a bowling ball running downhill. He skidded to a stop in the Waldorf Astoria, where I had acquired accommodations suitable for a Catholic literary quarterly, and demanded to know all about this business of a committee. He didn't seem certain we should go whole hog on *The Deputy*, pointing out, quite correctly, that it was "dramaturgically flawed."

I diplomatically suggested to Ed that nobody in New York knew or cared who he was, but that he could become famous overnight if he, a Catholic publisher, headed a committee to defend the Pope-baiting play. Keating became convinced of the rectitude of our course, and we spent the next thirty-six hours on and off the telephone and dashing about Manhattan collecting religious men of good will and conscience who hadn't already given their due bill to the devil. We managed to find a few prominent Protestants, like John C. Bennett, of the Union Theological Seminary, who would stand on the side of the angels against the best wishes of their own religious establishments. But we drew a blank on Catholic clerics. I talked to one auxiliary bishop, highly regarded for his liberalism, who told me he would rather endorse a company that put the picture of Jesus Christ on packages of contraceptives than get involved on the side of the author of *The Deputy*. We could not find a priest who would even answer the doorbell if he knew we were coming to ask him to put his name to such an infidel committee. In desperation I threw some Catholic laymen in the pot—Gordon Zahn, the sociologist, and John Howard Griffin, the novelist, agreed to serve as Catholic window dressing in lieu of the priests who had their heads stuck in the sand up to their ordained rumps. I also drafted some Jews who did not fear to serve—the late Rabbi Abraham Heschel, of the Jewish Theological Seminary, and Maxwell Geismar, the brilliant critic and literary historian—a wonderful man about whom I cannot marshal enough superlatives, who, from our chance meeting during the white-heat controversy over *The Deputy*, was to become almost instantly my closest friend, confidant, foster father and soul mate, and the most important intellectual influence on the developing *Ramparts*.

With a bit more padding, the "Ad Hoc Committee to Defend the Right of *The Deputy* to Be Heard" was born but a day after its conception. In the finest tradition of Potemkin villages, the Committee barely had as many members as words in its cumbersome title, but that mattered not. A committee had been born; scholarly men of conscience had stood up to be counted; those of religious ilk who would suppress the truth were now to be squelched. Armed with a press release, we marched out to do murder in the Cathedral.

All of this of course would be for naught if the daily press did not treat the late-blooming arrival of such a Committee as an event which turned the lopsided battle over *The Deputy* into an even fight—with important men of religion on both sides of the controversy. A burst of publicity to that effect would result in the desired effect of the public no longer viewing the portent of *The Deputy* as an example of bigotry and malice aforethought, but rather as the confusing object of yet another religious mishmash, and therefore of no concern to those secular authorities waiting in the wings for an excuse to close the play down.

Keating was worried. He was afraid that we would give a

party and that nobody would come. "It will be ruinous if we're ignored," he said, the night before the press conference to announce the Caesarean birth of our frail Committee. "It will be a disaster if the press doesn't come. A catastrophe. I'll be disgraced. Are you sure they are going to come?"

I said, Hell, I didn't know. Keating's face darkened as if in the shadow of a passing cloud. He paced about the living room of his Waldorf suite, delivering a depressing talk about how tough a town New York was, how hard it was to get any publicity there, how people were always calling press conferences in New York and being ignored, how Cardinal Spellman had agents planted in all the newspapers and how television stations would sabotage us, how we could be destroyed. . . .

Keating made me nervous. The press conference had taken on messianic proportions, with Wagnerian overtones of dread and doubt; the fate of the world hung somehow in the balance. I had never been to New York before, and didn't know what else to do to make sure a rabbit would pop out of the hat. I had already sent out a press release, and a telegram reminding everyone in New York City in possession of a pencil or camera of the next dawn's press conference. Hell's fire, I figured, another, longer telegram might further set astir the journalistic duck ponds of Manhattan. (I am a firm believer in telegrams; "Deliver, do not phone," is a most effective creed; few among us are jaded enough not to take notice of the flat-chested yellow carrier pigeon from Western Union.)

I locked myself away with a late edition of the Manhattan Yellow Pages and a bottle of Scotch whiskey and drafted a magnificent telegram, in length somewhere between the Gettysburg Address and the Declaration of Independence, and kept the Western Union lady on the telephone for nearly three hours, as I dictated to her the names and addresses of an eclectic group of invitees drawn at whim and whimsy from the Yellow Pages. I am no longer in possession of a complete list of those opinion-making journals which received a ramblingly urgent telegram the next morning inviting them to meet Edward M. Keating for Bloody Marys and Danish at the

Waldorf Astoria, but some stained notes indicate the nature of the constituency:

The American Organist, Bedside Nurse, Casket and Sunnyside, Detergent Age, Elementary Electronics, Floor Covering Weekly, Foreign Affairs, Greeting Card Magazine, Hebrew Weekly, Hardware Age, Hospital Management, Hot Rod Magazine, Irish Echo, Intimate Story, Iron Age, Jack and Jill, Jewish Braille Review, Journal of Nuclear Medicine, Kosher Food Guide, The Little Flower Magazine, Metal Finishing, Mobile Homes Magazine, Model Airplane News, Modern Concrete, New York Daily Fruit and Vegetable Reporter, Oriental Rug Magazine, Paris Match, The Polish Press Agency, *Personal Romances, Plastic Laminating, Professional Barber, Progressive Grocer, Refuse Removal Journal, Rubber Age, Saucer News, Scholastic Coach, Sexology, Solid Wastes Management,* and so on.

I asked the exhausted Western Union operator her name, as I wanted to send her one hundred roses; she declined, I believe suspecting baser motives. I crashed into bed, exhausted, to await the dawn, secure in the hope that Ed Keating would have the pleasure of the company of at least some ladies and gentlemen of the press in the morning; most of those papers had never been invited to a press conference at the Waldorf, let alone in a telegram from a Catholic publisher who was defending an anti-Catholic play against Jewish pressure groups.

The phone rang with the rising of the sun. It was Keating, wondering if I had "any news" about the news conference. I said I had sent out reminder telegrams scented with bay rum, and the rest was in the hands of the grim reaper. The press conference was at 11 A.M. in Keating's suite; at 10:50 there was nobody there but several ruby-eyed Cuban waiters who stood like salt shakers guarding what seemed like a mountain of Danish pastry and a cotton field of coffee cups and highball glasses. The minutes ticked on without visitors. Keating slumped on a couch, looking glum, staring blackly at the movable feast I had precipitously ordered.

At 10:58 he announced that nobody was coming. I got a drink for myself before they took the booze away.

At 11:03 A.M. the walls melted. There were suddenly hundreds of people piling electronic gear into the room; within five minutes there was standing room only, the food was gone, and we had sent down for more drink. The straight New York press had arrived en masse, but apparently my last telegram had flushed out a heavy representation from the journalistic hedgerows. A *Daily News* photographer told me this was the biggest press conference he'd seen since the last time Adlai Stevenson conceded. "How come so many people are interested in this guy?" he asked, pointing with his strobe at Keating. "The guy's running for Pope," I said.

Keating adapted quickly to success, changing in color from gloom-gray to a lilaceous, perspiring pink under the torrid television lights. I thought he handled quite well the potentially awkward question of why no other members of our blue ribbon committee had showed up at the press conference: Keating said that the room was too crowded. All through that night and the next day, Keating's passionate Catholic defense of *The Deputy* blocked out most of the Hochhuth hate news that had been inundating the New York media. MULTI-FAITH PLEAS MOUNT TO LET DEPUTY BE HEARD, said the *Herald Tribune*.

In the next few days other religious leaders began to dissociate themselves from the hysteria; Shumlin reported that the heaviest pressures to keep the play from opening had begun to ebb. Opening night came and went without benefit of disaster, although the audience was under something of a house arrest and no one went out for a drink at intermission. *The Deputy's* moral and political weight did not service its dramatic ballast. *Variety* wrapped it up in its own way: "It's hardly picture material, of course, and doubtful for the road or stock." Chanters and pickets lined the streets outside the theater, but the worst physical violence was when a pudgy man from the Brooklyn chapter of the VFW beat a brown-shirted Nazi over the head with a heavy crucifix.

That experiment in activist journalism which brought Ed Keating his first flash of fame became the prototype of the aggressive, extra-journalistic patterns of behavior that were a *Ramparts'* hallmark in the ensuing years—a constant string of press conferences, full-page newspaper advertisements,

committees, helicopter rentals, entrapments, and any and all
devious and inordinate means to make our journalistic efforts
effective in the face of the natural tendency of reasonable men
to ignore them.

For all that, the publisher did not recognize it as so historic
when he got the bill.

I walked into the paper's office some two months after *The
Deputy* battle to find Keating in a condition of tantrum. That
day the invoice had arrived from Western Union: $738 for
press telegrams sent to numerous publications in New York
City.

Keating was experiencing considerable difficulty accepting
that fact. I attempted to cool him down by putting the matter
in an historical perspective. I reminded him of what Mark
Twain had said of Andrew Carnegie: "He has bought fame
and paid cash for it." Pointing to the stack of Western Union
bills in his hand, I suggested, cautiously, that he had done it on
credit.

ROSARY BEAD RACISM

For all my base suspicions of the Church, I was long disabus-
ing myself of the notion, a set piece of my Catholic upbringing, that any and all secular criticism of the Church was rank
prejudice.

The first Catholic to convince me that the Church was, in
fact, something of a bitch was a black barber in Los Angeles.
He impressed me equally with the obvious depth of his faith
and with the painful chapter and verse of the sins his Church
was committing against his race. His name was Leon Aubry,
and in the early sixties in the City of the Angels, he was known
around the Cardinal's mansion as an uppity Catholic.

Leon Aubry's concern was not with segregated barber
chairs, rather with segregated communion rails. The barber
was representative of the transplanted Southern Negro
Catholic who grew up with the idea of a Black Catholic
Church and a White Catholic Church as an artifact of the
Confederacy and accepted it as a condition of saving his

soul—but later, migrating West, expected to find greener pastures in his Church, too. Instead, he encountered the same old fences in Southern California—religious hedgerows of racial discrimination growing alongside the freeways across the broad expanses of the rich and prosperous Los Angeles Archdiocese, under the Cardinal with a financial green thumb, James Francis McIntyre.

A former Wall Street stockbroker, who later took a strong position in commodity futures of Heaven, McIntyre ran his corner of the Catholic Church like the gigantic money-making machine that it was. Questioning his methods was as fruitful as arguing with success, and twice as unappreciated, as the Cardinal, nearing 80, took the act of kissing his ring as a metaphor for kissing his ass, and would countenance no behavior to the contrary. As for politics, His Eminence was said to be more comfortable inside a Masonic Temple than that expensive glass temple to socialism on the East River known as the United Nations.

Aubry had understood about segregation under color of law in Louisiana, but in Southern California he was nonplused at finding segregation under color of Catholicism. The typical parish in McIntyre's archdiocese was about as well integrated as a John Birch Society cell, and it was the Church's policy, actively and passively, to keep things that way. The Cardinal forbade those few of his priests who were so inclined to preach sermons about the Catholic doctrine on race lest it upset the white faithful. As black Catholic families moved into the neighborhood, pastors reacted as to the handiwork of the devil. And it was not just the white parishes which closed ranks; communities of Mexican-American Catholics—it being California, and they Spanish and all—felt very strongly about having been there first, before these "foreign" black Catholics migrating westward. The Mexicans were encouraged by their white pastors to fight intrusions. One elderly Irish priest told a protest meeting of his Mexican parishioners gathered in the church, "Don't worry, we have a plan for getting rid of the niggers."

Blacks were kept by economic preconditions out of the more ritzy white parishes, and those who did come to receive the Sacraments in Beverly Hills were accepted as the tokens they were. But in the middle-class parishes where the number of blacks approaching the communion rail grew (in the view of many pastors) alarmingly during the decade of the fifties—the church welcome mat was put out with all the subtlety of Ma and Pa Kettle making the revenue agents feel at home. White Catholics would discuss their delaying tactics over watery gin fizzes before Holy Name Society breakfasts. One popular tactic was for ushers to seat black parishioners together in one section at Mass. (One priest explained to me that there existed "apostolic" precedent for this practice since children were expected to sit together in one area at the "Children's Mass" so why shouldn't Negroes sit together?)

Gradually, some formerly white parishes, through massive shifts in the economic top soil of the neighborhood, became black parishes. When these parishes turned as black as an Ethiopian Christ, the Cardinal dealt with them, generously he felt, in what would most charitably be described as a "separate but equal" building program. He was especially proud of Verbum Dei, a new Catholic high school in Compton, an area of Los Angeles adjacent to, and as black as, Watts. "We have built a fine school for the Negroes out in Compton," he told a friend of Aubry's.

Lest one optimistically take the long view—that Cardinal McIntyre was an elderly, crotchety, rich old man who was the exception to the racial practices of the Roman Catholic Church—it should be immediately noted that he was, lamentably, no exception; rather, he was a more royal example of the rule.

Take, for example, Chicago—one of the most Catholic cities in the United States, except Boston, rumored as it is to be a suburb of the Vatican. Black Catholics in Chicago have their own sorrowful mysteries, dolefully similar to Los Angeles. The influx of blacks to Chicago came historically earlier and in larger numbers than to Los Angeles. The late Cardinal Mundelein of Chicago indicated the Church's attitude in these matters when in the twenties he invited a black order of missionaries, the Divine Word Fathers, to drop one of their assignments abroad and come and administer to the spiritual needs of the black natives in Chicago. (The Catholic Church maintained a "Commission of Catholic Missions Among the Colored and the Indians" in America, which issued an annual report as late as 1966.) This left Chicago's regular diocesan priests 99 and 44/100 percent white and free to continue attending the city's ethnically diverse multitudes, whose only common denominator was that they were white, poor and Catholic. In the fifties it was as easy for blacks to get into parochial schools in Chicago as into a country club in South Carolina. Chicago pastors used church facilities to organize whites-only "improvement associations" which would make sure that, should a Catholic move, he would only sell his home or rent his flat to another white Catholic, or a white Protestant, if God forbid it came to that.

The seeds of this rosary bead racism were to bear their sacrilegious fruit in the spectacle of young Catholic punks, scapulars and medals around their necks and wearing their parochial school sweat shirts, throwing rocks, taking the Lord's name in vain, and in other ways demonstrating against the civil rights demonstrators who invaded Cicero and the whites-only hot spots on the southwest side of Chicago in 1966.

It is axiomatically true that the Church of Rome moves slowly. But it has been on this earth almost 2,000 years, and it has yet to get around to doing anything serious about implementing Christ's teachings on race and equality. It took the Catholic Bishops of the United States four years to get up ecclesiastical steam to issue a flat-out proclamation against racial segregation and discrimination after the 1954 Supreme Court desegregation decision; then, having said it, most Bishops promptly forgot it, spiritual leaders to. some 50,000,000 hypocrites—good American Catholics all, whose religion made racial discrimination a no-no, but whose priests told them yes-yes with their eyes.

This was the great sham and scandal in the Catholic Church against which Leon Aubry and his fellow black Catholics began to take up nonviolent arms and give alms against in Los

Angeles. It is of interest that this uprising was mostly the work of Aubry's people—the transplanted Southern black Catholics. The "native son" blacks who had lived longer on the West Coast accepted the tacit segregation of their Church the way the blacks had in the South.

When I met Aubry he was in hot water up to his barber chair. He had been trying for six years to get an appointment with Cardinal McIntyre to discuss his grievances, but the closest he had come was a meeting with an epicene Monsignor who suggested it had been "arranged" for Aubry and his fellow malcontents to join the Knights of Columbus. So the barber and his black Catholic allies began to picket the baronial portals of exclusive Fremont Place, a private park for the rich in Los Angeles where the Cardinal's mansion is located. (Aubry and his group had the big black balls to sing "Holy God We Praise Thy Name," a bouncy hymn with a Gregorian sort of rhythm, while they stalked the Cardinal.) That sort of boat-rocking, even if you were white, was entirely out of bounds in Lotusland.

McIntyre labeled these black Southerners upsetting his flock as Catholic carpetbaggers—"outside groups," consisting of "half-whites and half-mongrels." The Cardinal did a memorable job on these upstarts, working them over with his pectoral cross in a way that hurt like hell but didn't leave bruises. The black families who had linked their names with Aubry's group became the sudden objects of pastoral attention. They began to receive visits from priests and nuns ostensibly to discuss their grievances—visits which were as oppressive and intimidating as they were frequent. One visiting nun stayed for 12 hours, just sitting in the living room, a crow dressed in black, fingering her rosary beads, until the family finally asked her to leave. These black Catholics were told that what they were doing was ruining the Church for everyone, hurting their own cause, and hurting their personal standing in the community, which could have severe social, financial repercussions. . . .

The barber ringleader got the full treatment. He had been cutting hair in the same shop in West Los Angeles for ten years, and the summer that he took up his beef with his

Cardinal, he got his first citation. The inspecting civil servant said that Aubry hadn't washed his hands properly before he went on to the next customer. Barbers usually wash their hands between haircuts about as thoroughly as surgeons did before Pasteur. The citation, and with it an implicit threat against the license which was his livelihood, came during Aubry's second "inspection" of that summer—followed by two more "inspections" and threats of citations. Within six weeks there were as many inspectors and bureaucrats coming into his shop to give him some sort of haircut as customers.

THE PRIEST WHO TRIED TO FIRE A CARDINAL

I knocked on Leon Aubry's basement door on a summer evening in 1964. Leon had taken a few days off work. Business was not too good. We walked through the basement, up a flight of cement stairs and across a short moonlit section of outdoor patio to a lean-to with latticework walls. Crowded inside was the Central Committee of the Southern California Catholic Underground.

The business of that night at the Los Angeles catacombs was carried on in a careless, chatty atmosphere that understated its seriousness. There wasn't a necktie or fully buttoned shirt to be seen, and Bermuda shorts and halters displayed a lot of Catholic legs and shoulders. The faithful strolled and slouched about, sipping beers and savoring the latest rumor.

Two priests walked in, dressed in full Roman-collared uniform. The reaction was as if two Centurion fellow travelers had spirited themselves into the midst of the Christians. There turned out to be cause for excitement because one of the priests announced that he was planning to commit ecclesiastical hara-kiri, and the other said he was on the verge.

One of them actually did it. Father William DuBay was shortly to become, by my record keeping, the first Catholic priest of the decade to go over the wall in full view of the public. Certainly, he was the only priest, in a decade of excess, who went so far as to try to fire his Cardinal.

DuBay was tall and the shy side of 30 with a few pimples still showing. He had the gait and gall of an intern. An assistant pastor in a largely black parish in Compton, a bedroom community within the boundaries of Los Angeles as the Jim Crow flies, he had been summoned to the Cardinal's lair, where he was told that if he persisted in preaching to black Catholics that it was a sin for white Catholics to discriminate against them, he would be suspended as a priest and his pay docked. "Cardinal McIntyre stated that there were many valid reasons for segregation and declared that 'After all, white parents have a right to protect their daughters,' " DuBay said.

The priest announced he was going to appeal directly to the Pope and ask His Holiness to replace the Cardinal. Squeals of excitement broke the sepulchral silence that had attended DuBay's blow-by-blow account of his meeting with the Cardinal. It fell my lot, as the supposed professional Catholic anarcho-syndicalist in attendance, to caution the priest, although dispensing caution is not my specialty. I suggested that Rome would not likely snap to attention at his petition, but the young priest said he had been studying the Canon Law of the Church and felt that there were grounds for his going over the Cardinal's head, and precedent that the Pope would respond affirmatively. I think the priest partially believed that. The cushion of some liberal hope that something should not be impossible, even though it is, is often the very spring that breaks the paralysis of caution and pushes a man to revolutionary action.

Three days later Father DuBay called a press conference. His hands were shaking as he read from a cable he had just sent Pope Paul VI. He had asked the Pope to remove the Cardinal Archbishop of Los Angeles from office, to bust him to Monsignor, as it were, for "gross malfeasance in office" and "inexcusable abuses" of authority in gagging his priests from preaching on race and pistol-whipping those who had tried.

The reaction of the press was typical of its kind. The way DuBay talked about McIntyre, the assignment editors of the daily blats and video bleeps weren't sure whether to give the story to the religious correspondent or the police beat. They knew something big was happening, but weren't sure what it was. In 1964, priests didn't wash the dirty vestments of the Catholic Church in public; even if he was right, the press didn't want to jump in and say so, fearful of offending the Catholic faithful.

The press therefore reported DuBay's charge and McIntyre's *pro forma* denial, and then ducked for cover. I asked one Southern California editor why he didn't seek out black Catholics to investigate their condition in light of DuBay's assertions; that would not be "objective," he said, since Negroes obviously had "an axe to grind" in the matter.

While Father DuBay waited in vain for a postcard from the Pope, the Cardinal, knowing the best way to kill off a story is to ignore it, retained his public silence—a silence that the Archdiocesan newspaper, *The Tidings*, suggested was in the tradition of Jesus versus Pilate. In the privacy of his Chancery, however, the Cardinal came down on Father DuBay like Genghis Khan collecting past due rent.

The impetuous padre, the din of liberal well-wishers still in his ears, his eyes still bright from the television lights, abruptly found himself standing in the center of a ballroom-sized chamber looking up at the Cardinal perched in the distance, a kewpie-doll-Christ on an elevated Marie Antoinette chair. The air was heavy with the nectarous smells of incense and revenge. Two hundred priests of the Archdiocese, witnesses on command of their Cardinal, not a one of them daring even to cough, had been art-directed in a semicircle around the priest on the carpet.

The Cardinal's Inquisitor, a Monsignor Hawkes, laid down the law to Father DuBay—the Canon Law, which, as Robert Blair Kaiser, a former Jesuit turned journalist explained it to me, is to jurisprudence as *Catch 22* is to logic. The priest, by delivering the forbidden sermons on race, had violated Canon Law 2331, the penalty for which was excommunication for one who "pertinaciously refuses to give obedience to legitimate precepts or prohibitions of the bishop." Under Canon Law, the sole judge of DuBay's guilt or innocence was his bishop, in this case the Cardinal, who if he did not wish to

put the Church to the expense of convening an ecclesiastical
court, could simply pronounce sentence there in that room,
selecting in his wisdom from a range of punishments which
included suspension from the priesthood, defrocking, or excommunication.

There was silence and the shuffling of black-shoed feet.
The Inquisitor was not finished. Father DuBay had told reporters that, should Cardinal McIntyre attempt to bring sanc-
tions against him for preaching against racism, he would seek
relief in the civil courts. Sue the Cardinal, indeed!

The Inquisitor read aloud from Canon 120, which renders
a Bishop immune from civil lawsuits. And the Church had not
left unattended the question of what should happen in the
event a person, in reckless disregard of Canon 120, sued a
Bishop. There was then Canon 2341, which provided that
such a person would be automatically excommunicated, instantaneous with the filing of a lawsuit. There was one final
thing. Excommunication under Canon 2341 came directly
from the Pope in Rome, so DuBay would have no recourse
against Cardinal McIntyre under the laws of the United
States—although he was welcome to try and sue the Pope if he
could find a lawyer crazy enough. Thus, even in the highly
unlikely event that DuBay was successful in a civil action
against the Los Angeles Archdiocese to restore his priestly
functions, it would be fruitless as he would have been long
gone from the Church, excommunicated by the Pope. How
was it *Dragnet* used to go? Dum de dum dum.

The priest could have thrown in his holy cloth and stalked
away from it all, but he wanted, more than liberty or honor, to
stay in the Church. Despite the walking horror that was his
Cardinal, DuBay still believed in the Catholic Church
—believed that it would survive the very revolutionary war he
was waging to change it, and forge on, a streamlined
monolith, the tin woodman receiving a heart, toward a new
era of serving man instead of merely saving mankind.

The Inquisitor asked DuBay which straw he wanted to pick;
the long straw was that he could remain a priest, on probation,
but could never again speak out in public, be interviewed, or

give or formulate opinions; he must obey the Cardinal in all things, including the proscription that the Catholic doctrine on race was fit only to be seen in theological texts but not heard in church.

DuBay nodded his assent to his Inquisitor. To seal the bargain, Father DuBay was led by the hand to kneel at the feet of Cardinal McIntyre and, with the 200 priests watching in silence, kissed the Cardinal's ring, the traditional gesture of Christian obedience.

The inquisition of William DuBay was not reported in the press. What was reported was a short announcement the next day from the Chancery office of the Los Angeles Archdiocese that the matter of Father DuBay had been "concluded," and that Father was going "on a retreat and then a vacation."

What happened thereafter to William DuBay is an object lesson in cooperation with the system. The Cardinal waited a month until the press interest had cooled, and then transferred DuBay from his black flock to a white parish where almost every car in the church parking lot on Sunday sported a Goldwater bumper strip. The Cardinal then waited another year and, when it was a safe bet that no one was looking, or cared any more, he suspended Father DuBay from the exercise of his priestly functions, i.e., kicked him out of the Church.

The priest later married a divorcée who had enough children for the both of them.

A decade has passed since Father DuBay's revolt, but little has changed. Cardinal McIntyre himself is gone, retiring to the pudgy salutes of the thousands of hard hats who received gainful employment building his schools and the best wishes of the Midas priests toiling in the Archdiocesan counting houses. There is another hand wearing the jeweled Bishop's ring at the tiller, but the course of the Ship of Church has not veered—it remains straight down the middle and angling to the right. The Catholic Church today no more exerts its moral and economic power to end racism than before. But the Church puts on a better face than it did in McIntyre's time, as prelates with better public relations savvy and sometimes more heart than McIntyre are calling the shots. The Church continues to treat racism as a political problem, not a moral one; it does just enough to protect its flanks from "interest group" criticism. Most American communion rails have been desegregated, to be sure; but the Church's heralded advances in this area are but retreats from visible sin, and have about as much effect on changing the institutionalized substructure of racism as the new flock of blacks appearing in television commercials has on improving the quality of life in the ghetto.

NEW FRIENDS

From Los Angeles, I went to Harlem, where I reported the riots of 1964 from a vantage point on a bar stool on Amsterdam Avenue and 126th Street. The change in point of view involved more than geography. Although *Ramparts* would continue to be described in the press as a "Catholic layman's magazine" for the next several years, we began, in that hot summer of 1964—the summer of Father DuBay's Inquisition was the summer of Harlem and the civil rights murders in Mississippi—the process of disengaging from the Catholic Church. The Church was a willing partner to the divorce. Even many radical Catholics were uneasy with *Ramparts'* kick-'em-in-the-ass style of bishop-baiting.

For me, the Church was a bridge to developing a political consciousness, although I did not know I was crossing that bridge until I had reached the other side. I became involved in issues such as racism and the war in Vietnam through the Church's complicity, and then went from the Catholic particular to the political universal. It was as if I first focused a Brownie camera on the Catholic Church—and then, stepping farther back (and left), began to see the picture as a whole. The Church was but one institution among many which had vested interests in the performance of the war and the maintenance of economic and social inequality. These institutions together made up that hydra-headed flatulence, the

"System," and I was soon off and running after the System, leaving the Church in the lurch.

It is somewhat ironic that *Ramparts* began to gain its greatest fame as a "Catholic" magazine at exactly the time that the paper's interest in the Church was waning and I was taking up what I thought were bigger fish to fry. It even fooled the *National Review*, a journal crawling with Romans. L. Brent Bozell and some *National Review* types launched a conservative Catholic magazine, *Future*, which Bozell announced as "an antidote to *Ramparts*." But the sighs of relief when *Ramparts* turned its guns to other targets came loudest from the Catholic liberals of the *Commonweal* school of journalism who were stylistically offended by what they would deride as the "Hinckle treatment" of smearing the Church. Those professional Catholics saw me as a lout from the wrong side of the San Francisco tracks lumbering mindlessly through the well-plowed and manicured fields they had planted of lay criticism, expressed with caution and dignity, of the clergy's handling of the Church. They became almost hysterical when Drew Pearson who, Quaker lout, didn't know better, began referring to me in columns as "a prominent Catholic layman."

Ramparts' storm-centered Catholicism early attracted many non-Catholic writers to it—kindred spirits who spawned new friendships and relationships which would provide the impetus to take the magazine out of the very Catholic orbit they so admired. These new friends, who gave me magnificent vistas of new enemies to conquer, were of a radical diversity that forbids summary. One led to another as in an atomic reaction, and mixed with some brute journalistic instincts, effected an astonishing series of changes—religious, intellectual, political, stylistic—in the formerly nice schoolgirl Catholic quarterly.

The nucleus for these new friends was Max Geismar. The distinguished literary historian forever endeared himself to me when I introduced him to Ed Keating, and Max fainted dead away on the restaurant floor of the Waldorf Astoria. Keating insisted Max rest the night in his suite. Max stayed in a bedroom, puking, while Keating sat in the living room telling Max's wife, Anne, his life story in the greatest of detail. Every time Keating came in the bedroom to see if Max felt well enough to talk, Max would start puking again. I went out on the pretext of moving the Geismars' car for them and went drinking for three hours. Keating was still talking when I came back. Anne Geismar hissed at me when Ed went in the bedroom, "You motherfucker, you stuck me here with this Catholic King Kong with diarrhea of the mouth." I loved her from that moment forward. We both had scatological minds, and would horrify Max with raunchily hilarious conversations about dingleberries and such. The Geismars became, and remain, my very favorite people. They have none of the self-righteousness and self-importance that makes the American left such a horror. Unlike the high priests of cant who make up his enemies in the American literary establishment, Max Geismar insisted that one can't separate politics and literature—that "art" is neither timeless nor classless the way the New Criticism attempts to neuterize it—Max calls it "the Higher and Higher criticism." Geismar's work over the decades has been a brilliant reaffirmation of the fine madness and love of life that is the great American tradition of Dreiser and Twain. He attacked the crinoline perversion of that tradition in the ultra worship of a social and sexual adolescent like Henry James by the dim-watted leading lights of the American literary establishment, who hate Max for telling them so brilliantly that they are the psychically walking wounded.

Over the years, my friendship with the Geismars, like any real love relationship, had its love-hate aspects; we recognized that and would laugh at it, too. I was always late going to visit them at their home in Harrison and one night, when I hadn't arrived by 11 o'clock, they turned out the lights and went to bed, just to show me. I had brought a giant salami as a peace offering and disgruntledly left it on the doorstep of the darkened house. The next morning Anne called me, almost unable to talk from laughing—their dog, Hankins, had gobbled down the entire salami and that morning had erupted in a Big Bertha barrage of farting that forced them to evacuate the house. After saying all this, I should report that, like all mortals, the Geismars are not perfect. They play tennis.

The Geismars brought into the paper's ken many writers who shared their radical politics and their love of life, people such as Truman Nelson, the novelist of the abolitionist movement, and Jakov Lind, the ribald novelist of his own wild Viennese-Jewish soul. Two friends of Max's were particularly important in developing the paper's tough-minded perspective in covering the domestic wars during the waning years of the civil rights movement. Their shared experiences give a better idea of my perspective about those years than any rendition of the familiar tune of how I got religion at Selma; I did, but more even than the experience of Selma, the friendship of two men—Conrad Lynn and John Griffin—made it possible for me to so readily understand a few years later what Eldridge Cleaver meant when he talked about the difference between white niggers and black niggers.

Conrad Lynn was a Clarence Darrow of lost causes, a brilliant lawyer with the spunk and sputter of a fired-up tea kettle, who paddled a lone canoe upstream against the political currents of the thirties, forties and fifties, defending unpopular causes before their time had come, being dealt losing cards from the stacked deck of the administration of justice, yet always raising the ante and staying in the game. Often his clients were those who sacrificed themselves on the altar of the propaganda of the deed, such as the Puerto Rican nationalists who shot up Congress in 1954, or the mixed bag of revolutionaries alleged to have plotted to blow up the Statue of Liberty. More often, his clients were people whose brand of pacifism or black activism was not on the approved list of the civil liberties or black establishments, such as pacifist Ruth Reynolds, framed for a term of years in a Puerto Rican jail in the early fifties, whose plight was shamefully ducked by the American Civil Liberties Union. Most of his clients suffered no such lack of publicity; usually, they had a big press but a bad press, such as Robert F. Williams, the black freedom-fighter of Monroe, North Carolina, later an exile and the author of the much-feared little book, *Negroes with Guns*,

whose ascent of the ladder of militancy began when he was
kicked out of the NAACP because he insisted on standing up
for his rights at a time when the only posture approved by the
millionaire morticians and other black bourgeois running the
NAACP was to stoop.

Conrad had done his share of busting over the years. The
lawyer for the first "Freedom Ride" South, he busted the
whites-in-front, blacks-to-the-rear seating pattern on the
buses of the rapid transit system of the Confederacy; he
busted the segregated lockers at Rockaway Beach, the
whites-only swimming pool at Palisades Park, and innumera-
ble other recreational and commercial conveniences of racism. In the doing, he'd been involved in more than his share
of police busts and headbusting.

Conrad's law offices were on downtown Broadway, where
he shared a suite in a vintage twenties building with his law
partner, Gene Ann Condon, an attractive Irish blonde some
decades younger and almost six inches taller than Conrad; a
girl of good IRA stock, she was no stranger to the company of
revolutionaries. The office was a legal lumberyard, with briefs
and files stacked in every conceivable cubic inch of space,
under chairs, on top of chairs, files and bookcases, piled askew
in corners as high as an elephant's eye.

Conrad took me on a wild ride to Harlem during the riots of
1964, where I was the only white reporter inside the Lenox
Avenue war offices of the Progressive Labor Party.

As we bounced along Riverside Drive with the top down on
Conrad's banged-up yellow Carmen Ghia convertible, going
up to Harlem, he was talking faster than the speed limit,
spinning out a story a mile—wild, hilarious tales from the
skeleton closets of radical politics, which he would astound-
ingly intermix with his personal sexual memorabilia. (Years
later Conrad sent me the manuscript of his unpublished au-
tobiography to read. I was amazed and delighted to find that
he hadn't changed his pattern of reminiscences, even in typescript. Interspersed and contemporaneous with his moving
accounts of the inner world of black and radical politics and
the effect of international leftist politics on the thirties and

forties were these painfully honest and at times purposefully amusing little memoirs of his sex life. He mentioned not only every girl he ever laid, but every girl he ever thought about laying. It was all in all the most enjoyable volume of political memoirs I have ever read, and I must mention one memorable incident from it, so as to perhaps spur a publisher on to print the book:

Conrad had just graduated from law school and begun practicing law, no small achievement for a black man then, but that triumph was as nothing to him compared with getting the girl of his desires, whom he had yearned for over a period of years, to go to bed with him. But at the critical moment his erection collapsed, and he was consumed with shame. The girl sullenly went to sleep, and Conrad describes how he lay there in the dark, tears of disgrace in his eyes, and he asks himself one of the great questions of all time: "Of what use was it having become a lawyer if I couldn't even fuck?" He reported that things had a happy ending, however, the next morning.

Ours was a heady, gale-force conversation, full of life and vitamins and gossip, and by the time that bumpy ride was over, I thought of Conrad Lynn as a soul brother, a rare free spirit who could battle the world without losing his ability to enjoy it. These were some of the stories he chose to tell on our way to our appointment in Harlem:

There was the time Conrad spent in the Army, "literally pounding shit"; he was handed a large mallet and ordered to keep a giant cesspool moving, a cruel and unusual punishment for the lawsuits, unpopular with the noncoms, that he kept filing, as a private, to desegregate the armed forces. Conrad told how, as a young lawyer, he drew up the papers for Adam Clayton Powell to buy a whites-only apartment house, which Powell kept whites only. He told me tales of "Scotic," a black shantytown which rose on a garbage dump in Nassau County in the late thirties, where destitute black families moved when they had nowhere else to go, lived in homes made from old packing crates and survived largely by picking through the garbage, living like animals off the waste of an affluent society. Conrad once appeared before the great

Judge Learned Hand, who, although retired and in his early
nineties, was still sitting as a Federal Circuit Appeals Judge.
Conrad was seeking bail for a Puerto Rican-nationalist fanatic,
an ex-lawyer who had shot a federal judge in the head during
a political trial. When Learned Hand heard what Conrad's
client had done, he rose and staggered from the courtroom,
one hand to his head, the other waving backwards signaling
No, No, No, before Conrad had a chance to say a word.
Finally, there was the weekend of Fidel Castro's visit to New
York to address the United Nations, when Conrad, working
for the Fair Play for Cuba Committee, was assigned to make
the arrangements so Fidel's party could move uptown from
fancy Manhattan to the Hotel Theresa in Harlem. The manager of the Theresa was less than overjoyed at the prospect,
and demanded a cash deposit of close to $1,000. It was Satur-
day night, the banks were shut, and Conrad was scratching his
head trying to figure where he could come up with that
amount of cash when he thought of the Harlem gamblers,
who all carried big rolls; so it was that a politically sympathetic
black gambler put up the money so Fidel Castro could move
up to Harlem. . . .

We were so caught up in these stories, Conrad in the telling
and I in the listening, that, even though I wasn't sure where we
were going, I regretfully broke into Conrad's stream of consciousness to ask if we hadn't missed the turn to Harlem,
which we had.

But Conrad was not the first nigger in the *Ramparts'* woodpile. That honor would go to John Howard Griffin—a most
extraordinary fellow, a one-man-band of virtue and a vir-
tuoso, who is, quite literally among other things, and at all of
these first rate—a novelist, essayist, musicologist, theologian,
expert in animal husbandry, public speaker, propagandist
and journalist-saint of the white man's struggle in the black
cause. Griffin is also a faith healer of himself, as the man has
had so many physical things wrong with him, among them
blindness and tumors from head to toe, yet has kept working
twenty hours a day, that he must rank as the eighth medical

wonder of the world—a cautious ranking on my part as I
forget the first seven.

"When I was a Negro . . ." John was always saying, because
he was one, for almost a year, a white man who took drugs and
dyes and baked himself under ultraviolet lamps to turn himself into a black man, so he could walk the streets in the South
and experience what it does to a man's soul to be black in this
society. He wrote about it in a book called *Black Like Me*, the
desperate, sensational attempt of one white man to convey to
other whites the reality of racism. What he didn't write in the
book was that the drugs he took to blacken his skin were to
cause him severe pain and Jobian medical complications for
years after—accelerating the growth of tumors, fortunately
nonmalignant but painful and dreadful, which were yet
another cross on top of a Calvary of medical problems, most
resulting from his being shot to pieces in the Pacific in World
War II. Griffin took all of this pain in silence; he was constantly on the go, driven by the vision he had during the 11
years of his life when he was totally blind, of a holocaust that
was coming because of the madness and evil of racism. He was
a determined Texan, out to make the world understand before it was too late, always driving himself too hard, as if he
were performing the collective penance for the sins of the
white race against the black, as if the very devil were chasing
after him to do good.

Blind or sighted, Griffin worked on like a metronome. He
was always trying to save somebody, himself last. A medical
student in France on the eve of the Second World War, he
spent two years working with the French Resistance smuggling Jews out of Germany and Austria. Griffin was lucky ducking German bullets, but later in the war, serving in the Air
Force in the Pacific, he wasn't so lucky. He was mustered out
with 5 percent of his sight remaining, the residue of head
wounds. By 1947 he was completely blind, and remained so
until his sight was partially restored a decade later after multiple operations. Some critics, whose cynicism is such they could
not believe a man as straight and sincere as John Griffin could
exist on this earth, and who therefore carped at *Black Like Me*

as some sort of gimmick, were to comment that the near-blind Griffin wore dark glasses because he wanted to be thought a movie star.

During his ten years in the dark, John studied music with the Benedictines in France and Thomistic philosophy with the Discalced Carmelites in America, settling in his native Texas where he took up animal husbandry, married, fathered three children, wrote two novels and an anthology of essays and journalism. Hardly a year after his sight was partly restored he went off to find a cooperative dermatologist to darken his skin; once he could see again, he wanted to see what it was like to be black.

If there is something wrong with Griffin it is that he is a goddamn saint, an insufferable Christian, a soft-spoken, gentle guy who never seems to think ill of anyone; he even prayed for those friends and neighbors who burnt him in effigy on the main street of his home town of Mansfield, Texas, when the word reached the local pool hall that he had gone and turned himself into a nigger.

Interestingly, for all his personal softness, Griffin's novels have a magnificent sense of evil; his books, which fairly exude brimstone, are as out of print as they are out of favor in some fashionable circles. (A short story of Griffin's was once printed in a creative writing "textbook"; he read the usual textbook-type questions at the end of the story such as "What does the author mean by this scene?" and said he couldn't answer a single one of them.)

The civil rights movement was one big integrationist Elks Club to John Griffin. He was constantly traveling about the country, speaking, wearing himself hoarse warning about what was coming in those too-short days before Watts and Detroit. He knew everyone who had so much as lifted a pinky against Jim Crow, and *Ramparts* made the acquaintance of them all—white Southerners who had long fought the good fight, such as John Henry Falk, the radio personality lost in the static of the fifties blacklists, and the late P. D. East, the integrationist editor of the *Petal Paper* of Mississippi; and, more in tune with our growing itch to get out of the frying pan of the Church and into the fire below, blacks who knew where the action was, such as Dick Gregory.

John Griffin, convert to Catholicism who bled for the pain of black men, was to gradually displace, by sheer moral weight, those other High Church converts who once bent Keating's ear.

5.

Radical Slick

THE PUBLISHER IS DOWN TO HIS LAST SHOPPING CENTER

"The Best of Everything is
what I want for everyone,
but it costs Millions."
—*Gully Jimson*

ON the night before the Thanksgiving of 1964 I was comfortably seated in the neo-Edwardian lobby of the Algonquin
Hotel in New York City having a drink with the publisher.
The occasion was pure ambrosia. I had just declared to him in
an outburst of statistical euphoria that we had "almost dou-
bled" our circulation—from 2,200 to 4,000 readers. The
transformation from a 2,000-plus-copy quarterly to a
4,000-copy monthly magazine was taking place under my
aegis, for which purpose I had just taken a six-month leave
from my secure job as a reporter for the San Francisco
Chronicle. It bothered me not a whit that we had to print
50,000 copies to sell 4,000. That was the publisher's problem.
Ramparts was his own expensive toy, but within the somewhat
stormy confines of what I took to be the natural eccentricity of
the very rich, I was being given reasonable access to play with
it, too.

Ed Keating's eccentricities were not of your ordinary common garden variety. One day a strange bill crossed my desk. It
was an invoice for $47 from a shoemaker, across which Keat-
ing had scribbled, "Editorial expenditure." Since I was nominally the executive editor, I asked him what it was about.

He confided that he had sent a young civil rights worker on
a secret undercover mission to Louisiana. His assignment was

89

to dig up proof that Leander Perez, the notorious seg-
regationist czar of Plaquemines Parish, had "colored blood" in
his veins. The proof was among some papers that Ed had
heard an old slave had hidden under a floorboard in one of
Perez's dungeons. Our spy was to infiltrate the dungeon, find
the floorboard and get away with the goods. The $47 was for
special alterations to his boots—the heels had been hollowed
out and a metal file and a compass hidden inside. If he was
captured by the evil Perez and locked in the dungeon, he
could saw his way out with the file and use his compass to
escape through the swamp.

I knew the legion of stories about the wacky ways of rich
publishers, and I doubted that there was anything Ed Keating
could do which would surprise me. I was wrong.

A glance across the table alerted me to the fact that my sense
of well-being was not shared by the man who was providing
for it. Ed Keating was crying.

I did what any sensible coward would do and pretended I
hadn't seen. I reached over and rang the little brass bell on the
battle-scarred oak cocktail table that summoned the waiter to
bring more drinks, which he eventually did, but that did not
effect any change in Keating. He was still crying.

I had never seen a millionaire cry. Finally, curiosity got the
better of prudence. I asked Ed if there was anything wrong.

Keating looked up from the spot across the lobby where his
blank gaze had been fixed.

"I'm broke," he said quietly.

"But Ed," I said, "you can't be broke. You're the publisher."

His abrupt statement was as immediately incomprehensible
to me as the national debt. Ed Keating was rich. He was
famous for being rich. He owned the magazine. I knew that he
had poured a lot of money into the quarterly *Ramparts*, but he
still had to be rich because he had just turned it into a monthly.
He had hired me. I had hired a staff. We were publishing. We
had all kinds of stories in the works. There were subscription
ads in the newspapers. At that moment there were thousands
of copies stacked in trucks on the way to the newsstands. We
had another issue going to press in two weeks. This was crazy.
It couldn't be. He couldn't be broke.

"But Ed," I tried again. "You're a *millionaire.*"

"I used to be," he said. "I spent it. It was my wife's money."

The business about the wife was equally unexpected and, for one of the few times in my compulsively chatty existence, the cliché was reality; I became speechless.

Keating asked what I thought he should do. My shock became part residual disbelief, part resentment that he might be telling the truth. I suggested that he should shut down the whole shooting match that very night, fire the staff by telegram, and see if he could get his deposit back from the phone company.

Keating glowered as if I were the one bringing him the bad news. He sat up, clanging the bell for more drinks, and began an impassioned speech, without any awareness of melodrama: "I just couldn't bring myself to close the magazine. It's too important to the Church. I must go on. There must be *something* that can be done to save it. There must be someone else who would be willing to put money in it besides me. Isn't there some way you can find someone to help me?"

I said that as improbable as such a likelihood was, even miracles took time, and it would be clearly impossible to do anything if we stopped publishing, which we most certainly would have to do if he couldn't even pay for the drinks we had just ordered.

I repeated, in a kind of dumbfounded rote, "You mean you really don't have *any* more money?"

Keating brightened a bit. "Well, I do have one shoppng center left. . . ."

I suppose I looked a little blank. Keating, explaining, became almost chipper: "It's only a medium-sized shopping center. It's in Santa Clara. It's got a mortgage on it, and there's a lawsuit I'd have to settle with one of the tenants, and I'd have to fix the air conditioning before I could sell it. But still in all it should net a little over a hundred thousand after that."

I said to the publisher that I did not want to be the person who told him to sell his last shopping center. But . . .

I found myself experiencing something of the peculiar merriment Jack London described as possessing men who are facing disaster. Back in a dark abscess of rationality I knew I

should be mad as hell at the deadbeat millionaire sitting across
from me who deliberately signed me up as first mate in the
launching of a journalistic Hindenburg. But there was something so pathetic and principled in his willingness to throw his
last shopping center into the pot that I instead told him to
cheer up, I'd think of something, it wasn't that bad, it could be
worse, everything would somehow work out all right. The
Optimist's Rosary: the five Euphoric Mysteries of Comfort.

Perhaps Keating saw the gleam of the disaster-lover in my
one good eye, or perhaps he was suddenly fatigued and
drained by his disclosure, but I noticed that his spirits were
falling almost inversely as mine were rising. "If you only knew
what hell I've been through, carrying this secret by myself," he
said. "You can't even imagine how exhausting it is." Keating
slumped in his chair. I waved at the waiter to bring the check,
and told Ed he should try and get a good night's sleep, even
think about taking a few days off to get some rest. . . . I was a
little surprised to find myself suddenly a combination father
goddam and co-conspirator. Keating kept looking at me as if I
didn't really understand, and I guess I didn't. "I can never get
away . . . from the stress . . . no matter where I go, the stress is
always with me."

I was about to suggest another drink for his stress when the
waiter came with the check and a small incident occurred that
was characteristic of the ambivalence, deference, envy, suspicion, and finally pathos of my extraordinary relationship with
Ed Keating over the next several years.

I picked up the check, signed it, wrote a handsome tip on
the back and handed it to the waiter, who nodded a gracious
assent and left us in silence.

Keating stared across the table at me. "Thank you," he said.

I thought he was being sarcastic; but no. He seemed
genuinely grateful that I had signed the check.

"But it's *your* money Ed," I said. "What are you thanking me
for? I just signed my room number. You're paying the hotel
bill."

"I know, I know," Keating said. "But I just like the way you
do it. You just pick the check up and . . . *sign* it. I could never
do anything like that."

I shrugged and mumbled something incoherent about there really being nothing to it.

The publisher of *Ramparts* magazine got up from his chair without another word and walked slowly across the empty lobby to the elevator, carrying his drink with him.

MONEY

WHEN I volunteered to find a way to save the paper, that was just talk. The only money I had ever raised was to pick up a quarter off the barroom floor.

However, when Ed Keating plunged forward with his convert's blind faith and actually sold his last shopping center to keep the good ship *Ramparts* afloat awhile longer, I was stricken with an acute attack of conscience. The least I could do was to go through the motions, although I was unsure as to what motions to make. I vaguely recalled as a teenager reading *Cash McCall* and other Cameron Hawley novels of big business intrigue, whipping through them to find the sex passages, and it seemed that the heroes were always demanding to see the books before pulling off some financial miracle to save the company. So I asked Keating to see the books.

That was an unnerving experience suited to a plot for an Alka-Seltzer commercial. The *Ramparts*' money story made as much sense as an eggshell omelette. Everything seemed scrambled together. I found what I guessed was a bill from Keating's psychiatrist stuck in with an invoice from the typesetter. Then I found out about Multex. That was the printing plant Keating had built from a mimeograph shop into a thirty-employee operation with a monster Heidelberg press purchased on the never-never plan. All this to print a quarterly magazine. Keating's idea was that the plant would take in regular printing work between issues and thus make enough money so that he could print the magazine free. Keating had lost some $200,000 on the deal by the time I began waving my arms in frantic semaphores to stop. One time, in an effort to turn the tide, Ed had the plant manager manage the magazine and Ed himself ran the printing opera-

tion, but things only got worse. His innovations were original
if costly. I once called Multex to talk to Keating, and a Swede
who couldn't speak English answered the phone. I finally got
Keating on the line and asked who the hell that guy was.
"That's the new sales manager," Keating said. I said what-
dayamean, Ed, he can't speak English. Keating told me that I
didn't understand the psychology of sales. "People will feel
sorry for him because he's a foreigner, and he'll get jobs the
ordinary American salesman wouldn't land." The Swede
eventually went to the briny deep with Multex.

The *Ramparts'* bank statement provided another jolt. The
bottom figure, in red ink, said something like $87,439.62 O.D.
I was not too familiar with overdrafts, as the banks I did
business with usually bounced my checks rather than extend-
ing themselves in aid of my profligacy. I called the *Ramparts'*
banker to ask what was this mistake about 87 grand O.D. He
said it was no mistake; that was the way Mr. Keating operated
the magazine. He put up blocks of U.S. Gypsum stock as
security, and the bank let him overdraw until it got nervous,
and then Keating would have to sell the stock. The banker
would often call Keating and ask him to sell, but Ed would
invariably ask him to wait awhile longer. He hated the idea of
having to sell, and kept piling up these overdrafts hoping the
stock would go up or the magazine would make money or a
third unlikely ifinstance. One time, while Keating was waiting,
the price of the stock dipped, and he lost a five-figure sum on
a forced sale.

The big picture was as bright as the Black Hole of Calcutta.
The paper had about 4,000 circulation and no income to
speak of, and a lot of the subscribers were priests who
wouldn't pay. It had been selling for $2 a copy on newsstands,
which meant that it wasn't selling. At that time it was already
some half a million dollars in the hole—not counting the
Multex $200,000—and the approximately $130,000 Keating
hoped to net out of the sale of the shopping center would last
barely a few months under the brave new monthly publishing
operation we had just launched unless the paper could find a
lot of credit somewhere, which I was not too sanguine about as
I had found some $50,000 to $60,000 of unpaid bills stuffed

in drawers. Those horrifying figures put Keating somewhere
near a million bucks in the hole, with no chance of getting it
back or of even keeping the doors open without finding
someone like himself to take his place in front of the money
urinal. The worse the situation looked, the more Keating
expressed optimism that I would find some way to work it out.
I figured he must know something I didn't know.

My first bright idea was to raid the Protestants. There was
no chance of *Ramparts* getting money from the Catholics, but I
thought perhaps the anti-Catholics might dig into their pockets to keep *Ramparts* pumping out graffiti about the Pope. I
went to the secular tabernacle of the Protestants and Others
United for the Separation of Church and State in Washington
to see if I could get the Know-Nothings to open their purses.
The P.A.O.U. functioned as the main anti-Catholic pressure
group in the capital, although its initials sounded to me like
one of those obscure anarchist sects in the Spanish Civil War. I
found it to be a syndicate of old ladies and stuffed shirts; the
Protestant decision-makers had starched collars and pinched
faces and were so cheap they washed the toilet paper and
hung it out to dry. No moola there.

On the rebound from that disappointment I came up with
an alternative plan for salvation. We would get *Ramparts* off its
awkward Catholic anti-Catholic hobby-horse and make it an
ecumenical magazine, in tune with the spirit of Pope John.
Keating seized on that tender idea with a fierce optimism. He
said he had the answer. *Ramparts* would become a
Protestant-Catholic-Jewish magazine. That way it could get
money from all three. He would appoint a Protestant and a
Jew along with himself as the editorial board. Keating called
this a "breakthrough"—a term he applied to ideas of varying
quality but which were all characterized by an apocalyptic
fervor. One got used to "breakthroughs" at *Ramparts*, which
came with the frequency and clamor of the crazy uncle's
cavalry charges in *Arsenic and Old Lace*.

Ramparts proceeded to follow that unsteady star for several
months. Keating named Arthur Cohen, the author and
former editor, and William Stringfellow, the lawyer and social
critic, as Jewish and Protestant members of the editorial

board, which was hampered in its functions by the fact that it hardly ever met. In the meantime I found a fund-raiser and made him publisher, a title Keating relinquished with some reluctance but conceded the fund-raiser's argument that he needed the proper cover if he was to have ease of entry to the vaults of the Protestant, Catholic and Jewish monies. The fund-raiser was Judson Chrisney, plucked from his position as chief money-raiser for the Atlantic Community Council, another High Protestant Eastern Establishment organization of vague purpose. Chrisney was a tweedy chap who had a face that would have taken second place in a Mount Rushmore contest. He was s-e-r-i-o-u-s about everything, and especially excited about the Protestant-Catholic-Jewish togetherness. He possessed a strong sense of general evangelism, and one day said to me that *Ramparts* was going to "bring morality back into the marketplace." I told him to save that stuff for the targets with checkbooks, but he was serious and proceeded to explain a game plan, the details of which have escaped me, just how and why that laudatory goal would be accomplished, and how we would all get rich in the doing. Chrisney got Keating personally to guarantee him a certain sum of money, and moved out to San Francisco, where he assumed his duties. He took a flat on the chic crooked part of Lombard Street, bought a Jaguar for town and country travel, and began writing letters to the New York *Times* and *Time*, making serious comment on matters of public concern, and calling for morality in the marketplace, signed by the Publisher of *Ramparts* magazine. The *Ramparts'* office in Menlo Park became stacked with editions of *Who's Who* and social directories of several cities, from which the new publisher made notations on recipe-sized ruled cards—the first job of fund-raising, he said, was to develop the proper "prospect list."

It was a little bit of the Atlantic Community Council in Menlo Park. Keating and I sat back in awe and wonder, waiting for the money to come in.

In November of 1964 *Ramparts* had just begun publishing as a monthly magazine—yet it appeared on the newsstands with a four-color advertisement for Pan American World

Airways ("That Wonderful Pan Am Feeling") on the back cover.

This was alas no sign of marketing recognition or financial stability, as the ad had been run for free. An account executive in Pan Am's Madison Avenue advertising agency, a good Catholic fellow, had, upon *Ramparts*' earnest entreaty, sent the color plates, figuring what was the harm in making a little Catholic magazine look good.

But the issue that had the glorious Pan Am ad on the back cover had on the front cover an unkind caricature of Barry Goldwater, the Republican candidate for President of the United States, as a rattlesnake. The snake was the handcraft of my friend Justin Murray, a former *Life* superartist, during the forties famous for his series of caricatures of politicians called "Birds of Our Time." He put down his pen when his eyes began to fail, and became a jazz drummer and full-time nature buff, raising God's unloved creatures such as fighting cocks and coyotes. An amusing fellow with a combative temperament (he once beat up Dick Contino for upstaging him in a Santa Rosa bar where they were both playing a gig), Justin through his half-blind eyes produced a memorable series of *Ramparts*' covers, including J. Edgar Hoover as a fag and Ho Chi Minh as George Washington crossing the Delaware.

Justin's Goldwater was regarded by many to be unfair, and held most heinously so by the higher management of Pan American, as one of the airline's top executives was a key financial mugwump in the Goldwater campaign.

The heavens trembled and the advertising man, in fear for his job, cabled that *Ramparts* must scrap the original plan of running free Pan Am ads on the back cover for six months and promise never, ever, to run that ad again; the color plates must be hurried back air express at Pan Am's insistence.

I cabled back several untruths: technical problems made such requests difficult if not impossible, and in any event very costly; the paper's covers were printed far ahead into the future; although *Ramparts* would consider returning the color plates (I had garnered an extra copy from the printer), that would be no guarantee, for the reasons stated, that the ad would not continue to appear.

There were hysterics from both client and ad agency when "That Wonderful World of Pan Am" materialized on *Ramparts'* December back cover. The agency finally sent a check, drawn on some black discretionary account of the type normally used to pay for abortions and such, for costs as were necessary to get that bloody ad off *Ramparts'* back cover. (I perversely ran it a third time, but only on the *inside* back cover, of the January issue; when Pan American complained I said they were lucky we had been able to get it inside from the outside.)

I thought it great sport that Pan American had had to pay us to stop running their ad. Keating had maintained an attitude of horrified detachment throughout these negotiations, and did not appear to share my joy in this sweet moment of victory; I asked him why. He gave me one of those looks that only a Protestant-at-heart can give, and asked me where I had learned to be such a cheerfully lying son of a bitch. "Jesus, Ed, I thought you knew," I said. "The Jesuits taught me."

That was a fairly typical moment in Dogpatch while we were all playing magazine, waiting for the money to arrive in the next mail. *Ramparts* was then housed in the Keating Building in Menlo Park, a one-story edifice that looked like a refrigerator crate laid sideways. It reminded me of the buildings the Atomic Energy Commission used to construct on testing sites in the Nevada desert and stock with canned goods and human dummies and then A-bomb to illustrate to the American public the wisdom of building fallout shelters. The building was ill fated from the start, and Keating was eventually forced to sell it to the Italian janitor.

When I arrived in Menlo Park to assume my duties as executive editor of *Ramparts* I found that I had a desk in a corner of the reception area, but instead of a chair I had an old toilet bowl, detached from its plumbing. I made inquiries about my seating arrangements. The office manager, a funny, brittle girl named Barbara Brown, explained that Keating had ripped up a purchase order she had put in for an expensive swivel chair. He told her, "I don't want any empire builders around here. Get Hinckle something cheap to sit on." That was her way of carrying out orders.

The *Ramparts'* staff at the time of my arrival resembled the waiting-room population of an outpatient clinic. One employee was a bull dike who kept trying to make it with one of the clerks, a girl with long stringy black hair, enormous weeping willow tits and a nose like a beer can opener. Another staffer was a red-headed overweight alcoholic who came to work mornings with "rum babas" for everyone, which she soaked with bourbon to sweeten the taste. The most efficient of the lot was a heroin addict who had just been released from federal custody in Lexington Hospital; she told Keating the scabs on her arm were from smallpox, and those of us who knew differently kept her secret. The art director was a pint-sized Australian named Peter Keep who played drums at night and doodled for money by day. One of the editorial assistants was a five-foot-two, frail girl of eighteen whose drunken father beat her every week when she took home the pay check because he insisted she was pocketing the deductions. The bookkeeper was a nice Jewish lady named Gertrude, who brought chicken soup to work and cracked funny jokes about the sewer the money was pouring into; she quit when Keating hired a German business manager who went around counting paper clips and asking the employees what "breed" they were.

I asked Keating where he got all those people. "Employment agencies," he said.

Harry Stiehl, the poet, was still nominally the editor but Keating was squeezing him out. Everyone was upset about that because Harry was such a sweet guy. He once moved from one apartment in Menlo Park to another a few blocks away and to save money moved his furniture entirely by bus, one day a lamp, the next a marble-topped table, the next a chair. Keating had docked his pay check the previous year for the cost of a special cream-colored paper the magazine used to print one of Harry's novella-length poems.

Keating's executive inner sanctum was constantly disrupted by someone dashing out to get him chocolate or orange juice

for his diabetes. For a time he was hiring a new secretary on
the average of about every two weeks, but he finally got one
who toughed it out, Leslie Timan, who stayed on to become
one of the heavy-duty *Ramparts'* editors in the years ahead.
Keating almost didn't hire Leslie because she had this socko
diamond wedding ring. He told Leslie that his wife wouldn't
want anyone working for him who had a diamond bigger than
hers. Leslie offered to take it off around the office, and got the
job.

Into this happy assemblage I began to infiltrate dissenters,
longhairs, and general shit disturbers who disrupted not only
the decorum of the Keating Building but also of quiet Menlo
Park. Paul Jacobs, the professional radical and bald-headed
author of *Is Curly Jewish*, began the commute from San Francisco to be a consulting editor.

Jacobs lived in San Francisco, as did most of the *Ramparts*
staff save those in far-off Berkeley. Such insular geography
was due partly to my own western chauvinism, partly because
the Bay Area had a natural, relatively unspoiled talent pool of
writers, photographers and artists—and partly because of the
peculiarly debilitating conditions of servitude in the artificial
trout pond of creativity that is Manhattan publishing. Whatever else *Ramparts* may have done, it ventilated the shibboleth
that a national magazine need be produced from New York.

One of the San Franciscans who helped *Ramparts* swing was
the great Hal Lipset, the private eye known among his fellow
gumshoes as the "private ear" for his proficiency in the modern art of electronic surveillance. (He once actually bugged a
martini olive.) When Hal came to editorial meetings he
brought his electronic vacuum cleaner with him and swept the
office for hidden bugs. I suspect *Ramparts* was the only
magazine of general circulation to have a private detective on
the masthead, and Lipset's devices figured significantly, behind the scenes, in many big stories. Hal was called upon in all
situations of potential peril. Once a package of dog shit dis-
guised as a bomb arrived in the lobby, addressed to Eldridge
Cleaver. The alarmed receptionist called Lipset, who hastened down and convinced her to take it to the bathroom
instead of the bomb squad.

Another consulting editor, Ralph J. Gleason, the respected *Chronicle* jazz columnist, was a media expert on Beatlemania and all-around counterculture buff. Gleason was in his mid-forties at the time of the rising of the sixties' cultural moon but was more enthusiastic over the implications of the new lifestyle alternatives than many of those living them. After Gleason wrote a particularly effusive *Ramparts'* cover story on Bob Dylan, a letter to the editor which was a classic of its kind arrived at the paper. It was from Arnold Passman, a historian specializing in the history of disc jockeys, who wanted to know if the rumor was true that the effusive Gleason was really "a 48-year-old schizophrenic who can't decide whether to split himself into three 16-year-olds or four 12-year-olds." Gleason, a good soul, took that without rancor, but his patience sagged at the squares hanging around Keating. The columnist just about bit through his pipe during one editorial meeting when Jim Colaianni, the ex-lay theologian Keating made managing editor because he had so many children, let it drop that he had driven some of his kids to the Cow Palace for a Beatles concert and waited for them out in the parking lot, listening to Gordon MacRae on the car radio. Gleason went cold with disbelief. "You mean you *really* stayed outside listening to some tin on the car radio when *you could be seeing the Beatles*? Man, you're putting me on. *Nobody* could be that un-hip." The managing editor nodded. Gleason, who was also a diabetic, poured himself a stiff shot of Keating's orange juice.

One interloper whose style especially rankled Ed Keating was Robert Scheer, at that time a black angel in the High Seraphim of Berkeley radicalism. Keating and I had a running argument over Scheer. I thought he was the most important guy on the staff because he knew all the dirt about Vietnam, but Keating considered him one cut above a doorknob-stealer.

I met Scheer under the most bourgeois of circumstances. Our wives, rather my wife, Denise, and his wife-to-be, Anne, were working at the same stock and bond house in San Francisco, and became buddies. The ladies then put us together, and we all were close friends and Scrabble partners throughout the amazing *Ramparts* buck and grind of the next five years. My friendship with Scheer was the more exceptional considering the differences in our personalities and backgrounds. I had never met anyone quite like Scheer. He was bright and formidable and arrogant, yet his arrogance had a soft edge—he had a curiously charming teddy bear quality about him, sort of an insecurity blanket, that, when you got to know him and he took it off, left the bare Scheer a warm and amusing person. Scheer was essentially an optimistic and affirmative spirit, although his optimism was tempered by an ingrown wariness that became at times a standard suspicion that the worst was going to happen (and, many of those times, it did). Scheer told me a story about growing up in the Bronx that explained some of these attributes. To pet an animal he had to stand in line at the Bronx Zoo, and once he got to pet one, he was told to move on quickly to give the next kid a chance. I also came to understand Scheer's deep-rooted competitiveness (which made him a damn good journalist) in terms of his four-year survival course in the left wing-Jewish intellectual Olympics at New York's City College, with its constant one-upmanship and leftist backstabbing. I was unable to even imagine the conditions of such a combatant world. But if I thought Scheer was from Mars, he thought I was from Pluto, with my imperious, fat-dumb-and-happy Irish attitude toward everything. One attribute we shared, perverse as it was, was the ability to function normally in chaos and crisis; to listen to our friends and relations, we were good at creating both.

Scheer claimed that he had known me back when I was a fascist pig. He remembered me as particularly disgusting during the great civil rights sit-in of 1962 at the Palace Hotel in San Francisco. I had covered the show for the *Chronicle* and was upset that the protesters had picked that historic hotel —where my grandfather's picture hung in one of the bars amid a rogues' gallery of Earthquake and Fire era alcoholics—rather than one of the newer and more vulgar tents around town. I did vaguely recall Scheer in the midst of the rabble on the lobby floor. This unkempt and long-haired person had his hand on the bare white leg of a particularly

well-groomed girl—a button-nosed pearl of Protestant features who didn't look as if she belonged in that distaff crowd.
She looked as if her father was a vice-president of the telephone company, which in fact he was. The girl was Anne
Weills, later Anne Scheer, and, by the gossipy standards of
comparative politics prevalent in the Berkeley left, was more
radical even than he.

The tale of the Palace sit-in later became a standard bedtime
story at the homesteads of rich leftists where Scheer and I
often camped on *Ramparts'* money-raising expeditions.
Scheer would recall how he looked up from his vantage point
on the floor, a cop's flat foot planted on his chest, and saw this
Brooks Brothers reporter from the *Chronicle* leaning against a
wall watching the carnage with a gin and tonic in his hand,
tsk-tsking because the protesters were getting the dust of
reality on his grandfather's picture. I would then stand up and
recite, in the tradition of Eliza telling the story of crossing the
ice, how I had once been a henchman of privilege, a captive of
the Pope, a cynic without redeeming social value, a person of
gypsylike abandon—until I joined *Ramparts* and came to see
the world the way it really was—so would the listener please
give *Ramparts* $25,000 to help us burn the candle at both ends.

Scheer had brushed himself up a bit since I first saw him on
the floor, but was still far out for Menlo Park in 1964. He was
sort of cherubic yet surly-looking and always wore the same
brown corduroy jacket, which was obscured at the shoulders
by a bush-length beard. If a cartoonist were to draw him,
Scheer would be just a pair of eyeglasses and a beard. He
drove the girls in the copy department mad because he wrote
on lined tablets, squeezing an incredible two rows of runic
scribble between each line. During one of our numerous
conversations about what manner of menace Scheer was, I
told Keating that I wanted to have Scheer around because I
thought he was smarter than I. Keating gave me a grave look.
"Never hire anyone smarter than you," he said. "They'll try
and take over." I finally carried the day by suggesting to
Keating that Scheer might be helpful in raising money from
liberals. Keating accepted this as a legitimate reason to take
whatever risk he thought Scheer represented.

The *Ramparts'* wampum situation necessitated occasionally utilizing barter as a means of exchange for talent. I worked out many such deals, but the most fun was with Jessica Mitford, who had an island to unload. Decca became a contributing editor to the paper, and we undertook a back-cover advertising campaign in glorious technicolor to smoke out a buyer for her real estate. The island was Inch Kenneth, a rump hunk of land in the Scottish Hebrides which afforded a sweeping view of the low-lying fog. The accommodations were in a stone-cold, ten-bedroomed castle of uncertain origin with faltering electricity and lights enough only to see where one was stumbling. Inch Kenneth was a pain in the *derrière* to reach, involving insular trains with splinters in the seats and carriage in unseaworthy boats. Once one arrived there was little to do but sit in the chill wet fog and prepare for the ordeal of the trip back. The island came into Decca's possession via her father. Even the Communist Party of England said no, thanks, when she offered to contribute it to the cause, but the idea of actually owning an island proved irresistible to many among the misguided in the *Ramparts'* audience. Decca had to deal with any number of imbeciles and wayfarers—one hotshot wanted to hold a rock festival on it—before she found a real person to buy the island—a doctor of sorts, if memory serves. The best advertising copy for Inch Kenneth had been written some time before by Dr. Johnson, after that gentleman had the misfortune of residing there for a night during his well-reported tour of the Hebrides with Boswell in 1776: "Sir, the only person who would wish to buy an island is the one who never owned one."

I thought we did such a smashing job unloading Inch Kenneth that I fancied the tale might impress other potential advertisers who might even pay *Ramparts* to run their ads, instead of vice versa. In that pursuit Scheer and I had many amusing luncheons with Decca and her buddy Sonia Orwell, where we hyped a scheme whereby Decca would be appointed Mistress of Advertising at *Ramparts*—she called it "Ramps"—and she and Sonia, a delightful and deadeye team if ever one there was—would Greyhound it about the states visiting the ranking capitalists of the land, affording them the treat of having high tea with two women of the classy intellectual left, wherein the captains of industry would be charmed into buying space in a publication that was enemy to their cause.

Like most good ideas at *Ramparts*, we never got around to doing it.

An unlikely pair who also scampered up the gangway of our sinking ship were Howard Gossage, the maverick advertising genius, and Gerry Feigen, a surgeon who was Gossage's sidekick. Unlikely is not a sufficient word to describe the pair; traffic slowed down when they crossed a street; heads turned when they walked into a public room. Feigen was shorter and a dark, saturnine-visaged, droopy-mustached man of metabolic moods who looked the prototype of the mad professor. Gossage was a but an inch-and-a-half taller but it seemed a foot—a demanding man with a chalky, bony face, sunken eyeballs resting cheerily in charcoal gray pouches of skin, a magnificently busted nose and wild-demon white hair, who chain-smoked Gauloises like a Pittsburgh chimney.

Feigen was a man of many trades, and master of all. In addition to his medical practice as one of the country's leading proctologists Feigen was, in no special order, a painter, television commentator, ventriloquist, lecturer, and world traveler. Feigen was also a white member of the Negro Press Association, globe-trotting buddy of Buckminster Fuller, and a tireless crusader against nuclear testing by anyone, friend or foe. Not one to stop at writing his Congressman, Feigen carried on a one-sided conversation with Nikita Khrushchev via classified ads—over 700 of them—in the personal columns of the *Chronicle*, in which he said things like: "Dear Nikita—fallout is no good for Russian bones, either; nyet?" He bought billboards all over San Francisco protesting General de Gaulle's plans to test a French H-bomb in the South Pacific. During a trip to Tahiti with Bucky Fuller, Feigen decided he would test the white man's capacity to suffer the native fire walk. The preparations were extensive, the coals red hot, the natives had gathered along the sides of the pit, and Dr. Feigen took off his shoes and walked across. "It didn't hurt at all," he said. A few hours later it became painfully clear that he had burned several layers of skin off the bottom of his feet. He got off the airplane in San Francisco with his feet wrapped in surgical dressing like two giant cones of white cotton candy. Feigen was waving a telegram which Gossage and I, knowing of his intentions to do the daring deed, had earlier sent him. Feigen claimed it was handed to him as he was carried by the awed natives away from the scene of his successful trip across the coals. The telegram said: "It was such a lovely fire I thought I'd walk."

Gossage was the Socrates of San Francisco. The visiting lions from Tom Wolfe to Terry-Thomas came to call on him in the magnificently restored old firehouse on Pacific Street that was his place of work, and for a time, when Howard and his buddy Herb Caen were both between marriages and batching it about town, place of residence. Gossage operated the Firehouse as if it were a French court, and he the captive king. He did everything first class—he ate, flew, wrote, talked, traveled first class. He believed every man should be comfortable while engaging in the necessary business of rescuing the world. He was at the same time as open and innocent as a doe-eyed calf and as crafty as a raunchy old owl. Howard was, nominally, in the advertising business. That at least was how he made his living, but he did it wholly on his own terms—first class—and with an originality of purpose and imagination that staggered the redundant minds of his profession. He was the inventor of Beethoven sweatshirts, the popularizer of Irish whiskey in America (he lived for a year in County Wicklow to get the taste of his task), and sky admiral of the Great Paper Airplane Contest of 1967. Those were but incidentals in Howard's life, commercial outputs which gained the rank of legend and a raft of copiers because of the strength of his stubborn originality. Gossage was forever stirring up the waters that his bread was cast upon. He had little use for the advertising industry and felt very uncomfortable and apologetic about doing what he was so damn good at.

Howard and I became friends when I told him, after listening to him bitch about getting out of the advertising business, that he wasn't *in* the advertising business at all—he was in the business of making ideas work. That was true. Gossage was

constantly seizing upon some idea that intrigued him and
then going to great lengths to make it happen, whether it was
convening a seminar on the subject of making San Francisco a
city-state or creating an international incident by helping unleash the Caribbean island of Anguilla from the bonds of
progress.

Gossage and Feigen met under clinical circumstances. Gossage was sick and another doctor had recommended an operation. Feigen examined him, listened to him talk for a few
hours, and then said that he didn't need an operation at
all—what he needed was to get rid of his partners. Feigen
helped Gossage divest himself of two business partners who,
he felt, were coasting on Howard's creativity. A man of suc-
cinct dismissals, Feigen said of one former Gossage partner:
"He had a bad relationship with his mirror." Of another, "The
guy came on as Jesus' brother—and the son of a bitch wasn't
even Jewish." Feigen himself became Gossage's partner, although not in the advertising business. They started an
amorphous company called "Generalists, Inc.," which was
described as a consulting organization, but Feigen preferred
another definition: "We're genius scouts." As such, the men of
Generalists, Inc. launched the sputtering comet of Marshall
McLuhan on the American scene. I wasn't sure what they
would do for *Ramparts*, but I hired the Generalists after
Feigen advanced the opinion, in his epigrammatic way, that
"You're not in the magazine business—you're in the crap-
detecting business." When I say hired I should note that,
except for a grand I got Keating to cough up in the beginning,
they never got paid a dime, and after a passage of years and
lawsuits, it ended up costing Feigen a lot of money.

He later referred to the *Ramparts* experience as going into a
soup kitchen and getting a butterfly's liver and two stewed
handkerchiefs to eat, and then having to pay $92 for the meal.

The first moves of Generalists, Inc. were to hire a new art
director and fire the publisher. Hiring the art director was
Gossage's idea, and firing the publisher was Keating's, who
wanted the title back.

The art director was Dugald Stermer, a Southern California beachboy turned to talent whom Gossage had singled out when judging an art directors' contest in Houston, where Stermer then worked for a concept factory. Stermer flew to San Francisco to talk. I told him I could only guarantee him three issues and then the whole thing would probably go bust. He asked if I was sure about the three issues. I said yes. He moved to San Francisco with his wife and a VW bus full of kids, another entry in the optimism derby. Stermer redesigned the paper into the trend-setting. Times-Roman-typography, Push Pin Studios-WPA, full-color-bleed prototype of new journalism trendiness that it was. Other magazines soon got the idea, and by the late 1960's one could line up *Evergreen Review, Harper's, Atlantic, New York* magazine, *Esquire* and *Ramparts* and be unable to tell the chicken from the egg.

Stermer wore several hats on top of his art director's beanie. He pitched in on the heavy money-raising chores, and was a general work horse in all departments. The square-jawed, talented Protestant thus provided the third force for an accidentally ecumenical triumverate of Stermer, Scheer and myself which developed, in true "Who's on first?" fashion, to run *Ramparts.* I was a bit taken aback when one day Dugald told me that he had converted to Catholicism, ending the lamentable trend toward secular balance that had set in at the journal.

Stermer and I always worked closely together on the layouts, a process of creativity by which I became familiar with some of the finer sides of the artistic sensibility. We once had a story bad-mouthing Pope Paul for the way he had trashed Pope John's open-door policy at Vatican City. I wanted to put Pope John on the cover with a tear running down his cheek. As an idea it was not the highest level of subtlety, although other magazines have since copied it, with other faces. We had difficulty finding an artist and Gossage suggested Barnaby Conrad, the writer, painter and San Francisco's expert bullfighter. I called Conrad, who said he would do it. He asked how much *Ramparts* paid for covers. I said five hundred dollars. Barnaby began to stall, and I thought he wanted more money. I said that five big ones was really all the paper could afford to go. There was a silence. "Well, all right, I'll do it for five hundred on the condition that you let me keep the painting," Conrad said. *Ramparts* usually kept the original art work used for stories, but I said I guessed it would be all right this one time.

"Why would you want to keep a painting of the Pope?" I asked.

"Well, that way I can paint out the tear and sell it later as a regular portrait," the artist explained.

Gossage referred to himself and Feigen as "the firing squad" because they seemed always to be firing the publisher. First it was Judson Chrisney, and then it was Keating himself, although he came back to be tossed out a second time. Gossage's way of firing someone was to make them think it was their idea to quit. He summoned Chrisney to the Firehouse conference room for a chat. The conference room was about three stories high with shuttered windows looking out over a wrought-iron balcony above a garden courtyard. The furniture was a couch as long as a freight train and a table as big around as a flying saucer. That was about it except for a two-by-four marble-topped table Gossage used as a writing desk. The room gave one a sense of free falling in space.

Feigen and Gossage gave Chrisney a long talk about why he was unhappy. Up until that point, Chrisney hadn't realized he was unhappy, but within an hour was caught up in conversation about the importance of liberation in a man's life and why *Ramparts* should make this big sacrifice of liberating him so he could do the great things that would really make him happy. Chrisney flew out of the conference room on the wings of his new freedom. Gossage reported a successful operation, but when I called Chrisney a few hours later some of the anesthesia was beginning to wear off. "You're a climbing Irish shit," he told me. "Do you know what I'm doing right now? I've got an eraser in my hand and my address book is open to the H's, and I'm rubbing you out of my life." With that, he hung up. I have never been told off better, before or since. The fund-raiser was gone and there was still no money to pick up the laundry, so I decided I'd better try to raise the dough myself. That decision was to keep me tooling about the country with a trick-or-treat bag for the rest of the decade.

One of the paid thinkers, I believe it was Denis de Rougemont, said of courtly love, "Whatever turns into a reality is no
longer love." It is much the same thing with raising money.
The expectation and the agony are the whole thing. When
and if you get the money, the actual coins are secondary, and
almost conducive of postpartum depression, because you
have spent the money in your head so many times over—or, if
you do things the way we did at *Ramparts* in those days, you
have already actually spent it, and the entire wretched mess is
but finding a willing Peter to pay a demanding Paul.

On a wet spring day in 1965 I set off for the rich forests of
Manhattan to find a money tree and chop it down. My traveling companion was Joe Ippolito, who had the unenviable task
of being Keating's accountant. Joe had become a good friend
and drinking buddy, and I prevailed on him to become—at
least temporarily—the controller of *Ramparts*. I didn't see how
anyone would invest money in a magazine which didn't have a
controller. We didn't know where to start, but Joe found a
place. He had been thumbing through a book that Chrisney
had left behind, *The History of Magazine Publishing*.

"Hey, look at this," Joe said, pointing out a passage. "It says
here that printers ended up owning a lot of the early
magazines because they were owed so much money that they
had to take stock." That gave us a clue as to where to begin: hit
up the printer.

The printer was a magnificently foul-mouthed Italian
named George Gambella who captained a fleet of web offset
presses in Long Island City. I had a good swearing and
screaming relationship with George, but he didn't cotton too
well to the idea of crossing the 59th Street Bridge to have
lunch at the Algonquin—"Why can't we eat in my
fuckingoffice?" His suspicions were heightened when we took
him to a private upstairs dining room. "Whatda we need a
private room for?" the printer wanted to know.

"We need room to chase you around the table, George,"
said the controller.

We explained our proposition, which entailed Gambella
putting up $100,000 either in cash, or in printing—we were
open about the details. The printer looked toward the door.

"Why me?" he asked, his voice a mix of panic and incredulity. "Somebody's got to be first George, and you're it," Joe explained.

"You guys," said the printer, "have got to be crazy."

Joe put his seat against the door. "Now let's talk this over sensibly, George." Two hours later the printer got out of the room after agreeing, albeit reluctantly, to take stock for $100,000 dollars of printing spread over five years *if* we were successful in raising an additional $400,000 of cash investment from other investors. He obviously thought we never had a prayer of raising the four hundred grand. George's conditional pledge gave him the considerable privilege of not investing, which privilege he later exercised, but Joe and I were nonetheless ecstatic—now we could say we had a hundred grand committed, and just yesterday we had nothing.

I telephoned Keating in Menlo Park. "Jesus, Ed, there's nothing to this fund-raising business. We've only been here a day and we already raised a hundred grand."

Scheer's glasses frosted over when we told him that Keating was broke and that he was going to have to help Joe and me raise the money to make his paycheck. Scheer grumbled that he knew it had been too good to be true. "Why should I help out Keating?" Scheer asked. "Look, Bob, if we don't raise the money we're going to have to fire people," said Joe diplomatically. Scheer pulled himself up to the tip of his New Left toes: "Well, in that case I want a written contract before I do a thing." We were standing at the crowded bar of P.J. Clark's in New York. Joe grabbed a brown paper bag that Scheer had with him and emptied several pocket books and half-eaten cookies onto the bar. "We'll give you a contract right now, Scheer," he said, and began writing "To Whom It May Concern" on the outside of the bag. "Is that legal?" Scheer wanted to know. I assured him that it would hold up in any court in the land. After some haggling over fine points of stock options and fringe benefits and other capitalist terminology that Scheer had acquainted himself with, we three signed the bag with great flourish. Scheer carefully folded it up and put it in his pocket. "Now don't spread this all over Berkeley," he warned.

The fourth member of our money-raising expedition was Sandy Levinson, an attractive girl who had done her master's thesis at Stanford on the civil rights movement and knew just about everyone on the left, old and new, in America. Sandy signed on as New York editor of the paper and between chasing down stories she flushed out fat partridges from the money thicket for us to ensnare, suffering many a pass from dirty old liberals in service of the cause.

We began by infiltrating SNCC fund-raising parties at the homes of rich Westchester Jews. We pretended to be boosting the cause but kept looking over people's shoulders to see the size of the checks they were writing.

I found there was left-wing gold rooted in pineapples, sewing machines, mattresses, zippers, plywood, soybeans, off-shore oil, General Motors and Hollywood—to name some pink fortunes—and we were soon deep into the concentric circles and interlocking directorates of the rich liberal-left. It was a very peculiar zoo. One man played the violin while we made our presentation to him. Another Midas, during the half hour we were delivering our pitch, busied himself trying to affix a wad of Kotex on the privates of his toy poodle, who, poor dear, was having her period. One millionaire explained as he passed the red caviar—instead of black, so as to save money, he confided—that he was a little short right then but he would like to do something to help out; he took out his checkbook and scribbled a check for $8 for a year's subscription. Another well-known rich man made his excuses about investing but said he wanted Scheer and me each to have a jar of pickled herring. We thanked him and left his penthouse clutching our cash flow projections in one hand and jar of herring in the other. Scheer said he was going to the Bronx to give his to his mother. I tried to palm my jar off on a cabbie for a tip, but he gave me a look like I was a dog poisoner and said he was going to call the cops.

After weeks of hearing sweet no-no's I had had it with the New York rich left, who clipped their Honeywell coupons by day and gave cheap-wine fund-raising parties for antiwar radicals by night. I decided to try our luck in Chicago, where we had a secret plan for scaling the monetary heights of Mount Hefner. The controller, Sandy, Scheer and I made a mad dash through black rain to catch a midnight plane on which we convened an insane strategy session around the table in the first-class section. I was pounding out some money gibberish on a portable typewriter while having a nosebleed that wouldn't stop. Joe was working over some revised projections on long green sheets of accounting paper lest we actually get in to make a pitch to Hefner. Scheer and Sandy were playing gin rummy. A horrible storm was bouncing the plane around like a pinball machine going on tilt; there were drinks splashing all over the place; my nose was pouring blood into the sea of booze and wet accounting papers awash on the table; and around that point I began to feel sorry that we had fired the fund-raiser. I got to Chicago in a foul, snarling mood and upon arrival at the Statler Hilton encountered a round cardboard box full of soap in the lobby—"DONATE SOAP HERE FOR OUR BOYS IN VIETNAM; HELP KEEP OUR G.I.'S CLEAN"—and kicked it down the up escalator.

The next day, still sore but sober, I visited the late A. C. Spectorsky, who was then running the *Playboy* tit circus, and told him of my plans to rip off his boss. He wished me luck, and provided *carte d'identité* for our demolition team to enter the *Playboy* mansion where somewhere on an upper floor the target was asleep. The trouble was that he always was asleep. Hefner's reclusive and eccentric working hours were legend, and no one seemed to know when the master would rise and be available. We hung around the mansion for several days, passing the hours skinny-dipping in the basement pool, watching off-duty bunnies set their curlers and pick their noses, cracking jokes with Shel Silverstein—always alert to the fact that somewhere above us the Man lay snoring, and might turn over and call for fiddlers and visitors.

We were swimming on the evening of the third day of our vigil when Scheer signaled me into one of the inner caves in the subterranean pool. "Something's happened," he said. "I've fallen in love with the Head Bunny." The Head Bunny? Scheer explained that she used to be in charge of hiring the girls but had graduated to the position of Hefner's bootjack and aide-de-camp. She was the only one who knew when he was asleep or awake, and, Scheer hinted, if his friendship with her continued to develop along its present course, he would soon be in a position to know when Hefner woke up. I asked Scheer when he was going to see her again. "Tonight," said Scheer. "Eleven o'clock. Tonight's the night."

We returned to the hotel in high spirits to wait for the magic hour. "Hey Scheer," said Joe Ippolito, "maybe you should have some oysters." Scheer said that he wasn't hungry. Joe picked up the phone and asked for room service. "You've got a heavy date tonight, Scheer. Some oysters would be good for you."

Everyone sat around watching Scheer eat his oysters. When he finished he emitted a little burp, and Joe picked up the telephone again and ordered another dozen oysters.

"But Joe, I don't like oysters that much," Scheer protested.

"Look, Scheer, anybody who has to spend the night with the Head Bunny better have a lot of oysters in him. You eat another plate. This is a business decision."

Scheer went along with the game for the second dozen oysters, but protested the accountant's intention to order yet another plate.

"I'm authorizing this as a legitimate business expense, Scheer. You eat some more oysters," the controller said.

"Come on, Joe, I can't eat another dozen oysters. I'll get sick," said Scheer.

"All right," the controller said to room service on the line, "just send a half-dozen oysters this time."

Scheer slurped down the 30th oyster. He said he was going to go to his room to rest up before his assignation.

I called Scheer the next morning. "How'd you do?"

"Shit," he said, "I was so stuffed from all those oysters that I fell asleep. I missed the date."

The upshot of our Chicago visit was that Scheer—who, traditionally Bronx-bred, had never as much as tasted an oyster before—discovered that he savored the slimy things, and now spends weekends digging up his own in Tomales Bay.

I was having a friendly conversation with Cora Weiss, a ranking New York peacenik, chatting up one grand thing or another that *Ramparts* was going to do to stop the war in Vietnam, when she expressed a degree of shock that the paper should be doing anything but deescalating its plans at the moment: "But *Ramparts* is in *debt*."

Cora of course knew that *Ramparts* was running on deficit financing because I had asked her if she thought her father, Sam Rubin, who was dripping in Fabergé perfume money, might put something in the pot. I replied, "For God's sake, Cora—*Ramparts* is only a couple of million in debt, but your enemy Lyndon Johnson is financing the whole goddamn war by running the country billions into debt! Scream at him, not at me!"

That slight exchange was altogether typical of the difference in perspectives between myself and what—for want of a more precise term—I will call the monied left (precious few of whom, as you will see, put a buck into *Ramparts*; which is not to say that I didn't try to get it from them). It was mostly a clash of style, although there were other differences, such as my affinity for the politics of the Black Panthers (Eldridge Cleaver vintage) over the suburbanite leftism of *Dissent*-type socialists. But it was primarily the style thing that made for stormy weather between me and the left—old as well as new. As William Safire, war refugee from official Washington to the political resettlement camp of the New York *Times* Op-Ed page, said while still in the earnest employ of the Watergate White House, "Atmosphere is substance."

As for the New Left: Many individuals in the movement were good friends of mine, but I had no patience with the boring dribble, self-important sense of purpose, and petty little personal power trips that characterized the New Left of the 1960's. In addition, the lot of them didn't drink. I just wanted to put out a paper; we were all against Vietnam, and as we agreed on most issues other than how to eat, drink, dress and live, the alliance, uneasy at times, was born. I cut the rhetoric out of their copy and whipped teams of New-Leftish researchers and reporters to root out facts rather than theories to support our mutual biases. It was not in the cards that the New Left would appreciate this city room approach to their ideologies, nor did they like the often perverse and occasionally sensational non-political side of *Ramparts*, which together with the New Leftism that filtered through the bar smoke made the paper the interesting example of functioning schizophrenia that it then was.

About the older left: There was something about *Ramparts* that gave them a twinge in the gut. The paper's mode of operating jarred their conceptions of the Uriah Heep posture of the left. If there is guilt connected with having lots of money, it was often assuaged by the wealthy ones sitting in a dirty cafeteria over a cup of watery tea and discussing with a group of the revolutionary dedicated the difficult and painstaking process of helping to raise $10,000 to print an antiwar brochure. The fat cat picks up the tab for the tea, but everyone at the table knows damn well he could just as easily pick up the whole 10 grand printing bill. They don't want advice; they want his money, but they're afraid to ask. His good left-wing deed done for the day, the pink fat cat then drives home—in a VW probably, perhaps a Pinto—to his $200,000 house in Westchester where there is an accountant in the basement poring over the dividends from his multimilliondollar portfolio (ITT, McDonald Aircraft, Con Edison and other low-profile profilers of the machinery of death—but no more Dow Chemical, which got too hot because of napalm and all). There is a natural contradiction in the idea of a rich left—the obvious clash of their class position with their avowed politics. However, since their giving to poor-boy leftist causes is buttressed in the comfortable expectation of losing, they can, without any conflict of principle, hang on to their money and their politics at the same time.

A difference of opinion developed between myself and many of the richer leftists over money—their money—which I suppose could be said to boil down to the fact that they wanted to hang on to it and I wanted to spend it. Also I have never been in a cafeteria in my life and it rankled beyond repair the sensibilities of some investors when I took them to lunch at the Four Seasons and paid for it with their money. A few individuals told me that the only time they really enjoyed their money was when I spent it on them, as their Puritan instincts would not allow them to treat themselves. (Of course if *Ramparts* had been anything other than a leftist magazine you would never have heard one word about the money thing; the paper was quite disconcertingly upfront about using the system and insisting on its share of the white man's privileges of the journalists on the other side of the political fence —while at the same time unreasonably attacking and vilifying the Establishment; this made people wonder what the paper was really about, and when they looked, they found me drinking at Elaine's.)

Ramparts was itself a contradiction in its own terms—a big-money, left-wing, professional publishing operation. It was clear that Chase Manhattan Bank was not the place to look for financing *Ramparts*, and I had no qualms about asking the rich left to cough up some risk capital. I didn't mind so much the multimillionaire pinkos saying no, but they rarely let it go at that—they would offer the advice—verbal jars of pickled herring—that *Ramparts* wouldn't need so much money if it didn't print on that expensive slick paper; it should use butcher paper like the *Nation*. Aside from missing the whole point of *Ramparts*—a slick, mass-media magazine of dissent rather than confirmation—it provoked me because I hate butcher paper so.

At any rate what we set out to do at *Ramparts* required a lot of capital. The left has never been accustomed, let alone comfortable, operating in the sort of crass commercial manner *Ramparts* represented. The main question about the magazine was whether we could get enough dough to have a fair shot at the brass ring. The odds were that we couldn't, and we didn't, but I did not see then, or now, why that should have kept us from trying.

It takes a lot of moola to fool around with national magazines, regardless of their politics. It takes even more if the paper is hell bent on shoving a hot poker up the rear end of the Establishment, as that editorial posture is not conducive to a massive influx of advertising dollars. The recent collapses of the politically uncontroversial *Life* and the brainchilded *Saturday Review* are instructive of the general perils, although a lot of people on the left still cherish the idea that *Ramparts* went under because I bought people drinks.

Jerry Piel of *Scientific American*, who is about the smartest man I know in publishing, once gave me a very rough rule of thumb of what it costs to launch a successful national magazine. He said it takes approximately $1 million to get each 100,000 of circulation, and that around 400,000 stable circulation is desirable if the magazine is going to have a reasonable chance of attracting enough advertising to allow it to make money. Those figures were operative only if you didn't make any mistakes. In the five years I ran *Ramparts*, in addition to Keating's million—which didn't exactly count, since he spent most of that when the paper was a 2,000-print quarterly—we raised another two million, give or take some; the highest circulation *Ramparts* reached was 250,000; so I suppose the paper was potentially somewhere in the ballpark, although we did make a lot of mistakes. In 1967, for instance, one editorial on Israel cost the paper $1 million—if you like *that* sort of example.

Once again, it's the old story of the monkey pissing into the cash register—it all runs into money. In this case, a lot of money. I figured that as long as I had to go to the bother of raising loot, I might as well try to raise enough to make the paper over into something more than the Catholic penny dreadful that it was. There was certainly no great call for another liberal magazine with Catholic flavoring, or, God forbid, yet another plain vanilla leftist sheet. The left-wing press such as it is in the United States has been the product of shadow circulation caves and butcher paper ghettos —magazines and newspapers of the committed, by the committed, and for the committed. The intramural left press poses no threat to the prevailing wisdom reflected and reinforced in the so-called "middle of the road" commercial media with all its stuffy egocentric nationalism. That point is, I daresay, not especially arguable, but one has to recall the sad story of the *Nation*'s printing the story of the Bay of Pigs preparations five months before the invasion and being almost totally ignored in its pitiable attempts to alert the rest of the American press to the story.

The experiment I tried with *Ramparts* was to attempt to break out of the circulation boundaries and audience of fellow basket-weavers of the traditional liberal-left press. The goal was to escalate dissent from the soapboxes to the newsstands of America. That the gamble succeeded, to the limited but still surprising extent that it did, is comment enough on the Big Sleep of American journalism through most of the sixties. If the rest of the gang had been halfway on the ball, there would have been no way for a cocky kid like *Ramparts* to muscle into the block.

The metamorphosis of *Ramparts* involved more than just slicking it up, although that of course was a key part of it: "Whatever you do, kid, always serve it with a little dressing," said George M. Cohan to Spencer Tracy—advice I have long valued. But an even more radical change than process color was the paper's approach to the truth, which, on the left, had been virtually synonymous with the correct "line." I barred such theoretical essays from *Ramparts*, and substituted old-fashioned muckraking journalism with its bias on the left but reporting facts—or to give my critics their day in court, purported facts—which made the political point stick. "There is nothing ideological about the facts," I would say to many a young leftist as I blue-penciled his theorems. Along with this hard-nosed approach to digging up dirt, *Ramparts* developed a branch of new journalism that interpolated social and political critiques with trendy you-were-there stylisms. And believing that the truth has to be marketed just like everything else in America, I promoted the blazes out of our stories so that the larger media, should it be inclined to ignore our screeds, à la the *Nation*, would find it difficult to do so.

This Kamikaze approach to journalism became known as "radical slick," a concept for which I have been variously credited (by *Women's Wear Daily*) and blamed (by the Washington *Post*) for inventing. It was on these terms of taking liberal-left journalism for a ride uptown that *Ramparts* went for broke.

Inasmuch as there have been such delicious rumors about where *Ramparts* did get its money I should proceed to set that record straight, although the truth is, alas, not as spicy as the speculation; and is it ever?

The first rich man to say yes to *Ramparts* was Irving Laucks, a vivacious 81-year-old who had a nine-year-old son, a millionaire to the tenth power and also a nice guy who specialized, in his words, in investing in "peace and women," with his rationale for the connection taking the clue from *Lysistrata*. Irving invented plywood. He told me about it one day. "I was just fooling around trying to figure a way to get this dingbatted wood to stick together, and then it stuck, and then I started a company, and then I sold the company and the patent to another company, and then some other company or other bought them, and then all of a sudden I was rich as Croesus." Irving oversaw his diverse efforts in the fields of women and peace from an office in Robert Hutchins' fancy think tank, the Center for the Study of Democratic Institutions, in sylvan Santa Barbara. The Center has doubtless made its contribution to the long uphill march of the Western intellect, but I found it estranged somewhat from reality. Housed in a magnificent villa in the rich Santa Barbara hills, the intellectual cat-and-mouse exercises at the Center (tape-recorded, lest a pearl drop) somehow reminded me of the Russian nobility having tea before the Revolution and discussing what must be done to improve the lot of the masses and reform the poultry-yard ethics of the Czar. A cagey fellow, Irving kept his eye on the think-tankers: "They're all hanging around expecting me to put a lot more money in this place," he said, his eyes full of mischief. "But I tell them my specialty is ending the war, and I'm awaiting and awatching to see what they can do to help me in my specialty. That gets 'em mighty nervous." Luncheon cocktails at the Center consisted entirely of dreadful Heublein premixed martinis, poured from the can, which the assembled intellectual lights made a gang rush for and sucked in at a furious pace until Hutchins tinkled his little bell and the men of the mind walked obediently into lunch. The 81-year-old millionaire would occasionally drive me down the hill to a Mexican restaurant in Monticello, "where we can get a real drink."

Irving put $75,000 in the paper, a welcome dollop in a several-hundred-thousand-dollar investment package we scraped together by the fall of 1965, just in time to keep the sheriff from the door. The term "package" sends fund-raisers reaching for the Maalox. The idea is that if a certain sum is necessary for a deal, then the various investors putting up the dough will not actually kick into the kitty until the entire amount guaranteed is forthcoming; the rationale is part that money loves company, part to counter the very real temptation to run like a bandit to the bank with the first check.

The investor who very sensibly insisted on that provision for *Ramparts'* first money was Bill Honig, an owner of the largest advertising firm in California, Honig, Cooper & Harrington, and a novelist on the side. Honig had been considering investing $100,000 in Max Ascoli's *Reporter*, but we saved him from that fate. He put the hundred grand in *Ramparts* instead, but with a tough business eye that helped the paper shape itself up so it at least had a chance to see the dawn. Honig became the head of *Ramparts'* embattled finance committee, and was a perfect brick during the rocky years ahead.

Bill Honig likes to tell one story, perhaps apocyphal, of the somewhat unorthodox settings for discussions about *Ramparts* finances. This particular time, he imagined that he felt some unmistakable pressure on him to consider perhaps putting in some more money. It was on a day that he made a routine visit to Dr. Feigen's medical office. The proctologist and the ad man were both members of *Ramparts* board of directors, and the small talk turned to money. As Bill tells the story, he was flat on an examination table with a cold sigmoidoscope up his rear end when Feigen made empathic just what dire shape the magazine was in—the boys really needed more money, and imagine, everything would be all right if *somebody* just invested another $100,000 in *Ramparts* right *now* (ouch!).

Next in line was Frederick Mitchell, a young (then 31) graduate student in ancient Aztec civilizations at Berkeley. Mitchell had been calling *Ramparts* for months, leaving messages that he wanted to talk to someone about investing in the magazine. No one ever called him back. I kept crumpling up his phone messages and throwing them in the dust bin. Anyone who would call up *Ramparts* and volunteer money could only be a crank, or worse. It was only in a moment of the most abject financial despair that Joe Ippolito and I decided to drive to Berkeley to visit the nuisance caller. I always knew when things were particularly bad because Joe would tell my wife, Denise, when she invariably asked how things were going, "Better not put any meat in the spaghetti sauce this week."

Mitchell lived in a huge-timbered Willis Polk-type house in the Berkeley hills. We got lost on the way, and stopped for a drink, and didn't ring Mitchell's doorbell until after 11 P.M. "Oh, I thought you weren't coming," Mitchell said, inviting us in. Mitchell was tall, with the demeanor of an altar boy and a slightly fey sense about him. I gave him the latest issue of *Ramparts*, which seemed to impress him mightily. I told him it was hot off the presses, which it was, but neglected to add that we had just bounced a $17,000 check to the printer to pay for it. We talked about the magazine for a while, and then Mitchell said, "I've always wanted to invest in a magazine. Do you think it would be all right if I invested a hundred thousand?"

"Well that's a nice round sum, Fred," Joe said.

Joe spent the next hour giving Mitchell a financial version of the Miranda warning. The magazine was in very bad shape, and he might lose his money. "Oh, I expected something like that," Mitchell said.

We got back to my house in San Francisco late that evening. Denise asked what had happened in Berkeley. "You can put the meat back in the spaghetti sauce," Joe said.

Before we could issue stock to Mitchell for his money the California Corporations Commissioner made him sign a somewhat embarrassing paper stating that he had full knowledge of *Ramparts'* financial condition and prospects but notwithstanding, he was over 21 and going to invest the money, anyway. Said Mitchell, reaching for his pen, "The only thing that's missing from this is the phrase 'of sound mind and body.' "

Keating did not hit it off too swimmingly with the new investors. For a reason I have never been able to comprehend, he sent Irving Laucks a several-paged, single-spaced letter criticizing his theory on peace and women. When the astonished Laucks telephoned to discuss the letter, Keating got into an argument with him on the phone and ended up telling the plywood king that he didn't know anything about peace or about women, either. Honig was quite concerned that before the new money went into the bank some sort of controls be established to insure that the publisher wouldn't do with their new money what he had done with his old money. Mitchell returned ashen faced from a luncheon with Keating and whispered to me that something was going to have to be done to keep "that man" from writing editorials.

Since Keating owned 100 percent of the stock—which had to be reshuffled and, as Wall Street says, "diluted" in order for the new investors to buy in—what is described in English novels of manners as an "awkward situation" developed. A fearsome round of discussions and negotiations ensued, and for a while it looked as if Keating might pull the walls of the temple down around him.

Finally Gossage, who loved to solve insoluble problems, stepped in the breach and after two days of brainstorming with Keating and Mitchell in separate rooms, announced what he called the ultimate solution: Keating would remain as publisher, but give up a block of his stock to the staff to vote. Then the new investors would buy in. That way, there would be three blocks of stock instead of two, and no one group would control any other group. And then while the paper was getting reorganized Keating would go off to run for Congress against Shirley Temple.

Gossage himself dictated the memorandum of agreement, then got all parties into his conference room and stood over them while they signed it. He ceremoniously handed Keating the gold pen used for the signing so Ed could keep it as a souvenir.

The scene that followed was one suited to a novelist's tastes. It was described in this way by novelist Earl Shorris in a piece in the Los Angeles *Times* magazine. He said it was a nonfiction piece, but I'm not sure that they believed him:

> Feigen, Gossage and others had been encouraging Keating to make the decision to enter the Democratic primary. During a meeting in Howard Gossage's office, they were successful.
>
> Keating, Feigen, Gossage, Hinckle and Stermer sat around the conference table in Gossage's private office. It is a room from Kafka. In one corner there is a couch, a coffee table and Gossage's desk and chair. Fifteen feet away, in the center of the room, is the conference table. The walls rise 20 feet or more.
>
> While Keating, Hinckle and Gossage talked, Feigen and Stermer slipped out of the room and into another part of the converted firehouse. There they made signs: *RAMPARTS LIVES, KEATING FOR CONGRESS, KEATING THE PEOPLE'S CHOICE*. They came back into the room carrying the signs and loudly humming a march. Hinckle and Gossage joined them. They marched around the conference table, where Keating still sat, all of them humming and bearing signs. When it was over, Keating had decided to enter the primary and Hinckle was running the magazine.

"WHAT GOOD IS FREEDOM OF THE PRESS IF THERE ISN'T ONE?"

The sixties was the decade when the frightened cry of "Timber!" was everywhere in the unclean air of publishing. The flow of competitive daily newspapers dried up, and magazines great and small fell like the trees chopped down for the paper to print them.

Now that the flagship *Life* has joined its lessers in the Sargasso Sea of bestilled publications, some conventional wisdom prevails as to how American publishing became trapped in such an economic rat hole: spiraling production costs, quadrupling postage rates, blood-sucking competition for advertising dollars from television, the general malaise of the economy, mass circulations sustained at uneconomical cutrates, the decline of print, et cetera. None of these reasons, to my way of thinking, explains the big picture. The man who, Cassandralike, doped out what was going to happen, long before the casualty lists began to mount, was Howard Gossage. Hardly anyone listened to him when he was alive and telling why so many papers were going to die. Now he is dead, and has the small epitaph of having been proved right.

Howard began to formulate his stone heresies, centering on the proposition that the reliance of publishing upon advertising was umbilic, transitory and fraught with peril, in the early sixties. He kept it up, and kept upping the ante, until he died in 1969; the decade previous, he had occupied himself throwing wooden chips in the porridge bowl of the advertising industry—here a deserved kick below the belt at the commission system, there a broadside at the billboard industry, here again a swipe at Smokey the Bear.

Howard hated Smokey the Bear.

Smokey was the American advertising industry's gift to the nation, the symbol of the industry's vaunted "public service" campaign, which had the stated purpose of reducing forest fires. Howard was aghast at the very idea that the advertising industry, which was responsible for so much of the glut and waste of consumerism and which had made of the country one giant depository for throw-away products including the automobile, so piously purported to be lending a helping hand to Old Mother Nature. In fact, Howard said, Smokey the Bear was inept and potentially disastrous in his job; Gossage had amassed considerable statistics to argue that the forests were better off when people weren't breaking their matches, as Smokey so often told them, because numerous small forest fires were part of the state of nature, and the "improvement" rendered by the anti-forest fire campaign had produced a situation where the forests were periled with massive and more ruinous "blockbuster" forest fires.

"It's a simple matter of kicking sleeping dogs awake," Howard would say, when asked the obvious by those among the incredulous who could not savvy why an advertising man would so consistently bite the hands that fed him.

I owe some dues to the tradition of oral history, or the memory of Boswell, since although Howard talked almost constantly about his media theories—at least, he did to me —he rarely got around to writing them down, except in bits and pieces, and then usually in the self-defeating format of speeches to the advertising fraternity, those pearls who came to hear Gossage tell them what swine they were in much the same way that white liberals, in the halcyon days of the civil rights movement, would crowd into some Greenwich Village arena for the soul-cleansing experience of hearing Leroi Jones tell them they were no-good white motherfuckers.

It is accordingly in the nature of things that, although Howard Gossage was, within his profession, perhaps the most famous maverick of recent decades, he is renowned, in Daniel Boorstin's phrase, "for being famous for being famous." Very few souls, except those few of us who lived the hurricane experience of being close to him, know what he really thought. That wealth should, I think, be shared.

Gossage's postulate was based, as with so many things he did, on a great line: "What good is freedom of the press if there isn't one?"—a quotation Gossage made up, but laid the authorship on A. J. Liebling. The quotation has a no doubt unprecedented use in the threnody of dead publications, or those about to die. Whenever Gossage employed these words, usually on the occasion of a publication's passing, he attributed them to the late Liebling, long *The New Yorker*'s resident bird dog of the press. Although Liebling never said that, it sounded like something he *might* have said, and that was good enough for Howard. "Otherwise, I'd be in the position of quoting myself," he said once, when I asked him why. (The attributing of bright things they were supposed to have said to people who had not in fact said them was one of his favorite pastimes. The definition of a consultant as a man who borrows your watch to tell you what time it is, and then charges you for it—I have heard him credit, on separate occasions, to three different friends, advertising men Carl Ally, Stan Freberg, and the late Nick Samstag, a valued co-conspirator.)

Liebling's non-quotation first surfaced as the headline on a Gossage ad in the New York *Times* on January 24, 1964. That was the day the *Times* folded its experimental Western Edition. Gossage was absolutely incensed that they were shutting it down, and paid $1,600 of his own money for the luxury of telling off the *Times* in its own pages. He wrote the ad for the last issue of the Western Edition, but the *Times* refused it. "They didn't want anything to rock the coffin," Howard said. Somehow, he talked them into running the ad, instead, in the regular New York edition of the *Times*, where the jelly-bean-munchers along Madison Avenue were dismayed at the point of his pique—that the *Times* had killed its Pacific Coast Edition without asking him, Howard Gossage, for permission. Gossage numbered himself a *Times* subscriber, one among the "90,000 other dead" Western Edition readers of the paper, and he felt that gave him some rights: "It seems quite wrong to me that a newspaper should go under while its readers still want it; what is a newspaper for if not for them?" He would have been willing to pay more money for the Western *Times*, Gossage said, and perhaps a lot of other readers would, too, had they been asked—perhaps enough so that the paper might not have had to die, at all; also, perhaps not, but at least the *Times* (or any other publisher) might have the decency to take its readers into its confidence before doing a nervy thing like dying. The publishing industry, Gossage declared, "has no more real notion of where its basic responsibility lies than a billy goat."

Howard believed that publishers had become quite piggish about Freedom of the Press, which they interpreted wholly as the freedom to publish. But, he argued, there was also such a thing as Freedom of the Press for the Reader. Nobody thought much about that, especially the readers, who were largely unaware that their Freedom of the Press had been taken from them by the clubbish and ill-starred reliance of almost all publishers upon advertising revenues to sustain life, or, conversely, bring on death:

"In this century we have seen effective control of our press shift from the public, for whom it presumably exists, to the advertiser, who merely uses it to sell wares to the public."

"Vell, Herr Doktor Goss-sage, ist dot not apparantk?" I once heard a German advertising man (West Germany, of course) ask the Master. "No!" said Gossage, leaping to his feet, eyes flashing, arms waving, his shock of white hair flowing back like an unraveling turban. No! he said in his magnificent stammer, the words coming out hyphenated, slowly, as in water torture, "No, bu-buu-buddy, it's not *ap-par-ent*—it's *ob-vi-ous*, and that's one hell of a big difference!"

What was obvious to Howard had aspects of a sacred mushroom. He had an uncanny ability to see the obvious, before anyone else, although not in the usual fashion of the self-deprecatory clap on the head: *"Mon Dieu!* All this time the letter was *here* on the sideboard!!" Gossage didn't merely see some pedestrian fact, such as the emperor having no clothes on, but rather some cosmic truth, a sudden blinding wisdom about the way things were that made everything else, related and interrelated, make some sort of grand, organic sense.

So it was with what Gossage saw as *obvious* about advertising, which was not just the truth about advertising but about communications, which was more than about communications, it had really to do with man's plight and man's fate, linked in so many ways to the definition and exchange and clash of ideas that was communications before the tinkerers and landlords and polluters of the media had at it. . . .

The German advertising man said he did not understand. No wonder, said Gossage, explaining the man's own incomprehension to him, "Loo-oook at it this way, bu-buu-buddy, *we don't know who discovered water, but we're pretty sure it wasn't a fish.*" That was another of Gossage's favorite quotations, a line of absolutely Delphic ambiguity. It came from his McLuhan Period, when he and Feigen were schlepping McLuhan around the country, introducing him as Mohammed to their friends ruling the media mountains. Gossage was always kind of translating for the potty prophet. . . . "What Marshall means by all that is this. . . ." But a lot was added in the translation, and McLuhan would look at Gossage like the Mad Hatter peering over the tea cup and say, in a voice that was part confused innocence, part modest genius, "Gee, Howard, that's exactly what I meant when I wasn't saying it."

The fish-didn't-discover-water line Gossage, after his fashion, occasionally credited to McLuhan, when the great man was in need of explanation, but the more frequent quotee was Father John Culkin, then a Jesuit and a McLuhanite, now an ex-Jesuit but I suspect still a McLuhanite. (If this book seems overpopulated by former Jesuits, it is because there are so many of them; there must be as many, almost, as ex-prisoners of war, but not anywhere near so many as sinus sufferers, to give an idea.) Culkin may have even actually said that, but primary authorship was as difficult to trace in quotations favored by Gossage as the authorship of the Dead Sea Scrolls. At any rate, what Gossage told the German, courtesy of the Jesuit, was that it was no wonder he knew zilch about what advertising really was, since he was *in it*: "You become aware of your environment only when you, somehow, get outside of it," he maintained.

The process, or posture, by which one could see one's own environment, or profession, or country, for what it really was—the fish looking in from outside the fish bowl—Howard called "extra-environmental" perception. That is the way a person oblivious to, or not conditioned by, his surroundings would see things. This intuitive capacity he explained by analogy to the color-blind aerial observers recruited during the Second World War because their color blindness enabled them to see things which were camouflaged to normally sighted eyes; Gossage thought it marvelous that these guys would look down at a quite ordinary stretch of landscape and say, "Hey, there's a gun emplacement!"

My faith in the obvious was never quite as strong as Howard's, so I saved these notes, taken from the Gossage, for a syllabus of errors, suitable for tacking on the front door of the cathedral of Madison Avenue.

Although most of us accept advertising as some sort of Providential Clock, taking its tick-tock from whatever Deity governs the market economy, the fact is that advertising is a relatively Johnny-come-lately. It did not exist in the mass-market form that we know it much before the First World War, and did not exist in much any form at all before the late nineteenth century.

But before advertising, there were newspapers and magazines. They were very much as we know them today, except of course that the pages were filled with news instead of paid hustle. Since they had almost no other source of revenue, the publications of that time lived or died by the reader's penny spent, and charged an honest price; if a publication costs five cents to produce, you can bet a publisher charged at least five cents for it, and hoped like hell that what his paper had to say was interesting enough to get enough people to pony up their nickels. It is no coincidence that the great muckraking magazines of American legend flourished under these game conditions; he who pays the piper calls the tune, and the only paymaster was their readers, who apparently liked what the muckrakers were playing.

If this was publishing's state of nature, advertising was its original sin. With the growth of consumer advertising early in this century, publishers found themselves in the sudden happy situation of getting income from both ends; and they enjoyed that mightily, as one will gravy.

At a point uncertain in time but no later than the flapper days of the post-World War I period, publishers took the fatal bite from the apple. Faced with rising costs, most publishers decided not to risk losing circulation by raising the price per copy accordingly. This decision was dictated by elemental greed, not charity toward the penny-pinching reader; the way publishers figured it, they could get more money from advertisers the more readers they had, so what the hell, why antagonize the customers when the advertisers were footing the bill?

"Well," said Gossage, "that tore it." The day a reader paid five cents for a publication that cost six cents to produce was the day, by Gossage's calculation, that he lost his economic freedom of the press.

Publishers soon became so hooked on the gravy of advertising that they could not do without it and, the first junkies, took to junk mail, discovering that they could "buy" readers, i.e., build up circulation, simply by lowering the subscription price, making it a loss leader while getting a handsome return from the advertisers—while it lasted.

The reader has paid dearly for all this. For one thing, he suffered the ultimate indignity that Western society can bestow upon its members: He became a consumer. The word consumer is another cigarette burn in the tablecloth of the English language that we can trace to the chain-smokers of Madison Avenue. When advertisers speak of consumers they think they mean people, but they don't. What they call a Consumer, is by Gossage's definition, "An anthropomorphic being designed to use whatever it is you have to sell—it will therefore be a grotesque on the order of the monsters of Hieronymus Bosch or Artzybasheff: all mouth or belly, but, in these days of automatic drive, just one foot."

For a second thing, the cheaper publications became to buy, the fewer of them there were around. Publications died right and left without regard to the fact that their subscribers were loyally paying their bills, or that their readers actually *liked* them. A newspaper reader who pays a dime for a paper that actually costs thirty-five cents to produce is being subsidized, and has as much to say about whether his favorite paper will live or die as he did about ending the war in Vietnam. Gossage's favorite illustration of the utter madness of publishing economics was that a newspaper or magazine was the only consumer product, from bubble gum to bras, where the selling price had no relation to the actual cost of production. It costs less, for instance, to have a magazine delivered at home than it does to buy it in the store; try that with milk.

Naturally, advertisers want to reach as many people as possible, but not necessarily in as many publications as possible. That can be rather expensive in, say, a town with six daily newspapers. Both wasteful duplication and *angst* about mak-

ing the right choices among the six papers would be eliminated if there were only, say, two daily newspapers, as the
advertisers could reach everybody who read the papers in
those two, saving the expense and bother of the other four.

Since Gossage began preaching his Apocalypse in the early
sixties, a veritable armada of newspapers and magazines has
gone down with circulations intact, so there is demonstrably
something to what he said.

The way Gossage figured it, "People don't read ads; they
read what interests them, and sometimes it is an ad." Similarly,
there is only one process of the flow of ideas and exchange of
information—"communications," which includes newspapers, radio, magazines, television, billboards and whatever
—and it is that entire process of information and mass education that advertising, in Gossage's phrase, has firmly by the
sweetbreads.

Whether advertising doesn't want or shouldn't have such
power over the press is immaterial. The fact is that it has it,
and Gossage's singular contribution to the pole-axed discussions of the narcoleptic state of mass media was to raise original questions about the responsibility that is implicit in such
enormous power. It is a question that is largely ducked in the
more popular critiques of the media; when Spiro Agnew
opened fire at the Eastern-Establishment types conducting
the press according to their own tunes, it is doubtful he was
thinking of the media buyers of Madison Avenue, who not
only pay for the orchestra and the sheet music, but also sub-
sidize the audience.

Advertising is generally assumed, even by its critics, to be
necessary to the economy. Gossage found that a highly questionable and undifferentiated assumption. "That's a crock of
sour owl shit," was the way he put it, with uncharacteristic
brevity. Although apologists for advertising say that it makes
the wheels go round, Gossage maintained that most advertising merely makes some wheels go round, and pretty dinky
wheels at that. The way he toted it up, over half of national
advertising goes for items which account for barely 5 percent
of the Gross National Product, and perhaps 2 percent of the
labor market: bulwarks of a strong and free economy such as

breakfast cereals, soaps, cosmetics, hair oils, toothpastes, deodorants, smokes, and booze. Taking television by itself, the figures are even more striking: fully two-thirds of television advertising is in those and kindred categories of fee-fo-fum.

"Viewed in its entirety, advertising is a seventeen-billion-dollar sledge hammer to drive a forty-nine-cent thumbtack," said Gossage.

The Constitutional guarantee of freedom of the press from government control tends to obscure other incursions that can equally limit the citizen's plurality of choice and content, and are therefore just as dangerous. That these incursions are economic rather than political makes them much harder to recognize, Gossage said, since politics is a *bad* word, but economics is a *nice* word. But *Star Trek* fans and other bereaved deprived of their favorite programs know there is an unseen Evil Hand at work. It is hard to conceive of television being such a mishmash if programs were not designed primarily to be attractive advertising "buys" geared to reach the largest gluttonous mass of unblinking consumers.

Howard believed in the power of analogy as a talisman which would ward off any lack of comprehension of his theories. He was constantly building elaborate analogy-castles in the sky, and none was more elaborate than his ultimate analogy of the process by which advertising shapes the content of the media it controls.

What has happened to television, he said, is what would happen to football if the hot dog vendors took over the game.

Gossage insisted that a good analogy should be capable of "being engraved on the head of a ten milligram Dexamyl tablet." This one is a little longer than that.

THE HOT DOG ANALOGY

by Howard Luck Gossage

(As told, at least one hundred times, to Hinckle)

Hot dogs are nice, but they are not the reason people go to the stadium. They go to see the game, but as long as they are there, why not have a hot dog?

That is also, somewhat, the operating principle of commercial television: Once the crowd is there to see the show, you also sell them something.

However, to get the big picture about television, you have to reverse the analogy: Suppose that the proceeds from hot dog sales were greater than ticket receipts. Moreover, hot dog-wise it is more profitable to have a full stadium, even if you have to let spectators in for nothing, or at greatly reduced admission, than to charge full admissions to a smaller crowd of die-hard fans, who are the only ones who regularly show up when the home team is on a losing streak, anyway.

This would shortly affect the complexion of the audience, and eventually the game, because it's never quite the same thing when you get it free, and the type of people who are willing to pay for their pleasure expect a different quality of show than those who get it on the cheap. But as we are now only interested in numbers, things would be going along famously; the stadium is packed and the bleachers happy, even though by getting in for free the spectators have been demoted from fans to potential hot dog consumers.

Now, along comes that old spoilsport, economics: High football production costs make it necessary to bring in more money, and, as it is impractical to call in the Pinkertons to bust up the players' union, increased volume is the only answer to the profits to which you have become accustomed. However, once the spectators have become accustomed to seeing games for nothing, you certainly can't expect them to *pay*. And Phase III of the Federal Price Controls has a mean thing about hot dogs, so you can't raise the price of them, much. The only thing to do is to sell *more* hot dogs.

The simplest marketing solution is to create ten-minute intermissions between quarters, on top of the traditional half-time break, so the fans can better stretch their pocketbooks and hear their stomachs growling. But, so as not to extend the game so much that it runs over into the game which immediately follows in the same stadium —the late game—five minutes are chopped off each period.

So spectators wandered in and out the open gates with varying degrees of interest; and sometimes hardly anybody was interested, even for free; attendance dwindled. To cope with that, the games that pulled the biggest and most enthusiastic crowds were studied for their successful formats. Soon, all games were alike—including a mandatory five interceptions, one bloody field free-for-all, and an upset victory in the last ten seconds by a forty-yard pass or seventy-yard run, interchangeable so the suspense did not become monotonous.

Thus, football would be a sort of open-air television; the analogy wasn't perfect, Howard admitted, because if you wanted to escape the hot dog vendors during intermissions you had to walk a half mile to the bathroom.

Gossage developed this thought while lecturing as a visiting professor at Penn State in 1962. When he expounded at his usual length about it, he inevitably got into a discussion of the "rights" of advertisers versus those of the spectators. One insistent coed, like the dreadful little girl who recited to a captive Lewis Carroll during a long carriage ride the entire text of *The Hunting of the Snark*, kept arguing that advertisers had the right to control what was on television, because after all, they paid for it. Howard asked her if she thought that hot dog vendors had the right to control the university's football games. "Of course," she said, "if they paid my way in."

When Gossage got annoyed his stammers came on like
jackhammers, his spectacles would perch up on the edge of his
nose—an epic, beat-up nose that suggested the bumps and
grinds and contours of a freeway interchange collapsed in an
earthquake.

"But what right have they got to pay your way in?" he
fumed. "Whose football game is it? Whose stadium is it?
Whose university is it? It's yours. It doesn't *belong* to the hot
dog vendors, it belongs to you; and so do our communications
media."

Broadcasting is most arguably a public utility, using as it
does the public air for private profit; but Howard was upset
that the Federal Communications Commission, while accepting this proposition to the extent of regulating broadcasting license applications, shied from the even more basic issue
of regulating the advertising industry, which had more control over the content of broadcasting than the station owners
or the networks themselves, since Madison Avenue was paying everybody's way.

To the insistent coed who argued that advertisers who pay
the piper have the right to call the tunes Lawrence Welk plays,
Gossage's reply was, baloney; advertising got itself into that
position by default, and it was a default that had become
self-perpetuating. It had been that way for so long that people
just didn't realize it could be any other way. Yet the day was
long past when anyone would argue that any private industry,
such as electricity or transportation or telephones, could do
what it wanted with a public necessity, or necessary public
convenience, that it wholly controlled; but only Gossage
thought of communications, and advertising, in the same way.

Gossage had the sauce to tell the advertising industry that it
had the responsibility to inform the public just what terrible
shape the mass media was in because of its dependence on,
and connivance with, advertising. Instead of running all those
"public service" ads in favor of U.S. Savings Bonds, or coming
out four-square against forest fires, Howard wanted the ad
boys to mount a massive campaign to get the price of newspapers and magazines up to a realistic, fair figure (and to get
overinflated circulations, accordingly, down). Gossage even

invented a catchy, advertising-type name for it: Pay Reading. "We have to put over the idea that a newspaper is worth at least as much as a package of cigarettes," he often said.

Throughout the sixties, when advertisers were flocking to the happy land of television at the expense of the mass magazines they had helped create, Gossage told them they were little better than murderers, and not even mercy killers; in league with greedy publishers, ad men had gotten the reading public hooked on cheap magazines, which meant there were fewer magazines, with less difference between them—and now they were killing the publications that they had so artificially kept alive, pulling the plug from the kidney machine, without so much as a tip of the hat to the widowed reading public. The least the advertising industry could do, Howard said, was to tidy up the graveyard and attempt to put American publishing back in the more or less healthy state it was in before Madison Avenue subverted it.

Gossage had harsher readjustments to suggest for the nation's favorite whipping boy, TV, which ill-used the same air space. Since the TV channels were owned by the citizens, and the owners were merely licensed to operate them in the public interest, who was it who said the stations ever had the right to *interrupt* programs with commercial announcements, which could just as well be bunched between programs while people went to the bathroom? It was only that the considerable profits of the stations were even more considerable that way, and they did it only because they got away with it—more precisely because the FCC let them get away with it.

As it was inconceivable that a good newspaper or magazine would allow an advertiser to sponsor its articles, so, Gossage argued, it should be with television—advertisers should take pot luck as to when and where their TV spots ran, somewhat along the lines of the system operative on the English commercial channels, where ads are grouped on a rotating basis between programs and there is no such animal as commercial "sponsorship" of a show.

That was the type of thing Gossage used to tell advertising men; it is little wonder they didn't listen. He tried to explain to the lords of advertising that reform was in their own self-interest, that so many lousy ads cluttering up the tube was counterproductive for their clients, that people were turned off by advertising domination, that Madison Avenue should renew itself by strangling the golden calf; but his fellow Hot Dog Vendors didn't listen to that, either.

At times, when he would get discouraged, Gossage would look out the window at a gray San Francisco day, his eagle face wrinkled up in a frown, and say, "To explain responsibility to advertising men is like trying to convince an eight-year-old that sexual intercourse is more fun than a chocolate ice cream cone."

THE NEW JERUSALEM

The hippies grew up in my backyard. I did not find them good neighbors.

It was nothing personal. I thought it terrific, in the early days of the Haight-Ashbury, that love children could put a dime in a parking meter and lie down in the street for an hour's suntan (thirty minutes for a nickel) and most people would be careful not to run over them.

I wrote a *Ramparts'* cover story about the hippies at an early stage in the counterculture's development that gained me the reputation, not entirely without warrant, of Billy Goat Gruff to the love generation. Some of the flower children went so far as to say they wanted to kick the shit out of me. For one thing, they took umbrage at what I said about their father goddamn, Timothy Leary.

In 1967 he was still a guru in Brooks Brothers clothing. His tweedy suit was Brooks Brothers '54, the paisley tie more J. Press contemporary, and the carved-bone Egyptian mandala hanging around his neck had to be about 2,000 years old. Dr. Timothy Leary, BA University of Alabama, PhD University of California, LSD Cuernavaca, and 86'd Harvard, was out for a night on the town in San Francisco, and tireless proselytizer that he was, he invited me along, even though I had expressed some doubts about his act.

The mission for the night was for Leary to scout somebody else's act, a Swami's at that, who was turning on the hippies at the Avalon Ballroom by leading them in hour-long Hindu chants without stopping appreciably for breath. The Avalon was one of the two great, drafty ballrooms where San Francisco hippies, hippie-hangers-on and young hippies-to-be congregated each weekend to participate in the psychedelic rock and light shows that in the sixties were as much a part of San Francisco as cable cars.

This dance was a benefit for the new Swami, recently installed in a Haight-Ashbury storefront, with a fair passage sign from Allen Ginsberg, whom he had bumped into in India. The hippies were turning out to see just what the Swami's *schtick* was, but Dr. Leary had a different purpose. He had a professional interest in turning people on, and here was this Swami, doing it with just a chant, without pills, like it was natural childbirth or something.

The word professional is not used lightly. There was a large group of professionals servicing and stimulating the hippie world—in reporting the Haight-Ashbury I called these men merchant princes—and Timothy Leary was the pretender to the hippie throne.

Dr. Leary claimed to have launched the first indigenous religion in America, Aimee Semple McPherson in drag. Leary, who identified himself as a "prophet," had recently played the Bay Area in his LSD road show, where he sold $4 seats to lots of squares but few hippies (Dr. Leary's pitch was to the straight world), showed a technicolor movie billed as simulating an LSD experience (it was big on close-ups of enlarged blood vessels), burned incense, dressed like a holy man in white cotton pajamas, and told everybody to "turn on, tune in, and drop out." Leary was not to be dismissed as a cross between a white Father Divine and Nietzsche, no matter how tempting the analogy. He made a substantial historical contribution to the psychedelic scene in America, although his arrest records may figure more prominently than his philosophy in future histories.

Since he first bit into the sacred psychedelic mushroom while lounging beside a swimming pool in Cuernavaca, Leary has been hounded by the consequences of his act. He discovered LSD and was booted out of Harvard for experimenting a little too widely with it among the undergraduate population, and was asked to leave several foreign countries for roughly the same reasons. When I knew him, he was temporarily but comfortably ensconced in a turned-on millionaire friend's estate near Poughkeepsie, New York, while awaiting judicial determination of a 30-year prison sentence for transporting a half-ounce of grass across the Rio Grande without paying the Texas marijuana tax, which had not been enforced since the time of the Lone Ranger.

If he were asked to contribute to the "L" volume of the World Book Encyclopedia, Leary would no doubt sum up his work as "having turned on American culture," though his actual accomplishments are somewhat more prosaic. Together with Richard Alpert, who was to Dr. Leary what Herb Klein was to Richard Nixon, Leary wrote an article in May, 1962, in, surprise, *The Bulletin of the Atomic Scientists*. The article warned that in event of war, the Russians were likely to douse all our reservoirs with LSD in order to make people so complacent that they wouldn't particularly care about being invaded, and as a civil defense precaution we ought to do it ourselves first—you know, douse our own reservoirs—so that when the Reds got *their* chance the country would know just what was coming off. It was back to the old drawing board after that article, but Alpert and Dr. Leary made their main contribution to the incredibly swift spread of LSD through the nation in 1964 by the simple act of publishing a formula for LSD—all that was needed by any enterprising housewife with a B average in high school chemistry and an inclination for black market activity. It would have been easier to take Dr. Leary seriously if he could have overcome his penchant for treating LSD as a patent snake-bite medicine.

I found an enlightening example of this panacea philosophy back among the truss ads in the September, 1966, issue of *Playboy*. In the midst of a lengthy interview when, as will happen in *Playboy*, the subject got around to sex, Leary was all answers. "An LSD session that does not involve an ultimate merging with a person of the opposite sex isn't really complete," he said, a facet of the drug he neglected to mention to the Methodist ladies he was attempting to turn on in Stockton, California. But this time, Dr. Leary was out to turn on the *Playboy* audience.

The following selection from the interview is reprinted in its entirety. Italics are *Playboy*'s.

PLAYBOY: We've heard that some women who ordinarily have difficulty achieving orgasm find themselves capable of multiple orgasms under LSD. Is that true?

LEARY: In a carefully prepared, loving LSD session, a woman will inevitably have several hundred orgasms.

PLAYBOY: Several *hundred?*

LEARY: Yes. Several hundred.

After recovering from that intelligence, the *Playboy* interviewer, phrasing the question as diplomatically as possible, asked Dr. Leary if he got much, being such a handsome LSD turn-on figure. Dr. Leary allowed that women were always falling over him, but responded with the modesty of a Pope: "Any charismatic person who is conscious of his own mythic potency awakens this basic hunger in women and pays reverence to it at the level that is harmonious and appropriate at the time."

Dr. Leary also said that LSD is a "specific *cure* for homosexuality."

The final measure of the tilt of Dr. Leary's windmill, his no doubt earnest claim to be the prophet of the hippie generation, must be made by weighing his beliefs against his frequent and urgent pleas to young people to "drop out of politics, protest, petitions and pickets" and join his "new religion" where, he said,

"You have to be out of your mind to pray."

Perhaps, and quite probably so.

I decided the paper should check out the roots of the New Jerusalem. The question was what, if anything, the hippie phenomena represented besides a pleasant excursion into love, fun and flowers by the overprivileged middle-class kids who comprised the bulk of the hippie overpopulation in the Haight.

The big highs had been in 1965 and 1966, when the San Francisco Mime Troop under the brilliant Ronnie Davis was putting on free theater in the parks, the Diggers had surfaced to put out free food, and the great Human Be-In was looked upon in many quarters as truly the be-all and end-all for humankind. But by 1967, when I wrote some unkind words about what was happening to the love generation, new troops had occupied the Haight to degrade, corrupt and loot the original hippie idealists. One factor was the ascendancy of the merchant princes and media and marketing hypsters who in the space of a few years ripped off an entire generation. Another bad seed was a recessive gene from San Francisco's other heralded renaissance of a decade previous, the Beat Generation. About that, Allen Ginsberg had some input.

Ginsberg began by talking about an evening in 1955—a moment of incubation for the Beatniks, who represented the most thorough repudiation of American middlebrow culture since the expatriates made for Paris in the 1930's. A group of men who were to be in the vanguard of the Beat Generation had gathered at the 6 Gallery on Fillmore Street for a poetry reading moderated by Kenneth Rexroth, a respectable leftish intellectual who was later to become the Public Defender of the Beats. Lawrence Ferlinghetti was in the audience, and so were Jack Kerouac and his then sidekick, Neal Cassady, the Tristram Shandy of the Beat Generation. They were listening to Michael McClure, Phil Lamantia, Gary Snyder and Philip Whalen read their poetry. Ginsberg was there, too, and read a section of the still unfinished "Howl," a poem that would become a Declaration of Independence for the Beats.

Ginsberg is too nice a guy to stress this point, but two quite different strains in the underground movement of the fifties were represented at this salient gathering. One trend was distinctly fascist, which can be found in Kerouac's writing, and is characterized by a nihilism and totalitarian insistence on action for action's sake, often accompanied by a Superman concept. That strain can be traced, running deeper and less silent, into the hippie scene. The recipients of this heritage were Ken Kesey and his friends, the Hell's Angels, and, in a more subtle but no less menacing way, the LSD *Mein Kampf* of

Timothy Leary. When the Hell's Angels rumbled by, Kesey welcomed them with LSD. "We're in the same business. You break people's bones, I break people's heads," he told the Angels, who thereupon became regular studs in the Haight-Ashbury roughhouse.

The other, dominant, side of the Beats was a cultural reaction to the existential brinkmanship forced on them by the Cold War, and a lively attack on the prevailing rhetoric of complacency and self-satisfaction that pervaded the literary establishment. Led by men like Ginsberg and Ferlinghetti, the early Beats weighed America by its words and deeds, and found it pennyweight. They took upon themselves the role of conscience for the machine. They rejected all values and when, in attempting to carve a new creative force, they told America to "go fuck itself," America reacted, predictably, with an obscenity trial.

The early distant warnings of the drug-based culture that would dominate the Haight-Ashbury a decade later were there in the early days of North Beach. Marijuana was as popular as Coke at a Baptist wedding, and the available hallucinogens—peyote and mescaline—were part of the Beat rebellion. Gary Snyder, poet, mountain climber, formal Yamabushi Buddhist, and one of the few leaders of the hippie scene who retained his purity of purpose, first experimented with peyote while living with the Indian tribe of the same name in 1948; Ginsberg first took it in New York in 1951; Lamantia, Kerouac and Cassady were turned on by Beat impresario Hymie D'Angolo at his Big Sur retreat in 1952. And Beat parties, whether they served peyote, marijuana or near beer, were rituals, community sacraments, precursing the hippie rituals of the sixties.

Those were some of the hand-me-downs, for bad and good, that the hippies got from the Beats. The two generations of noncomformists shared a good deal, but their attitude toward the dominant society they were both opting out of could not have been more dissimilar. The Beats fought to remain out of and above commercial America, and lost; the hippies, at least commercially, not only accepted assimilation, they swallowed it whole.

Almost every society susceptible to the adjective "advanced" has allowed, usually with a perfunctory tsk-tsk, the sons and daughters of its more privileged classes to drop out and cut up. If one reads the history of Russia before the Revolution one will find a similarity of gamesmanship among the bored and alienated bourgeois youth. What I found objectionable about the hippies—or rather about some hippie promoters—was the attempt to make a serious political stance out of goofing off. Dropping out *was* the revolution; non-politics was the most serious politics.

One of the leading merchandisers of this counterculture bullshit was *Rolling Stone*, the rock culture tabloid that was started by two disgruntled *Ramparts* types. One of them was Jann Wenner, then a fat and pudgy kid hanging around the office. Wenner was considerably frustrated by my oafish refusal to print his dope and rock stories in the magazine, as I considered rock reporting as a state of the journalistic art on a level with Ben Gay ads. *Rolling Stone* has since become successful on its own rock journalism terms, and Wenner's co-believers in the counterculture press have attempted to cannibalize him for being so successful while they remain failures. Those underground press types who view Wenner as Goebbels look upon me as Hitler, and several articles dinging young Wenner for ripping off the rock revolution described him, in the ultimate insult, as having been "created" by me. The truth of the matter is that I hardly knew the kid; and the only thing *Ramparts* gave him to help start his paper was a bottle of rubber cement to paste up the first issue, and I screamed about *that*.

The second *Ramparts'* evacuee to the *Rolling Stone* was Ralph Gleason, who resigned in a fury over my hippie article which dinged much that he held holy. Gleason said he quit because I quoted him in the article without interviewing him, which was true; he neglected to mention that what I quoted was a column he had written, and that is not the same nasty, but I will let the lumping stand as I liked having the Gleason on the paper (I once offered him a year's salary, in escrow, to quit his *Chronicle* column for *Ramparts*, but he said no; smart) and am sorry that

I dumped on his flower children without giving him a chance to defend the little fascists.

Since the blood-fest of Altamont in December of 1969 —Pearl Harbor to the Woodstock Generation, I called it at the time, but I probably should have said Waterloo—no one is mouthing much more about the glories of the "love revolution." When the hippie cultists argued that people should drop out of the unrewarding task of steering society, they left the driving to the likes of the Hell's Angels. And Altamont showed that one of the results of dropping out can be getting beat up.

The only Haight-Ashbury stars who seem to be still functioning are those, such as Gary Snyder and Allen Ginsberg, who had their own credentials outside of hippiedom. For a time it looked like Emmet Grogan might have staying power—the Diggers was a good idea and he carried it off outrageously well—but when he couldn't make the rhetoric of a wholly cooperative subculture a reality, he opted to give up on the reality and take solace in the high of rhetoric and fancy, until now the poor fellow has become totally a figment of his own imagination.

EARLY BLOOMING REVISIONISM

The Irish storyteller Frank O'Connor warned that books which begin with a recounting of Irish history tend to remain unread. That caution is no doubt applicable to the general subject of America's involvement in Vietnam. Yet Vietnam was one of the subjects *Ramparts* went at with a meat-ax, and I must chat it up sufficiently to explain the process of conversion, peculiar to the sixties, to an early blooming revisionism; one thing, as they say, led to another.

It began, as with most baptisms of fire at the paper, in an earnest attempt to hang something on the Catholic Church. We set out looking to lay some of the blame for Vietnam at the silken slippers of the Pope; we succeeded only in implicating Cardinal Spellman.

We found that not since the days of the Papal States, when Popes rode at the heads of their own armies, has a Prince of the Church been so intimately involved in the arranging of a war than Cardinal Spellman in the origins of the Vietnam conflict.

The Cardinal worked overtime to help condition American opinion to the necessity of Uncle Sam's assuming the Christian colonial burden of the decamping French in Southeast Asia. He was an early sponsor of the Catholic mandarin Ngo Dinh Diem, who lived under the Cardinal's approbation in New Jersey and New York seminaries in the early fifties, while Spellman used his influence to open Washington doors to the then little-known Vietnamese politician-in-exile. When Diem was named Premier in 1954 and consolidated his power with United States money and guns, he proceeded to turn official Saigon into something approximating an Indochinese Vatican City. The ranking jobs in the army and government were given to Catholics, the fringe Catholic philosophy of personalism was elevated to a kind of state religion, and the yellow and white flag of the Vatican fluttered from flagpoles in rural Catholic enclaves; all the while, Diem made life miserable for the Buddhists who comprised the majority of the population. This seemed to Spellman's liking, as the New York Cardinal began to fly in and out of Saigon as if it were a satellite parish of his diocese. Diem ordered army units to work through the night preparing triumphal arches for the Cardinal's visits. The American Catholic Relief Agency gave over $35,000,000 in aid to the refugee Catholics who formed the base of Diem's support in that predominately Buddhist and Confucianist country, and Spellman personally intervened when Eisenhower, in a wavering moment in 1955, considered dumping Diem.

When Diem's little Spain in Vietnam began to fall apart and Washington had to send in American troops to cover its lies, Spellman spent every Christmas with our boys, whom he called, with no apparent intention of hyperbole, "soldiers of Christ."

The extensive Catholic influence in establishing and supporting the Diem dictatorship—and helping disguise its real

nature to the American people—remains a little-known aspect of the overall Vietnam debacle. It was a story on which we
cut our journalistic teeth at *Ramparts*. Among American journalists, only Drew Pearson had the anti-clerical nerve to repeat our allegations in print. *Ramparts'* membership in the
Catholic Press Association was not renewed the next year.
When I inquired why, the Press Association officials explained that it was not because of Cardinal Spellman, or that
we had earlier vilified the sainted memory of Dr. Tom Dooley.
It was rather that *Ramparts* had drifted out of the Catholic
orbit into the secular. Too many Jews on the staff, and all that.

The Jew responsible for *Ramparts'* Spellman-baiting was of
course Robert Scheer, one of the first American intellectuals
to put the lie to the official mythology for U.S. involvement in
Vietnam. In the fall of 1964 Scheer was completing almost two
years of research and interviews in both America and Vietnam, attempting to pin down just how our country got involved in a land war in Southeast Asia—just the way
Eisenhower said it shouldn't. His study was being prepared
for publication as a landmark and prophetic report for the
Center for the Study of Democratic Institutions. When Scheer
told me that supercautious editors at the Center were leaving
out "a lot of the good stuff," I hired him. (*Realist* editor Paul
Krassner paid part of Scheer's way to Vietnam with proceeds
from the sale of "Fuck Communism" bumper strips.) Keating
was reluctantly satisfied with proving a Vietnam conspiracy as
far as Cardinal Spellman, and sent Scheer East to investigate
the Knights of Columbus.

The Spellman-Diem axis was one of several Vietnam connections reported by *Ramparts* during a mid-60's frenzy of
muckraking contemporary history, utilizing Scheer's pioneer-
ing research on Vietnam as a taking-off point. We didn't
realize it then, but we were engaging in what later came to be
known as revisionism, although *Ramparts* went at it more in
the fashion of police reporting and our end product was not
quite as grim as the contemporary real thing. It was, for us, a
rather heady, pre-paranoia period of traveling beagle-nosed
about the country, sniffing out Vietnam villains who were still
willing to talk about their disastrous good intentions.

In the process we afforded some of our New Left
researchers—New York's City College Jewish intellectuals
—the rare experience of reading back issues of the Neanderthal Catholic Brooklyn *Tablet*. We interviewed scores of
souls, conspirators and innocents alike, as the circle of in-
crimination and guilt by association with the propaganda
cloud-cover over Diem's dictatorship widened beyond
Catholics as such to several ideologically chummy circles with
all the identifying characteristics of interlocking directorates.
In today's vernacular they would be called branches of the
Eastern liberal establishment. We then called them the "Vietnam Lobby," which at least had the benefit of brevity. Our
research into the private, extra-governmental political pressures for American involvement in Vietnam centered on the
period from the mid-fifties to the early sixties—the quite
extraordinary years when the disaster of Vietnam was sizzling
in the oven, but no one seemed to know anything was burning
until the damage had been done. The glimmer of reality
seemed only to reach the American television public by the
light of Buddhists burning themselves in protest in the streets
of Saigon.

It required another ten years from the time the American
public became aware that everything was not A-OK in Vietnam until the Nixon-Kissinger putative withdrawal with all
the grace of the Grinch that stole Christmas. The United
States ended up losing, and lying about it; meanwhile most
everyone else involved lost, too—most of all, the Vietnamese
people, those surviving, whose land was turned into a brown-
out by the grace of American hardware.

Now that the Pentagon Papers have been published, and
the uninspiring tale of Washington's deceit and folly in
Southeast Asia has begun the tedious process of unraveling
—the full story will doubtless take most of the seventies to be
told, for better or worse—there seems little call in this volume
to recite at length *Ramparts*' one-sided contributions during
the sixties to the national debate over Washington's war
policies. Although *Ramparts* was the leading journal in the
United States against the war, a good many of the things we
printed were also said, and often said better, by others in the

front lines of that domestic war against the war in Vietnam.
Any exercise in I-Told-You-So seems to me, at this point,
before even all the shouting has died down, a bit redundant.

I didn't catch on to what was happening in Vietnam until
after John Kennedy had done his dirt over there. From there
on I horsewhipped the printers in the haste to vilify Johnson
and then Nixon—whose Vietnam game plans were about as
different as Tweedledum and Tweedledee. Much of what my
paper accused LBJ and his successor to the throne of having
done, or planning to do in Vietnam, has now been calmly
documented in the Pentagon Papers—a coolly horrifying
reading experience—which even illuminates the objectivity
with which the national security managers considered the
option and exercise of what was previously only an hysterical
leftist charge: genocide.

The recriminations and judgments will be coming down for
years, and perhaps we will be able to put a bow around it in
time for America to celebrate its 200th birthday in 1976, if it
still dares. Perhaps, also, America will by then be discussing
granting its war criminals amnesty, along with its draft dodgers. That might be good. Retribution, right or left, can be a
bloody bore.

Yet still those early *Ramparts'* stories linger on. The *Wall
Street Journal*, in an editorial titled "Those Thriving Conspiracy Theories," in its edition of September 1, 1972, expressed some concern that "a well-known TV actor charged
that the U.S. entered the Vietnam war because of the Roman
Catholic clergy and officials of a Midwestern university." The
Journal kindly did not mention the name of the actor, but I bet
I know where he got his information; he read it in *Ramparts*.
The Church, in particular in the person of Cardinal Spellman, and Michigan State University, which we exposed as
providing academic cloud-cover for the CIA in Saigon, were
two of the paper's favorite objects of Vietnam pillory. To be
fair to our side, which the *Journal* doubtless tried to be, we
didn't say that His Eminence or Michigan State was behind the
United States' breaking and entering in Vietnam. We said the
Cardinal and the university both had roles in encouraging

and effecting Washington's covert policies in Vietnam and in keeping from the American public for many years the real nature of the "miracle of democracy" being wrought in Saigon. It was those good citizens who engaged in that cover-up whom we referred to, *en banc*, as the Vietnam Lobby.

The nice thing about tracking down Vietnam Lobby people in the mid-sixties was that they were then still as upfront about their enthusiasms as Giants fans. Their dream of reason had bred a nightmare, but they were able to recall with nostalgia their participation in arranging the fate of a less advantaged people. They meant well, these Americans; don't missionaries always?

They were, at least personally, certainly not the monsters we made them out to be in print. Typical, although more fashionable and charming than most, was William vanden Heuvel. He carried off the Camelot style with more grace than his good friend and political cohort, the ofttimes grumpy Robert Kennedy. When I met vanden Heuvel he was in the free fall zone of 35, and already his career read like a patented example of the American dream. Born of immigrant Dutch parents, he had combined a precocious law career with prestigious political appointments, made a marriage that augured well for his financial and social success, and was enjoying an exciting life of intimacy with political power, the affluent society, New York parlor intellectualism, and other characteristics of monied liberalism.

Vanden Heuvel was then married to the editor-authoress Jean Stein, the daughter of Music Company of America founder Jules Stein. They had lived in the Dakota but were so socially secure they moved across the street so they could have more room. I sat with vanden Heuvel during a long afternoon in October of 1965 in his comfortable den, which had been swimmingly done in decorator curtains that covered up most of the books. He was puffing on a cigar, a lock of brown hair fallen Kennedy-style over his forehead, his horn-rimmed glasses resting on his nose, and reading aloud from typewritten sheets in a battered black binder —the pages of a diary he had kept in Indochina some twelve years before. His diary explained something of the thinking of the bright and progressive Americans like himself who helped paddle the United States up the creek of Vietnam.

In an irony of chronology and fate, vanden Heuvel, although dry behind the ears politically and only in his early twenties, played a role in the decision-making that got us into Vietnam. He became an aide to General "Wild Bill" Donovan when the former wartime OSS director was appointed Ambassador to Thailand in 1953. The general was upset over the extensive U.S. financial support of the French colonial war. He believed that America should cater to the nationalistic aspirations of the Vietnamese—but unfortunately all the Vietnamese nationalists on the horizon were Communists. The general's young aide soon found himself torn between antipathy for Communism and disdain of French colonialism. The young New Yorker and the old war-horse general soon began talking about the desirability of finding a "non-Communist nationalistic alternative" to Ho Chi Minh. It was vanden Heuvel's fate to stumble across a warm body to fit the bill. He was in northeast Thailand, checking on some Vietnamese war refugees encamped there, when he found, in many of the refugee huts, pictures of Jesus, Ho Chi Minh, and another Vietnamese he had never seen before. The third man was Ngo Dinh Diem, who, vanden Heuvel quickly found out, was an ardent anti-Communist—and his picture was on the wall next to Ho Chi Minh!

The young aide hastened back to General Donovan and said he had found their nationalistic alternative. Donovan had never heard of Diem, but anybody would do at the moment. He told vanden Heuvel to write a memorandum to Senator Mike Mansfield, an old Indochina hand, suggesting Diem as a possible man Washington might boost. A few weeks later, according to vanden Heuvel's diary, Mansfield gave a pro-Diem Senate speech. The general then went to work on the State Department, and Donovan and his aide went to Saigon to see what support they could raise for Diem, but the trip proved a bummer. The only people who backed Diem were former collaborators with the French colonial government —as had been, for a time in the 30's, Diem himself.

It seemed no contradiction to the two Americans that their

candidate for a popular "nationalist alternative" against the
Communists might not be so popular since he had sat out the
very 20-year war against the French that his rival, Ho Chi
Minh, had fought and become a national hero by winning.

Vanden Heuvel wrote in his diary on June 3, 1954: "The
Saigon Embassy does not seem to be nearly as enthusiastic as I
was about Ngo Diem. He was described to me as a fanatic, but
my feelings are that the right kind of fanatic is not going to be
harmful in this situation. . . ."

Diem of course became, with American backing, premier of
South Vietnam. And Bill vanden Heuvel returned to the
United States to rise in liberal political circles and join the
American Friends of Vietnam.

The American Friends of Vietnam had the typical organi-
zational letterhead with a string of impressive names running
in small print down the side. The Friends list was virtually a
roll call of the liberal center: Senators John F. Kennedy and
Richard Neuberger, intellectuals Max Lerner and Arthur
Schlesinger, Jr., Representatives Emmanuel Celler and Edna
Kelly, diplomat Angier Biddle Duke, and so on. For balance,
there was Socialist Norman Thomas and the ultra-
conservative J. Bracken Lee. And two famous generals, "Wild
Bill" Donovan and "Iron Mike" O'Daniel, were co-chairmen.

The American Friends of Vietnam was not exactly your
typical eleemosynary organization. One member of the executive committee, Harold Oram, a New York fund-raiser
and public relations man, was on Diem's payroll at $3,000 a
month, plus expenses, and was registered in Washington
—along with at least one other official of the Friends—as a
foreign agent of the Republic of Vietnam.

The primary function of the Friends was, in fact, a public
relations function—to convince the American press, and
through the press the American public, that Diem was creating a "showcase of democracy" in Vietnam.

Mr. Oram had to earn his $3,000 a month. Diem was not the
easiest man to keep popular, and the first task was to package
Diem as a commodity palatable to the American public. The
packaging operation assumed grand proportions during
Diem's triumphal "official visit" to the United States in 1957.

Diem landed aboard President Eisenhower's personal plane, addressed a joint session of Congress, then took off for New York and breakfast with Cardinal Spellman. Mayor Wagner hailed him as the man "to whom freedom is the very breath of life itself." At a dinner co-sponsored by the American Friends of Vietnam, Angier Biddle Duke presented Diem with the Admiral Richard E. Byrd Award for "inspired leadership in the cause of the free world."

It was one nifty packaging job, considering that at the time Diem was lopping off heads left and right at home. Diem's American advisers covered that little excess by taking care that his speeches were liberally salted with democratic clichés.

The "Friends" was the formal part of what *Ramparts* called the Vietnam Lobby. The lobby specialized in the "miracle" myths. Everything that Diem did, or attempted, was described as a miracle. Articles in American magazines, from the *Reporter* to *Look,* hailed the "miracles" of political stability, land reform, refugee settlement and economic development allegedly achieved by the Diem regime.

The most double-think proposition was that the free elections for Vietnam, as called for in the Geneva Agreements, were simply a means of enslaving the free people of Vietnam: since the Communist-backed Viet Minh would almost certainly win, the United States was actually striking a blow for freedom by keeping the people of Vietnam from holding a national election. Such was the theme of an editorial in *Life* magazine in 1956. We were "saving" the Vietnamese from themselves, and at the same time teaching them the golden way of American democracy through Diem's "showcase" government. This type of rationale Kipling used to write poems about.

The most widespread of these myths was the refugee myth. The dramatic story of one million refugees fleeing to the south from the Communist north supported the theory of Diem's regime as the sanctuary of freedom. Naive, well-meaning publicists like Dr. Tom Dooley projected this view with considerable success in the United States. But what Americans did not know was that the refugees were almost all Catholics—many of whom had fought with the French against the Communist Viet Minh—and who had been told by their village priests that they could get better treatment under the Catholic Diem. These refugees, settled and well cared for through extensive American aid, became a privileged Catholic minority in South Vietnam and Diem's base of popular support. U.S. dollars were administered to Vietnamese Catholics by American Catholics, through the vehicle of the Catholic Relief Service. Dollar aid to the refugee Catholics, around which Diem based his government, averaged $89 per person—this in a nation where the annual per capita income (for the non-Catholic majority) was $85.

The lobby floated a myth for almost every occasion. In the early 1960's, when Diem's unpopularity could no longer be cosmeticized, the rationale for his problems (adopted by the Kennedy administration for its increases in U.S. military commitment) was the myth of "aggression from the North"—a long-heralded concept which the Pentagon Papers have effectively pooh-poohed—aggression that was said to have wrecked Diem's "progressive" programs, and even forced him to adopt some regrettable but necessary totalitarian means—only temporarily, of course.

From there one can follow the familiar bouncing ball in the history books.

"THE WHOLE THING WAS A LIE!"

In February of 1966, Special Forces Master Sergeant Donald W. Duncan quit in uniform on the cover of *Ramparts*. For the occasion he wore his Bronze Star, South Vietnamese Silver Star, Combat Infantry Badge and United States Army Air Medal, along with a pound of overseas ribbons, topped off by his green beret. Duncan thus became, to the extent of my limited knowledge of military history, the first American war hero to leave the army under such circumstances. "I Quit!" said Sgt. Duncan on the cover: "The whole thing was a lie!"

Duncan had a leathery, handsome face, star-blue eyes and the posture of a ten-gun salute. If he hadn't turned against the war and allowed me to put his impressive puss in radical slick process color on the cover, it would have been the perfect image for a Green Beret recruiting poster. Duncan, a former treetopper, was a half-brother of Mitzi Gaynor. A career soldier with six years in the Special Forces—part of it as a recruiting officer, he looked the part so well—Duncan was as gung-ho anti-Communist as a Green Beret can be when he went to Vietnam in 1964. Eighteen months later he was still anti-Communist but not so gung-ho; a hero soldier, he turned down a U. S. Silver Star, the Legion of Merit and a battlefield commission to captain to return to the States and tell the story of the lies he had lived and the American principles he saw shattered in the bomb craterland his country was making of Vietnam. "Anti-Communism is a lousy substitute for democracy," said Duncan.

Duncan was assigned by the Special Forces in July of 1965 to brief then Secretary of Defense Robert McNamara on his combat observations of the effectiveness of massive American bombing in War Zone D. The Green Beret told the Defense Secretary that the bombing was a dud, militarily. "Unless dropped in a hip pocket it was only effective in destroying housing areas"—i.e., wiping out villages, killing and maiming civilians, and creating infinitely more Viet Cong than it eliminated. McNamara turned to General Westmoreland, who was sitting next to Duncan. "I guess we still have a small reaction problem," he said.

The intervening years have so sadly accustomed us to Vietnam horror stories that it is a memory test to recall just how stunning it was back in 1966 for a Green Beret to stand up and sound off about Americans engaging in torture, sending secret assassination teams into Laos and North Vietnam, faking body counts, and indiscriminately bombing civilians. It occasioned all the more howls at the Pentagon when *Ramparts* prefaced Duncan's story with a full-page blow-up of an official Letter of Appreciation to him from Colonel William A. McKean, Commanding Officer, 5th Special Forces Group (Airborne), 1st Special Forces, expressing "my appreciation for your outstanding presentation of facts and information of Special Forces activities to the Honorable Robert S. McNamara."

Scheer encountered Duncan in Berkeley, where the Master Sgt. was knocking on the doors of peace groups and having some difficulty getting across to the professionally suspicious peaceniks that the tanned and rugged-looking fellow in the yellow cardigan golf sweater wasn't a double agent but a real Green Beret hero with a bomb to drop about the war. Scheer brought him across the Bay to San Francisco, where we held the soldier a virtual prisoner in a Chinese restaurant for six hours while debriefing him, and then placed him under house arrest for four days to produce his war memoirs.

Duncan's apostasy was the first in an extraordinary string of career turnabouts whose confessional literature *Ramparts* published. FBI agents, CIA agents, intellectually-compromised professors and mercenaries-for-hire followed the Green Beret in airing their transgressions in print. A few months after Duncan said, "The whole thing was a lie," *Ramparts* published the memoirs of a former Special Agent of the FBI, which were titled "I Was a Burglar, Wiretapper, Bugger and Spy for the FBI." It was characteristic of these renascent individualists that—although their entire world view had shifted—their psyches remained unchanged. Suddenly on the left side of the fence, they were as constant to their training and life-styles as they had been on the right. They remained straight arrows, although flying in the opposite direction. Many of them stayed on at *Ramparts*, where I found honest work for them. Duncan became the Military Editor.

But as Duncan was the first of this rare breed, I was unsure how far to go with him. I needn't have worried. I oafishly assumed that he couldn't write, since he was but an unlettered GI. After several chaotic days of reciting into tape recorders and Dictaphones and having the stenographers make goo-goo eyes at him, Duncan asked, modestly, if he might try his hand at writing it down. The next day he handed me a quarter pound of yellow legal paper filled with ball-point scrawl. It read like a cross between Ernie Pyle and Thucydides on the Peloponnesian War. "I'll be darned," said Peter Collier, an English graduate student turned *Ramparts* editor, "if that soldier can't write."

We had immediate need of Duncan's Special Forces skills. The *Ramparts* edition for which he was the cover boy was written in my home in San Francisco, as I was becoming weary of driving down the Peninsula to the *Ramparts* office in the Keating Building in Menlo Park, where the action wasn't. Late one evening Duncan was in an upstairs bedroom with his tape recorders, I was in the kitchen pounding out an epic-length muckraking piece on the basket-case city of Oakland which was to run in the same issue (two weeks after that article appeared the mayor of Oakland was indicted and the police chief resigned), and typewriters were aclatter throughout the house when the hum of industry was disturbed by a scream from the dining room. My secretary, a proper English girl named Maureen Stock, had been typing on the dining room table and looked out the window into the garden to see a strange man playing footsie with his penis. "I first thought he was sharpening a pencil," she said, "but then I realized it wasn't a pencil." Duncan bounded downstairs like the Viet Cong themselves were attacking and crashed through the back door in ferocious Green Beret fashion to give the hapless exhibitionist the fright of his life.

There was some concern that the Master Sergeant might crack under the strain of a hostile press corps belting him with questions about becoming a renegade hero. Gossage thought it a good idea to have a "dry run" press conference to test Duncan's nerve under verbal fire. The Silver Star nominee survived several hours on a stool in Gossage's conference room with a floodlight on his face, sweating through psychologically-loaded questions yelled out by Feigen and Gossage from the other end of the cavernous room. When Duncan braved the lions of the Washington press corps a few weeks later, he was as relaxed as a three-term senator. "We aren't the freedom fighters," Duncan replied to a patriotic questioner, "we are the Russian tanks blasting the hopes of an Asian Hungary." To mark the occasion of Duncan surfacing as the first antiwar war hero of Vietnam, I ran a full-page advertisement in the New York *Times* of a poster-sized picture of Duncan quitting on the cover of *Ramparts*, with the splendid headline underneath:

WHY WE WILL SEND YOU THIS ISSUE
AIR MAIL SPECIAL DELIVERY, FREE

"How can a magazine [*Ramparts*] with almost no advertising and a small circulation afford full-page ads in the New York *Times*, a massive mail campaign, and the services of a New York public relations agency to handle the Duncan business?" asked the *Army Times*, in a bellicose editorial.

That was a good question. The *Army Times*' nasty was typical of the deep suspicion and bewilderment with which the press greeted *Ramparts* cometlike ascendancy on the national scene. For a paper that began life in debt and grew up gasping for money, *Ramparts* seemed slicker than *Vogue* and as omnipresent as *Time*. The answer was so simple that few people believed the way I did it—which was on nerve and credit. The only thing *Ramparts* couldn't afford was to miss, and it averaged a lucky percentage of bull's-eyes. The full-page newspaper advertisements that became *Ramparts*' hallmark were the collaboration of Gossage, Stermer and myself, and we were able to keep running them because they usually brought back in subscriptions what they cost. I either scraped up the ad cash in advance, or piggybacked on a friendly advertising agency's credit and paid it off when the money came in. The mailing campaigns were similarly successful, achieving whopping percentage returns—sometimes in the four- and five-percent range—that created a cash flow which I used to buy stamps for more mailings. I wrote the letters, and the mailings were brilliantly engineered by Bert Garmise, a New York publishing consultant who plugged admirably through many trying years of *Ramparts*' financial hiccups and became a good friend—so much so that I often mused that the biggest favor I could do my friend Bert would be to fire him. The prodigious amount of ink *Ramparts* got in the press was in large part the work of the ever-hustling Marc Stone, whose one-man public relations agency was on the payroll, and whose paychecks from *Ramparts* bounced on occasion, just like everyone else's. The dark secret of *Ramparts*' publishing show was one constant cash juggling act; once I got the balls into the air I had to keep juggling them until they finally came down on my head.

Ex-Sergeant Duncan was perversely responsible for *Ramparts'* sudden emergence on the national newsstands. The newsstand business is about the biggest closed club this side of Sicily, and it is the devil's own proposition to get a new publication through the minefields of lethargy and corruption impeding access to the corner cigar store. Until the Duncan issue, *Ramparts* was for all practical purposes distributed only on the West Coast, and that only through the extraordinary aid and comfort of Lou Swift of San Francisco—the George Washington of independent distributors, a grand old man who for over half a century has been the champion of free enterprise for a free press in the West—and neighborly souls in the business such as Shig Murao, Manager of City Lights bookstore. But around the rest of the country the paper was as easy to find as first editions of *Finnegans Wake*. The national magazine distributors were all headquartered in Manhattan, where I would regularly camp on their doorsteps, a one-eyed moocher hoping to find a businessman to assent to the unlikely proposition of shipping 100,000 copies of a radical Catholic antiwar sensationalist rag to just the right pockets of unrest in the country. When *Ramparts* finally landed a newsstand distributor, it was entirely a case of mistaken identity. The general manager of one of those estimable concerns had just perfunctorily dismissed our entreaty when his door banged open and in lurched the chairman of his board of directors, weaving like a sloop in a hurricane from the effects of what appeared to be a ten-martini lunch. His half-inch thick glasses appeared to be on upside down and the carnation in the buttonhole of his blue blazer had died from alcohol poisoning. The chairman grabbed the copy of *Ramparts* with Duncan on the cover that was lying on the manager's desk. "Now this is wonderful!" he exclaimed. "It's a pleasure to see a magazine that has the guts to put one of our fighting men on the cover at a time when all these punky kids and peaceniks are criticizing our boys in Vietnam." The chairman banged out the door, leaving irrevocable orders to distribute the patriotic paper called *Ramparts*. (Regrettably, we did not do business with that distributor, but used the chairman's offer to talk one of his rivals into taking the mag on.)

Duncan's disclosures earned banner headlines throughout the country, so one might think *Ramparts* was lucky to get the story. Not so. It was more the case that we were the only ones that thought it was a story. A month before *Ramparts* appeared with Duncan on the cover, the Master Sergeant spoke before some 20,000 people at a Berkeley Vietnam Day rally. He told the same story he told in *Ramparts*. All the local and national media—newspapers, news magazines, television networks—had reporters at the rally. But no one reported the words of the conscience-stricken war hero. There was an automatic disposition on the part of the press that no "news," save a dope bust or a riot, could come out of a propaganda rally.

That professional myopia was part of that Big Sleep of Journalism to which I made previous reference. It was all the more odd—and revealing—because it was, in one respect, not ideological. It had a lot to do with style and the peculiarly American presumption of reasonableness. A soldier at a peace rally was ignored, but the same soldier in full color on the slick cover of *Ramparts*, with the same words he proclaimed in scruffy Berkeley, commercially heralded as worthy of attention with a full-page paid advertisement in the New York *Times*—that was suddenly a national story of front-page magnitude.

The don't-rock-the-boat style of the press was part of the dominant style of phony reasonableness that set the perimeters of the Cold War consensus: work from within; don't vilify or embarrass the government; father knows best. These assumptions of what was "responsible"—which were as pervasive in academic and institutional life as in the press—amounted to a modern Hegelianism. Hegel's system completely dominated intellectual life during the early 19th century in Western Europe. Hegelian assumptions were assumed to be the only ones possible. Intellectual challenge and inquiry were limited to compounding Hegel's answers instead of questioning them. It took the ill-mannered Kierkegaard, who kept screaming in class about Hegel having holes in his shoes, so how could he be perfect, to again raise the nettling hackles of the individual. Kierkegaard was hated by the academicians, who had a stake in leaving undisturbed the system they had pegged their careers on. Sound familiar?

If that sounds argumentative, it is quite demonstrable, as there is no clearer or sadder example of the Cold War hibernation of the American press than the war in Vietnam.

The press's own performance has been smoke-screened recently by the largely irrelevant hoopla over the Pentagon Papers. The Pentagon Papers are concerned with Richard Nixon's attempts to limit the First Amendment. They have little to do with the question of how the American press *exercised* the First Amendment during the ignoble years the Pentagon Papers cover. That is entirely another story, and one the press would not appear anxious to tell on itself. The United States installed a classic client state in Vietnam, yet Americans had the opposite impression from reading their newspapers. Successive American presidents illegally and deliberately escalated the war, yet with rare exceptions—such as the reporting of Homer Bigart from Vietnam in 1962—the American public was not made aware of the increasing American military commitment. When things went from bad to worse in Vietnam, the press generally supported the increased U.S. military role on the fictitious grounds of "aggression" from North Vietnam—for which, as the Pentagon Papers have shown, there was not a scintilla of evidence. The people who were speaking out against the war in the United States were treated as neurotics or Narodniks by the media. It was not until the waning years of the decade that some of the press began to raise some of the essential questions about the government's war policies that any kid who had stayed up all night at a Vietnam teach-in knew by heart years before.

There is little solace in the irony that the New York *Times* and the Washington *Post*—two newspapers that editorially supported and encouraged U.S. Vietnam policies during the sixties—were to publish the Pentagon Papers, which showed those policies to be lies. It is instructive now to look back at the *Times*'s editorials chiding Bertrand Russell for having the nerve to criticize America's use of napalm and defoliation in Vietnam, or the *Post*'s blasts at Buddhist "extremists" who were protesting too much against the Washington-backed dictatorships in Saigon. But it is unfair to single out the *Times* and the *Post*, because almost every major media outlet in the United States subscribed to American war policy in Southeast Asia. Despite the long march of folly during the decade, the press remained inclined to give the government more than the benefit of a doubt. Even My Lai received initially cool treatment from the mass media. The underlying view of the press was expressed by James Reston in a 1961 column about "the imperative necessity of organizing the West to confront the new communist empire." Vietnam was seen by Americans as a head-on clash with the Reds—a sort of cowboys and Indians extension of World War II. As the *Times* editorialized in September of 1963, Vietnam was a war "from which we cannot retreat and which we dare not lose." Although the history of American journalism in this century has not been overburdened with the performance of its putative fourth estate duty of acting as an independent check and balance on the activities of government, with Vietnam the press ventured perilously close to becoming a virtual fourth branch of government. It is a good thing Richard Nixon had the means to put it back at arm's length.

What critical reporting there was about Vietnam dealt with questions of the efficiency or practicality of the means of American policy but did not question its ends. It is a measure of the level of press criticism of America's great Vietnam misadventure that David Halberstam was awarded the Pulitzer Prize in 1964 for calling Madame Nhu a bitch. Halberstam, long the war's most celebrated critic, chastised the corrupt Nhu family and poked the wind machines of the General's public relations machinery while still accepting the basic ideological tenets of American policy. In an *Esquire* interview in 1964 Halberstam worried that "this pretty little country will be lost." In his earlier book, *The Making of a Quagmire*, said Halberstam the war critic: "The lesson to be learned from Vietnam is that we must get in earlier, be shrewder and force the other side to practice the self deception."

I would not nitpick Halberstam were it not for his recent and nauseating criticisms of those liberal Establishment types

who made America's Vietnam policy—that they were the victims of some weepy, ill-defined hubris that kept them from
seeing the fatal flaw in the whole undertaking—that he for-
mulates in his trendy best seller, *The Best and the Brightest,*
which must rank as one of the great bullshit books of all time.
Halberstam adroitly skips over the fact that the American
press establishment had its own best and brightest in Vietnam
(not the least of them Halberstam) during those years of
folly—a decade of electronic, plugged-in and satellited reporting that exhibited the same arrogance or, if we must,
hubris of the ideology of the men whom Halberstam now so
artfully brushes with the vanishing cream of tragedy.

In recent years the quality of input provided to the thinking
public by the guardians of that public's right to know has little
to recommend itself outside of suggesting we might need a
muckraking study of the way the press reported the war. The
media not only failed to point out what are now taken to be the
commonplace truths about the developing Vietnam disaster,
but for a round inglorious decade it did the government's
propaganda work for it. The liberal magazines during this
period were the worst of the lot; that concept of Vietnam as
"the miracle of democracy in Asia"—a phrase to treasure
—came from the *New Leader,* which, along with the *Reporter*
and other journals of liberal orientation, promoted the view
that Vietnam was a set piece of triumph for American-
exported democracy. It was this view—with no significant
dissenting—that one will find in the American press during
the sixties, from the now extinct trinity of *Look, Life* and the
Saturday Evening Post to Spiro Agnew's Eastern Establishment
dailies.

As journalist Richard Harris wrote recently, the Nixon-
Agnew complaint that the press manages the news is inaccu-
rate; more often, the press mismanages the news.

BOGART PROFESSORS AND WITTY KIDDIES

We have come a long way since that day when staunch
Henry Stimson, Herbert Hoover's Secretary of State, closed

down the State Department cryptographic office—which housed the intelligence system built up during World War I—with the announcement, "Gentlemen don't read other people's mail."

By the mid-sixties, to employ an anachronism, it was becoming perfectly clear just how far America had gone down the road to where the cloak and dagger was replacing the stars and stripes. Bill Cosby played a likable CIA agent in a popular video series, but that was about the only good press the CIA could count on. After the Bay of Pigs, the term CIA became in common usage a pejorative adjective. Pop books such as *The Secret Government* were published which purported to reveal the scope of the spy agency's secretive derring-do abroad. It seemed the CIA had a license, in the name of freedom, to commit mayhem on an international level, and a budget of untold millions with which it could get away with murder, among other things.

Along with many others who had imbibed deeply of the popular wisdom, I had no liberal illusions left as to what the CIA might be about.

That is, I thought I had no illusions. I was wrong.

For the one thing that no one then dreamed was that the CIA would be about its dirty tricks *within* the United States. Its enabling legislation clearly denied the CIA any domestic operations. That was the province of the FBI, which was trouble enough. It had become the conventional liberal critique of the CIA that it had gone beyond the bounds of legitimate intelligence-gathering and into secretive foreign policy-making to which neither the people nor the Congress were privy. The CIA's covert operations abroad were said to pervert the independence and free choice of other peoples.

Then *Ramparts* disclosed, in a series of exposés in 1966 and 1967 that made the paper crackle and snap on the newsstands, that the CIA was about the same perversions in the United States—recycling intellectuals, co-opting universities, buying labor unions, renting students. We uncovered the secret CIA tunnels to the board rooms of the mightiest and the bell towers of the loftiest of American institutions, and found the Agency susceptible to the journalistic metaphor of Drano run amok—it was everywhere outside the kitchen sink of intelligence where it belonged.

Henry Stimson would not have approved.

"What the hell is a university doing buying guns, anyway?"—tag line to *Ramparts'* April, 1966, account of Michigan State University's activities in Vietnam.

Gary Wills called them the "Bogart Professors"—academics who, tiring of the humdrum of college routine, discovered the wonderful world of exciting government contracts. They found travel, money, adventure and a Big-Man-On-Campus-type prestige in hiring their social-science expertise out for fun jobs on behalf of the Fatherland in Washington. The glamorous project loomed more important than the bright student, and in a number of parvenu universities, the budgets of entire departments became dependent on grants and contracts to do the government's Cold War business. This was quite consistent with the outer direction of the American university in recent decades. For that, a tip of the freshman propeller beanie to Harold Stassen and Clark Kerr: Stassen, as head of the International Cooperation Administration in the fifties, pushed the concept that American universities should be tapped as "manpower reservoirs" for the extension of Americanism abroad. Kerr, the Mussolini of Berkeley, came up with the bright idea that the great state universities should become "service stations" to society. Somewhere along the line academic principle and academic independence went the way of professors wearing cloaks and mortarboards. Universities became institutions on the make, and new standards developed for professorial upward mobility. The "publish or perish" mode gave way to the idea that to make it, a professor had to be an "operator." He had to have contacts in Washington and be able to swing a sweetheart deal at taxpayers' expense for his department, or at the least for himself.

Examples of these activist, "operator"-type professors would include the late Eugene "Bud" Burdick, the author of *The Ugly American* (and probably the only professor ever to make a television beer commercial, and in scuba diving gear at that), and Wesley Fishel of Michigan State University, who

tooled around Saigon in the 1950's in his own high-octane limousine and lived in a villa grander even than the American
ambassador's, but those were the lesser of his accomplishments. For no other academician has ever achieved Fishel's
score of getting his university to come through with enough
professors, police experts and U.S.-bought-and-paid-for
guns to help secure a dictatorship for an old friend—Ngo
Dinh Diem, whom he'd known when they both were losers.

Fishel was the head of Michigan State University's six-year,
$26-million-dollar assistance project to the Diem government,
which did everything from write the paper "Constitution" for
his dictatorship to train his secret police in the advanced
paraphernalia of modern police state technology. Michigan
State, in addition, provided a front for CIA agents to operate
in Saigon, and went so far in its efforts to please that it gave
academic rank to some of the spies.

Ramparts stripped the academic cloud-cover from the
Michigan State Vietnam project with a scurrilous cover depict-
ing Madame Nhu as a busty Michigan State cheerleader (one
of the "factual errors" propounded by critics attempting to
ding the article was that Madame Nhu did not, in fact, have tits
that big).

East Lansing, Michigan, the home of Michigan State, is
hardly a Midwestern Paris, but the visiting professors got a
taste of the high life in Saigon. They lived, rent free, in the
well-appointed villas of the former French colonials, hung
around the pool at the Circle Sportiff, the elegant colonial
country club, and even learned to go tiger hunting. Meanwhile the drip-dry professorial wives gave their dishpan
hands to Vietnamese servants at 30 bucks a month.

Bogart professors were paid well, too. Their campus
salaries were annualized by adding 33 percent of their base
pay. They then received an "incentive increase" of 10 percent.
In addition to that there was a "hardship" increase of 25
percent. At these rates if a professor was earning $9,000 just
for teaching classes back in Michigan, he received a salary of
$16,500 for a year of "advising" in Vietnam. That was only the
beginning. Each professor would also get a housing allow-
ance, round-trip first-class flights for his entire family and

free shipment to Asia of his household furniture and the family car, and the MSU families were entitled to use the American commissary, where the best booze came at $2 a bottle. During their tours of duty in Saigon, the professors were also exempted from paying U.S. income taxes. A thrift-minded professor could spend a few years in Saigon and return to East Lansing (the long way, via Germany, to pick up a new Mercedes as some of them did) with $20,000 cash in his pocket.

Their Bogart experience in Vietnam also did wonders for the professors' tenure. Despite the activist nature of their work in Vietnam and the lack of any substantial scholarly research during the project, two-thirds of the MSU faculty members who went to Saigon got promotions during or shortly after their tour of duty. Wesley Fishel made it to full professor.

Ramparts' peek into the high life among the initiated was provided by a drop-out Bogart professor, Stanley Sheinbaum. Stanley turned off the Bogart syndrome when three South Vietnamese police officials—the people Michigan State was "advising"—tried to enlist his aid in a plot to murder a fourth policeman; they thought the deed might be done at its prophylactic best in the States rather than in Vietnam. Stanley warned the intended victim, who escaped, but it was out of the frying pan into the fire, as the man was executed in Saigon a few years later, anyway, by Diem's successor, on charges of having assassinated several Vietnamese—perhaps his would-be murderers.

Stanley began to ask himself what he, a member of the Department of Economics at Michigan State University, was doing mixed up in such foreign intrigue. It was a question few of his colleagues in the Vietnam project allowed themselves the luxury of asking. Then Stanley found out about the CIA, a secret he came across when he was told by a university administrator that it "wouldn't be necessary" for him to check the academic qualifications of three men being hired for the Vietnam project and given academic rank. Their papers said they came from the "Department of the Army," but they soon became known to the professors in the project as CIA agents.

Stanley became an editor of *Ramparts* after we ran the story in which he exposed himself. He was a hard worker on the paper, delivering the goods on targets from the Warren Commission to the Greek junta (in which he got me involved in a considerable madness with Melina Mercouri and what seemed like five thousand warring Greek exile groups). Sheinbaum married one of the movie Warner's daughters, Betty, a sculptress in her own right who had nothing in common with Hollywood. I then asked Stanley if *he* wanted to be publisher, an appointment he graciously declined.

Stanley never quite got over the tawdry assignment he and his fellow professors took on in Vietnam: "Looking back I'm appalled how supposed intellectuals [Aren't academicians supposed to be intellectuals?] could have been so uncritical about what they [we] were doing." What the professors were doing was helping set up the machinery of a dictatorship under the guise of a democracy. Since the United States was barred by the Geneva Accords from maintaining too high a profile in Vietnam, it fell to the professors to shore up Diem's wavering regime. They assumed the responsibility for almost the entire apparatus of state and security: the functioning of the civil service and police bureaucracy, the shaping up of a 50,000-man "militia," even the supplying, via AID (Agency for International Development) purchase orders, of guns and ammunition for the Saigon police, the civil guard, the palace police and Diem's dreaded "VBI"—an organization known as a Vietnamese Gestapo to critics and as Vietnamese FBI to friends.

The professors carried out the gargantuan task of rebuilding the entire state police apparatus, from traffic cop to "interrogation expert," as loyal servants of the Diem government. This was essential to maintaining the absentee aristocrat in office, since he had no popular base of support and could only stay in power through repressive means.

It is small wonder the university would have preferred that its role in Vietnam remain unwritten history. It did its best to see that it did. The incriminating evidence was buried in a manner that required the talents of one more versed in archaeology than investigative reporting. While rooting about in a dusty corner of the Berkeley library stacks, Scheer came across a pile of papers donated to the university by the widow of a professor who had served on the Michigan State Vietnam project. No one had bothered to catalogue the documents, which included the official "progress reports" the professors in Saigon sent back to East Lansing. They provided the first documentation of the true nature of Michigan State's "assistance" project, and stand today as a rather expressive summary of the conditions of academic servitude in the Cold War:

April 17, 1956: The training of the commando squads of Saigon-Cholon police in riot control formations has continued during the month. . . . A report on riots and unlawful assembly is nearing completion.

June 5, 1957: Training of the Presidential Security Guard in revolver shooting began during the month. Thirty-four VBI agents completed the revolver course.

September 11, 1957: Eight hundred pairs of Peerless handcuffs arrived in Saigon, but distribution is being delayed pending arrival of four hundred additional cuffs.

February 17, 1958: The Palace Guard is being put through another class in revolver training. . . .

To cry CIA was one thing; to prove it another. Although there had been rumors of CIA involvement with Michigan State for years—Scheer suggested as much in his pamphlet about Vietnam—it had never made a story because, if asked, MSU officials flatly denied it; and no soul in the know seemed willing to say anything to the contrary.

Then Sheinbaum, after a memorable meeting with Scheer in a Berkeley parking lot, agreed to write the preface to the *Ramparts* exposé of his former employer. I sent the magazine's research editor, Sol Stern, to East Lansing to snoop. He found records of what had once been Michigan State's proudest overseas project in discard piles in the basement of the library. Stern began sorting through the old files with the persistence of the former graduate student that he was, and what he uncovered made the university's further denials inoperative, and put the story on the front page of the New York *Times*—buried in the university stacks was a hard-cover report by two professors in the project, with the catchy title "Technical Assistance in Vietnam: The Michigan State University Experience," which reviewed, in stuffy, anal-retentive professorial fashion, every aspect of the Vietnam project, including the role of the CIA: "USOM [United States Operations Mission] also absorbed at this time [1959] the CIA unit that had been operating within MSUG [Michigan State University Group]."

With that, it was all over but the shouting.

Professor Wesley Fishel, out of a job in Saigon after his buddy Diem got bumped off in 1963, continued to make the Bogart circuit, commuting between East Lansing and Washington to advise the State Department on Vietnam policy-making. In December of 1965, Fishel announced to the press that he had organized a petition—signed by 1,900 American professors—in support of U.S. policy in Vietnam. Fishel said of his petition: "Most of the teachers of government, foreign policy, and international affairs support U.S. policy or accept it as necessary."

Perhaps, in any final analysis, that is the Nicene Creed of the Bogart Professor.

"This is one of the saddest times our government has had. . . ."
—Vice President Hubert Humphrey, February 20, 1967, on the *Ramparts* disclosures of secret CIA subsidies to American student leaders.

On Valentine's Day of 1967 we caught the CIA *in flagrante delicto* with another innocent coed. This time it was the National Student Association, the oldest and largest organization of students in the country, a left-leaning domestic congress run by longhairs in vests and Joe College operators who, unbeknownst to the faithful back on campus, were trafficking in CIA coin and jetting to faraway places with strange-sounding names to spy on foreign students. The CIA under-cover connection was no simple seduction. It was a fifteen-year bedding down between the spooks and the student lead-ers, at a yearly tab of hundreds of thousands of taxpayers' dollars funneled by the blank-check artists of the CIA through a labyrinth of conduits, fronts and foundations. This network was further revealed as a Pandora's box of money dimensions in the tens of millions paid secretly by the CIA to scores of famous American institutions quick to do the bid-ding of the patriarch in Langley, Virginia.

The resulting fuss was memorable even by Washington standards. Capitol Hill liberals introduced resolutions shim-mering with Day-Glo outrage. The White House pledged to investigate the secret tentacles of the CIA octopus. Conserva-tives were near to rug-chewing. Barry Goldwater said it all smacked of socialism. The Young Americans for Freedom demanded equal secret subsidies for conservative groups. *Human Events*, the rightist weekly, was beside itself attempting to explain why the Communist-controlled *Ramparts* would want to harm the Communist-controlled CIA.

President Johnson ordered an immediate end to CIA covert subsidies to student groups and resorted to the time-honored bureaucratic dodge of appointing a committee —with a Fair Witness such as CIA director Richard Helms as one of the members—to investigate charges of the CIA run-ning wild in the domestic sector. The tempo increased as hundreds of newsmen lined up at the Internal Revenue Ser-vice to scour the records of foundations revealed in *Ramparts* as CIA conduits, to find what other groups had received funnymoney. Reporters traded off foundation tax returns like bubble gum cards, and the orgy of disclosures continued for weeks in the press. Almost everybody got dirty. The Na-tional Council of Churches. The American Newspaper Guild. The International Commission of Jurists. The American Friends of the Middle East. The United Auto Workers. The National Education Association. The International Retail Clerks. The Asia Foundation. The National Newman Club. The African-American Institute. The Congress for Cultural

Freedom. The Synod of Bishops of the Russian Church Outside Russia. The American Federation of State, County and
Municipal Employees. People-to-People, Inc., etc.

Since the mid-fifties, the CIA had had its helping hand in
the till, and a hand at the tiller, of an imperial cross section of
presumably independent American institutions. With Bourbon complacency, the CIA had not changed its "covers" all
those years—in itself a violation of one of the cardinal principles of good intelligence work—its whole stacked deck came
apart all at once, and the fallout was something fierce.
Newsweek branded it the CIA's "most damaging scandal since
the Bay of Pigs," and said that to high CIA officials "almost
as galling as the story was the vehicle of its disclosure—*Ramparts.*" Walter Lippmann, anticipating a phrase
that was to become a household word in the seventies, called
upon the CIA to cease and desist such "dirty tricks."

Barely two months before, I had shared a piece of chocolate
cake with a nervous young man in a mid-afternoon-empty
corner of the Algonquin dining room. He was Michael Wood,
a 24-year-old Pomona College dropout, a civil rights worker
in Watts before the apocalypse, and a former fund-raiser for
the National Student Association. Wood was fidgety and
run-down, a psychological war refugee from himself after a
year-long battle with his conscience over whether he should
betray his buddies by telling me the story he had finally, in a
state of napkin-wringing earnestness, decided to unfold. I
had sat through my fair share of sessions with phantoms and
finks who revealed for spite or money (usually both) what they
righteously considered would be the Big Story of the year.
Although this turned out to be no gross exaggeration in
Wood's case, his deportment was normal for someone with
sour grapes to sell. Even when they are straight, as was Wood,
such assassins of their own past are plagued by Raskolnikov's
dance. They have difficulty sitting still. They twist their necks.
Their eyes have a malarial glaze. They're guilty about what
they did—and equally guilty about informing on their
friends, past and present, who may still be doing it. They are
caught between a need to do some good that may live on after

them and fear of some evil that may be interred with their bones.

Wood's story was not one calculated to instill faith in the skeptic. He recited a glossary of the CIA pillow talk that he said the "fellas" who worked for the "company" used when dealing with those "kiddies" who were "witty." He said "Covert Action Division No. Five" of the CIA's Plans Divisions gave the orders. The "witty" students all had government security clearances. They received draft deferments for an "occupation vital to national interests." Each student took a National Security oath under pain of prison to keep the 15-year secret of how government green kept youthful pinks in clover. Fascinating, as Mr. Spock would say.

What will happen, I inquired of my informant, if the "company" finds out you spilled the beans. Wood said he had not taken the oath, so they couldn't put him in jail. But he had heard that the CIA was forging his psychiatric records so people would think he was a nut. I ordered the kid another piece of chocolate cake. The last time I heard a story with so many punch lines was when a lady with a funny hat told me about the caves under Disneyland where Orange County patriots convened kangaroo courts for Rad-Libs. I took the witty kiddie puzzle to a friend and counselor (also a counselor-at-law), Eleanor Jackson Piel, a director of *Ramparts* and a gracious and bright lady whom I often consulted on matters of state. I also shared the puzzle with Marcus Raskin, a *Ramparts* Washington editor and co-director of the Institute for Policy Studies, the Washington think tank which during the sixties was something of a left wing David to the Rand Corporation's Goliath. We found ourselves stumped by the confounding question of what the CIA would want with a bunch of left-wing longhairs.

The answer, as it unraveled later, involved a history lesson in a still little-known domestic Thermidor of the Cold War. The CIA during the McCarthyite fifties became a political sanctuary for achievement-oriented liberals. While the ADA-types and the Arthur Schlesinger model liberal kewpie dolls battled fascism by protecting their right flank with domestic

Red-baiting and Cold War one-upmanship, the Ivy League delinquents who fled to the CIA—liberal lawyers, business-men, academics, games-playing craftsmen—hatched a master plan of Germanic ambition that entailed nothing less than clandestine political control of the international operations of all important American professional and cultural organiza-tions: journalists, educators, jurists, businessmen, et al. The standing CIA subsidy to the National Student Association was but one slice of a very complex pie. The goal was to pick out and manipulate developing leaders in Third World nations whose careers would be affected by the technical and economic aid provided by such international professional cli-ques, and to use Americans with leftist credentials to influence inevitable leftward trends in non-Communist countries in a moderate direction compatible with American hegemony. The cost of holding such subtle reins of empire was quite dear, yet it was only one among many CIA Herculean tools for keeping the world in imperial balance. If all else failed, the medicine ball passed to the old-line OSS hands in the CIA, who would employ much nastier means to achieve its clandes-tine ends.

To effect its sophisticated international string-pulling the CIA needed many of the same domestic lefties HUAC wanted for different purposes. The lumpen right wingers in HUAC didn't know the difference between a Social Democrat and a Spartacist, but the CIA did. It used those anti-Communist left intellectuals who, during the fifties and most of the sixties, ruled the roost of American academic, cultural, peacenik and labor organizations, along with many internationalist-minded Eastern businessmen, to police and propogate the American empire abroad. The web of American private interests thus financed by the CIA afforded the propaganda edge of brag-ging at international gatherings that independent private citi-zens stood up for America, while Communist nations "con-trolled" their representatives. It was the Eagle Scouts vs. the Manchurian Candidates, and who would guess that the Eagle Scouts were on the come?

Ramparts security leaked like a bad kidney. The CIA knew we were onto their game before we had time to discover what it really was. Doors slammed in the faces of our inquiring reporters. We traced the nonprofit foundations Wood named as CIA "conduits" as far as the large law firms that facelessly administrated the funds, refusing to say to whom the money went or where it came from. "Some of our records were rained on. They melted together," said an official of the Kentfield Fund, which, along with four other CIA funds of safe Protestant nomenclature—Borden, Price, Beacon and, perversely, Edsel—were not even on the IRS list of tax-exempt foundations. The blank walls were impressive. A CIA front never gave directly to the ultimate recipient but passed the money through other CIA funds and one or more legitimate foundations, where funnymoney was washed with clean money, much in the manner of a mob "laundry" operation.

Fortunately, Wood had lifted the NSA's financial records. I sent a team of New Left accountants out to reconstruct the flow of the spy money. The little rascals sharpened their hatchets and came back with a bag full of biographies of former OSS and Naval Intelligence types on the boards of the suspect CIA fronts, but that didn't prove much except guilt by association, which I had to remind them we were supposed to be against. I hope it will not diminish the fond expectations of any future practitioners of the sport to observe that investigative journalism is one part drudgery and one part waiting in the rain for streetcars—with the glamorous writing done, to borrow a phrase from Ronald Firbank, "in hotels with the bed unmade at the back of the chair." The amount of drudgery can make a difference. To the frequent vexation of my associates, I would pound the table and demand research into every conceivable aspect of a story. At times the ancillary material turned out to be more important than the original story, as was the case with the witty kiddies of the NSA.

Thus an August 31, 1964, story in the New York *Times*, about a row between feisty Texas Congressman Wright Patman and the IRS over the suspect financial dealings of the do-good J. M. Kaplan Fund, which saved Carnegie Hall and promoted free Shakespeare in Central Park, provided the key to uncover the CIA's secret subsidies to students as spies. Patman was holding hearings on the IRS's notoriously lax policing of nonprofit foundations. He created a one-day storm when he unexpectedly accused the CIA of interfering to keep the IRS from pursuing possible multimillion-dollar tax violations by the Kaplan Fund because it was being used as a conduit for "foreign operations of the CIA." Before anyone could shut him up, the angry Patman blurted out the names of several phony foundations he said the CIA used to run money through the Kaplan Fund and other foundations. Among those certified as CIA fronts were those very funds still plugging money into the National Student Association. I was astounded that the highly paid metallurgists of the CIA had not even bothered to change their covers after they had been revealed. At that, perhaps they were encouraged in their lethargy by the competitive Washington press corps which, in 1964, did not consider the existence of the CIA "conduits" secretly passing taxpayers' money to private American organizations worth an investigative phone call or two to see who was getting the dough.

Some time later, over a drink, I asked Tom Wicker whether the *Times* had really known about such CIA domestic funding all along but had not printed it for the same patriotic reasons they held off the story on the Bay of Pigs invasion. Tom said no. He had been in the Washington Bureau when the *Times*—a short while before *Ramparts* kicked off the CIA exposés that the *Times* was to front-page for two weeks —produced a long series on the CIA that purported to tell all; as far as he knew, nobody knew about the NSA or the CIA's domestic Marshall Plan. Wicker groaned a Carolinian groan when I told him that I had gotten the proof of the pudding off his own front page.

(The original J. M. Kaplan matter was quickly dropped by Congressman Patman after a closed-door meeting with representatives of the CIA and IRS. Patman announced he would "delve no further." *Ramparts* tried, unsuccessfully, to answer the quite intriguing questions left by Patman—not the least being whether there was such a thing as "the CIA Exemption," which would not be on your routine income tax form. Multimillionaire financier J. M. Kaplan, a capitalist buccaneer of the old school, was a Caribbean molasses baron who diver-

sified and became a Democratic party sugar daddy. His career
suggests a marriage of sugar politics and Cold War politics,
with fighting in-laws in the IRS and CIA. There is also a
strange nephew in the woodpile: Joel David Kaplan, who
served ten years in a Mexican prison on a James Bond-type
murder charge and then made a daring helicopter jailbreak in
1971. [I became an intimate of the jailbird, but that is all
another story.] During the *Ramparts* years, we huffed and
puffed at J. M. Kaplan to no avail, yanking one story, preparing another, and the exterminating angel eventually did the
paper in before we collected enough dirt fit to print. But I
have kept notes, and hope springs eternal.

With the CIA funding of the students pinned down, I
unleashed the *Ramparts*' juggernaut of radical researchers,
who sawed through the tax returns and interlocking directorates of the CIA fronts like so many termites in a toothpick
factory. They emerged with damning facts clenched between
their teeth. One of our Cambridge researchers, the widely
feared Mike Ansara, known as the Red scourge of
Harvard—a lad viewed with particular alarm by right-wing
newsletters because his wife was the granddaughter of
Charles Merrill, of the stockbroker Merrills—used his
Brahmin contacts to elicit the testimony from the president of
a prominent New England foundation that agents of the CIA
had asked him to serve as one of their secret "conduits,"
revealing many other "patriotic" foundations as among those
so cooperating. His foundation, citing a "19th century sense
of morality," turned the spy boys down cold.

Ansara was one of a ferociously resourceful crew of radical
academics who delivered the goods backing up almost every
important *Ramparts* investigation. Without them, the paper
never could have produced the distinctly political variety of
new journalism at which *Ramparts* at times excelled. (The
scarlet honor roll of the *Ramparts* devils who did the investigative scout work included the likes of John Spitzer, Dan Schec-
ter, Robert Avakian, Lee Webb, David Kolodney, Kit and
Tuck Weills, Mark Libarle, Jan Austin, Michael Locker, Reese
Ehrlich, Steve Chain, David Goldstein and H. Indian Cohen.
Three of these individuals happened to be nonsanguineous

relations to Scheer and myself. The frequent rumors of nepotism at *Ramparts* were referred as a matter of staff procedure to my sister, whose job it was to scotch them.)

It seemed time to brace the student leaders. I asked Ed Schwartz, an NSA vice president and its left-wing leading light, to come to my house. He complained that he was busy organizing a Berkeley riot against the firing of Clark Kerr. When I told him what I wanted to discuss he rushed across the Bay. Over a game of darts, which I played for the water torture angles, I laid out, dart-*thump*, dart-*thump*, what we knew. Schwartz did not deny the CIA relationship. But he argued through most of the night that I shouldn't print the story. It would destroy the NSA. The CIA would retaliate against the students. Innocent people would be hurt. The CIA money was used for valuable liberal projects, even helping organize Vietnam teach-ins. He might lose his draft deferment. And so on.

The next day, in Washington, the same arguments were made by other NSA leaders to Sol Stern, who was writing the story. They actually advanced the intriguing contention that such a disclosure would be damaging to the enlightened men of the "liberal" internationalistic wing of the CIA who were willing to provide clandestine money to domestic progressive causes.

I was unaware at the time that the student leaders were simultaneously meeting with their CIA contacts at a motel in Arlington, Virginia. The CIA came up with a plan that, under normal circumstances, might well have avoided those aspects of the expose that the agency feared most. The student leaders were to call a press conference weeks in advance of the *Ramparts* publication date to expose themselves. They would reveal that the CIA, years before, had given some money to NSA—but that such deplorable funding had been terminated by recent student leadership. The hope was that by the time *Ramparts* came out, its cranky left-wing charges would seem stale and, in CIA language, "fully deniable." The secret of the actual extent of the CIA clandestine network into American institutions would be saved. Better the NSA dirty itself a bit than the lid come off the United Auto Workers.

To effect this plan, the CIA asked the students to plant an informant in *Ramparts*, who was to provide the muckrakers with further "details," while keeping the agency advised of our progress toward the press. The CIA story was still being written, and the press date a week away. We had, however, a plant of our own in the NSA inner sanctum. On Saturday, Scheer called me on an emergency frequency from Chicago, where he had just received word from our spy about the impending press conference, secretly scheduled for the next Tuesday.

I was damned if I was going to let the CIA scoop me. I bought full-page advertisements in the Tuesday editions of the New York *Times* and Washington *Post* to scoop myself, which seemed a preferable alternative.

"In its March issue, *Ramparts* magazine will document how the CIA has infiltrated and subverted the world of American student leaders, over the past fifteen years," read the Valentine's Day ad copy.

On Monday afternoon the student leaders were in conference with the CIA men preparing for the morrow's press conference when a New York *Times* Washington Bureau man telephoned with some pertinent queries about the ad appearing in its next morning's editions. The students panicked. They bolted from the CIA men. After a hurried caucus, they called in the press and admitted—everything. They even said the CIA had "pressured" them to deny the truth of the charges.

The usual procedure for political exposés is that the denial of the charges carries as much, usually more, weight than the charges. The ensuing confusion tends to cover up potential damage. The lid came off the CIA's domestic sneak act because, for once, the denial syndrome became inoperative.

For its expose of the CIA, *Ramparts* received the George Polk Memorial Award for Excellence in Journalism. The award cited *Ramparts*' "explosive revival of the great muckraking tradition." At the risk that future historians of journalism might think slightly less of our achievement, I should point

out that it was really the unprecedented, unconditional surrender of the accused—as the students were caught in the
very act of the cover-up—that brought about the serial disclosures that so humiliated the CIA.

It is a rare thing in this business when you say bang and
somebody says I'm dead.

COUP D'ETAT IN A HOUSE OF CARDS

> *"Having wonderful time. Wish you*
> *were here instead of me."*
> —Richard Halliburton,
> the last radiogram from his
> Japanese junk before it was lost in
> mid-Pacific in 1939.

Ramparts, during the downslide of the sixties, gained the
dubious distinction of being known as the largest institution
on the New Left, even though the New Left—as a concept
about as cohesive as marbles boiled in butter—disavowed
institutions in general and *Ramparts* in particular. The paper
reached a peak circulation of a quarter-million, a paid staff of
fifty, and an annual income from subscriptions, newsstand
sales, book publishing and tax loss swindling of some
$2,000,000—almost sufficient to meet operating expenses but
insufficient to cope with its debt, a snake pit of turned-off
investors and curdled creditors who early began to whipsaw
Ramparts in the manner of the tail wagging the dog. Such
tribulations were part of the price of fame. *Ramparts* joined
the Audit Bureau of Circulation, and some of us kingfish
made *Who's Who in America*. The year it went bankrupt I
gained the additional honor of being listed in *Who's Who in
Finance and Industry*.

Feigen called *Ramparts* "the primal scream." It was, at the
least, frantic. The bigger the paper became, the more broke it
seemed to be. A growing magazine guzzles lots of money, and
I sent the editors running around the country between editions to borrow cups full of moola. It was all one big rush, and
some people got trampled in the process.

"Hin-Hin-Hin-Hinckle," Gossage would say, in his eloquent stammer, "you've got a trail of bodies behind you
stacked up like cordwood." I suppose that will be my epitaph,
although as Lenny said in *Of Mice and Men*, after he ended up
strangling the girl because he wanted to pet her hair the way
he petted a bunny rabbit, I didn't mean to hurt anybody. I just
naturally assumed that everyone on the paper would of
course be willing and able to run a four-minute mile every
day, and when someone fell by the wayside exhausted or with
a broken leg, I looked upon it, with a neutral detachment, as
an example of natural selection at work. I ran the paper with a
sort of Israeli toughness about what had to be done, driving
our wayward bus at comet speed, getting across the necessary
hurdles at any cost, while the passengers were bounced
around in the rear and occasionally thrown out a window.

I would rarely fire anyone. If people became superfluous I
would tend to ignore them and give their work to others,
leaving them ostracized in never-never land with nothing to
do but twiddle their thumbs and throw darts at my picture.
There were those who became especially embittered, among
them Ed Keating, at the water torture treatment they felt they
suffered at my behest, and I can understand why. The decent
thing to do would have been to fire people rather than leave
them just hanging around, but I was too much of a born
coward to do that.

The level of chaos at *Ramparts* defies summation outside the
analogy of an underdeveloped country. The growth rate was
enormous, there were always vital supplies missing, we had a
negative balance of payments, we were constantly under
siege, et cetera. It was a force-fed chaos, as I kept pushing
things further than they would normally go. I would often be
displeased with an issue ready to go to press, and would think
nothing of ripping it apart at the last moment, rewriting
flabby copy, redoing layouts, creating a new cover story out of
whole cloth while the printer sputtered about deadlines and
the loyal staff inhaled Dexamils to stay awake during the
ordeal. I simply saw no excuse to produce a mediocre issue
just because I and the other editors had to spend three weeks
out of four keeping the financial roof from falling in; let our

more slothful, well-financed, corporately stable competition take four weeks to publish a monthly; *Ramparts* would beat them at their own idiot magazine game even if I had only one week to do the job, which was often the case. As a crisis-ridden monthly, *Ramparts* became almost contemporary with the weeklies—at times scooping up stories that left *Time* and *Newsweek* with nothing to do but follow our lead in their next week's editions. In a typical apology to the readers, I explained why I twice held up an issue which had been scheduled to come out around the time of LBJ's abdication, then butted up against Martin Luther King's assassination, "so you wouldn't be reading about Johnson's chances for reelection and the future of nonviolence."

From the outside looking in, *Ramparts* was as slick and sharp as its newsstand competitors, but inside it was all Marat/Sade. I simply refused to compromise with reality, and it is testament to the extraordinary punishment that the human body and the corporate body alike can take that *Ramparts* kept cracking out the demon issues that it did—until, of course, it eventually fell apart under the strain. There were naturally mistakes made under such pressure, but the ones that got into print, I was fond of pointing out, were never of the magnitude of the *Newsweek* cover that had the eye patch on General Dayan's *good* eye.

The financial administration of *Ramparts* was if anything more frantic. The business department was a virtual revolving door shuffling lost souls who would walk in relatively stable, and walk out fingering steel balls. The lone money manager who survived the roller coaster was Robert Kaldenbach, a former Berkeley city Auditor who rode the ups and downs all the way through the bankruptcy courts and emerged to write a book on "How to Go Bankrupt and Rip Off the System." The bane of the toilers in the accounting vineyards was the *Ramparts* budget—an impressive and quite incomprehensible computer print out which I changed as often as a Penn Central timetable. The budget proved a singular frustation to those with ostensible responsibilities in the business department, since it had little to do with the rabbit-from-the-hat financial tricks with which I kept the paper alive for five years.

In 1966, for instance, *Ramparts'* survival depended on the simple proposition of not paying its printing bill. I was rather proud of that feat, which Bill Honig and I engineered during a five-hour, fifteen-martini lunch with the printer, a chap whom we had not paid in seven months. When lunch was over we had talked the printer into loaning *Ramparts* $270,000 so we could pay his bill, and then—because we were paid up—we talked him into advancing another $100,000 of credit. I hired the printer's daughter in gratitude, and she turned out to be one of our hardest-working employees.

The business types were distressed over my apparent ability to play contradictory roles—those of raising the money and planning the budgets, and spending the money and ignoring the budgets. I have never been possessed of what Karl Jaspers once described as "the immoderate desire for security." There have accordingly over the years been many amusing stories in the popular prints about my various excesses in the performance of my corporate duties. Most of them are true, although there is one I wish to correct for the record. It appeared in the New York *Times* Magazine in a wonderful hatchet story on *Ramparts*. In one of those internecine moments that make life at the *Times* so interesting, the Sunday department people wanted a story that would embarrass the news department people—who had given all that publicity to *Ramparts*. They assigned Jim Ridgeway, who was a good choice as he had several times been scooped by me when he was an editor of the *New Republic*. Ridgeway, an honest and blunt fellow, called me while writing the story and said that the *Times* people wanted even *more* horror stories about money; I obliged. But the one I wish to correct is the *Times'* report that I once, during an airline strike, flew from Chicago to Paris to get to New York. In fact, I flew from San Francisco to Paris to get to New York. If I had been in Chicago, I would have just taken a cab.

One *Ramparts* money story is indicative of the way it was. Marc Stone, who ran the paper's New York office, was constantly fretting over the size of *Ramparts* phone bill. He finally talked me into buying a money-saving telex system linking *Ramparts* in San Francisco with the printer in Denver and the

office in New York. After much travail and expense the tel-
exes were installed. The first message that clattered over the
telex was from Marc Stone in New York. It read: "Tell Warren
to call me immediately."

Keating came back from running for Congress (he lost the
Shirley Temple primary) to a fundamentally different
magazine from the *Ramparts* he had started. The old angry
Catholicism was gone, and in its place a quasi-New Leftish
muckraking in fierce pursuit of the Vietnam war and anything else corrupt about America. I had moved the paper
lock, stock and cartons of overdue bills to San Francisco—a
move Keating did not appreciate, as now he had to drive up
the peninsula to work, instead of the staff, most of whom lived
in Berkeley and San Francisco, driving down. "Menlo Park,
California, when you really think about it, is a ridiculous place
to publish a magazine," I explained in a moving notice to the
readers. The staff had changed totally from the Catholic
harem to which Keating was accustomed; he sat in on editorial
meetings, staring across the table at the hated Scheer caucus-
ing with his New Left cadre, and found he had little to say and
little to do with the editorial policy of the magazine he had
created and was, as far as the outside world knew, its publisher. Moreover, new investors' money was providing for the
payroll checks, including Keating's, which he now needed to
feed his kids, since he had sold the family jewels for the old
Ramparts. He was hard put to understand why the new investors would want to begrudge him that weekly check, which
they did, in fact, begrudge him. Keating was later to accuse
Scheer, Stermer and me of plotting with the investors against
him. The fact was, although he would never believe it, that we
fought with the investors to keep them from canning him.
Dick Russell—a Connecticut businessman who brought bags
of Singer Sewing Machine heiress money to the paper in
1967—a nice guy personally but as a businessman the distilled
essence of Attila the Hun, wanted to throw Keating out of his
office and off the payroll. Russell said that the publisher was
no longer contributing anything to the magazine. I men-

tioned that he had contributed a million bucks, but that didn't impress Russell.

The offices in the paper's new camping grounds, a squat, ugly, brown building on the edge of San Francisco's topless-bottomless nightclub strip, were a cornucopia of eccentricity, variously painted mustard, raspberry, white, green and/or lemon. But Keating's office was the most bizarre of all. He got Barbara Brown, *Ramparts'* first office manager, who had long since fled the madness, to return to the scene of the crime and decorate it for him. He told her he wanted a "pad—just like Hefner's." He got a pad—heavy curtains shut out the light; there was a black rug on the floor thick enough for a small dog to get lost in; and instead of a desk there were imitation black leather couches and swivel-balloon chairs that you could sit in up to your eyeballs. The place looked like the waiting room in a sperm bank. "They're going to cut me up," Keating told Barbara Brown. "I've got to do something to retain my identity—this is my last chance."

The storm broke over drinks with Arnold Toynbee. Jessica Mitford was having a little bash for the great man at her Oakland home. The left wing in the East Bay is a cozy little lot, and all those with good table manners were in attendance. Scheer, who was something of a neighbor of Decca and her husband, Bob Treuhaft, was trying to exert his territorial rights to get me to stop talking to Toynbee about Thomas Aquinas so he could ask a question about Marshal Tito, when Decca pulled me out of the group. "I say, Hink Three, there seems to be a bit of a blackout call for you on the phone in the kitchen."

The call was from Dick Russell, the money man in Connecticut. He said he had just received a message that the entire three-man business department *and* Keating were flying to see him the next day to present evidence of my many transgressions and to propose a new course of management for the paper. Russell was coolly angry, and speaking formally: "They asked me to keep this secret from you, but I replied that I would inform you of their actions immediately. I am not

interested in seeing them; I will not see them if they persist in
coming, which I advised them not to do. I am well aware of
your excesses, but I consider them insignificant in the context
of your contributions to the magazine as a whole. You hold
four men's jobs, and there is no one around to replace you in
even one of them. Had you taken my advice and gotten rid of
Mr. Keating, who in my opinion is a negative asset, this situation would never have arisen. However, you have my complete support. I believe we have more stock control at the
moment than Keating, but I'm not certain. He may be able to
acquire proxies. Also I have no idea of how many votes he may
muster on the Board of Directors. You have a palace revolt on
your hands, and you should take whatever measures are required to squelch it."

I thanked Russell for the warning and for his support, and
went back to the living room, where I said a hurried good-bye
to the eminent Dr. T.

Scheer came up and asked if anything was wrong. He shuddered when I told him. I knew what had happened: the
average age in the business department, which saw the bills
stack up, was 40. The average age in the editorial department,
which spent the money, was about 23. It was the den mothers
vs. the cub pack.

In addition, I had staffed the business department with
refugees from reality, as real businessmen seemed to run
from *Ramparts* as from a hoard of red ants. Among the refugees was Hank Marchman, a 350-pound computer expert.
Marchman was so fat he couldn't get in the toilet door in the
office and had to waddle up the street to a gas station to pee.
He had to sleep sitting up, and occupied two first-class seats on
an airplane—one for each bun. His wife was skinny and frail
and the talk around the office was how they ever made it, if
ever. Feigen kept telling Marchman that he'd be dead within
six months if he didn't have radical surgery to tie off his
intestines so he could chew food but not digest it. Marchman
would sit gobbling chocolate bars while listening to Feigen
predict his imminent death. He said he had been tossed out of
his own computer firm that had been doing *Ramparts'* circulation work because the paper hadn't paid the bill. But he stole a

copy of the tape with all the subscribers' names on it, so we hired him.

Marchman was one of those in the revolt. Another was Jim Colaianni, the lay theologian Keating had made managing editor. I tried to fire him, but felt sorry when he told me about all his kids and about how it wasn't his fault he hadn't done a good job because Keating had given him orders to hide all the manuscripts from me. Old softy, I gave him a job in the business department. The third person was Don Rothenberg, a fund-raiser of the old left whom Scheer had brought aboard to help sell advertising and raise money. I could see the three of them sitting around by themselves sorting through the Diners Club bills, planning a revolution.

I told Scheer that in my opinion his buddy Don Rothenberg, unable to restrain the impulse to maneuver for power in the byzantine old left tradition, had put Keating up to this.

Scheer at that point made a rather disparaging remark about the old left. (But he later forgave Rothenberg for his putative plotting, and went on to become Berkeley-style friends and neighbors with him, thereby absolving the suspect, by association, of all guilt.)

I went home and called Keating. Helen Keating answered the phone. I chatted with her pleasantly for a few minutes about her kids and such, unable to restrain the thought the whole while that it had been her money that had gone down the *Ramparts* drain. Finally I asked if Ed was there. "Oh, sure," she said, "I'll put him on."

There was a considerable pause. Keating's voice finally came on the wire. "Yes?"

I told Ed of Russell's call, of his declamation that he would not meet with him, and suggested that I should drive down that night so we could work out this problem before it grew into something that could affect the magazine.

Keating said that he wasn't going to give me a chance to "sweet talk" him into anything. He wouldn't see me unless he was surrounded by wagon trains of lawyers. He kept calling me "big boy," like in a gangster movie, and said he was going to "get me." He kept asking if I was sweating and squirming. "You'd better say your prayers, big boy," he said, hanging up.

That was so much for sweet reason.

I have long dreaded telling the story of the alley fight that ensued, as I can only provide an embattled combatant's account, and would be sore put striving for objectivity—even if I achieved it, no one, naturally, would believe me, and that would be most fretful.

But, happily, Decca Mitford sent me a copy of a memo she wrote to Gossage around the time of the blow-up. It is both complex and amusing and certainly captures the enigmatic temper of what she calls the "Rampartian" era. I have decided, with her permission, to print it here, as it is rather fair to all sides, and certainly gives Scheer and me a well-deserved kick or two that might otherwise be missing, wrongly so, from this chronicle.

Everything you read between the lines is true.

28 April, 1967

Dear Howard,

I thought I should send you an account of yesterday's meeting, to add to yr. no doubt voluminous files on the Rampartian blow-up.

As you know, the meeting was originally called (before the blow-up) to discuss the resignations of Paul Jacobs and Ralph Gleason from the Editorial Bd. After these were reported in Herb Caen's column, it occurred to me that others might follow suit, to the detriment of the mag, unless some of the beefs were aired and corrected. So I visualized a sort of Contributing Editors Defense League meeting at which the transgressions of Hink III and Scheer could be brought to their attention, in hopes they might reform a bit.

The complaints one hears in general from authors range from sloppiness (losing manuscripts, failing to pay authors, a fire-alarm approach to stories which results in mistakes) to the more serious one of exploiting and using

people, then throwing them overboard when their usefulness is at an end. And while we all know that
Hink/Scheer are brilliant young bandits doing an extraordinary job, and that their ruthless handling of people
may be the necessary other-side-of-coin to their flair and
forward thrust, nobody wants to be on the receiving end
of it, if you see what one means—so that the danger is that
people will start drawing away for fear of getting run
over.

Before the meeting I talked with both Paul and Ralph.
Paul's main complaint was the firealarmishness that led to
amateurishness and inaccuracies—he feared that one day
these qualities would lead to some sort of explosion (since
obviously the Establishment would like naught better
than to get Ramparts). Paul said he admires Ramparts
and would always be willing to write for them etc. but
didn't want to be so closely connected with the operation.

Ralph's criticisms were a lot stronger, in fact he was
very bitter about the way he has been treated—and
others. To wit: He was not consulted about the Hippie
article, which was full of inaccuracies. He was originally
supposed to write this article but Hink III went ahead
without his knowledge, 1st thing he knew about it was
when it was in print. In February, he wrote a furious
letter of resignation and demanded that this letter shld.
be printed in the mag. He got no acknowledgment, nobody contacted him at all, it was never printed. He thinks
that Donovan Bess got a similarly raw deal, was dropped
from the masthead without consultation. Also he said
they were beastly to Keating, and that Keating walked
around with a haunted look; "don't be surprised if you
read in the paper one day that Keating has committed
suicide," Ralph said. There was much more along this
line, and a good deal of son-of-a-bitching etc. I asked
Ralph if he would come to a meeting with Hink/Scheer,
he said he wasn't sure but certainly *not* if it were held at
Ramparts' office, he'd never set foot in that place again.
He was, in a word, simply *furious* with the lot of them.

Well, to my *extreme* astonishment, not one word of all

this came out at the meeting yesterday. On the contrary
Ralph was giving all sorts of expert advice on how to
handle the press (offered to call Abe Mellinkoff to pave
the way for a Chronicle interview with Hink/Scheer), was
predicting how Keating might jump next—and how he
could best be forestalled—might he bring in Pinkerton
men to invade the Ramparts offices? Get an injunction?
etc. etc. He volunteered to talk with Newsweek etc. about
his own resignation, to assure the press it had naught to
do with the current blow-up. Paul drew up a statement
for the press expressing his support of Hink/ Scheer.
And so it went. (This didn't surprise me on Paul's part,
because as I said he wasn't angry or bitter at Hink/Scheer
so much as irritated by aforementioned sloppiness.)

Needless to say we never did get to the original subject
matter for which the mtg. was called. I mean, nobody
wanted to: we listened, riveted, to Hink's report of the
Executive Board meeting.

I think the Hink strategy of private vilification and
public sweetness is working pretty well (that bit in today's
Chron. about how we shall miss our esteemed founder).
At the meeting, he said that Keating is clinically insane;
also, that Don Rothenberg seems to have been the mas-
termind behind the takeover plot.

Now, regardless of the truthfulness of the charges
against these chaps, it seems obvious to me that if it had to
come to a choice between Hink/Scheer and Keating
—well, I mean there simply *is* no choice; Hink/Scheer *are*
the mag, the creators of everything that's so splendid
about it. (This, perhaps, accounts for the rallying-round
of Ralph Gleason and Paul Jacobs.) But one does wish
they could be a trifle less Animal-Farmish about it.

I don't know Keating especially well, but I do know
Don Rothenberg. I first met him last summer during the
election campaign, and more recently have been working
with him on the ad-gathering. He strikes me as a very
principled, able sort of person. Furthermore he always
had nothing but the highest praise for Hink/Scheer. I
gave him plenty of openings to be critical of them, too, by

discussing the authors' beefs etc. with him; but he never specially picked up on this, on the contrary he tended to defend them on the grounds of being excessively over-worked and young and reckless and all that sort of thing. (I said all of this at the meeting, by the way.) Nor do I think he had any personal desire to "seize power." Seize power for what (I asked Scheer), did you think he had editorial ambitions? Scheer said that yes, he certainly did! In fact was always coming up with story suggestions, five of them a week. Well, honestly. That was the tone of much that was said at the meeting—putting these sinister constructions on what were really pretty ordinary actions.

Rothenberg's version of the power-grab thing is, of course, a lot more innocent. The proposal for the meeting with Russell arose (says he) out of concern about the financial instability of the mag, a desire to save Hink/Scheer from themselves in effect— wiser and older heads would institute a more regular control of funds, and would also insist upon implementation of a prior Board decision about all this. (No point in my going into any more detail on this aspect, but that was the gist of it.) I told Rothenberg I thought it was all a bloody silly scheme, *and* not his style of work, to try to cook up this meeting behind Hinckle's back, whatever the motives. First he sort of agreed that it was lousy judgment; now he says that on thinking it all over, it was the only thing he and Keating could have done, because endless meetings on the financial matters with Hinckle had been held, he had ignored the decisions that came out of these meetings, and so on. Again, no point in me trying to paraphrase and re-member all the ins and outs of this, because you can get it directly from Rothenberg if you are interested. But in trying to make up my mind as to whether Rothenberg was being Wicked or Stupid about engineering this meeting with Russell, I have come to the conclusion that he was being Stupid.

Rothenberg says that since the Crisis, that is since Monday, his one aim has been to act as a moderating force on Keating.* Thus, he forestalled K. from going to

the press at once with his version of the *histoire*; he has
been closeted with Keating for the purpose of trying to
prevent him from doing anything that might wreck the
mag. I tend to believe this because the whole training and
background of a person like Rothenberg would lead him
to try and be a peacemaker amongst warring left factions.
(The United Front, remember? I once had a secretary
who always misspelled that as Untied Front, which is what
this all is fast becoming.)

Mal Burnstein, who knows Rothenberg well and in fact
introduced him to Scheer (I think), agrees with me about
him. As for this pish-tosh that he might be CIA-
connected (dropped shruggingly by Scheer at one point)
both Mal & I think that is ridiculous.

Now, lest you think that this is by way of being a
Rothenberg Defense League Manifesto, it isn't. I think
that Rothenberg's best self defense is to fade out fast and
to stop trying to save people from themselves; he'll only
get further clobbered if he keeps it up.

So I guess it's an anti-further-clobbering manifesto.
The awful thing is that in a way I have a certain built-in
affinity for the rather frightful methods of Hink/
Scheer—that is, I can distinctly remember being equally
ghastly to people when I was their age and younger, and
very much enjoying the outmanuevering of real or imagined enemies. What made it all so splendid was, of
course (as in their case), that it was done in a righteous
cause.

But my quarrel with them is not just that I have gradually become a Dear Old Soul. It is simply that I fear that if
they keep up the ruthless, trampling-on-people bit,
they'll drive away a lot of talent and support that right-
fully belongs with Ramparts. Nobody wants to stop them
from being tough realists; but I do think they should
avoid any further decimation of the civilian population—and especially stop bombing their own side by
mistake.

I should add that I, personally, have not suffered any
of these dire things. On the contrary I find Hink/ Scheer

marvelously good company, clever, funny, all the things we like. Also they laugh at one's jokes which is always such a smashing quality.

> *Love from*
> *Decca*   R.S.V.P.!

*Also he is *livid* because of the kicking-around Keating got.

p.s. Sorry about the excessive length of this—you probably stopped reading it pages ago. But in case you are still there, Bob just brought the NY Times story about the Ramparts thing. (I must say I *shrieked* at the part about the man with a hollow shoe and concealed compass for finding his way out of the slave camp.) Howard, the McCarthy reference. Hink III made the same point, come to think of it, in our meeting; that Keating kept saying "Point of Order!" just like in the McCarthy hearings. But who, one wonders, were cast in the role of Cohn and Schine at that meeting? Also, Hinckle said that Keating disrupted the proceedings by insisting on a tape-recording or some sort of transcript. Which, to my mind, is some slight proof he might be clinically sane, because no-one in their right mind (speaking for *moi*) would go in to such a meeting *without* having the proceedings recorded! Don't you rather agree?

Well, it's all fascinating and frightful; I only trust that Ramparts will survive it. Do be thinking of something clever to be done. I suppose it is too late in the day to start a Squares for Ramparts committee. The requisites for joining such a committee would be an affidavit signed by at least 5 known-to-be-square people to the effect that the candidate is a generally well-disposed old thing, in favour of peace at almost all costs, yet kindly to individuals; in favour of legalized abortion yet not an abortionist. No. Whilst thinking of the requisites I can see the whole thing is hopeless, so don't let's do that.

Over to you. . . .

(I should hasten to add here that although Ed Keating and I have had our differences, I would attribute them more to the characteristic of fierce stubbornness that we both shared rather than to any kind of insanity on his part or, as far as I know, on my part. [My rationality has of course at times been seriously questioned by reasonable men, but I take solace in Nietzsche's dictum, loosely translated, that there is hardly such a thing as insanity in individuals, although in political parties, nations and epochs it is the rule.])

The New York *Times* story referred to by Decca was a piece by Marty Arnold, direct from the scene of the crime. Arnold arrived in San Francisco the morning after the palace revolt began, a fact which we naturally but unsuccessfully attempted to keep from him. He had been dispatched by then national editor Claude Sitton with express instructions to find out where *Ramparts* was *really* getting its money, and whether it was Moscow or Peking gold that was involved. I expressed amazement that the *Times* would send a reporter from New York as, just a few weeks before, they had run a long front-page, top-of-the-fold feature on *Ramparts*. The story had been written by Wally Turner, the *Times* San Francisco-based investigative reporter, and one of the best diggers in the business; Wally somehow tracked down every major investor in the magazine—he had the story of every *sou*. But the *Times* management in New York, perhaps feeling a bit guilty that they had helped create a monster by giving the paper so much publicity, couldn't believe the whole *Ramparts* money thing could be that innocent, and had sent yet another man to try, try again. (I later heard from another *Times*man that the impetus for the second investigation came down from Clifton Daniel, who had heard from someone on high in Washington that *Ramparts* had "definite" ties to foreign capital.)

After a few days hanging around the paper, Arnold realized what a funnyfarm the place really was. I showed him the books and, with nothing to do but confirm Turner's earlier account of *Ramparts'* financing for his incredulous bosses, he began to enjoy himself immensely with the intrigue and plotting leading up to the climactic board meeting. We were attempting desperately to keep the revolt out of the papers, while still hoping to avoid a shoot-out with Keating. Marty began interviewing the staff while desperate attempts continued to squelch the revolt. In the confusion, the New York *Times* man found out every closet skeleton and nasty about the paper; he even wheedled the story of Keating and the hollowed heel out of Scheer, although I suspect Scheer had ulterior motives in letting it drop.

When High Noon arrived, Arnold filed a blow-by-blow account of the fight, rich to the very details of the traumatic board room scene, with Keating hollering "point of order" every five minutes. We had tried down to the wire to talk Ed out of the showdown he demanded. Bill Honig met with him an hour before the meeting and went over the list of new stockholders, pointing out that Keating no longer held a majority. The new stockholders were united against him, and the only vote he would have on the board of directors was his own. There was no way he could succeed in his announced attempt to take over control of the magazine. Honig said he and the other investors would be willing to meet with Keating to discuss his grievances if he would only call off the showdown meeting. Keating told Honig that he had it all wrong, and that *he* was the one who was going to do the throwing out, not be thrown out.

At that point even Gossage, the eternal peacemaker, decided there was nothing to do but relax and enjoy the war. Before the critical vote, Keating delivered a stern warning that he would hold each of the directors personally financially responsible if they voted against him. He looked directly at June Degnan, an investor and one of the wealthier people on the board. "Move the question," June said icily. Keating lost, 13-1.

"They threw me out like an old shoe," he said.

6.

Give Us This Day Our Paranoia

THE JOLLY GREEN GIANT

PARANOIA is a little like dog shit. Once you step in it, you can never be sure it is not still with you. You try to scrape it off your shoe and walk on, looking back frequently to see if you are leaving any tracks, continually sniffing the air around your own person so as to be doubly sure, pitting one sense competitively against another, challenging the nose to be sensitive to what the eye cannot see. But you are never certain, and therefore, become more cautious about reality; you learn to live with paranoia, if not enjoy it somewhat. Dan Greenburg, the funny writer, once explained to me that *of course* he was paranoid. "You'd be paranoid, too," he said, "if you had so many people constantly plotting against you." When I told Greenburg I'd heard that one before, he said *of course*—he'd made it up and people were always stealing his lines.

To live it and love it is one way of dealing with the presence. There is another, but it has not proved particularly efficacious since the day the Emperor was sighted without his clothes. You pretend—or really believe—it matters not which, as the result is the same—that the dog doo isn't there, you press on, leaving tracks across people's rugs and hardwood floors, generally creating a stink, and giving the impression of being some sort of a nut.

That last was the way the District Attorney of New Orleans, Jim Garrison, handled his paranoia. I cannot fault him for it,

197

as no man I have known had more legitimate reasons to
become paranoid than Garrison; there actually were people
constantly plotting against him.

My last communication with Garrison was on November 5,
1968. It was not untypical. I was interrupted in mid-
explanation to an unhappy investor (Keating's stormy depar-
ture had not helped the money-raising situation). The investor was turning a tinge yellow at my suggestion that the only
way to insure the return of the $20,000 he had previously
loaned *Ramparts* was to cover his bet with an additional
$50,000. The interruption was an emergency long-distance
telephone call from New Orleans.

The caller was in no mood to inquire about the weather.
"This is urgent," Jim Garrison said. "Can you take this in your
mailroom? They'd never think to tap the mailroom extension."

I excused myself to go to the mailroom for a moment on a
matter of high priority and left the investor, sputtering like a
referee without a whistle, alone with the latest negative balance sheets. In the mailroom, two bearded Berkeleyite mail
boys were running the postage machine under the influence
of marijuana. I told them to take a walk around the block and
get high on company time, and locked the door behind them.

Garrison began talking when I picked up the mailroom
extension: "This is risky, but I have little choice. It is imperative that I get this information to you now. Important new
evidence has surfaced. Those Texas oilmen do not appear to
be involved in President Kennedy's murder in the way we first
thought. It was the Military-Industrial Complex that put up
the money for the assassination—but as far as we can tell, the
conspiracy was limited to the aerospace wing. I've got the
names of three companies and their employees who were
involved in setting up the President's murder. Do you have a
pencil?"

I wrote down the names of the three defense contractors
—Garrison identified them as Lockheed, Boeing, and General Dynamics—and the names of those executives in their
employ whom the District Attorney said had been instrumen-

tal in the murder of Jack Kennedy. I also logged a good deal of
information about a mysterious minister who was supposed to
have crossed the border into Mexico with Lee Harvey Oswald
shortly before the assassination; the man wasn't a minister at
all, Garrison said, but an executive with a major defense
supplier, in clerical disguise. I knew little about ministers
crossing the Rio Grande with Oswald —but after several years
of fielding the dizzying details of the Kennedy assassination, I
had learned to leave closed Pandora's boxes lie; I didn't ask.

I said that I had everything down, and Garrison said a
hurried good-bye: "It's poor security procedure to use the
phone, but the situation warrants the risk. Get this information to Bill Turner. He'll know what to do about the minister. I
wanted you to have this, in case something happens. . . ."

I unlocked the mailroom door, and returned to my office.
The investor was gone.

I typed up a brief memorandum of the facts as Garrison
had relayed them and burned my notes in an oversized
ashtray I used for such purposes. I Xeroxed one copy of the
memo, which I mailed to myself in care of a post office box in
the name of Walter Snelling, a friendly, non-political bartender in the far-removed country town of Cotati, California,
where I routinely sent copies of all supersecret _Ramparts_
documents. That night I hand delivered the original to Bill
Turner, the former FBI agent in charge of the magazine's
investigation of the Warren Commission. Turner had drilled
me in a little G-Man security lingo. According to our code, I
called him at home and said something about a new vacuum
cleaner. He replied that he'd be right over, and said he would
meet me at the bar at Trader Vic's, which meant that I was to
actually meet him at Blanco's, a dimly lit Filipino bar on the
fringe of Chinatown, where we often held secret meetings.

That was the way we did things in those days.

"Those days" encompassed several years of sniffing, as Sam
Goldwyn might say, along the greenhorn trail of red herrings
in the 26 volumes of the Report of the President's Commission
on the Assassination of President Kennedy. We began asking
rude questions in 1965, and by 1968, with paranoia in full
bloom, we had divided almost everyone, by some sort of

conspiracy litmus test, into "them" and "us." Even "us" was subdivided into good guys, not-so-good-guys, dangerous fanatics and fifth columnists. We ended up seeing "them" lurking behind every potted plant rented by the CIA; and, occasionally, we found a real spook in the shadows.

I met Garrison on a brisk, moonswept summer evening in 1967 at attorney Melvin Belli's penthouse pad, which sits atop a sagging building on Telegraph Hill like a diamond collar on a dented can. It was the New Orleans DA's first visit to San Francisco. Belli, who assumed the luckless defense of Jack Ruby after other lawyers had run away when Ruby began talking about cancer juice being injected in his veins, had invited the locals to hear Garrison's views on the assassination.

Belli doesn't sneeze without putting on a show, and the setting was adequate for staging *Aida*. The equivalent of several cable-car-loads of lawyers, police brass, newsmen and other San Francisco opinion-makers of smart chic and dowdy chic were munching rack of lamb and sucking in cocktails on Belli's vast bricked terrace hanging assover the Bay, looking in through glass walls to the half-bookish, half-bare-Zen-exhibitionist décor of the penthouse.

Garrison rose to the occasion. He was the essential frontier lawman—ectomorphic, taciturn, handsome, charming, dramatic in a properly low-keyed way. He spoke in the slightest of Southern drawls, just loud enough to be heard over the hoot of foghorns out in the Bay. He presented factually, without the hint of an opinion, a most incredible story of conspiracy, murder, and ineffectual conspiracy to cover the conspiracy—a story that was kerosene at the roots of the legitimacy of our system of government. Garrison rattled off dates, names, contradictory citations from the Warren Report, and extraordinary new evidence his New Orleans investigation had uncovered.

The DA was cool, sharp, informed, confident, convincing. He didn't leave a confirmed scoffer in the audience. A nervous lady in a low-cut print dress said something about how could high people in government be involved in such a thing. Garrison, who uses historical metaphors the way a tubercular does cough drops, replied: "Honorable men did in Caesar, Madam." His delivery brought a usually emotionless, grumpy Hearst reporter to his feet: "But, Mr. Garrison, if you're right, why it could destroy the government!" The DA replied with the calm of the frontier populist, Fess Parker explaining how to hitch a buckboard: "Well, sir, if telling the truth to the people of this country means that all the marble pillars of government in Washington will fall to the ground tonight; well, then, we'll just have to build ourselves a new government the next morning, maybe a little farther out West."

Garrison's official guide for the evening was an 18-year-old North Beach topless dancer with horn-rimmed glasses and well-buttressed breasts, assigned by his hosts to show him San Francisco's version of Bourbon Street. She looked at Jim doelike with unbridled admiration, a condition of enrapture shared, in varying degrees, by many among the rooftop assembly. The fresh converts to the cause of doubting Tomism waited to shake the DA's hand, standing around rubbing their goose bumps as the familiar early wet chill of a San Francisco summer fog closed in on the evening. Jim Garrison had put on one hell of a performance.

I wasn't sure, that night, if the New Orleans DA was on the right track, or merely enjoying his own show. But I took an immediate liking to him. I have learned to measure people who are uncompromisingly serious in their public pursuits, as Garrison was, by those standards of private weights and measures adjudicated by the late Humphrey Bogart—do they drink, are they able to laugh at themselves, can they appreciate a good time. If not—if they exhibit no capacity to value people other than through the prism of usefulness to the Cause—then beware: They are those monsters of purpose known as missionaries, and will as surely as not boil the baby to purify the bath water, or shove you off a subway platform to stop a speeding train; the same brown bag of constipation is toted by all those who are unable to enjoy the world while changing it, or, worse, while saving it.

I have been fated in many causes to be on the same side as the missionaries, but I suffer being around them. Humorlessness in pursuit of principle is no virtue. Having been involved in certain common efforts dear to the puritan heart of the New Left, I have grown drearily accustomed to having creeps as allies. Most of the ideological tinkers who populate the marching and clam chowder societies of the coming revolution tend to view an ice cold martini as the last refuge of fascism.

Thus I said an alleluia that in Jim Garrison—glass of bourbon in his left hand, the scales of justice in his right—a good wild man with the attendant majestic virtues and vices, there was finally a high roller on our side and a District Attorney at that.

In New Orleans the DA is called the "Jolly Green Giant." Jim Garrison is tall enough, and normally jolly enough, and in his dealing with a cheating government and an ambush-primed press in the months and years of his assassination investigation, he showed himself green enough to earn the title, whatever the significance of the original sobriquet.

Garrison was a member in good standing of the law enforcement establishment. A Lieutenant Colonel in the Louisiana National Guard, a conservative individualist who read Ayn Rand without wincing, sought after by other DA's as a popular drinking companion at their national Dick Tracy conventions, he was known as a tough, racket-busting, if flamboyant, DA who knew how to run a tight ship without making New Orleans a dull town.

Things began to change after Garrison read the 26 volumes of the Warren Report, and put them back on the shelf convinced that something was haywire. He decided to investigate Lee Harvey Oswald's activities in New Orleans prior to the assassination—a trail which soon led the DA across state lines, and into a theory that the assassination was carried out by anti-Castro paramilitary types under supervision of persons with past, or present, CIA connections. Rebuffed by Washington in his requests for assistance through normal channels, Garrison turned to private sources to fund his inquiry, which had rapidly grown as far beyond the capacity of the New Orleans District Attorney's staff as a moon flight would be to a

Piper-Cub manufacturer. Several of New Orleans' substantial citizens put up the money for their DA's far-flung activities. With that bittersweet sense of humor peculiar to the town, they called their special fund "Truth or Consequences, Inc." It might as well have been called Trick or Treat.

When the DA dialed the wrong number of the assassination, he not only found himself portrayed in the national media as some sort of Captain Crunch, but discovered, to his anger, that he had been cut off from all the room service of law enforcement. Other states refused to honor normal extradition requests for his key suspects. He could not even get routine cooperation from the FBI on fingerprint checks, let alone access to important records of the original assassination investigation secreted away in the National Archives; those documents not "classified" were crudely reported as "missing." When, in retaliation, he subpoenaed FBI agents to testify, they refused, invoking Department of Justice Order 32464, better known as executive immunity, that catchall doctrine to prevent the asking of embarrassing questions.

Garrison's reflex reaction to trouble was to brush it off with the subtlety of a bull swatting a fly. The resounding slap could be heard far out in the bayous, and was a familiar sound around New Orleans; the city's Criminal Court judges once collectively sued Garrison for defamation because of his constant references to them as "the sacred cows of India." Garrison's response to attacks from the press or brickbats from Washington was to counterattack with a startling, if unsubstantiated, revelation or a hint of impending arrests. The Grand Guignol qualities that made Garrison so popular and, until recently, reelectable in New Orleans, where he brought a little Mardi Gras what-the-hell to everyday politics, provided the media with the raw material to make a Faust, or a fool, of the Jolly Green Giant.

I have no ambition in this book to write the history of the fall of Rome, that is of New Orleans, which under Garrison became the epicenter of the Kennedy assassination empire. That is better left to the future historians of disaster and metaphysicians of collapse. Nor am I about to re-create Garrison's case, or argue those theories of his which are recyclable from the dust bin; others will undoubtedly do that, since conspiracy theories, unlike old soldiers, never really fade away; someone is forever coming along to give them a fresh coat of paint.

But the nationwide grass-roots reinvestigation of the Kennedy assassination was an extraordinary phenomenon of an extraordinary decade. Some elements of its rise and fall may be instructive for the future, as those years remain of note as the longest running siege of acute paranoia yet imagined. We inhaled conspiracies like Sen-Sen, yet we had cause to sweeten our breath. There was the probable conspiracy to murder John F. Kennedy. There was the certain conspiracy to manufacture sanitary answers to the unanswered questions of his assassination. Finally, there was the self-destructive paranoia of the anti-conspiracy conspirators; among them, Jim Garrison was like Jesus Christ, and toward the end, he saw himself surrounded by puckered Judases.

To put the paranoia in proper perspective it is best to go back a few years. At least at the beginning, everything made a suspicious sort of sense.

THE "SLEUTHS"

Ramparts' lengthy and unrequited affair with the problematics of the Kennedy assassination began some two years after the foul deed, and lasted sufficiently long to stir the murders of Robert Kennedy and Martin Luther King into the thick conspiracy soup. All three killings had bothersome elements of similarity other than guns and ready-to-wear assassins —but whether such similarities were but unfunny coincidences of the grim reaper, or the spoor of conspiracy, singular or plural, remains a question without a satisfactory answer; only a firm maybe.

The pursuit of a truth other than that constructed by the authorities is itself a story of loose ends and dangling participles, held together by the spirit gum of theory. It is not only the government which has had difficulty proving conspiracy cases. But the last time anyone bothered to take a poll on the subject, a sizable majority of the American public did not believe the Warren Report—although a substantial number of that majority did not feel the investigation should be reopened, either, which can be taken as an index of the base common sense of the populace along the lines of letting sleeping dogs, or dead Presidents, lie.

I was not overanxious to get involved in the Kennedy assassination hoopla. Inasmuch as *Ramparts* had recently distinguished itself by floating a conspiracy linking the Roman Catholic Church to the war in Vietnam, I figured it might be well to take a breather on conspiracy stories. Yet it was impossible to believe the Warren Report. Anyone who has read those twenty-six volumes (I gave up at about number eighteen; enough was enough) knows that the function of the Warren Commission was not to ferret out the truth, but to put the citizens at ease that there was no conspiracy; the two goals may not necessarily be mutually exclusive, although in the case of John Kennedy's murder I believe that they were.

The Warren Report's chiropractic explanation of how a lone gunman did it was violative of the laws of physics, probability, forensic pathology, Aristotelian logic, and Newton's second law of motion—but I will not replay that broken record here. It will suffice to say that if you believed the "superbullet" theory, you believed the Warren Commission. "Superbullet" was invented by the commission to explain away their own investigators' conclusion that a lone gunman shooting from where Oswald was said to have been had time to get off only three shots as the Presidential limousine passed; yet Kennedy was hit twice, Connally once, and one shot missed. To explain that, the commission came up with the legerdemain of the "magic bullet," as it was called even by the commission's defenders.

The first bullet, said the alchemists in the commission's employ, winged through Kennedy's neck and then, whipping about like a speeding spermatozoon in a sex education film, hit Connally in the back, came out his chest, plowed through his wrist, and, vicious bastard that it was, then pounced down into his thigh. The second bullet had missed, and the Zapruder film made painfully clear that it was the third shot that exploded the President's head; therefore, the commission reasoned, the first bullet had to be a Tarzan bullet.

The commissioners obviously thought better of calling it Tarzan so some dullard renamed it Bullet No. 399. The commission just grinned and bore the fact that energetic Bullet No. 399 was found on a stretcher at Parkland Hospital, after its cruise through the two politicians' bodies, and it was as good as new—head unflattened, lead intact, not a scratch on it. The ballistics experts shrugged their shoulders, since bullets usually get all banged up if they hit even one person, once; No. 399 hit two persons four times. In response to that quandary, the commission performed some experiments with anesthetized goats, but I will spare the details. The magic bullet theory also got into trouble with the naked eye school of facts. If one is ghoulish enough to watch the famed home movies of the shooting taken by Dallas dressmaker Abraham Zapruder, one sees Kennedy's hands going up to his throat as the first bullet hits him; but Connally just sits there, bovine, serene, looking the other way, a perfect statue—unblinking at the very second the Warren Commission insisted that the Tarzan bullet was hacking and tearing through his body.

Now that LBJ has gone to the great roundup in the sky and his aides are writing for publication, we learn that Johnson himself thought the Warren Commission was full of beans. Of course he was in a position to know something we all didn't.

The man in charge of *Ramparts'* investigation of the failure of the Warren Commission to investigate adequately the murder of the 35th President of the United States was Bill Turner, a ten-year veteran of the FBI turned author.

Turner was a nice Catholic boy from Buffalo and a former semipro hockey player, perfect soup meat for the FBI pot; but he was possessed of a fatal streak of independence, and had made the mistake of criticizing the fingernail-cleaning procedures and other obeisance drills so characteristic of Hoover's FBI. He also raised inquiries which, although polite, were not considered in the "best interests" of the Bureau—such as why FBI field offices spent so much time dummying up stolen car statistics, a meaningless record of accomplishment which is to the FBI what body counts are to American commanders in Vietnam, and so little time digging into organized crime. Turner's file bulged with perfunctory congratulatory letters from Hoover on the Special Agent's crime-busting proficiency as a "sound man," which is FBI talk for an electronic bugger, but he was nonetheless punished, by a month's suspension without pay, for his uppityness in asking to discuss his criticisms of the Bureau with J. Edgar himself, a request regarded by the FBI Gauleiters as in the realm of asking for a second bowl of porridge.

As is routinely expected of the person similarly punished in Anglican seminaries or symphony orchestras, Turner was expected to follow an unwritten code of courtly and contrite acceptance of the higher authority justly invoked against him, and exhibit his thankfulness by volunteering for unpaid menial duties around the office, like offering to drive the wife of the Special Agent in Charge to the gynecologist. Turner, instead, went to the Unemployment Office, signed up to get paid during his forced idleness, and took off for a skiing holiday in Aspen.

Retribution came swiftly. Turner was shuttled to the fun spot of Knoxville, Tennessee, where he was not allowed to go outside the city limits on a case, a hindrance in investigating crimes across state lines. At that time there was talk about the alleged intentions of Hoover's nominal boss, Attorney General Robert Kennedy, to lay Kennedy gloves on the FBI's autocratic operations. So Turner wrote the Attorney General, asking that his blackballing by Hoover's lackeys be investigated; he received in return a collect telegram from Bobby, telling him to take such matters up directly with the Director of the FBI. Turner began scratching out lengthy letters to Senators and Congressmen of his acquaintance, suggesting a Congressional inquiry into the mythology of the FBI, and relating certain factual matters tending to create an impression of the Bureau as a cross between an incompetent Gestapo and the Keystone Cops.

Turner was subsequently fired for conduct unbecoming a eunuch. He hired Washington attorney Edward Bennett Williams to sue the Bureau, a fight which went all the way to the

Supreme Court on points of law involving the Congressional and public right to receive information about the malfunctioning of the executive branch without the executive branch interfering by chopping off the head of the word giver. Turner lost. But he caused the FBI such pain in the doing, in the form of highly embarrassing testimony from former FBI men about the absurdities, peccadilloes, institutionalized narcissism and cardboard efficiency of Hoover's private army, that he could in some honesty call the whole thing tit for tat.

Along the way his career metamorphosed, caterpillar-into-flying-object, from cop/bugger to muckraker maintaining journalistic surveillance over the advances and excesses of law enforcement—another editor in the *Ramparts* tradition of career turnarounds.

One evening at a *Ramparts* party Turner was chatting with Bob Treuhaft, Decca Mitford's husband. Treuhaft is a prominent left-wing lawyer in Oakland. Turner kept saying that he was sure they had met before, but Treuhaft kept saying no, he was certain they hadn't, although he was pleased to make the acquaintance. Suddenly Turner put his glass down and said, "Now I remember! It's your voice that's so familiar. When I was in the bureau I used to tap your phone."

With Turner on deck, I went looking for a rope long enough to string up Earl Warren. Some of the people who crashed our lynching party left me with ambivalent feelings about the sanity of our cause. There was a sudden input of bodies from a distaff circle of humanity known as the "sleuths"—volunteers who came out of the woodwork of society to finish the detective work the Warren Commission had left undone. They were an odd lot by any standard of measurement. Some were charlatans or publicity hounds, but most were honest and subdued; the typical "sleuth" was more the concerned suburban housewife than the big city hustler. Some were more paranoid than others, but all shared, to some degree, the paranoia which was the state of nature of their enterprise. This condition was abetted by the wrath of all officialdom, which seemed to descend on their work, a circle of hostility which was completed by the rancor and sarcasm of most of the media.

The sleuths were connected by a grass-roots communications network which was constantly abuzz with gossip and news of the latest "discovery" or new theory. *Ramparts'* interest in the assassination spread like news of a new disease at a convention of hypochondriacs. The *Ramparts* office on San Francisco's topless strip soon became a library, research center, information retrieval system, office, and all-night hot dog stand for free-lance assassination buffs. Many of these amateur crime busters were quite as strange as those they suspected of the crime. But though their methods were unorthodox, they often came up with extraordinary information. An additional attraction to the financially anemic *Ramparts* was that it was all for free. The sleuths worked for the sheer joy of it; in return one was expected to exhibit consummate interest in the details of their handiwork, which at times was a high price to pay. I was forever being stopped in a hallway, or cornered in the office bistro to be subjected to the minutiae of Oswald's alleged love affair with Jack Ruby. One of the most horrific experiences of my life was when a dogged female sleuth trapped me in the men's room, where I was sitting in the loo in a particularly compromised and gaseous state the morning after a long evening of drinking. She lounged against the urinal, lecturing me for half an hour through the stall door about the conspiratorial significance of Oswald's having shaved off all his pubic hair.

The assassination investigation seemed at times like a pageant staged by Busby Berkeley—if I had to cast the Carmen Miranda role, I would give it to Mark Lane. Lane was the New York lawyer and lecture artist who, before Garrison, was chief honcho among the Warren Commission critics. He was one of those people to whom I took an instant and irrational dislike. (Another is the dreadful Al Lowenstein, that boy scout of reform politicians.) I am hard put to explain why; demurring to the laws of slander, I can only cop out to brute instinct. Were I a dog, I would have growled when Lane came around. ("Watch out for the guys who come in fast," Cookie Picetti once told me, meaning that the type of guy who comes through the front door in a hurry, talking a busy streak as he breezes up to the bar, is invariably going to borrow money or

cash a check that will go to the moon and bounce back.)
Perhaps it was Lane's speed that turned me off. He moved
about the world at a roadrunner's pace, a commercially-
minded crusader, developing President Kennedy's murder
into a solid multi-media property. Lane produced a book,
Rush to Judgment, which sold like a Bible beachball at a Baptist
resort; a movie of the same name, which consisted largely of
on the street interviews with witnesses who said Oswald went
thisaway, not thataway; and a long-playing record on which,
for the price of an LP, you could hear Lane's testimony to the
Warren Commission—consisting, if my recollection is correct,
of Lane telling the commission he knew something they didn't
know, but couldn't tell them what it was.

Lane's paranoia had a show-biz cloak-and-dagger frosting;
while making his movie, he slunk around Dallas under an
alias, as if that would fool those conspirators who had been
smart enough to bump off the President and get away with it.
Lane had a tendency to grab bits of evidence like a sea gull
swooping down to snap up a fish, swallowing it whole without
taking time to see if it was anything digestible. This procedure
got Lane in trouble in 1970 when the Kennedy assassination
business was experiencing a recession, and Lane decided to
diversify into the fertile field of Vietnam atrocities. He wrote a
book purporting to be based on interviews with American
soldiers who admitted to various barbarisms and tortures; the
gimmick was that the soldiers did not take refuge in anonym-
ity, but allowed Lane to print their names. However, Neil
Sheehan, ace war correspondent for the New York *Times*,
revealed in a blitzing review of Lane's book, that the
muckraker's report of an alleged Nazi working the Vietnam
atrocity circuit on behalf of Uncle Sam—one of Lane's soldiers
"confessed" that his father was a former blood-lust S.S. officer
serving as a United States Army Colonel in Vietnam—was
deficient in that the Nazi did not possess name, rank or serial
number in the U.S. Army.

For every stridulous Batman there looms a sibilant Robin.
Mark Lane's congener and rival for star billing was Ralph
Schoenman, who surfaced in the assassination business as the

volunteer head of the London office of Lane's "Citizens' Committee of Inquiry." There is scarcely a left wing cause the doorway of which Schoenman has not darkened. He was possessed of a rabbity energy which reminded me of the line of John Barrymore's in Gene Fowler's grand biography of the actor, when Barrymore talks about the rain that "beats with the persistence of an unpaid madam at our door." Schoenman was an indefatigable meddler, a whirling dervish in three-quarter time, a salute without a flag; he circled the globe hundreds of times during the sixties, establishing a reputation as a sort of Red Baron of international unpopular causes. Schoenman was Bertrand Russell's confidential secretary during Russell's last years, and proved a vexatious cross for the great man. The last thing Russell wrote in his life was a personal white paper dissociating himself from many of his aide's statements and activities in his behalf; he had it published posthumously, presumably so that Schoenman could not follow him to the grave. Ralph's capacity to sire dislike was greater than that of any person I have known; Sartre was said to gargle after speaking with him.

Schoenman thrust himself into the Warren Commission controversy in 1965 by bursting through the door of the apartment of Edward Jay Epstein, then a quiet Cornell graduate student hard at work on his uncomplimentary study of the piecemeal procedures of the Warren Commission, which was later to receive notoriety as the book *Inquest*. Epstein had found the FBI report of the Kennedy autopsy that contradicted the Warren Report's lone assassin thesis buried among the hundreds of miles of Kennedy Assassination papers in the National Archives. Schoenman, falsely identifying himself to Epstein as an English publisher, dashed in and demanded a copy of the hot FBI report. Epstein refused, and Schoenman began rummaging through desk drawers, almost pushing the stuffing out of the pillows, and generally behaving as if he were a Florida hurricane just blown in the door. Epstein said he had to yell police to get Schoenman to leave.

Such a stormy visitation from the Radical Opposition must have had a trumatic effect on the cautious and refined graduate student. Epstein, once he could sleep nights without having nightmares about Schoenman, finished writing his book, which made a barnyard joke of the methods and procedures of the Warren Commission. Yet, at the end of this careful document so destructive of the commission's work, Epstein abandoned the discipline of reason for the certainty of intuition. He implied that, despite the fact that he had just proved the commission was not competent to resolve with any certainty if it was raining, its gratuitous assumption that Oswald was the lone assassin was probably the right one, in the first place. The commission's defenders bent over gratefully to accept the graduate student's whiplashes in order to rejoice in the warm glow of his leap to faith. *Inquest* was popularly and controversially received as a biting attack on the Warren Commission. It was, in fact, something else—a secular masterpiece in the classic tradition of Christian apologetics: The writer one-ups the Saracens in his attacks on the foibles of orthodoxy and then, after finding so many things wrong, the writer still believes! Is this not in itself a proof? (Epstein's work was in the tradition of apologists for the Roman Catholic Church who for centuries have suggested that if an institution so filled with fraud, deceit, and corruption could survive all these years without foundering in some Sargasso Sea of dead religions, then that must mean that it is God's One, True Church. How else could it possibly overcome its own dissoluteness?)

Epstein advanced to a new calling, staked on his credentials as a "reasonable" critic of the Warren Commission, as *The New Yorker's* resident debunker of unkempt enemies of the Liberal Establishment. His targets, to date, have been as diverse as District Attorney Jim Garrison and The Black Panther Party for Self-Defense. Perhaps one day Epstein will get it all out of his system by debunking Ralph Shoenman.

While the paper's drawbridges were up against the likes of Schoenman and Lane, the door was open to most everyone else who would throw rocks at the glass house of the Warren Commission. Some pretty funny people came to dinner, and many stayed for a year; some even longer. The roll call of the sleuths contained as many eclectic models as a used car lot. There was Shirley Harris Martin, a fortyish, blue-eyed mother of four, of Hominy, Oklahoma, who was so impressed with John F. Kennedy that she converted to Catholicism in 1960, and when he was shot three years later, dedicated her life to solving the mystery of who had done in her co-religionist. She must have been doing something right, since she was followed by the Dallas cops every time she ventured there to do some sleuthing. A kindly lady, she saved any number of stray dogs from the Oklahoma poundman; she named various of the animals hanging around the house in honor of her fellow sleuths: "Anne-Lise," for Mark Lane's Danish wife; "Vince," for Vincent Salandria, a crew-cut Philadelphia lawyer, one of the earliest questioners of the commission, who exhibited more staying power than many of the sleuths, and stayed with Jim Garrison to the bitter end—an end, some of Salandria's critics among the sleuths say, which was hastened by his "purging" the others in Garrison's camp; the dog "Jonesy" was named after Jones Harris, a rich New York bachelor, said to be the son of Ruth Gordon, who kept his hand in the East Coast operations of the assassination investigators from a command post on the second floor of his elegant Manhattan town house.

The sleuth women outnumbered the sleuth men more than two to one. There was Maggie Field, a nice Beverly Hills lady who was thought to be dying of cancer, but didn't. She had a big house with a swimming pool and a pack of German shepherds. Maggie once dressed her teenage son as Lee Harvey Oswald with a gun stuck in his belt, a rifle in his left hand and copies of the Communist Party *Worker* and the Trotskyite *Militant* in his right hand—Oswald's alarmist pose in the famous incriminating picture printed on the cover of *Life*. Fellow sleuths then took pictures of her son as Oswald, in the hope that their photographs would show up the *Life* picture as a fake, Oswald's head grafted on the body of a poseur, but nothing developed. We provided Maggie with the alias of Marjorie Deschamps for her sleuthing activities. Her stock-broker husband feared becoming the laughingstock of Spring Street—Los Angeles' Wall Street—should word get around that all those assassination freaks were camping out in his backyard, where Mark Lane could often be found floating around in the pool, which he used as a combination office-

bathtub when in Lotusland. Queen Bee among the sleuth ladies was Sylvia Meagher, a widow who worked for the United Nations as a researcher but spent another eight hours a
day clipping and sorting all the bad news about the assassination. Her knowledge of the Warren Report was reputed to be
the most exhaustive and she functioned as the mistress of the
court of last resort of disputes among the sleuths. Among
other females in the assassination juggernaut were Ellen Ray,
a shapely, redheaded Manhattan film maker who twice had
secret documents stolen from her on planes from New Orleans to New York, and Mae Brussels, a sixtyish Carmel
grandmother who took up the assassination as her hobby and
was still going strong, as late as 1974, with a weekly radio
program of conspiracy news that has a high audience rating in
the Big Sur area.

Like feuding Democrats, hardly a one of the sleuths ever
had a nice thing to say about another one. Harold Weisberg, a
Maryland gentleman farmer-sleuth, stated flatly that the
other sleuths were "counterfeiting" his work. In addition to
pounding out his best selling *Whitewash* and its sequels, I
remember reading somewhere that Weisberg was the proud
father of a stillborn brainchild called "Geese for Peace," a
project developed for the Peace Corps which had to do with
geese converting waste into protein. Weisberg said his experiments with the geese were ruined by low-flying helicopters.
Surpassing Weisberg in the capacity to be unloved was David
Lifton, a pushy UCLA engineering student who was known as
"Blowup," since his specialty was enlarging photographs of
Dealey Plaza taken the morning of the assassination and finding figures lurking in the background. Lifton did not like to
hear no for an answer and was persistent in insisting that one
pick out the figure of a man among a forest of black and white
dots in a twenty-times enlargement of a Polaroid snapshot of
Dealey Plaza he toted around like a billboard paster going to
work. It all looked like one huge Rorschach test to me, but one
of our staff writers swore that if you looked at the blow-up
long enough you could make out the figure of a man wearing
a Prussian helmet. Lifton also contributed the "one of the
trees is missing" theory to the literature of the assassination.
By comparing blown-up photographs of Dealey Plaza taken at

a later date to photos taken on November 22, 1963, Lifton discerned that a tree in the famous grassy knoll area was there on November 22, but gone thereafter; this inevitably gave rise to speculation that the missing tree had been camouflage for a sniper.

Of all these ruminations my favorite assassination theory is one floated by Oswald's mother, Mark Lane's client. She explained what had happened that day in Dallas by advancing the theory that Kennedy and Connally shot each other during a political argument in the car.

At the height of the Warren Commission frenzy the paper's office began to take on the appearance of a Grand Central Station for assassination freaks. A small mob of volunteers was in the office day and night searching for the needle in the assassination haystack—the metaphor for piles of files, annotated volumes of evidence and testimony, photographic blow-ups and other tools of the paranoia trade stacked in the hallways.

These conspiratorial-minded interlopers were treated by *Ramparts'* regular New Left staffers like Arabs squatting in at the Tel Aviv Hilton. Scheer took particular umbrage. He regarded the sleuths as a gang of hysterics, ghouls and fetishists who had taken to hanging around his ice cream parlor.

Scheer's attitude was even minded compared with that of most of the left, which exhibited an eagerness bordering on anxiety to accept the Warren Commission's word and be done with it. This was a singular exception to the left's general posture of never taking the government at its word about anything, and I discerned an underlying unarticulated fear—of a witch hunt if not a pogrom—should a new investigation reveal Kennedy as the victim of a leftist plot.

For all the fuss being made by the fourth estate and the political opposition—those titular guardians of the truth —one would think the governmental foul-up had been on the level of the Department of Agriculture being in error in a pamphlet on the reproduction cycle of the boll weevil, instead of the President being bumped off and the public's right to know massacred. The hurry-up Warren Report had been slammed together to meet Lyndon Johnson's political deadline for a "lone assassin" verdict so his predecessor's murder would not be a political issue in the 1964 elections. This miasma was deepened by a bewildering inventory of classified and missing documents, missing X-rays, missing film frames—a Punch and Judy Show of suppressed evidence. I found this especially galling since all the government had to do was declassify the controversial material—such as the Kennedy autopsy records and supporting X-rays—and it could have settled once and for all the most serious challenges to the Warren Commission's verdict, and saved everyone concerned, defenders and attackers, those years of frustration, rumor, conspiracy-mongering, and unresolved doubt.

Over foot-stamping opposition from the left wing of *Ramparts*, I fed the sleuths their vitamins and let them plunge ahead with reconstructing the Warren Commission's boondoggle. There seemed to me little else to do but to keep drilling until we either hit a rock or struck oil. It was tedious work, until we lucked across the King Tut curse.

TEN MYSTERIOUS DEATHS

Once, during a boring panel discussion I responded to a witless question about what "school of editing" I belonged to by answering, "The Nero Wolfe School." I explained that while it was perhaps true that Nero Wolfe never edited much of anything except the small print on the bottom of orchid bulb packages, I nevertheless believed his approach to work to be efficacious and instructive for other disciplines, in particular that of the editor. To be a good editor requires as much the calm doping out of what will move people's minds as blue penciling a writer's words, and both require sitting still. Wolfe just sat on his fat duff and did what detectives are supposed to do, solve mysteries, without ever going anywhere, getting hit on the head, fornicating, climbing in windows or any of the hog wallow that detectives perform between the covers of paperback novels. However, many denizens of the print business seem to feel that meeting the public is an important element of influencing the public. This is to my mind a nonsensical proposition, leading to the circle-jerk intellectual cocktail party circuit and campus lecture tour binges. The lecturing thing has always baffled and horrified me. Many editors and writers of my acquaintance seem to spend as much or more time talking, for money, about what they do than actually doing it; this may boost their pocketbooks or egos, but is of little aid or comfort in actually writing or editing, as such public chitchat is an exhausting indulgence which can only be pursued, as the right wing is wont to say, at the cost of sapping the vital juices. That is one no-no of the Nero Wolfe school. Another is the equally silly belief in nervous movement, going places, seeing things, having meetings, and other trappings of professional persiflage, as somehow contributing to making a good editor—a calling which is, after all, nine-tenths intuition and one-tenth alchemy, with an infinitesimal percentage of burglary. Excessive wayfaring brings with it the unwholesome exposure to strange bars and strange beds, which is productive of melancholy. I therefore avoid traveling, whenever possible, other than to a favorite tavern to read the papers and plot the next move against the world.

It was thus an extraordinary business which brought me, kicking and screaming, to Dallas toward summer's end, 1966. Dallas in August was as dismal as Sunday in heaven, as Marcel Aymé wrote of another time and place. I doubt that anything other than a King Tut's curse could have inspired me to make the trip.

"Death Shall Come on Swift Wings to Him That Touches the Tomb of the Pharaoh": There had been fourteen deaths since King Tut's tomb was opened in 1923, fifteen if you want to include Marilyn Monroe, who was said to have died with a fat gem in her jewel box that had originally been snatched from the sarcophagus of the Tut. But now a small-town newspaper editor near Dallas was said to have uncovered a Kennedy version of the King Tut curse.

The newspaper editor was Penn Jones, Jr., of Midlothian, a small former cotton town some twenty-five miles out of Dallas. The sleuths said he had discovered at least thirteen deaths that were mysteriously related to the assassination of President Kennedy. Disbelieving, I had called John Howard Griffin, a neighbor, Texas style, of Jones, living only some forty miles distant. I asked if he knew this Penn Jones, and if so, what sort of a nut was he? John knew him well. "Penn's a good fellow," he said. "He's the scrappiest editor in Texas. If he says there's been a series of deaths, I'm sure there's substance to it." John Griffin would say something nice about a man who had just run over him, but he would never misstate a fact, or give a false impression; if he took the King Tut's curse in stride, then there had to be something to it.

But if there was something to this one, I was saying disagreeably to myself on the way to the airport, then we may as well check out that rumor that Hitler was alive and living with the Hopi Indians.

Sometimes, only sometimes, the wildest stories turn out to be true. This was one of those times.

The Texas School Book Depository, a pedestrian building even by Dallas standards, was both monument to the assassination carnage and a beacon to its continuing controversy. Three of us who had come to Dallas stood genuflectory fashion in front of it. With me were two *Ramparts* editors working on the assassination—Stanley Sheinbaum of Michigan State University fame, and David Welsh, a former Detroit *News* reporter who had covered the South for *Ramparts* and was gearing up to cover Southeast Asia for the paper; meanwhile, he shared with Gene Marine baby-sitting responsibility on that frenetic part of the paper that had come to be known as the "sleuth desk."

Penn Jones had insisted we "soak up the atmosphere" of the Dallas assassination shrines before making the half hour drive to Midlothian. We dutifully poked around atop the grassy knoll, urinated in a seedy alley near Jack Ruby's boarded-up Carousel Club, visited Oswald's former rooming house in the sprawling Oak Cliff section of Dallas, an entire suburb of ill-repute, and went through the sleuths' checklist of curtsies, handsprings toward the East and such that assassination pilgrims are supposed to perform in Mecca. When those stations of the cross were at last completed, we rented a wheezing Hertz machine which poked along amid the diesel trucks and vintage automobiles, most of them candidates for the

Bonnie and Clyde prop department, that crowded the two-lane blacktop to Midlothian.

Midlothian (population 1,521) was a whistle-stop without a train, a dusty, tree-lined town of modest brick and frame houses. The Midlothian *Mirror* was a weekly, six-page journal which successfully defied all the laws of typography. It was printed on strange, coarse newsprint which had the look of a recycling experiment that had failed. The Midlothian *Mirror* was the genuine item, an indigenous, atavistic frontier weekly which covered the boredom of Midlothian like its dust. Its fighting editor, Penn Jones, Jr., was of a dying breed of populist prairie journalists, an editor who was part *Front Page,* part *Grapes of Wrath.* He had received Southern Illinois University's Elijah Parish Lovejoy Award for Courage in Journalism for beating up a Bircher on his composing room floor. His newspaper appeared to be the only functioning anti-Establishment voice in the shadow of Dallas. Penn's wife ran the linotype, and he did everything else—from writing the editorials to boarding up the front window after receiving a letter to the editor in the form of a firebomb. Penn looked like a wash-and-wear version of Burgess Meredith. He was five foot five, his weathered face had an unfinished texture, as if sandblasted out of balsa wood, and his uneven, receding hairline was semi-crew cut in a style scalped by amateur Indians.

John Griffin had called him "scrappy," and God perhaps had Penn Jones in mind when he created the word. When the city paved the streets in the black section of Midlothian with a gravel loaded with rusty nails, Penn not only wrote about it—he dug some 50 pounds of nails out of the streets and put them on display in his office window for all the world to see. When a lieutenant in the Dallas police department offered Penn the lucrative job of printing the regional KKK newspaper, Penn told him to go to hell. "Half the cops in Dallas belong to the KKK or the Birch society," he said. Penn pledged allegiance to no creed but the truth, which (his corny country parlance gave a dignity to the cliché) he called the "cross and grail" of the newspaperman. He was a card-carrying member of Genuine America and proud of it: he had landed at Salerno with the fighting Texas 36th Infantry in World War II; his collection of barbed wire was the largest, he said modestly, in the continental United States; his pudgy son was the drum major for the University of Michigan marching band. He was especially proud of the esteem in which he was held by his fellow country editors in the Southwest and Midwest, who viewed him as something of a cross between William Allen White and the Green Hornet. When the Frederick, Colorado, *Farmer and Miner* called Penn Jones "the most courageous newspaperman of our time" for his editorials on the assassination in Dallas, that meant more to Penn than the day Walter Cronkite came to take his picture.

I asked Penn why he put out such a crusading newspaper in a place like Midlothian. "This is the only newspaper which cares about Midlothian. If I left, nobody would care."

This man, this prime-rib slice of middle America, swore on a stack of Bibles that a dozen or more people connected with the assassination had met mysterious deaths in its aftermath—and that more deaths were in the cards.

We drove out to Penn's ranch to talk. He wanted to show us his hand-made waterwheel; he boasted it was the only working waterwheel in Ellis County, although it took a kick and a run up the hill to the pump to get it going. Penn found the necessaries and a quart of branch water in a hingeless cupboard in the ranch's ramshackle main cabin, and we sat down to listen to the waterwheel chug in the distance as the editor discoursed in narrative detail on the spidery, black world of Texas politics. He described the several Dallases: the jet stream, superchic, millionaire liberal fashion-plate Dallas of department store owner Stanley Marcus; the fanatic, paramilitary billionaire right-wing Dallas of General Edwin Walker; the crawling lowlife of cheap punks, pimps and perverts in the dingy Dallas of Jack Ruby; the corrupt, stetson-sporting, justice-for-sale, penny-arcade official Dallas. He talked of the "Texas Mafia," those pot-bellied bosom buddies of Lyndon Johnson, the middlemen who also got theirs off the top, who could fix everything from a speeding ticket to a murder charge; of Bill Brammer, Lyndon's former aide who had the poor sense to write a good novel, *The Gay Place,* about

LBJ's world, and how LBJ had destroyed him, crumpled the man up and thrown him away like a used pack of cigarettes.

Penn was just getting warmed up about Dallas by the time he got down to the grit of the assassination. He estimated that he had spent "several thousand hours" reading and knocking on doors, asking questions, attempting to connect the dots in the puzzle left by the Warren Commission. "The Warren Report," he said decisively, "wasn't worth the paper it was printed on." He was not averse to backing up that statement. He ticked off a list of social contacts between Ruby and Dallas police officer Jefferson Davis Tippit, and then between Oswald, who shot Tippit, and Ruby, who shot Oswald, that read like a computer matchmaker's dream datebook. There was the testimony of Oswald's landlady, Earlene Roberts, that a Dallas police car had pulled up in front of the rooming house shortly after the assassination, while Oswald was inside, and honked twice, in some sort of signal, then drove off; Oswald left via the front door a few moments later. There was a list as long as a tattooed man's arm of Oswald's FBI contacts in Texas and New Orleans. And stories like that of Julia Ann Mercer, an eyewitness who was told to deny what she had sworn in writing to the Dallas County Sheriff's Office, and was never called as a witness before the Warren Commission; she had seen a man with a rifle case get out of a green pickup truck and walk up the hill to the grassy knoll above Dealey Plaza minutes before the assassination—the driver of the pickup, she said, was Jack Ruby.

We sat transfixed, listening over the *chung-plung, chung-plung* of the waterwheel to his verbal catalogue of the sins and omissions of the Warren Commission. "I've got a million of them," Penn said. One of the strangest was the story of Rose Chermi. According to police reports Penn had dug up, Ms. Chermi, a lady of less than tender years and experience, had been thrown from a moving automobile near Eunice, Louisiana, on November 20, 1963. A passing good Samaritan picked her up and drove her to a hospital, where she angrily volunteered information to the effect that she was in the employ of Dallas nightclub owner, Jack Ruby, and had been driving to Florida with two of Ruby's men to pick up a

load of narcotics for their boss; during an argument, one of
the men had shoved her out the door of the speeding car. She
also volunteered the information that President Kennedy and
other officials were going to be killed on their impending visit
to Dallas but two days hence. No one took her seriously. After
the assassination, the Eunice authorities thought a little differently and Rose Chermi was questioned further. Shown a
news story the day after Ruby shot Oswald, which quoted
Ruby as denying having previously known Oswald, she
laughed out loud. "They were bed mates," she said. What
further information, if any, Rose Chermi provided was not
later found in the official records of Eunice, Louisiana. And
l'affair Chermi somehow escaped the attention of the Warren
Commission.

When Penn went looking for Rose, he found that she had
been killed by an unidentified hit and run driver, on September 4, 1965, while walking along the side of a highway
near Big Sandy, Texas.

"So that's one of the mysterious deaths," I said.

Penn looked at me as if I were some sensation-mongering
big city journalist.

"Nope," he said. "Not yet, anyway. She's dead all right. But I
haven't finished checking her case out."

No rush, he said. There were plenty of other, duly certified,
mysterious deaths. And there'd be plenty more where they
came from, no doubt; he reckoned he'd be working on the
assassination the rest of his life, there was that much to do.

The tiny Texas editor discussed such matters with the calm
of a reporter who had his scoop down pat, and was just waiting
for the man from Pall Mall cigarettes to come along and give
him its $500 Big Story award. Curses, like rivers, have to start
somewhere, and the string of mysterious deaths connected
with the Kennedy assassination was traced by Penn Jones to a
fateful meeting at Jack Ruby's apartment on Sunday,
November 24, 1963—the night that Ruby shot Oswald. Penn
discovered that three of the five people present at that meeting had died in a mysterious manner afterwards. It was this
discovery which started the Mysterious Death clock ticking.
When we talked, in 1966, the count was around thirteen or

fourteen; Penn's latest tabulation, as of 1974, has the number at one hundred or more. Granted the actuarial tables and hardening of the arteries, that list still amounts, at the least, to a bit of a curse. The first fatalities are instructive of the lot. The two newspapermen who were at Ruby's apartment that night died—by all fair-trade applications of the adverb —mysteriously within a year. Jim Koethe, a reporter for the Dallas *Times Herald,* was killed, as Ed Sanders would say, chop-chop, by a karate blow in the neck when he stepped out of the shower the morning of September 21, 1964. His apartment was ransacked, and two notebooks filled with information on the assassination were taken. The second reporter, Bill Hunter, of the Long Beach *Press Telegram,* was shot to death by a cop while sitting at his desk in the press room of the Long Beach Public Safety Building six months later. Two Long Beach police detectives confessed that they had been horsing around, playing cops and robbers with loaded guns, when one cop dropped his gun and it went off, killing Hunter with a bullet through the heart. The cops were convicted of involuntary manslaughter, but sentence was suspended. The third dead man who had been at Ruby's apartment that night was Tom Howard, a Dallas professional character who, as Ruby's first attorney, had proclaimed that his client should get the Congressional Medal of Honor for shooting Oswald. In 1964, Howard, a healthy and gregarious fellow, began to act in a very nervous manner, then reportedly died of a heart attack at the ripe old age of 48. No autopsy was performed.

From there, Penn Jones's list of dead people who had some connection with the assassination began to balloon:

Nancy Jane Mooney, a stripper at Jack Ruby's Carousel Club, the mother of four, jailed on a disturbing the peace charge, was found hanged by her own toreador pants in her cell in the Dallas City Jail. (In addition to having worked for Ruby, Nancy Jane's tie to the assassination investigation was as the prime alibi for an individual accused of shooting a used car salesman in the head; the salesman had seen a man with a gun fleeing the scene where officer Tippit was shot—and said the man was not Oswald; when he recovered from his wound, and after consulting at length with General Edwin Walker, the car salesman changed his story and said the man with the gun was Oswald, after all, just like the Warren Commission said.)

Housepainter Hank Killam, the husband of Wanda, Ruby's favorite B-girl, and the buddy of a man who lived in the same roominghouse with Oswald, massacred himself on Valentine's Day, 1964, by falling through a plate glass window and severing his jugular vein.

Cab driver William Whaley, who drove Oswald from the Kennedy murder scene, died in a weird head-on collision in 1965. He was the first Dallas cabbie to be killed in action since 1937.

Edward Benavides, the brother and lookalike to an eyewitness to the killing of officer Tippit, was shot in the back of the head in a Dallas beer joint in 1964; when a relative, dissatisfied with the police classification of the shooting as "unsolved," began to poke around on his own, someone took two potshots at him.

The list went on much in the same fashion. The only exception to the editor's scientistlike restraint in naming a person as a mysterious death was the bitchy matter of Dorothy Kilgallen. Penn just couldn't get over the fact that she was the only reporter ever to interview Jack Ruby alone—with no official or unofficial interlopers; just before she died she had been going around New York telling friends that she was about to "bust the Kennedy assassination wide open." She was found dead in bed, reportedly of too many cocktails made of one part alcohol to three parts barbiturates. The thing that freaked Penn was that Miss Kilgallen died on November 8, 1965—the night the lights went out in New York. Fair to jumping up and down over this coincidence, Penn wrote an editorial in the Midlothian *Mirror* titled: "Was It A Mickey?"

"Find out," I asked David Welsh in the plane on our way back to San Francisco, "if all those people are really dead."

Meanwhile, back at *Ramparts'* drydock in San Francisco, there was an armada of sleuths afloat on Dexedrine, attempting to meet the deadline for the November issue, in time to observe the third anniversary of the assassination. They were preparing an encyclopedic broadside against the Warren Commission as "merchants of alibis," to borrow a phrase of the great Mike Gold, that one-man Addison and Steele of American Communist letters. This Song of the Sleuths would be of such sweet clarity as to compel the reopening of the assassination investigation.

Consistent with *Ramparts'* operating procedures, we had a cover before we had a story. Stermer had procured an official color photograph of Jack Kennedy—chin propped on hand, handsome beaver teeth smiling, money-pouch bags around the eyes, comate hairdo shining with vigor. It was a visage suitable for a Camelot airmail stamp. Stermer sent it to a local jigsaw puzzle manufacturer with instructions to make a puzzle out of the picture of the martyred President. We figured the jigsaw maker for a Republican, since he got the finished puzzle back to us, as several boors in the office noted, in jig time. Before sending it off to the engraver, the art director removed a few pieces from the bottom of the puzzle, for dramatic effect. Keating wanted to improve on the idea and take pieces out of JFK's head, exactly where he had been shot. Stermer refused, and after considerable pushing and pulling of Kennedy jigsaw pieces, the art director carried the day. The assassination-puzzle cover ready, I waited for the sleuths to deliver their giant speckled egg so long in gestation; the time had come to crack open the Warren Commission.

The sleuths' manuscript was a monument to the irrelevance of logic. Slightly less bulky than the Manhattan Yellow Pages, our counterthesis was as academic, convoluted and tautological as the Warren Report itself. It was a goddamn legal brief; I wanted something that would get people talking about the Warren Report with the cynicism they did about the weather report. All public opinion polls and other scientific ilk belong in the same cocked hat; they are loaded in the first place, since they weight the question simply by bringing it up. In my book, the only reliable indicator of what is weighing on the national consciousness is what people are talking about in neighborhood bars. The books that had come out criticizing the Warren Report had stirred the nation's intellectuals but left the masses becalmed. I wanted to churn the bars.

I stuck my head in the door of David Welsh's office. "Did you find out if all those people are dead?"

"So far, ten check out. Ten dead," he said.

"Ten's enough," I said. "Pin it all on Penn Jones."

I threw out the 30,000 plus words of sleuth sweat and tears. To purple gazes of hate and small gurgling sounds of rage from the sleuths, I ripped apart the entire magazine and, over the weekend it was scheduled to go to press, inserted a special section of Penn Jones's "mysterious death" editorials from the Midlothian *Mirror*. It was accompanied by Welsh's report, titled "In the Shadow of Dallas," which related with spartan objectivity the story of how the small-town newspaper editor in Texas had discovered a series of deaths related to the assassination of President Kennedy, and that all these people were, indeed, dead. The tone was that of *Dragnet*: slightly incredulous but respectful of the facts. We included Dorothy Kilgallen on the list of those mysteriously dead—but with a question mark after her name. I rewrote the lead for the Kilgallen section in a manner conducive to the raising of an interesting rumor, but not a flag:

"We know of no serious person who really believes that the death of Dorothy Kilgallen, the gossip columnist, was related to the Kennedy assassination. Still . . ."

Amnesia is said to be curable by a good hit on the head; national amnesia may be no different, as the use of King Tut's hammer proved most effective. The "mysterious deaths" became an overnight sensation. *Ramparts* sold out, and went back on the presses. Penn Jones found himself catapulted to the status of instant folk hero. Walter Cronkite dispatched a film crew to Midlothian and devoted long segments of three consecutive CBS newscasts to Penn Jones's Big Story. European newspapers ran scare headlines, while many American papers editorialized against anyone taking seriously such sagebrush rumors—but in denying a conspiracy the press found itself in the unexpected position of promoting a curse. Mysterious deaths were suddenly reported everywhere, from the gruel dished up in drug-store tabloids, to the mass slicks; *Cosmopolitan* reprinted the *Ramparts* story in its conspiratorial entirety, which was one of the last acts of the old management before Helen Gurley Brown took over and began asking men to take off their clothes in the centerfold. Some time later I was in a proletarian bar in outer Brooklyn, and, over a beer, I heard a toothless old lady tell the fellow next to her about "all these people who got murdered down in Texas because they knew who killed President Kennedy"—I knew then that the national consciousness barrier had been cracked.

The sleuths were unhappy. Although I had got a good national buzz going in their cause, they were so upset at my trashing their manuscript that had I brought the sun whirling down to the crowd at Fatima on their behalf, I doubt they would have approved. Missionaries like to control the process of conversion, and do not always find miracles to their taste. David Lifton, the supersleuth, sat grumping in my office one afternoon while I attempted to explain that it is necessary to break the ice before you can go swimming in winter; now that people were talking about the assassination in neighborhood pubs, the public attention span for considering the Warren Commission's misfeasance had been sufficiently expanded so that people might even be willing to look at one of his blow-ups and see a rifleman in the bushes.

Unable to appeal to any higher authority, I retreated to citing Hinckle's Laws of Advocacy Journalism, which I had made up that instant, just to shut him up:

"Listen, buddy," I said, "if you can't prove a conspiracy, settle for a curse."

Finally, a regrettable incident occurred which caused me to be drummed out of the ranks of the sleuths.

A book review came into the office that was a rather funny satire on the excess of insignificant detail and latent necrophilia in the ballooning literature of criticism of the Warren Report. It was in the form of a review of a nonexistent book, *Time of Assassins,* allegedly a privately published, four-volume work printed on slick paper and written by a Franco-Russian sociologist of Levittown, New York, one Ulov G. K. Leboeuf. The satire had been written by Jacob Brackman and Faye Levine. It skirted the absurd in a somewhat heavy-handed fashion, praising the fictional author Leboeuf for linking the

Kennedy assassination with the deaths of Aldous Huxley, Marilyn Monroe and Adlai Stevenson, and tied in the conspiracy with George Hamilton's "evasion" of the draft and Ben Bella's ascent to power. But it was worth a chuckle, and the paper had been grim lately, so—to Scheer's great joy—I decided to run it, and in the book review section, lest we belabor the obvious. Besides, the mysterious deaths story was running in that issue and I thought it might confuse the readers if the spoof was in the body of the paper along with the spook story.

The "book" was listed thus in *Ramparts* in the time-honored book review fashion:

TIME OF ASSASSINS by ULOV G. K. LEBOEUF. Levittown, N.Y.: Ulov G.K. Leboeuf. 4 Vols. I: 495 pp., II: 387 pp., III: 691 pp., IV: 460 pp. $24.

The November issue of *Ramparts* appeared on the newsstands in Manhattan on a Tuesday. By Wednesday evening, Bookmasters had received over 100 orders for the $24 set of *Time of Assassins*. The demand increased geometrically each day. The *Ramparts* switchboard in San Francisco was besieged with long-distance calls from readers who couldn't find "Leboeuf" in their local bookstores, and from hungry booksellers who wanted to stock such a hot item but couldn't raise the author and publisher in Levittown information. Over three hundred people sent checks for $24 to *Ramparts* in an effort to acquire the hard-to-get volumes. My sister, Marianne (aka Vampira), a roving *Ramparts* editor in charge of trouble, drew the duty of writing all three hundred souls, returning their money and explaining in the nicest possible way that they had been had.

Within the ranks of booksellers and Kennedy assassination enthusiasts, "Leboeuf" created the same kind of havoc that Orson Welles' notorious Mercury Theatre broadcast of *War of the Worlds* did in certain panicked hamlets in New Jersey. That was to say nothing of the reaction within the ranks of the sleuths themselves, who recognized the review for the fraud and deceit that it of course was and reacted with angina pectoris, chain letters of canceled subscriptions, historical analogies to Pearl Harbor, and cursory threats of physical violence. The cold unbridled fury of the sleuths was given its most eloquent statement in a letter from Sylvia Meagher, who wrote that the publication of such a sordid lampoon "places you in the same camp with the outright pornographers and other befouled merchants who are assassins of the human spirit."

I wrote a monthly column in the front of the magazine with the standing title "Apologia," and there I apologized to one and all for the laying of so unexpected an egg. I thought that would be the end of it; but I was wrong. "Leboeuf" would not die from a simple declaration of its nonexistence. A month later, the Boston *Globe* ran a front-page feature story on the critics of the Warren Commission by two investigative reporters who had been assigned to dig into the controversy and give the readers the straight poop. The reporters ridiculed most of the critics, including and especially *Ramparts*, as irresponsible and unbelievable. Nevertheless, the *Globe*'s article postulated that the assassination inquiry should be reopened anyway, because despite crackpots such as *Ramparts*, substantive questions had been raised in serious and responsible works on the assassination—among them the interesting new study of sociologist Ulov G.K. Lcbocuf of Levittown. . . .

A year later, the paper was sued for libel for the one and only time in my five years' stewardship. The service was from Texas, and the complainant a janitor in Parkland Hospital in Dallas, one Darrell Tomlinson. Mr. Tomlinson was the man who found the Warren Commission s Bullet No. 399, the superbullet, on Governor Connally's stretcher. He was so mentioned in the Warren Report, and correctly identified in the Leboeuf book review, but from there the satirists had run amuck, implicating the janitor in the fantasy-plot through his "clubfooted wife named Mary from whom he was divorced," and who was said to actually be, through a very complicated lineage, a second cousin to Jack Ruby; and living secretly in Las Vegas "as the commonlaw wife of one Officer Toasty," an FBI agent the satirists linked sexually to Oswald.

The lawsuit asked for a perfunctory million dollars. I

passed the matter on to Bruce Stilson, our libel lawyer, who reported that the action by the distressed Mr. Tomlinson included among the defendants a San Diego book publisher, Publishers Export, Inc., which had recently distributed a book on the Kennedy assassination titled *Oswald Alone?* The authors of *Oswald Alone?* had apparently been impressed by the non-existent Leboeuf's credentials as a scholar and investigator—so much so that they had gone Leboeuf one better and suggested conclusions in their book, based on the "coincidences" of Leboeuf's fictional evidence, that the sage of Levittown himself had not dared to make.

Thus Mr. Tomlinson alleged in his formal complaint that, in spite of the fact that his former wife was *not* club-footed *nor* named Mary, and that he had never used an alias let alone been known by the name of one "Artemis Heverford" (as he was identified in the satirical review), he "has received and been subjected to many insults and abuses from various persons by telephone or otherwise from all parts of the United States as a result of said statements to the extent that he has been required to avoid most telephone communications and obtain a non-listed telephone number; that his life has been threatened as a result thereof by anonymous calls at all hours of the night; all of which has caused. . . . . stress of mind and mental anguish. . . . ."

It is sobering testimony to the state of investigative journalism in San Diego that the authors of *Oswald Alone?*, unable to find Leboeuf's four-volume work in the library, were undeterred in their zeal—even unto listing *Time of Assassins* by Ulov G. K. Leboeuf in their bibliography, citing the *Ramparts* fictitious book review as documentation.

Stilson hired Dean Carlton of Dallas as local counsel, and together they were able to obtain a dismissal of the lawsuit against *Ramparts* on the technical ground that the magazine was so unpopular in Texas that it did not sell enough copies there to establish it as doing business in that state. The judge who determined the case was United States District Judge Sarah T. Hughes, whose previous connection with the Kennedy assassination was her swearing in of Lyndon B. Johnson aboard Air Force One.

THE MINUTEMEN WANT TO HELP

My political education around this time was advanced by learning the distinction between left-wing Minutemen and right-wing Minutemen. Far from being a relatively cohesive block of lunatics, the gun-toting paramilitary right was split between the anti-Communist Minutemen, in some relative position approximating a left on the fanatical right, and the late George Lincoln Rockwell's American Nazis, located farthest to the racist and anti-Semitic right, with those armed bigots operating under sheeted cover of the Ku Klux Klan somewhere toward the middle—liberals on this bizarre spectrum.

Turner was my mentor in all this, having somehow gained the confidence of Robert DePugh, the head Minuteman, after doing a *Ramparts* article on the right-wing gun slingers. Turner wrote that the Minutemen were a dangerous, well-organized, well-financed, well-armed and well-disciplined assembly of vicious right-wing commandos with the human compassion of electric eels. The Minutemen seemed genuinely pleased by this description, and thought Turner a regular fellow for taking issue with his former boss, J. Edgar Hoover, who had recently pooh-poohed the Minutemen as a "paper organization" that was no threat to national security, unlike the very real menace of that gaggle of incendiaries in the W. E. B. Du Bois Clubs. When Turner wrote that the Minutemen had twenty times the members and eight hundred times the weapons that the FBI credited them with, he had himself a friend for life in DePugh. Militant right-wingers are like that: They don't care if people like them, they just want them to be scared pissless of them.

DePugh was a balding veterinarian who took good care of the cats and dogs in Norborne, Missouri, a town distinguished by the stanzas of the Hail Mary being posted on Burma Shave signs along its main highway. The veterinarian once invented a Molotov cocktail which utilized Tampax for a wick; I found the idea irresistible, but, even though Turner brought back explicit directions from DePugh, I never could get the hang of fixing the Tampax wick on the bottle.

As the Lord says in *The Green Pastures*, even bein' Gawd ain't
a bed of roses. DePugh, who considered himself a responsible
extremist, was worried sick over the uncontrolled activities of
Minutemen "defector" groups which were springing up
around the nation like weeds along a highway. These renegade riflemen had bolted the organization's central authority, drifting off toward the sign of the Horst Wessel, or becoming freelance sharpshooters for hire against any target veer-
ing leftward from the American Medical Association. DePugh
complained that he had to spend too much time dashing
about the country breaking up unauthorized snipings, instead
of tending to the important Minuteman business of secreting
caches of arms and ammunition and establishing gun-making
workshops in strategic hiding places in preparation for the
invasion of the Red Menace. (The workshops were deemed
especially important since the fifth columnists running the
government would of course cut off the people's access to
automatic weapons, and it would become necessary to fabri-
cate them. "It is better to buy one lathe," said DePugh, in the
solemn manner of Father Christopher talking about lighting
one candle, "than a dozen machine guns.")

The Minutemen leader had recently nipped two rump
Minutemen ambushes in the bud. The targets were Senator J.
William Fulbright and Stanley Marcus of Dallas. The contracts on both men, DePugh said, had been put out by certain
spoiled billionaires in Dallas—one of whom had turned out to
be a nut using an alias who was put in an asylum after his check
bounced. Then there was the messy business of a Minuteman
plot to dump cyanide in the ventilators at the United Nations.
That had gone as far as the purchase of ten gallons of potas-
sium cynaide when it was discovered by DePugh loyalists who,
not wishing to bother the boss, had arranged to punish the
cyanide deviationists by shooting them in a room lined with
butcher paper, so as not to bloody up the floor. But the cops
got wind of it and everybody was arrested. A mother cat with
too many kittens, DePugh was having a rough time keeping
track of his illegitimate offspring, and no wonder: A former
Minuteman told Turner that there were only some 8,000
mainline Minutemen in the country—and some 80,000 ex-

Minutemen and neo-Minutemen in splinter groups and
Eagle-worshipping societies, over which the main lodge had
lost all control.

Now their leader had yet another concern: He suspected
that some of his fallen away riflemen who had drifted off to
the Nazi sandbars along the shore of Southern California had
been part of a rifle team shooting at President Kennedy at
Dallas. Master Marksman DePugh scoffed at the idea of Oswald scoring those hits on his own; his opinion was that the
President had been caught in a "classic guerrilla crossfire" at
Dealey Plaza.

DePugh was so concerned about cleaning up his
organization's act that he offered *Ramparts* the resources of
the Minutemen's extensive intelligence system—the Minutemen said they had infiltrated both the American Nazi Party
and the FBI—and access to its carefully guarded card files of
Gold Star right-wing fanatics, which confidential records
were chemically coated to self-destruct in the event of a government raid. DePugh's objection to the Kennedy assassination was technical and legal, not political; I had the impression
that he would not have minded the business of bumping off
Kennedy had it been done according to Minutemen
regulations—but such suspicions about one another are
properly suppressed by wartime allies. His tender of help was
quite earnest, and we accepted it in the good faith it was
offered.

I timidly asked a favor that the Minutemen might do the
paper. The decibel count of paranoia in our offices had
reached a new high pitch with the recent arrival of a letter,
signed by "The California Minutemen," which warned in the
time-honored rhetoric of death threats that time was running
out for the editors of *Ramparts* unless they changed their
"nefarious ways." I hoped some conciliatory word from the
Moses of the Minutemen might calm the staff jitters. Word
came down from the Rockies that we should not fear and, sure
enough, it was later discovered that "The California Minutemen" was an organization with a membership of one, a cranky
San Francisco mailman who had begun delivering death
threats to everyone in the town whom he didn't like. (One

other request was less favored. I was drooling at the thought of those Minutemen card files—a bonanza of guilt by association for cross-checking routine questions of paranoia. But discreet inquiries about *Ramparts* footing the bill to put the whole system on a computer for instant reference were gently rebuffed.)

The Minutemen showed themselves to be as much doers as talkers, which is something that cannot be said of their ideological opposites on the left. When Turner and Bill Boxley, an investigator from Garrison's staff, scoured the briar patches of Southern California in search of a missing link to the assassination, the Minutemen were as helpful as could be. They provided *carte d'identité* to sundry Minutemen units, and to the armed religious camps with whom DePugh was engaged in intraservice rivalry on the right. One was "The Church of Jesus Christ-Christian," the hyphen-Christian being a signal that a dirty Jew like Jesus couldn't get in the door; this fundamentalist Church worshipped the gods of race prejudice, and the Church-sponsored radio programs in Florida and California logged over one million mucus-eared listeners; the more devout among the faithful spent their worship hours in close military drill, preparing for the Inevitable. Some members of the sect even made threats of bodily harm to Billy Graham in 1961 when the minister committed the sin of playing golf with JFK.

But the DePugh follower who drank of the deepest waters was the Reverend Dallas Roquemore, a Californian who went around looking in stables, as he was certain that the Russians were buying up all of our horses to merge with all of their horses to mount a Cossack-style attack on Southern California, rendering automobiles and armored cars alike useless on the jammed freeways. Roquemore was accidentally shot to death when he sneaked up behind a Minutemen recruit to test his reactions—which were good.

Turner dined out for some time with stories of the Eric Ambler style "security" precautions taken for meetings with these Woody Allen militarists, most of whom seemed to live at home with their mothers. One meeting with an Orange County choirmaster and Minutemen executive was moved to three different sites—first from his house, where his mother nervously said he wasn't home as the back door slammed, then to a coffee shop, where an underwear salesman of harried appearance came up and whispered the number of a room in a nearby motel. There Turner and the New Orleans detective were frisked by a bodyguard wearing a plaid hunting jacket and a Dodgers' cap. Everyone in the room was told to toss his gun on the bed—a friendly precaution that is customary in some circles of the paramilitary right. Garrison's man tossed in his Police Special .38, which made Turner the only one in the room without a gun to put in the kitty. When the Minutemen leader walked into the room, the first thing he told Turner was what a great article he had written about what menacing bastards the Minutemen were.

DePugh assigned his best Sherlock Holmes types to the riddle of Dealey Plaza. They came up with a clue that Watson would have saluted. Rifle clubs are to Minutemen as kennel clubs are to dog fanciers, and DePugh's investigators located a rifle buff who had found a singular device discarded on the ground in Dealey Plaza the day of the assassination—an ingeniously constructed piece of plastic piping which the rifle experts said was used to stuff down a rifle barrel for the purpose of changing its bore. DePugh was excited by this discovery, because it meant that the bullets from Oswald's rifle—the only concrete evidence linking him to the assassination—could have been rigged to be fired from more technically proficient rifles in the hands of marksmen, and after the shooting was over the only evidence left would be Oswald's incriminating bullets.

Regrettably, the Minutemen were not able to pursue this line of investigation, and the telltale piece of plastic tubing was somehow lost to posterity, when FBI agents arrested DePugh on Missouri bail-jumping charges at his New Mexico hideout near the rustic town of Truth or Consequences. (That was the real name.)

DePugh then spent several years as a resident in federal prison in Atlanta where, he once wrote Turner, those Minutemen inside beat the John Birch Society, 1-0, in softball.

If the good neighbor policy of the paramilitary right did not seem peculiar to me at the time, it was because I had stepped through the looking glass into that shadow world of intelligence derring-do where the bizarre became the commonplace, and half truths were the only constructive grammar. The real thing was not as tidy as the classy spy fiction of John Le Carré and Noel Behn would have it. The only constants were corruption and degeneracy, and there was more double-dealing and double-crossing among compatriots than those classy tricks intelligence services play on one another in the movies.

It was a technicolor nightmare, and it was anything but slick. The shadow nucleus of the Kennedy assassination seemed surrounded by a clownish penumbra—a kaleidoscope of swamp mists and strange noises night and day, where there was no black or white but only vile oranges and purples smothered in gray—an undulating demiworld of never clearing fog, formed by the confluence of the hot air of Caribbean intrigue with the chill jet stream of Cold War politics, hanging damp and sticky over the southeastern rim of the United States.

The professional scum who had CIA meal tickets—errand boys, cheap-shot artists, blackmailed homosexuals, cooperating crazies, ex-cops lusting after red blood and low-life thrills—seemed to thrive in this absurd climate, where their intelligence covers gave them immunity to make an illegal buck on the side, sometimes with official approbation; if smuggling guns or dope was their "cover," they pocketed the profits. The mess had more levels than the Moscow subway. The atmosphere of intelligence and organized crime was further complicated by political vibrations from the foot-stamping restlessness of those thousands of illegal soldiers on American soil, professed freedom fighters for a capitalist Cuba, who, lured by the propaganda of armed return and by the CIA's largesse, remained bivouacked in cheap rooming houses and swamp holes along that ninth-inning stretch of the Gulf of Mexico from the Petticoat Junction of New Orleans to the Caribbean Cold War capital of Miami. These beached *gusanos* had cash in their pockets and guns in their hands, but nowhere to go and nothing to do. Inevitably, many of them drifted into such profitable mischief as high-stakes dope-importing, gun-running, Caribbean black-marketeering, and general backstabbing for hire. They also fell in with various American fringe groups—frenzied anti-Communists of paramilitary bent—with whom the stranded Cuban guerrillas shared feelings of betrayal and bitterness toward Washington.

(The Cubans, I believe, had objective cause for their anger. They were suckered by the CIA into smoking the long pipe of overthrowing Castro and then left stranded on the beaches at the Bay of Pigs. Similarly, Washington encouraged masses of Cubans to leave home—creating a refugee population of over half a million in the Greater Miami Area alone—but when it became clear that Castro, despite the CIA, was there to stay, the American Government was unwilling to accept responsibility for the unassimilated refugee population it had caused to be so artificially encamped on the shores of the world's greatest melting pot. Many Cubans regarded it as an exercise in black humor when Congress finally got around to passing a Cuban refugee aid bill that exempted exiled Cubans from paying U.S. income taxes—if they could find a job to earn any money not to pay taxes on.)

In this mosaic of intrigue few facts could be certain, but we learned enough to establish the unrebuttable presumption that the Warren Commission had covered up the involvement of U.S. clandestine intelligence operations in the Kennedy assassination; of the jillion things that remained uncertain, the most troubling was whether the government cover-up had been motivated by embarrassment or complicity.

At any rate, the intelligence backgrounds of both minor and major characters in the assassination drama were inescapable, although their individual stories often were unsuitable for *Night Gallery* on grounds of unbelievability.

If some of the assassination stories we stumbled across had overtones of Kafka, others were more Marquis de Sade. Queen bee of the bizarre types was David Ferrie, a homosex-

ual of fantastic ways. Garrison's inquest centered for a time on
Ferrie's ubiquitous role in the web of strange circumstances of
the assassination. Garrison once called him "one of history's
most important individuals." Certainly he was one of history's
strangest. A former Eastern Airlines pilot fired for leading
too active a gay life at 30,000 feet, Ferrie became an apostle of
theological anti-Communism. He declared himself to be a
priest of the Apostolic Orthodox Old Catholic Church, a
curious sect catering to the paranoid right and upwardly-
mobile homosexuals. Ferrie kept vestments, a crucifix, chalice
and other priestly artifacts in his crowded New Orleans
apartment—along with military supplies including Army
field telephones, guns, flares and 100-pound ordnance
bombs. Ferrie was also an amateur cancer researcher of some
repute and kept caged mice for his experiments. He was the
type of weirdo the CIA seemed to find useful. By profession
an instructor in the Louisiana Civil Air Patrol, he trained
Cuban pilots in Guatemala for the Bay of Pigs. Ferrie himself
made several solo fire-bombing raids on the island republic in
1961, piloting a Piper Apache owned by Eladio del Valle, an
ex-Batista henchman who escaped with considerable loot and
became involved in narcotics trafficking. Ferrie was once involved in a bizarre plot involving, of all things, a homosexual
who played the organ in the officers' mess in Fort Benning,
Georgia; other homosexuals branded him a witch hunter for
the CIA, who entrapped gay officers in compromising posi-
tions and then turned them over to the CIA, which blackmailed them into doing things they shouldn't. Ferrie was also
an investigator for a New Orleans detective agency run by a
former New Orleans police chief as a private anti-Communist
intelligence service. The pilot was often seen with exiled Cubans who wore military fatigues, and he once loaned Lee
Harvey Oswald his New Orleans library card.

    Garrison had connected Ferrie with half the suspicious
characters indexed in the Warren Report, and was planning
to arrest him when he was found dead in his apartment, either
of an embolism or a karate chop. The day Ferrie was found
dead in New Orleans, his boss, del Valle, was found dead in

Miami, shot in the heart and his head split in half by a machete, but that was of course a coincidence.

My eyebrows ached from rising at the ooo-la-la life styles of the CIA types we found submerged in the intelligence swamp surrounding the assassination, and I began to wonder what the heralded CIA "connection" was all about.

Silly boy, an espionage-wise and cynical friend said to me, did you think the CIA was running a tennis club?

My friend was from a distinguished Eastern seaboard family. He had worked for the CIA for ten years, before concluding that his father had been right when he told him he was rich enough not to work for a living if he didn't care to, and never mind the bourgeois conventions about having a job. He therefore retired, at 41, to write novels and hike in the Adirondacks.

Although we did not agree about many things politically, he was more than happy to set me straight about the CIA. He proceeded to give me a proper dressing down for my naïveté. Was I some sort of a Protestant dope like John Lindsay, who thought the world could be straightened out with *Robert's Rules of Order*? He said he would straighten me out about the Kennedy assassination theories and countertheories. I must warn the reader that his interpretation is about as favorable to the CIA as it is possible to be under the circumstances. He put it to me thus:

"The movies have fancied up the spy business, and the adventure-hungry academics who joined the agency have given it an Ivy League frosting, but the filling is rotten like a cream puff filled with pus. In some ways, it has to be like that. Spies must operate in the scumbelt of humanity cinching the world; the scum attracts the weak, and weakness is the backbone of intelligence. Without weakness and greed there would be no spies or counterspies. The system depends on the bribe and blackmail—those are the basic tools of intelligence, the pen and pencil, the hammer and sickle—but they can only be applied to soft spots. If you can't find a soft spot, you make one: That's why agents employ the corrupt to compromise the weak, when necessary. Where else would the fishermen of espionage search for their minnows but in the pools of miscast and misfit humanity? These people have no existence to be proud of, so they are willing to change it for the purposes of a job. And, they are expendable.

"It is a rotten business, to be sure, but the name of the game is results—and a satisfactory result is just maintaining the status quo. You shouldn't be surprised that a lot of people have to spy, and people even have to die, and a lot of dredge go under the bridge unnoticed, just to keep things the way they are—between nations, and between intelligence establishments. Those people in the business who still have consciences tell themselves that in a rotten world, it becomes necessary to spread a little more rot, just for the limited but desperate purpose of keeping the whole shebang from collapsing of its own dry rot."

I asked if he thought the CIA would go so far as to kill the President.

Negative, my friend said. Highly unlikely, anyway. "Intelligence is not in the business of overthrowing the government. If the CIA ever bumped a President, they'd have a war with the Pentagon for ultimate power. They need the President as a buffer; the executive is something to influence and manipulate, not destroy. Even a hostile President isn't that much trouble for the CIA. These guys have got staying power. Look how long Hoover hung around, and he didn't have half the shit on people that the Agency has in its files."

Well, then, I asked, could individual agents, or their hangers-on have done it?

"Of course. It wouldn't surprise me. Oswald obviously had an intelligence background. And the CIA in the sixties was spread as thin and was as long and as screwed up as a tapeworm. If it wiped its ass it couldn't be sure if it was its own hand that was doing it.

"The CIA kept all those poor Cubans on the string for years after the Bay of Pigs—it had them running around all over the place, using the CIA's guns and money for God knows what. Most of them ended up in narcotics or smuggling of some kind. It's not unlikely, either, that some agency guys would work out a deal on the side with them. Opium smuggling was standard operating procedure for CIA and Air America guys in Southeast Asia. It was a goddamn fringe benefit.

"But you can be sure of this. If any of the CIA people, regulars or fly-by-nights, were involved in any way in the assassination, the CIA would cover it up. And that isn't just a matter of complicity—it's a matter of survival for them. Even the involvement of minor agents acting unilaterally would open such a public can of worms that the Agency could never go fishing the same way again.

"Now, I'll bet on this too: The CIA would take care of those people privately. Their eyeballs would be on somebody's cuff links. But at the same time the agency would do anything they had to—even kill—to keep the lid on."

I must confess that *Ramparts* contributed little toward reducing the smog of alarmism hanging over Garrison's investigation when I ran a cover on the DA which was half a tightly-cropped picture of his studious face, the other half, in large type, this out-of-context quotation from Garrison: *"Who appointed Ramsey Clark, who has done his best to torpedo the investigation of the case? Who controls the CIA? Who controls the FBI? Who controls the Archives where this evidence is locked up for so long that it is unlikely that there is anybody in this room who will be alive when it is released? This is really your property and the property of the people of this country. Who has the arrogance and the brass to prevent the people from seeing the evidence? Who indeed?*

"The one man who has profited most from the assassination—your friendly President, Lyndon Johnson!"

With the exception of the unlikely bedfellows of *Ramparts, Playboy,* and the *New York Review of Books,* Garrison had a solidly hostile national press. Among the sidebars of history to the Kennedy assassination, it has always struck me that the most singular was the cooperation of the government and the major media to sanctify the sleight of hand of the Warren Commission and to dump on its critics. This began long before Garrison got in the act. Of course those were the halcyon days before the Pentagon Papers, when cooperation and gentlemanly agreement were the rule of thumb between the Eastern Establishment's media branch in New York and its governmental apparatus in Washington.

Much of the beating Garrison took from the media was his own fault. When his investigation became bogged down in the intelligence swamp which was the real milieu of the assassination, Garrison adopted the practice, inadvisable for a swamp guide, of grabbing some slimy green thing out of the water and holding it up for the press to see, as if that showed how the ecology of the swamp worked. The denouement of the Garrison story belongs to the tradition of *Waiting for Godot,* except that we are still waiting. The more viperous among the sleuths now maintain that the CIA "got" to the DA, but I think not. The truth is considerably more commonplace. The blue meanies got to Jim. Angered by his Faustian sparring matches with the press, distraught from defections within his own staff of investigators, frustrated by the refusal of other states to extradite his suspects, physically run down from a recurrent bad back, yet propelled forward by the high octane of paranoia, Garrison eschewed the probably hopeless alternative of amassing sufficient evidence of the government's cover-up of its intelligence agencies' involvement to get Washington to reopen formally the assassination investigation.

The prosecutor in him rising with his temper, Garrison elected to go for the kill. Since he could not get to many of his prime suspects, he opted to hang it all on Clay Shaw, the New Orleans businessman he had put in the dock for alleged complicity in the assassination. As Garrison escalated his pronouncements during the long waiting period before the trial, the guilt or innocence of Shaw became synonymous in the public mind with the truth or falsity of the assassination probe.

I was worried, and sent Sidney Zion, a former Assistant U.S. Attorney, then a legal correspondent for the New York *Times* and then a friend, to New Orleans to check out Garrison's case. Zion came back scratching his balding head. "Idono," he said, "if Jim's got what he says he's got on that guy, he's got a hellofa case; but he wouldn't show me what he had."

It took two years for the Shaw case to get to trial, a period during which many people lost interest, among them, seemingly, Jim Garrison. He went through the motions of pursuing the investigation, but when the trial date arrived, Jim turned his big case over to an assistant district attorney, barely showing up in the courtroom, except to make a dramatic midnight summation to the jury. As powerful as Jim's oration was, the jury seemed more impressed by the admission of one of the witnesses for the prosecution, who said he had been hypnotized over 100 times by his "enemies." It returned an acquittal. Garrison then turned around and rearrested Shaw for perjury, on the ground that, among other things, he had lied under oath by saying that he was not guilty as charged.

Despite the collapse of Garrison's investigation, the government has continued to act as if he knows something they don't want others to know. In July of 1971 the DA was indicted by a federal grand jury on charges of taking bribes to protect illegal pinball games in New Orleans. Attorney General John Mitchell himself announced the indictment. The media coverage of the DA surrendering himself to federal agents was as extensive as that for Mardi Gras.

The press somehow missed a considerably more significant Garrison story some ten months later. In May of 1972, the government's main witness against the DA formally recanted his testimony and said that the whole pinball charge was a frame-up engineered by the Department of Justice. In an interview televised in Canada by the Canadian Broadcasting Company, but blacked out in the United States, the witness said that in return for swearing a false affidavit against Garrison, the Justice Department had supplied him with a false name and a false birth certificate for his son and sent him to Canada where he had an $18,000-a-year job with General Motors—but never had to do any work because the salary was his "pay off." The Justice Department had no comment to inquiries from the Canadian press. Most American papers didn't ask. [Jim was eventually found innocent.]

That is far too glum a note on which to end about Jim Garrison. He is a remarkable piece of Americana, wild and imperfect man that he is.

There is one Garrison story that cheers me up. It was at a time that the conspiracy bubble was just beginning to crumple. The District Attorneys' Association—sort of the Elks Club of big and little city DA's—was holding one of its many national gatherings in fun New Orleans, and most of the nation's DA's were there.

The main event was a dinner-dance-soiree for the DA's and their wives in the ballroom of the Royal Orleans Hotel. Garrison, as the host District Attorney, was scheduled to speak. The program committee had elicited a solemn promise from Garrison's chief aide that Jim's remarks to his fellow DA's would deal with subjects other than the Kennedy assassination.

The afternoon of the dinner, Jim met with the program committee. He was excited. A "major break" had developed in his investigation in Dallas, he said, which he would announce during his speech that evening. His fellow District Attorneys reminded Jim of the pledge to assassination silence. But he was not to be put off. He said he was going to say whatever he wanted to say, and that was that.

The other DA's reluctantly told their host that if he insisted, they would have to take him off the speakers' program.

"This is my town," said Garrison. "You just go ahead and see what happens if you don't let me speak."

The DA's said they were very sorry. . . .

Garrison went directly to the hotel kitchen and summoned the manager. He told him to padlock the doors to the ballroom. The dinner for eight hundred was off.

The distraught manager asked what was he going to do with the steaks. "Give them to the Little Sisters of the Poor," Garrison said. "I'm sending over a truck."

The law enforcement executives and their wives found the ballroom padlocked that night, and no food in the hotel cupboard. Garrison, at the time of this unsettling discovery, was having a few reporters in for drinks at his hospitality suite.

The irate head of the DA's committee burst in and demanded an explanation.

Garrison glanced up, took an extra breath, and said in a friendly drawl, "I don't speak, you don't eat."

THE MYSTERY OF THE BLACK BOOKS

> "Just because you're paranoid doesn't mean you aren't being followed."
> —*Thomas Pynchon*

Somewhere back in the primordial ooze of the Garrison investigation there lingers a story that has never been told before. It is not an assassination story, it is primarily a mystery story, and it is not even a story about Garrison himself, although his interests at the time spurred on the events. There have been good reasons for the long silence of the participants, or victims, as the telling places certain people where they perhaps should not have been, and involves the violation, or alleged violation, of several laws of the land, among them those proscribing the unauthorized dealings by private citizens with the governments of unfriendly foreign powers. By now, though, Richard Nixon the Elder has left pecker tracks all over those previously clear ground rules, and one no longer knows if one is dealing with an old enemy or a new friend until one picks up the morning paper. So I will be indiscreet.

In the New Orleans summer of 1968, Bill Turner was chewing the conspiracy fat with Jim Garrison and enjoying a Southern bourbon without benefit of mint. Turner suggested that it would be nice to know what the Russians knew about the murder of John F. Kennedy. Assuming that they didn't do it, they doubtless had a pretty good idea who did.

The thought of the KGB's bulging files on the CIA lit Garrison up like the White House Christmas tree on opening night. But a frown browned out his enthusiasm. "Even if they'd cooperate," the DA said, "we could never make the approach from my office. The wolves out there would never stop howling if they caught us asking the time of day of the KGB."

Never mind that, said Turner, *Ramparts* would make the Russians an offer they couldn't refuse. . . .

It was a week later. Turner was having coffee in a San Francisco beanery with a young man who had no name. He was the shady side of thirty-five, tall, tanned, sandy-haired, with high, raw cheekbones and polished turquoise eyes. He was not a professional mystery man, although he was mysterious about his profession, and it would be as accurate to say he had several names as none, because names to him were as paper plates, to be used and then discarded. His primary employment, in the year and a half that we had known him, was that of a contract combat pilot for the CIA. He flew a Douglas B-26 out of Miami on itinerant bombing raids against the Cuban coastline. His targets were usually pedestrian objects such as oil tanks, although once he made a pass over a Russian-built radar installation. He had also flown aerial reconnaissance missions over Cuba out of Central and South American airfields.

He had flown and fought in many other places in the world at the drop of a dollar. His disillusion with the CIA began when he worked for them in the Congo. "You can rescue nuns," the Agency had told him. He found himself shooting up supply boats instead. But he kept flying, partly for the money, which was good, partly because he was hooked on adventure, and the CIA was the big Connection.

It is testimony to the perverseness of his world that —although he came to see himself as working for the bad guys, an employment he was loath to give up because he enjoyed the means if not the end—his dangerous compulsion to simultaneously do something for the good guys was limited by his inability to find any. He had once tried an undercover assignment for the federal narcs, but their bumbling ways nearly got him killed. Given the paucity of angels, he latched onto *Ramparts* as a reasonable alternative to evil and a place where double agents were granted instant status as war heroes. As often as he was in the office, and visiting our homes, there remained a restive quality about him, a separateness, as if he were lonely out there in the cold and wanted companionship, yet didn't want to come all the way in.

We called him Hill. At least that was the name by which he was known to everyone on the paper, including one of the secretaries with whom he took up housekeeping between derrings-do. But he had a name for every day of the week. He was Bill Bridges when he worked in Miami, until, he said, he became too hot and the CIA decided to "kill off" Bridges by simulating a plane crash at sea, thus discouraging the spoilsports in the FAA from inquiring further into the checkered history of Bridges' flight plans. He had several newspaper clippings reporting his own death, which he would exhibit with the eager shyness of someone showing you an appendix scar or bottled gallstone. He was also known as Jones, also as Montgomery, also as several other people. But by any name he was, as Damon Runyon said about those types who stand out among other types of their type, the "genuine item."

Hill loved adventure, and second only to that he loved talking about adventure. However, his exploits were made of far sterner stuff than imagination. A walking scrapbook, he showed Turner a news clipping of his latest CIA exploit, dated but a week before their coffee date. HAITI CALLS ON U.N. TO HALT BOMBINGS the headline read. Two geriatric B-25's had flown over Port-au-Prince, dropped a few bombs which missed the Presidential Palace by several yards, and then landed some thirty Haitian exile commandos to the north at Cap-Haïtien, who subsequently held a radio station for a few hours before they were chased into the hills by the Tonton Macoute.

It wasn't much of an air raid by *Twelve O'Clock High* standards, but Hill, who piloted one of the B-25's, explained why the CIA would want to bother bombing a broken-down dictator like Duvalier. It made a CIA-sort of sense. The scenario was for Haitian exiles, supplemented and directed by CIA freedom fighters from central casting, to overthrow old man

Duvalier. That would get a good press, as everyone knew he was a miserable bastard. The Free Republic of Haiti would then accept as naturalized citizens those large numbers of displaced Cubans who had been giving the CIA such a headache by hanging around Miami. Thus stocked, this artificial trout pond of a republic would proceed to drive Castro to the wall, gradually knocking out Cuba's defenses by low-flying bomber attacks across the narrow windward passage separating the two islands, and the amphibious landing of teams of saboteurs and Fuller Brush salesmen of insurrection. With a little bit of luck, Castro would crack under the pressure, or be faced with no alternative but that of counterattacking Haiti. That would mean war in the Caribbean, and the United States could come to the defense of its new democratic neighbor Haiti, and thereby land the Marines in Cuba—all on the up and up. It was not a bad plot, as evil plots go, and for all I know it's still in the CIA's Out Basket.

Hill was the man we tapped to send to the Russians.

Anyone who has seen a good spy movie knows how to get in touch with the KGB. All you do is go to a Russian Embassy and ask to see the Second Secretary, who is invariably the resident Soviet intelligence chief. (If you're looking in an American Embassy for the CIA, best try the Cultural Attaché first.)

Anyway, that's what we did. And it worked.

There was, however, some hesitation before the fateful knock at the KGB door. Hill quite understandably gave thought to the damage possible to his CIA meal ticket, or his person, lest word get back to Langley, Virginia, that one of their pilots was fraternizing with the enemy. But the lure of rubbing noses with the KGB eventually overshadowed any cautionary reserves in his nature. When he said he was ready to go, we took extreme steps to insure that the man with no name would leave no trail should any untoward or unfortunate event occur while he was dealing with the enemy. We bought his airline ticket with cash, so it could not be traced back to *Ramparts*. We even shook him down for incriminating matchbook covers. When we were satisfied he could not be connected to any organization in America, save perhaps the

CIA, he boarded a jet for Mexico City, on his way along the yellow brick road to see the wizard of espionage at the Russian Embassy. It had been agreed all around that the act of asking to borrow a cup of intelligence from the KGB had best take place in another country.

By the estimate of the *Reader's Digest,* the Russian Embassy in Mexico City is "one of the world's great sanctuaries of subversion." It has the appearance of a giant cuckoo clock that has been put under house arrest. A gray Victorian mansion bedecked with gingerbread cupolas, it is cut off from the outside world by grounds dotted with peach trees and patrolled by sentries with a do-not-touch look about them, who are in turn cut off from the street by an iron fence unsuitable for pole vaulting. The twenty-four-hour work of the Embassy is carried out behind shuttered windows to the sound of crickets at night, melting into the click and whir of camera shutters by day, as most of the handsome houses across the street on the Calzada de Tacubaya are apparently in the possession of camera bugs of various intelligence services who have made a hobby of photographing everyone including the milkman who approaches the Russian Embassy. Not to be outdone, the Russians also photograph everyone who comes through their main gate, and occasionally even photograph the hidden photographers across the street.

Hill walked chin high through the moat of cameras. Once inside, he asked to see someone who could get word back to Moscow. He was ushered to a monastic waiting room. A stocky, owl-eyed man with the look of a well-groomed card mechanic soon entered, blinking in a formal, quizzical manner which gave the impression that he only blinked during working hours.

The visitor introduced himself as the undercover emissary that he was and explained the peculiar circumstances of his mission. The Russian warily asked for the camera which hung around Hill's neck, and said he would return it when their conversation was completed. Hill got it back later, "in better working order than when I gave it to him."

The Russian and the young American without a name talked for two hours. Hill explained Garrison's theory of the assassination, and the Russian nodded on occasion at the mention of the CIA. Hill made his plea for "sanitized" information from the KGB files on Oswald and others.

"Our assumption is that you must have information about these matters that we do not," he said.

The Russian rose from his seat unblinking. He asked Hill where he was staying, and suggested he stick to his hotel and not do too much touring. "It may be necessary for you to stay in Mexico City for a few days."

Hill was followed when he left the Embassy for the hotel. "They used a tail on a tail," he said. "It was a very professional job."

When Hill went down to dinner that evening, a burly man in a rumpled suit sat down directly across from his table, making no pretense that he was doing anything but watching Hill. Hill sent him a complimentary vodka, and the big man smiled, displaying several gold teeth in a setting of black teeth.

The man was there again the second night. On the third day, Hill received a request to visit the Embassy.

The Russian was blinking again. He spoke in careful, circumventive, translated-from-the-Martian phrases, as if his every word were being broadcast that instant to a stadium full of hostile people. His caution was taken by Hill as some sort of a signal, because the Russian hardly said anything more than, "Don't call us, we'll call you."

"What you request is not impossible. But it is not necessary that it will happen. The only way that it could possibly occur is in a way that would be most unexpected, and untraceable to its source. Something might be left in your hands, for instance, by a visitor to your country. That is all for now."

The official smiled, extended his hand, and gave Hill his camera. "Do you like books?" he asked. Hill said that he did. The Russian gave him several books, "all about how the East and West could get along together." Hill reached in his knapsack. The only reading material he had was a Robert Crumb comic book, which he presented to the appreciative Second Secretary, who, expressing unfamiliarity with some of Crumb's idiom, in particular the phrase, "Gimmee some reds," said he would have it translated.

Hill was en route back to San Francisco when there occurred one of those bollixes that come from too much sucking on the snow cone of paranoia. He was about to go through customs in the crowded Los Angeles International Airport, one of the seven plastic wonders of the world, when he suddenly found himself staring into the bloodshot recesses of my own one good eye. Hill came up and gave me what I suppose was the password for his secret mission. He instantly assumed that my unexpected presence in the customs area was meant to head him off at the pass from some certain disaster that had befallen our comrades.

He repeated the password. I looked at him as if he were panhandling in Swahili. I snarled something nasty and incoherent to the effect that if he shaved his legs he might get a job in the chorus of the *Nutcracker Suite*. The atomic pile behind his turquoise eyes flared into critical mass, and he stepped back as if his toes had just dissolved before his eyes. He was gone before I could remember who he was, for if truth be told, I had forgotten—so hung over and generally dissipated was I, an empty egg carton that had just been helped off the plane from Ireland, whence I had fled in a deep funk to drink my way through the apocalypse of turning thirty. I was twenty-nine when I left and a human junk heap when I returned, and could not even recognize the most unforgettable person I had ever met. But Hill knew none of that. Believing my catatonic hello to be a signal that we were all in the gravest peril, he went underground from his underground assignment. That began a carnival of pixilation, a lost weekend of paranoia. The *Ramparts* people assumed Hill's disappearance meant death, or a double-cross. Hill, seeing no report of our arrest under the Espionage Act in the papers, assumed the government was suppressing the news until they hunted him down. Each non-fact reinforced another non-fact, with me not speaking all the while lest the aftertaste of Guinness escape my mouth.

It was straightened out several hundred corkscrews later. But it was a Seconal letdown when we learned, upon Hill's belated surfacing, that all we could do was wait some more for some sign from the KGB that might or might not come.

The only concrete result of that traumatic mission to the

Russian Embassy was an invitation for the editors of *Ramparts* to attend the Red Army Ball in Mexico City, which was graciously declined.

Sometime later, Jim Garrison took a long-distance call in his New Orleans office. The caller identified himself as the traveling representative of the Frontiers Publishing Company of Geneva. That firm had, the caller said, an important four-volume original work on the Kennedy assassination which was about to be published in Europe. Would Mr. Garrison be interested in seeing the manuscript? Yeah, sure, send it, Garrison said, hanging up. Another nut.

The United States mails deposited a fat package in the New Orleans District Attorney's office. It contained three thick volumes of manuscript, each bound in black.

When this manuscript later emerged in book form, its title was *Farewell America*. The author, according to the book jacket, was James Hepburn, a thirty-four-year-old writer, former acquaintance of Jacqueline Bouvier, and former student at the London School of Economics and the Institute of Political Studies in Paris.

Garrison took one look, and called *Ramparts* to say that the Miracle of Fatima had occurred. Instead of a lovely lady, the creator had sent down something to read.

The next day a courier arrived from New Orleans lugging a Xerox of the sign from the KGB. It was a heavy sign: a thousand-odd pages of flawless typescript, as if part of an IBM demonstration at a convention of old-maid office managers, or from the Pope. Book manuscripts normally have at the minimum a few peanut butter and jelly stains on them, not to mention hen scratchings and other placental alterations. No author since the dawn of movable type has got himself together enough to dam the babbling brook of creativity, settle the last word and position the final comma, and then had the time or the money to completely and perfectly retype his manuscript before sending it to the publishers, or they to the printers. This masterpiece of the touch system was patently the product of some boiler-plate rewrite bank in the basement of an intelligence factory.

The content of the manuscript confirmed the validity of that superficial assessment of its origin. Garrison was amazed that the unheard-of Geneva publishing outfit had as well-developed and documented a conspiracy theory as Garrison's own—with many of the same villains by name, and others of the same faces, but different aliases. The shock waves were equally as great at *Ramparts.* The mystery manuscript was as sprinkled with details as an ice cream cone dipped in chocolate jimmies. There were names and addresses, where relevant, about the clandestine operations of the Central Intelligence Agency. Much of the information was of the type that could only come from the CIA's own files or from the dossiers of a rival intelligence network. For instance, it was revealed that the CIA maintained a training center for saboteurs on Saipan Island in the Marianas, and that the Agency had exactly 28 agents in Iceland, working out of two offices, one at the American Embassy in Reykjavik, the other at the U.S. military base at Keflavik.

A *Ramparts* team of New Left researchers had been digging into the internal operations of the CIA for the better part of a year and had scavenged numerous scraps of available information, save whatever was tattooed on the inside of John McCone's belly button. A large part of the material in our files was unknown to the general press or public. But these manicured pages so inexplicably handed down from the mountain repeated, in a matter-of-fact manner, many of our zealously acquired CIA supersecrets—and revealed many more, all of which subsequently checked out. Whoever James Hepburn was, he had reliable sources of information about the inner workings of American intelligence.

The poop on the CIA was plotted in with the subtlety of a Vincent Price movie. The book's text gasped for breath as it crawled through hills and valleys created by mountainous footnotes, which were as jam-packed as a lifeboat with whole file drawers full of classified data. The manuscript revealed the locations of secret CIA schools for sabotage; exposed CIA-owned newspapers, radio stations and publishing houses in Cyprus, Beirut, Aden, Jordan, Kenya and other countries in Africa, the Middle East and the Far East; named the CIA's clandestine commercial "covers" in the United States, and recorded the Agency's role as co-director of the Eisenhower Administration, and examined its links—through Kermit Roosevelt in the fifties and John McCone in the sixties—to the oil industry. Among other epithets, the manuscript alleged that former "specialists" for the CIA's DCA (Department of Covert Activity) were members of an assassination "team" at Dallas.

Similar working details were disclosed about the KGB, the assessments being quite favorable. "In the domain of pure intelligence, the KGB is superior to the CIA." This supported our belief that the manuscript had been typed on Russian typewriters fitted with American characters.

Many sections of the book were non sequiturs which reminded me of Groucho Marx's line in *Duck Soup*: "A child of five would understand this. Send somebody to fetch a child of five." The gratuitous mention of a 1931 Paris detective story by an author who used the premonitory pseudonym "Oswald Dallas" made at least impish sense. But I couldn't figure the humor of numerous out-of-context references to Roy Cohn, the former boy witch hunter, whose selected quotations merited several vague footnotes with citations such as, "Roy Cohn, at the Stork Club in 1963."

Later, after we had gone scuba diving in the black waters of the manuscript's authorship, much of this strangeness was to be cleared up somewhat, as was the motivation behind a puzzling chapter alleging shocking Secret Service foul-ups which made the Dallas assassination almost a pushover. The critique amounted to a white paper on the deficiencies of the Secret Service, and was obviously prepared by someone very much on the Inside. There was a rather bitter attack on the competence of Kennedy White House aide Kenny O'Donnell, who supervised the security arrangements. The unsubstantiated attack made little sense as the mystery book went on to provide a lengthy analysis of the demonstrably superior security arrangements of other nations, particularly France and Russia, for protecting the lives of their chief executives. There was a puzzling hurrah for Daniel P. Moynihan, a professional thinker of moderate means, who so far as I knew had zero to do with guarding the President: "Only Daniel P. Moynihan, a former longshoreman, had some idea of such things."

The thesis of the mystery text was that of John F. Kennedy as the good guy-golden boy of American democracy, whose honest policies were so at odds with the power-mad and corrupt CIA and its billionaire oilmen kingmakers that he was accordingly snuffed. But by whom?

The three-volume manuscript was accompanied by a cryptic note: If we were interested in seeing the fourth volume, we should cable a law firm in Geneva, and arrangements would be made. An obvious deduction, Watson: The fourth volume would name the murderers.

We cabled. We waited. A week later Garrison telephoned: "You know that fourth volume? Well, it just walked in the door."

There was to be a further complication. The messenger who had arrived in New Orleans from Geneva did not have the final volume with him. We would have to send a representative to Geneva to inspect it in person.

At that, I began to wonder if this was a present from the KGB, or a booby trap from somebody else.

Garrison immediately dispatched an emissary to Geneva to collect the tainted goods. Selected for this delicate task was Steve Jaffe, the peach fuzz side of twenty-five, who had already established a reputation as a professional photographer and was envied by other assassination sleuths because he had credentials from Garrison authorizing him a special investigator for the District Attorney's office, and was so registered in Baton Rouge.

In Geneva, Jaffe discovered that the office of Frontiers Publishing was a desk in a large Swiss law firm that specialized in representing Swiss banks. The most concrete information the law firm would provide was that Frontiers was a Liechtenstein corporation. The real headquarters, Jaffe was told, were in Paris. Jaffe went to Paris.

The Paris editorial offices of the elusive Frontiers were in the modern offices of a famous international law firm. Nobody was minding the store but lawyers. It was explained to

Jaffe that important "financial interests" were behind the publishing of the book. At one point, the smarmy suggestion was dropped that the Kennedy family itself had underwritten part of the costs.

Jaffe had been asked to interview the author, James Hepburn, and question him about his sources.

The answer came from Paris: It is impossible to meet the author. The author is a "composite."

As my friend Tupper Saussy, the composer, once wrote, "I turned on the Today show and wished it were yesterday." Additional communications across the Atlantic weaved back and forth like carrier pigeons drunk on elderberries. Such facts or suppositions of fact as emerged made only one thing clear to me: we were shadowboxing with a high-level intelligence operation—although no longer necessarily the KGB. French intelligence was suddenly in the running; even the ubiquitous CIA became suspect.

Farewell America was published in Germany, with fanfare but without the missing final volume, and became a moderate best seller. The phony book was syndicated in *Bild*, Germany's largest daily newspaper, which is owned by Axel Springer, who is not exactly a raving Bolshevik. Why would Springer authenticate such a KGB plant? The inevitable suspicion arose that this might be a triple-decker CIA cake with Ian Fleming icing to somehow entrap *Ramparts*.

Further investigation revealed that Frontiers Publishing Company of Vaduz, Liechtenstein, had never published a book before, and had no apparent plans to publish anything else in the future.

Farewell America was then published in France in a handsome edition by Frontiers. The review in *L'Express* was quoted on the book's jacket ". . . . the most violent indictment ever written by a man about his country, out of love for that country." Not a bad notice for a composite.

Jaffe reported that he had tracked down the publisher of Frontiers. He identified him as one Michel. According to the curriculum vitae supplied to Jaffe, Michel had been the publisher of a French women's magazine, in the early sixties.

Before that, he had been a combat officer in the French army in Indochina, had studied at Harvard for a time, and had attended the French Diplomatic Training School. Jaffe said that Michel was the key to the preparation of the mystery book and added his opinion, which he said was not totally unconfirmed by Michel, that the "Publisher" was highly placed in French intelligence.

Whoever he was, the "Publisher" knew his way around the Elysée Palace.

When Jaffe asked him for some authentication of the material in the book, Michel whisked him into the Elysée Palace and into the private office of the Director of the French Secret Service, André Ducret.

Ducret was most gracious to the young American. He said that the Secret Service of France had indeed provided certain information for parts of *Farewell America*. He gave Jaffe photographs and diagrams hand-drawn on his personal stationery supplementing the criticisms of the American Secret Service made in the book. Ducret also told Jaffe that he had knowledge of the weapon that had actually been used in the Kennedy assassination—which was not the dime store rifle the Warren Commission said Oswald fired.

Jaffe asked the Secret Service head if there was any chance of getting a letter to General de Gaulle. Ducret said it was certainly possible, although he had no way of knowing if the General would have time to send an answer. Jaffe gave Ducret a letter stating the gist of his mission, and inquiring into whatever clarification was possible on the role of the French government in the publication of the book.

Ducret said he would personally take Jaffe's letter to General de Gaulle. He returned about fifteen minutes later and handed Jaffe De Gaulle's engraved card, with a personal note scribbled on it:

GENERAL DE GAULLE

Je suis très sensible à la
confiance que vous m'exprimez

The head of the French Secret Service also told Jaffe in so many words, just how important that he, too, thought both Jaffe's mission and Garrison's investigation were, and how

France appreciated their efforts. Jaffe left the Elysée Palace, equally impressed and puzzled.

Michel indicated that the "documents" on which the book was based were locked up for safekeeping in a Liechtenstein bank vault. However, he said Jaffe was in luck as one of the sources, a French intelligence agent known as "Phillipe," was in town. Michel said that Phillipe had interviewed a member of the paramilitary sharpshooting team that had murdered Kennedy at Dealey Plaza. At midnight, Michel drove Jaffe to the Club Kama, a dingy Latin Quarter bar, to have a drink with the spook.

Phillipe spoke only in metaphor. Most of his metaphors were about the Hotel Luna in Mexico City, which he implied had—in the assassination year of 1963—a "Cuban band," whose musicians had dangerous "instruments."

Then Michel said there was just one little thing more before we got to see the fourth volume with the yellow pages listing Kennedy's murderers. Frontiers was anxious to publish *Farewell America* in America—and wanted *Ramparts* to publish it, just as Axel Springer had been so kind to have done in Germany.

It seemed time either to retreat or send in reinforcements, so I bludgeoned Larry Bensky, the current victim on the sacrificial altar of the *Ramparts* Managing Editor's chair, into catching a night plane to Paris. Bensky was not all that happy about going, since he had been a founder of a Franco-American antiwar group during his previous residence as an editor of the *Paris Review* and had reason to think the French police would be watching him.

Bensky found Michel to be a very average-looking Frenchman, a chain smoker of Gitanes, a chain lover of women, with a strong taste for luxury, a seemingly inexhaustible supply of pocket money, and many flashily dressed friends with nice apartments and no visible means of support. He was an expert in "pillow-talk intelligence," having been assigned by French intelligence, with its concern for industrial counterespionage, to infiltrate the social circles of the oil industry in New York and Texas by seducing the daughters of the petroleum magnates. "I learned English to fuck them," the Frenchman told Bensky.

The French intelligence agent came on as an orgy freak, or, more precisely, he came on as a combination self-voyeur and fetishist about being an orgy freak. He sat in Paris sidewalk cafés ostentatiously picking his teeth, and otherwise acting the part of Terry-Thomas playing the stud. His conversation was that of an after-dinner speaker in a bordello catering to civil servants. He would preface intimate accounts of the sexual proclivities of prominent politicians with the phrase, "It is known in French intelligence that . . . ," then proceed to the nitty gritty about several American politicians and their boy-friends.

Michel was in other ways the perfection of rottenness. He pulled off one of the meanest ploys in the book of dirty tricks: He deliberately got one of our men the clap. The victim was a *Ramparts* lad who had been standing by in Paris, another innocent New Leftie abroad. Michel apparently convinced his young victim that sexual intercourse was a prerequisite to commercial intercourse in Paris and that their discussions could best be held during nightly visitations to Paris whorehouses in which he was a stockholder. There our lad received a sexual mickey. Relying on the young American's pride not to cry uncle, the fiendish Michel stepped up the whoring pace, putting his negotiating partner at the disadvan-tage of extreme physical and psychological discomfort. Bensky arrived just in time to put a halt to this slow torture, which he learned about only by accident. The lad met him at the airport and on the way into Paris asked Bensky to wait for a minute in the cab while he ran up to a doctor's office to get a "vaccination." After the meter had ticked by twenty minutes, Bensky, figuring even *Ramparts'* expense accounts did not have that elasticity, paid off the driver and wandered upstairs. After several wrong numbers in doctors' offices, he found the innocent American, all blushing red, pale white, and de-pressed blue, sitting uncomfortably on a folding chair in a VD clinic. The embarrassed investigator confessed his plight, which was redundant in light of his surroundings. He perked up a bit when Bensky explained to him, Captain Ahab to

Penrod, that his extended discomfort was not due to inex-
perience or bad luck but a trap of the devil, in all his cunning.

Benksy ducked Michel's efforts to lure him to the
whorehouses, where he was certain a trap lay germinating for
him, pleading a Benedictine vow of celibacy from a previous
incarnation, and instead maneuvered the Frenchman into
successive cat-and-mouse encounter sessions of drinking cognac in bistros of Bensky's choice. On the third night, he beat
the Frenchman at the endurance game. As the sensuous intelligence agent wandered drunkenly around the bistro, having
left his jacket on the chair, Bensky went through his pockets,
discovering business cards and press cards in several identities, only a few of them in Michel's own name, and a British
passport in yet another name.

Bensky dropped these identities on Michel in subsequent
conversations, which caused the Frenchman to raise ever so
slightly his egg-skin eyebrows and compliment the Managing
Editor on *Ramparts'* "excellent sources" of information.

Back home, we at last developed a good hunch about who
was dealing in the bridge game in which *Ramparts* was playing
a dummy hand. The droopy fleur-de-lis of French intelligence overshadowed the cardboard publishing house of
Frontiers, but that in itself was of little specific help in tracing
the river of data in *Farewell America* to its source, because the
French SDECE was so notoriously, and almost hilariously,
riddled with KGB double agents that as a matter of course
Frenchmen were offered vodka before wine at international
spy gatherings.

There were also some noisy cross signals indicating that the
book's brewmasters might be in the private sector of international espionage. A dandruff-collared crew of former French
spies, tossed in the garbage when the rotten apple that had
been French intelligence was drawn and quartered after
World War II, had been hired en bloc by the French oil cartel.
The paté of flab around their midsections was strengthened
by the addition of Marseilles thugs and floating assassins to
their number, creating a relatively sophisticated and mean
chorus line of Harry Palmers in berets, ready to do whatever

was necessary so that the Frenchies might gain a bigger share of the world oil lamp, Standard Oil be damned.

This was something by the way of cherries on the matzos, as the SDECE itself assumed as a prime part of its raison d'être the protection and furtherance of French petroleum interests. (It remains an object of bar bets in Paris whether it was the SDECE proper or the freelance French oil agents who erased Enrico Mattei, the Italian oil magnate whose North African holdings encroached on French vital interests, and who conveniently perished in a plane crash near Milan in 1962 which had the suspicious markings of that other political plane crash of General Sikorski off Gibraltar in 1943, in which Winston Churchill was alleged to have pulled the fatal cotter pin.) At any rate, such types as these, who possessed sufficient rough magic to make the Moroccan leftist Ben Barka disappear from the Left Bank and from the face of the earth in 1965, had the financing if not the suavity (that apparently was Michel's function) to palm off *Farewell America* on the public libraries of the world. This was something they might wish to do inasmuch as the book contained between its hard covers considerable dirt on the American oil industry, including the not very nice suggestion that the kingpins of American petroleum got together to knock off the President of the United States.

It sounds mad, I know, but when you get into it, and down to it, all real madness takes place in some factual context. The French are not the only ones who have found other uses for old spies. Everywhere, former intelligence agents for hire constitute a black belt of overprivileged crud. What really goes on in the world is made all the more dreadfully complicated when one becomes aware of the existence of this private half-world on top, or rather beneath, that other half-world of officially sanitized clandestine intelligence work and subversion.

We never learned for certain whether Michel worked for the French intelligence, with or without its KGB brandy float, or for the Watergate division of French private intelligence, or, for that matter, for some other squad of Flying Dutchmen. Someone substantial was paying his whoring and typesetting bills. He admitted to being a plant but would not say who potted him. All his identities were phony. He had never been the publisher of a French magazine. But in his earnest efforts to get *Ramparts* to publish his thing Michel did clear up several of the minor mysteries about the black books. He said the extraordinary detail about the CIA had come from the files of the SDECE, which of course kept tabs on the competition. The information in the book about the KGB had come from the same source; he denied it came directly from the KGB. The nasty details about the American petroleum industry were the product of the same files and from Michel's own years of spying and snookering his way into the inner social circles of the filthy oil rich. He also explained the derivation of some of his most scarlet name-dropping. Michel's imagination took him to the heights of drugstore fiction. The nonplusing references to Roy Cohn, for instance, were explained as a simple matter of "friendship"—Michel claimed to have become great buddies with Cohn while working the stud circuit in Eastern seaboard millionaire playgrounds. To hear the Frenchman tell the tale, he and Roy were something of a frogman team of cunnilingus experts who made many successful forays together in the dangerous waters off East Hampton; therefore, one nice guy to another, the spy put his friend's name in his book. (I later asked Cohn about this; he said he recalled no such person and that the whole story smacked of a left-wing lie.)

Michel also came clean that the name James Hepburn, the pseudoauthor of *Farewell America*, was of a metasexual derivation. James was the French *J'aime*, and Hepburn from the actress Audrey Hepburn, with whom Michel professed, without substantiation, to once having dated, and for whom he had kept a soft spot in his black heart, even though, he said, his affection was unreciprocated.

On the basis of this less than complete information, *Ramparts* purchased an option to publish *Farewell America* in America, paying for it with a postdated check drawn on a bank with which we no longer had an account. I had never bounced a check on an intelligence agency before and it seemed somehow a fair idea. If the truth be told, the cables I was sending

Bensky urging him to hurry up and make haste so we could go
to press with James Hepburn's exclusive were in that gray area
between little white lies and big black lies. It was in for a dime,
in for a dollar, and I couldn't see the harm in hanging tough
and trying to find out just who had gone to all this expense
and effort to bloody up the good name of the CIA and
eminent American oilmen such as H. L. Hunt, the billionaire
brown-bagger whom James Hepburn, the pseudoauthor, had
defamed in terms I would be loath to repeat even about
someone poorer than Hunt.

There being no Geneva Convention of publishing, I figured that if the culprits coughed up Volume Four, with the
names and numbers of the players in the Dallas assassination
bowl, and if we succeeded in pinning the goods on one intelligence agency as opposed to another, then we could screw
James Hepburn and run the story with its proper
by-line—"Who Killed Kennedy, by the KGB." I thought that
would make a terrific *Ramparts* cover.

Under prodding, the proprietorship of Frontiers Publishing came clean as to their most extraordinary source: the
material on the internal foul-ups of the Secret Service
—detailed down to the number of bourbons a Secret Serv-
iceman had had the night before and how many aspirins he
took the morning after—was hand delivered from the inner
councils of the Kennedy family. The chapter was based on a
private, unpublished and undistributed memorandum prepared for Attorney General Robert Kennedy after his
brother's murder. Bobby had convened a select committee the
day after the assassination, which was to conduct a secret
investigation of the Secret Service, independent of the work
of other federal agencies such as the FBI or the CIA.

For RFK's first thought had been that the person responsible for his brother's death was his old enemy, Jimmy Hoffa.

Michel said the committee's report had been written by
Daniel Moynihan. It excoriated the Secret Service for organi-
zational and functional deficiencies, but it also cleared Hoffa
of any involvement in any plot. Once he was assured that his
nemesis hadn't done it, Bobby apparently lost all interest in
the investigation. He didn't even turn the report over to the

Warren Commission, although it was far more critical of the Secret Service than the eventual Warren Report.

This memorandum had lain hidden somewhere in the file cabinets of Camelot ever since. Through "personal friendships" developed within the Kennedy inner circle—Michel would not say with whom—it had come to rest in the hands of French intelligence, which had made such expert use of it.

Such was the root of the strangest one-liner in the inscrutable text of the espionage classic *Farewell America*: "Only Daniel Moynihan, a former longshoreman, had some idea of such things."

We were of course sworn to secrecy because of the "extreme sensitivity" of this confidence, a trust I violated in a flash by bracing Moynihan. At first he refused to talk. This was not wholly unreasonable of him, as a tart invitation to a liberal intellectual of the stripe of Daniel Moynihan from the Katzenjammer Kids of *Ramparts* would naturally raise suspicions of New Left entrapment. However, a second telephone call to his Cambridge home, in which the subject matter of the desired discussion was mentioned, brought him flying down to New York, where a *Ramparts* Face the Nation panel had hastily assembled.

Moynihan almost swallowed his bow tie when briefed on what we knew. He vehemently denied knowing the man known as Michel, or any French cockfighter, but he would not deny his secret mission for Bobby. He would not confirm it, either. He became fidgety and begged permission to use a telephone for some private calls. "I have to ask some people," he said. Twenty minutes later a slightly more composed Moynihan reappeared, announced that he had no intention of discussing this matter with us, and made a less than graceful exit. We presumed he was under homing instructions beamed from some transmitter still functioning in the ruins of Camelot.

That is everything there is to know about the mystery of the black books except who did it.

Bensky returned from the Paris talks with little more substantial than a fervent dislike for the other side. When pressed to the wall, Michel handed over the long-awaited "fourth volume," which consisted of one double-spaced page. Here is what it said:

"THE MAN OF NOVEMBER FIFTH"

"The choice made by the people of the United States on November 5th, 1968, will have profound and far-reaching consequences for the life, liberty and happiness of the universe. The peoples of the earth are awaiting new decisions. The man of November 5th cannot escape the conflicts of the modern world. If he chooses to ignore them, he will only delay their consequences. If he is prepared to confront them, he can overcome them.

"John and Robert Kennedy had the courage to meet these problems and break down the doors to the future. They were stopped by the frightened confederates of the traditions on which they infringed.

"When John Fitzgerald Kennedy's head exploded, it was for some the signal for toasts. The funeral did not go unnoticed. One November morning the cannon boomed, the Panama Canal was closed, flags flew at half-mast, and even Andrei Gromyko wept. Adlai Stevenson declared that he would bear the sorrow of his death till the day of his own, and the Special Forces added a black band to their green berets. Almost five years passed, and another bullet shattered the brain and stopped the heart of another Kennedy who had taken up the fight.

"There was another funeral. Once again the Green Berets formed the Honor Guard; once again the Stars and Stripes flew at half-mast. On an evening in June, Robert Kennedy joined his brother beneath the hill at Arlington, and those who pass by can bring them flowers.

"The tombs are splendid, but the scores have not been settled.

"Who killed them?

"And why?"

It is perhaps indicative of the nature of the real knowledge of the Kennedy assassinations on the part of the authors of

Farewell America that their manuscript finally ended on a question mark.

At that, the book remained chock-full of an odd lot of goodies. Stalemated in the attempt to determine to which intelligence agency to award the by-line, I adopted a new tactic which, in retrospect, may have been counter-productive: I told the truth. Frontiers Publishing was informed via its Geneva, Paris and Vaduz, Liechtenstein, addresses that *Ramparts* would regretfully not publish its book as it would not tell us which brand name of espionage it represented. Michel replied, in something of a snit, that Frontiers would publish the book itself in America, as it had successfully done elsewhere. They proceeded to print a hard-cover, 418-page English-language edition of *Farewell America* in Belgium which was air-freighted to Canada, warehoused and prepared for distribution in America.

For reasons best known to Frontiers—a publishing firm which, needless to say, has ceased to answer its telephones —the book was never brought into the United States. I fear now that its failure to surface may have had something to do with my promise to Michel to "write about" the book when it was published in the United States. I meant that as a promise, not a threat, but it may have been interpreted otherwise.

The plot died lingering. A month after the events just described, Michel showed up in California. He telephoned Bill Turner, who had been Jaffe's contact man. Turner was getting ready to fly to New York, but offered to stop by Michel's hotel on the way to the airport. Hill—our supersecret emissary—was driving Turner to the airport, and he joined the meeting. The encounter was light on substantive conversation, but the next evening Michel called Hill, who had let it slip that he was staying in Sausalito, and said that he was leaving town but had "a present" for the gang at *Ramparts*. Typically, although the Frenchman was staying at the Fairmont Hotel, the present was in the hands of the bell captain of the St. Francis Hotel. From the bellboy Hill retrieved a can of 16-mm film. It was a print of the famous Zapruder film, at that time off-limits to the world at large and under lock and key in the vaults of the National Archives in Washington and at *Life* magazine, which had paid Zapruder a tidy sum for all the prints in existence.

Bensky volunteered the most articulate explanation of these strange goings-on. The Bensky Theory is the product of his tiptoeing through the intelligence poppy fields of Paris without getting dizzy from the fragrance. He believes Michel was working with a politicized wing of the French intelligence service which had become the last bastion of gainful employment for various supporters of the right-wing militarists who lost out to reality in the French Indochina and Algerian colonial wars. These types were all young-to-middle-aged rightist playboys of the intelligence world, grinning fascists with souped-up cars and a hand in the till of private business deals, of whom Michel was a specimen. A thinking cult among their number, anxious to develop some ploy that would appeal to De Gaulle, hit upon the black books to worm their way into favor. The General was of course very anti-American, but was known to have achieved something of a personal rapprochement with Jack Kennedy, whom he liked and whom he was convinced was the murder victim of a conspiracy within the United States. General de Gaulle was also extremely concerned about France's future sources of energy, which he saw at the mercy of the American and British petroleum cartels. Industrial counterespionage, both oil and nuclear, was an important function of French intelligence. The object of the black books, therefore, was to show De Gaulle that he was right in his views about the conspiracy to kill Kennedy, and at the same time create a scandal both in Europe and the United States by linking the hated American oilmen to the assassination. Neat, no?

There are differences of opinion about the Bensky Theory, but I will refrain. If that was the purpose of the black books, the perpetrators were at least partially successful. They managed to con the largest daily newspaper in Germany and newsmagazine in France into buying their poke, not to mention thousands of book buyers in both countries who were taken along for the ride. And although *Farewell America* has never been reviewed or written about in the United States, for reasons now familiar to the readers of this history, numerous copies of the book have somehow wormed their way into the public libraries and card catalogs of the nation, including the Library of Congress (Catalog Card Number 68-57391).

I do not know what happened to the shipment of books in Canada, except that six hundred of them ended up in Bill Turner's basement. Michel had asked him at their breakfast tête-à-tête if Turner would like "some copies" of the book. Turner said sure. Two months later he received a notice from a freight forwarder in San Francisco that they were holding something for him. It was a considerable poundage of *Farewell America*, sent via Montreal to Turner's San Rafael home. Turner refused to accept the skid of books, since there was a $282 shipping tag to be paid, and he did not feel like subsidizing a foreign government to that amount. He so notified Michel. Michel wired back telling him where to pick up money to pay the shipping cost. Following Michel's instructions, Hill went to a Swiss bank in San Francisco and got the money.

So the ex-FBI man keeps the only known extant stash of the black books next to his lawn mower. It is a slowly dwindling pile, as he is constantly bothered by requests to send copies through the mail. Most of these orders come from bookstores near college campuses, one shop apparently getting his address from another. He mails out a dozen or more copies each month, at $8.95 a pop. The Los Angeles Public Library bought five copies.

7.

The Relics of St. Che

SISYPHUS WITH JOY

THE New Left is not generally known for its religious sensibilities. There was, however, one event, in the later years of the sixties, which amounted to nothing less than a Passion Play for the revolutionary faithful—the long-running drama of the disappearance, jungle capture, martyrdom and elevation to sainthood of Ernesto (Che) Guevara. *Ramparts* was fated to play a key, if accustomed, part in the denouement of this drama: that of the spoiler. But for once we were on the side of the angels, or at least, if that be too presumptuous, of the soul of the dearly departed.

Che's secular canonization was marred by a scramble for his relics, a process not unusual in the making of a saint, but which became in Che's case an unlikely tug of war over whether his killers should profit from the prime memento of his death, his personal Diary.

The tinhorn Bolivian generals who had murdered Che planned to make political and financial gain by selling his personal effects to the highest bidder, and the CIA had its inevitable thumb on the scales as chief auctioneer. This made for a state of affairs violative of what Howard Gossage referred to as "the decent opinion of mankind." I am pleased to report that things did not go as they planned, and that I had a hand, in the precision of the cliché, in throwing a monkey wrench into the works.

269

The news of Che Guevara's death brought forth a great clatter of hooves and rattle of breastplates. The noise was testimony to the deceased's commanding position in the folklore of the sixties. Che's attraction for the young radicals was a narcotic similar to Marshall McLuhan's pull on the decade's fashionable intellectuals; both proferred self-defining systems with all the conveniences of slogans, instant theories: The medium is the message; the job of the revolutionary is to make revolution. Che's do-it-now gospel of revolution was perfectly tempered to the moral activism and impatience with the encumbrances of theory that were the essence of the New Left; with Che, struggle created politics, not vice versa; Che was Sisyphus with joy, with everyone pushing the rock in different directions.

Naturally, capitalists would not be assumed to approve of such a free-for-all call to revolutionary activity. But if one thought that Communists would, one would have another think coming, and be due a lesson in the cautious tree-climbing of orthodox Marxist-Leninism. Che's enemies were as much on the left as on the right, and the concern of both camps, upon his demise, was to twist the facts of his life and death, along with the words of his Diary, so as to judge him a failure, a revolutionary stumblebum who would have little power to live on, in myth, as a beacon to sibling re-volutionaries. Che's admirers of course wished differently, and this story is about the arm wrestling that ensued. It is in many ways a quintessential story of the sixties, and it is typical of the decade that the heroes have hickeys, and the villains are more crummy than appalling. The only larger than life figure is St. Che himself, and he a Saint-errant at that.

Che's last, lost crusade in Bolivia was chivalric in its purpose and conduct, though in romance nearer to Shelley than to Lancelot. These qualities were so apart from the values of the real world, right or left, so pure, and therefore so rare, that Che acquired a unique value to friends and enemies alike. He became a myth even before he became a corpse, and was treated, by both friend and foe, as some sort of revolutionary blue-chip stamp; some wanted to cash him in by killing him; others to gain revolutionary brownie points by helping him.

His friends did not do him as much harm as his enemies, but not so much good, either. Such is often the luck of saints.

Among his friends, there was no one more typical, or a better introduction, than Jules Régis Debray—the French Marxist who barged in on Che in his guerrilla solitude in the jungle, and was to complicate the traveling revolutionary's life, and by some accounts, inadvertently to hasten his death.

DR. GUEVARA, MEET MR. DEBRAY

For the New Left, it was an event on the level of Stanley Meets Livingstone: In the steaming Bolivian hinterlands, the young French intellectual, short, thin, with a slight urban pot belly and looking rather sheepish in his fatigues, fresh from the civilization of Havana and from writing a book about Castro's revolutionary theory, had arrived in an awkward and dangerous manner at the secret guerrilla front to ask Che Guevara a few questions. But he had come with Fidel's blessings, and he was to be accommodated as best the difficult circumstances would allow.

So in the middle of the guerrilla theater of war, in March of 1967, Che Guevara took time out to annotate a copy of Régis Debray's thin volume, as told to him by Fidel, of revisionist Marxist-Leninism, *Revolution in the Revolution*. Che had then been a missing person for almost two years, and the international press had indulged in the silliest speculations as to his whereabouts, dead or alive—placing Che in a shallow grave in Cuba, the result of a contract put out on him, Mafia-style, by a jealous Fidel; suggesting Che as the undercover Big Brother of the Red Guards in China; reporting Che as having gone over the wall to the lucrative business of debriefing himself to Western intelligence services at the standing rate of $10,000 an hour.

Since his disappearance in 1965, the Argentine doctor turned Cuban revolutionary leader had actually been first in the Congo, where he was thwarted in piecing the Humpty Dumpty forces of Patrice Lumumba back together again, and then back to Cuba where, bored with the inexorable bureaucracy that had settled in like a low fog to dampen the ardor of the revolution, he received Fidel's blessing for his great guerrilla experiment in Bolivia which, if successful, he believed would mean two, three, many Vietnams in South America.

But for all the world knew then, Che might have been playing pinochle in Peru, Indiana. It was thus a considerable achievement for the interloping Frenchman to find Che Guevara, and for such a bookish purpose. However cogent Che's criticisms might have been of Debray's work, they would appear to be lost to revolutionary posterity since Che's copy of the book was captured along with his person, and appears to have suffered much the same fate.

Debray was captured before Che, and found himself in some difficulty pleading the equivalent of the First Amendment to his Bolivian captors. At the peak of the ensuing international hullabaloo over Debray's imprisonment, a group of French journalists dispatched a petition to Bolivia's then chief man-of-iron, General René Barrientos Ortuño, demanding that the young French intellectual be granted recognition as the world's first "guerrilla correspondent," and thereby treated with the same amenities as the older model war correspondents of conflicts past.

Ramparts was typically guilty of the overreaction of the left at the fate of the bumbling Frenchman, who of course meant well, but might as well have left a trail of bread crumbs for the Bolivian soldiers and their American Green Beret "advisers" who were busy pinning down Che's location for the kill. We all signed the proper "save Debray" gang letters to the *New York Review of Books* (in that inane tradition of multi-signatory letters to the *Review* protesting some faraway outrage against civil liberties in Bolivia or Uganda or some other lesser land without the Anglo-Saxon law, but presumably susceptible to the whippersnap sting of New York intellectuals). *Ramparts* put Debray on the cover, an impressionistic portrait in seaweed green and red, with the French Marxist looking a cross between Jesus Christ and James Dean. We excerpted, in our best Book-of-the-Month-Club manner, Debray's *Revolution in the Revolution,* which read like a Rumanian tractor manual.

Castro reviewed Debray's book with one of his famous

shaggy-bear shrugs, which was largely interpreted at court to mean that the book was just about what a French intellectual would be expected to make of his ideas, but about as close as anyone was likely to come to Fidel's theorizing until Fidel himself got around to taking pen in hand. After his book was published in Havana, Debray kept hanging around Fidel, asking questions. Whether it was for material for a second volume, or just to get the industrious Frenchman out of his hair, the Premier finally allowed Debray to venture off to the guerrilla front in Bolivia to get Che Guevara's opinion of it all.

The unfortunate Frenchman spent the better part of four years in uncomfortable Bolivian clinks, all for the offense of rushing in, where others had feared to tread, to touch the hem of St. Che's gown. He was finally released on Christmas Eve of 1970, and seemed himself a bit confused at all the fuss he had occasioned.

Debray's return to Havana was more that of a groundhog who had overslept than a prodigal son. Left-wing politics are as mercurial as Paris fashions; in a few seasons, everything had changed as drastically as bosoms going out and buttocks coming in. Che of course was dead, and he had posthumously sliced up the Frenchman in his Diary, the publication of which was *Ramparts'* big scoop of 1968, but which gave us cause to regret that Jesus Christ part of our 1967 Régis Debray cover, if not the James Dean part, too. Che in his Diary did not seem too happy about Debray's "desperation" to leave the guerrilla band not so very long after he had arrived, and wrote that he had warned the Frenchman of the dangers of making such haste. This led many interpreters of the Diary to conclude that Debray, by his botched reentry to civilization, to some degree contributed, in a negligent manner, to the luckless chain of events that led to Che's capture and death. Castro, in an introduction to the Diary, gave lip service to explaining the "inconsistency" of Che's attitude toward Debray, but the thing that rang truest about the explanation was that Che was pissed off at the Frenchie.

Debray encountered other back-to-the-drawing-board-type realities. Urban guerrilla warfare, which he had discounted as ineffective in his 1967 revolutionary manual, had

become the rage of the late sixties in both South and North
America. As for the other Cuba-type Marxist-Leninist
heresies that Debray had promulgated as the wave of the
future, Fidel Castro, his Word-Giver, had found himself
trapped in a Russian economic bear hug, and necessarily
grinning and bearing it, toed the thin red line of orthodoxy.
This occasioned an outpouring of books and articles heavily
critical of Castro from bitchy socialists and writers more "left"
than Debray. And the same varsity rowing crew of intellectuals who had signed letters in the *New York Review of Books*
throughout the sixties in earnest support of Castro's Cuba,
had suddenly discovered, upon Fidel's bopping a kindred
Cuban poet on the head, that there were no ACLU-type civil
liberties in the left's most favored nation; now they were
signing the same sort of group letter, in the same journal,
attacking their former hero, Fidel.

Debray has had a generally good press. No less a professional wiseman than C. L. Sulzberger of the New York *Times*
called for the breaking out of champagne upon news of
Debray's imminent release from jail in December of 1970:
Debray's release, Sulzberger wrote, would give an experienced, seasoned leader to the New Left in the West! With such
notices he should be able to withstand readily the tale of a
French Marxist in Fidel Castro's Court, with which I wish to
conclude his ambivalent role in this history. Russell Stetler, a
friend of mine who at the time was working as Bertrand
Russell's private secretary, recalls that a traveling emissary
from Russell's foundation visited Debray in prison in the
dusty Bolivian village of Camiri in 1967 to bring the usual box
of chocolates and ask if there was any message for the outside
world. Debray did not seem in any great need of stores, as his
mother, a conservative Paris city-councilwoman, had been
sending over French wines so the prisoner could maintain a
taste of home. But Debray implored Russell's man to get an
urgent message to Castro: Fidel must do something, anything,
to free him. He had had it with being a world leftist hero, and
asked that Castro barter his freedom by trading any number
of political prisoners.

The message was duly delivered to Fidel, who gave no

particular acknowledgment of it at the time of receipt, but did have occasion to refer to the young Frenchman in one of his marathon stadium addresses to the Cuban body politic a few weeks later.

"I have received a message from our imprisoned comrade Régis Debray," Castro told the crowd, amid great cheering. "He has informed me that he has elected to remain in jail until the revolution is successful in Bolivia!" Fidel's sentence was punctuated with gargantuan roars of approval from the Cuban masses, and such are the snails and puppydog tails that reputations on the left are made of.

THE ANATOMY OF AN AUCTION

Scheer had a friend arriving in a hurry from La Paz. She had just torpedoed the negotiations for Che's Diary; she had also found out how Che actually died. That was more than sufficient for an invitation to a midnight supper, so late of a San Francisco evening Scheer and I sat cracking our knuckles in Trader Vic's and listening to ribald tales of confusion and pranksterism and raw horror stories in the broken English —not really broken, just bent, in the French way—of Michele Ray.

Miss Ray bears introducing. Were this a photo book I could save words. She is a former Chanel model. She is also a former race car driver. She combined the attributes of these two professions in her third, that of superjournalist. She journeyed to Vietnam in 1966 and rapidly gained the standing with Paris photoplay magazines and leftish weeklies that Marguerite Higgins, the lady news- and war-hawk, had with the New York *Tribune* in its publishing days; the difference was that Miss Higgins did not wear miniskirts while on duty and did not consider revolutionaries anything to flirt with, let alone embrace. Michele Ray's thing as a newsperson was that she could charm the stripes off a zebra. She went about the journalism business with the determined enthusiasm and guile and all the equipment of a successful Miss Universe contestant. She was captured by the Viet Cong, but during the three weeks she was held prisoner she did most of the captivating. The pajama-clad soldiers came to view her as a cross between Joan of Arc and Snow White and she responded in kind with a gushy essay titled "I'm in Love with the V.C." If her politics were sectarian her charm was not; the American soldiers also came to wax sentimental, with an affection bordering on awe if tainted by lust, over the winsome French correspondent who waltzed into combat zones as casually as if she were going to have a dress fitted. The GI's went so far as to name an offensive in her honor—"Operation Michele."

Michele was dressed in a jungle-green jumper that blended into the restaurant background of bamboo and potted plants in such a way that her face seemed to float, an independent, quizzical existence in the leafery. She had just that night landed in San Francisco from Bolivia but seemed fresh as an orchid from the box; even the bags under her eyes had the right curves. The combat zone from which she had returned, victorious in the opening battle of the war over the Che Diary, was that of La Paz—the altitudinous de facto capital of Bolivia, a country which, even by the almanac standards of comparative poverty and *Putschs* in South America, argues to be its poorest and most unstable republic. The scene in La Paz in the late fall of 1967 was that of a forties Sidney Greenstreet movie, complete with a Presidential Palace and "luxury" hotel named, with a bravado a movie scenario writer might balk at, the "Copacabana." There the Yankee traders gathered in the lobby to give evil eyes to one another while a dozen Peter Lorres ran back and forth to the Palace, where the leaders of the Bolivian people waited for them to cross with silver the palms outstretched behind their backs.

The stakes were sufficiently high. Che, alive, had already outdistanced the original Beethoven as the teenagers' most favored image on silk-screened sweatshirts, and his death had naturally increased his value. Che's martyred image was supporting a minor but flourishing industry of books, records, posters and other paraphernalia of making a buck off the revolution. Che's Diary was widely considered to be the biggest potential capital gain of all, and when the secret got around that it was for sale, publishers and other artisans of risk capital made for La Paz like blackbirds to the pie.

If one accepts the common image of publishers as bandits, La Paz by mid-November of 1967 resembled the host city to an international convention of the Pancho Villa Society. The morning line of *Publishers Weekly* was in on the Che Guevara act: Germany's *Stern,* France's *L'Express,* England's *Daily Mail,* the New York *Times,* a hatful of American book publishers, and sundry leading newspapers and magazines from most every country utilizing movable type. The smell of money was in the rarefied air. The big publishers' men were bidding as if they were a bunch of speed freaks playing bridge. But there were complications, most of them stemming from the fact that the two Bolivian statesmen who would profit most from the Diary's publication could not get their act together. One general wanted his picture on the cover, the other wanted to art-direct the inside of the book; one general wanted payment in cash, the other wanted at least partial payment in a numbered Swiss bank account, et cetera.

Michele's arrival on the scene was fashionably late. The haggling was pretty much completed, and the word among those competing grave robbers who feared they had lost out on the booty was that the Diary was going, and for all practical purposes gone, for a sum in moonshot range of $200,000, to Magnum, an international consortium of photographers and others, which had in turn negotiated world serialization to the New York *Times* and its European counterparts. That that expected event did not come to pass was later attributed, by her friends and enemies alike, at least partially to Miss Ray.

She explained to Scheer and me that she had scuttled the opening round of the grotesque auction. "That Hungarian," she said, while cheerfully sipping a Mai Tai, "he thinks I am Mata Hari."

The Hungarian of reference was Andrew St. George, the *éminence grise* of the Diary negotiations. A world traveler, adventurer and writer, St. George was to the CIA in the sixties what Lanny Budd of Upton Sinclair's forties' novels was to FDR. By profession a journalist, St. George seemed to enjoy

the extraordinary relationship to journalism that Johnny
Stompanato had to the movies. He always seemed to show up
where the action was—as much a participant as a reporter. He
was in the Sierra with Fidel and Che, and was sent to America
by Fidel in December of 1958 with an urgent message to the
State Department requesting that Washington keep hands off
in the impending rebel victory. St. George later had a falling
out with the rebel leaders, and Che, in his earlier Diary of the
Cuban revolution, referred to him as an "agent of the FBI"
who visited the *guerrilleros* in the Sierra Maestra. St. George
then became a paramilitary journalist for *Life*, accompanying,
and sometimes sinking with, the CIA-backed Cuban exile sea
raiders on their fruitless but continual Miami-based raids
against the mainland. In 1966, St. George was in the middle of
CBS' quite preposterous "sponsorship" of an abortive invasion of Haiti that starred the likes of Rolando Masferrer, the
much feared former Batista gunslinger. The invasion ended
with Masferrer and others indicted by a Miami grand jury,
and CBS under investigation by a House subcommittee for
allegedly interfering in the internal affairs of another country.

St. George's role as a middleman in the sale of Che's Bolivian Diary had a certain irony in that Che was, once, his
friend. The Hungarian has admitted that this fact gave him
sleepless nights and indigestion, but said that he did it for the
money, not the CIA. (CIA officials have in fact attacked him
bitterly in Senate hearings for various men's-adventure-
magazine stories disclosing one CIA operation or the other.)
St. George now spends so much time denying he is a CIA
agent that, naturally, everyone believes that he is. Even his
wife of twenty years, who knows better, sometimes thinks so.
He said he once was suffering from hemorrhoids, and his wife
suggested that he "go to Walter Reed" (the government hospital). "Those people in Washington must have some sort of a
medical plan for guys like you," she said, as the bleeding
Hungarian screamed a pained protest.

St. George, at the peak of his Johnny-on-the-spot form,
materialized in La Paz shortly after the Diary had been discovered in Che's saddlebag. Who asked whom to take the

first bite of the apple is not known, but St. George was one of the commercial catalysts prompting the decision of Bolivia's ruling generals to pass an ex post facto law declaring the Diary of the man they had murdered an "asset" of the State and putting it out to the highest bidder.

A Bolivian interior minister, a frenetic chap named Antonio Arguedas Mendieta, later double-crossed his bosses by sending a photocopy of the Diary to Fidel Castro, and said he did it to spite the CIA, which, he said, played around with his country as if it were a Lionel train. The minister said that the CIA's brainstorm about Che's Diary was to have it published with a packaging and annotation that made it a document of revolutionary failure rather than of romance—and the circus of publishers bidding big money for the Diary as the hot literary property of the year would bolster the political value of the doctored document the CIA wished to lay on the reading public.

The opening bets and raises were all on the table, and the Magnum consortium was about to rake in the chips when Michele put on her Mata Hari wig, and went to the Palace to see President René Barrientos Ortuño. "The diary in the hands of the United States is like the Koran in the hands of the infidels," she told him. Barrientos looked at her as if she were a television rerun. Michele shifted to a less political tack, announcing that she represented a French publishing house which wished to purchase the Diary. She said that her boss would be mad at her if she came all the way to Bolivia and didn't get to bid. Besides, if the Americans knew they had competition, they might raise their price. Now the President indicated that she might be talking his languge. He told Michele to go ahead and bid. That was not as simple a process as it might sound; first, she had to appear before the "Diary Commission."

Bolivia's Diary Commission was something special even to the horse opera bureaucracy of underdeveloped countries. It approximated a real life version of the up-front racist characterization the old *Mission Impossible* shows used to give to bumpkins and greedy civil servants in "foreign" countries of vague Latin American or Eastern European geography. The balance of power in Bolivia was held by two rival generals who distrusted one another, so the Diary Commission consisted of two rival members who sat all day in a room darkened from the heat and glared at each other. Michele sat with them in the stuffy dark for two hours to give the impression of negotiating. The talk was mostly about the overendowed Ford Mustang one of the two had imported, but had no place to drive it as Bolivia then had only some 4,000 miles of paved road, and those mostly bad, so he had to make do with speed shifting around the Prado in La Paz. The Diary Commission even tried to sell Michele a movie. Once Che's band of Marxist men had been captured in the jungle, the Army, in a maneuver out of M*A*S*H, "re-created" the shoot-out with the guerrillas while state cameramen captured it all on film, which they handcrafted into a bizarre documentary with background music spliced in from a Frito Bandito commercial. The film was going for a song, but there were no takers.

A lady with funny money to spend can be the devil's own negotiator. Michele shut her eyes and bid $80,000 for the Diary, for openers; the implication was that she was prepared to go considerably higher. She hoped the bid would be sufficient to get her in the game, while not so dramatic that the generals or the competition would bother to check to see if she really had the money which, of course, she did not. When Michele left Paris she had mentioned in passing to a friend, the publisher Jean Jacques Pauvert, that if she could she would pick up Che's Diary for him, to keep it out of the hands of the Americans. Pauvert had nodded an absent-minded assent, as if she had said she would pick him up a souvenir ashtray at the airport. Michele cabled Pauvert: "$80,000 bid." She hoped he would understand the message in the spirit of good clean Monopoly fun. She knew her cable would be read by her American competitors, as one of the conveniences of graverobbing in La Paz was that replicas of all telegraphic and telephonic communications to and from Bolivia were available, for a price, to anyone with the price. Hotel rooms were also searched, on a basis more regular than the maid service,

by the Bolivian secret service, which likewise made reports of
its investigations available on a commercial basis.

General Alfredo Ovando Candaná, chief of the Bolivian
Armed Forces, the other seat of intellect holding down the
seesaw of power in Bolivia, summoned Michele to his
presence. He said that she had disturbed the confident
equilibrium of the high bidders. They had occasioned the
American Embassy to provide him with detailed "intelligence
reports" on everything she had written, her travels during the
past five years, her friends—even how much she had in the
bank. General Ovando then told her the bottom line: Her
offer was too low. He said the Americans had offered
$200,000, a figure which included royalties. However, he was
not ecstatic over a royalty agreement, there being no guarantee, given the unstable nature of Bolivian politics, who would
be around to enjoy the dividend checks. She should make a
better offer in cash; he would give her a little time.

Michele was no longer sure just who was conning whom.
She suspected that Ovando suspected she didn't have the
Bolivian equivalent of a pot to urinate in. But it was to his
advantage to have her in the bidding, as that might scare the
Americans into upping the ante. Since there was nothing to
lose but Magnum's money, she decided to bluff on. She went
to a La Paz lawyer and had him draw up a contract offering
$400,000, which, she correctly assumed, would not remain
the best-kept secret in the capital. Word of her move sent the
wolves running to cable their home lairs about putting up
more cash. Michele then proved herself a formidable agent of
chaos by leaking the story of the mad bidding to *Agence
France-Presse*. The extraordinary gathering in La Paz had
remained at least a nominal secret, meaning that those segments of the news media in the know had not reported it to the
reading public during the long November of negotiations.
The story broke in France, occasioning howls of protest, both
against Magnum and the hapless Pauvert, who learned upon
picking up a newspaper that he had "offered" $400,000.
"Poor Pauvert," said Michele, "I think I almost gave him a
heart attack."

The French publisher cabled her to withdraw. That day she had an appointment with Ovando at four o'clock, and the Magnum people at five, to enter revised bids for the Diary. The Magnum consortium representatives were waiting in Ovando's anteroom when she came in: St. George, Juan De Onis of the New York *Times,* and Don Schanche, a former editorial heavy at the *Saturday Evening Post* and *Holiday* turned hard-nosed free lance, who had gone to La Paz to put a ribbon on the package for Magnum. As she walked into the general's anteroom, her three competitors smiled smugly; she knew that they had a copy of Pauvert's cable and expected her to announce her defeat. But Ovando was also smiling, and fingering a cable—which she later discovered was Pauvert's withdrawal—and told Michele that he hoped she was still in the bidding; she said yes, of course. With a smile as broad as the Bolivian *Altiplano*, he told the men from Magnum: *"Que no*! Michele hasn't come to withdraw, but to confirm her offer. You had better raise yours, gentlemen." They stared at the folded cable in Ovando's hand, uncertain whether he, too, was bluffing, or whether there had been yet another moneygram that they hadn't seen.

While Magnum's men on the spot were sorting things out, the French partners in the consortium, blanching at the bad publicity, announced that they were withdrawing. Then some American book publishers who had bid large sums to Magnum for the book rights began to waver, the flurry of sudden publicity having raised the ominous possibility of an international copyright fight between Che's heirs and his murderers. Michele also made public Bolivia's plans for alterations and additions to the Diary text, which had by that time degenerated from the sly sugar-coating that the CIA wanted to demands for the inclusion of whole cream puffs in honor of the generals.

So many vultures finally flew the coop that the Magnum deal collapsed. St. George began muttering about Michele as a Mata Hari and/or Tokyo Rose for Cuba, and *Newsweek* later reported, that "a comely Cuban agent" had a hand in wrecking the negotiations. That was our girl.

Michele got quickly out of La Paz, which had become a

dangerous place to be, as one could get hit by the bottom falling out of the Diary market.

THE ANATOMY OF AN EXECUTION

We know more about how John Dillinger met his end than about Che Guevara. Such information as surfaced at the time of Che's death, early in October of 1967, was insufficient to fill a Scrabble board. It also carried with it the presumption that someone was cheating.

Reports emanating from government jawbones of Bolivia first said that Che was killed instantly during a guerrilla shoot-out with the army; then, rather, that Che did not die instantly, and was able to admit his identity before expiring; rather, that he died seven to eight hours later, of two bullet wounds, at a military post which had no surgical facilities; rather, that he lived for twelve to fourteen hours after his capture, then died in a schoolhouse in a small Bolivian village from blood loss from nine bullet wounds; rather, that Che was only superficially wounded in the clash with the army, but was executed a day later. All but the last were official versions. The accounts of the disposition of his body were no more plausible. It was first announced that Che had been secretly buried in an unmarked grave. It was then announced that Che had been cremated, that his ashes had been buried in an unmarked hole, but that his hands first had been cut off for purposes of identification—an identification curiously confirmed by "experts" in Washington, D.C. It was later reported, and casually denied, that Che's body had been carted off by the CIA to points unknown, presumably to guard against relic hunters.

With the zeal of Rosicrucians searching for Atlantis, we made haste at *Ramparts* to uncover the true facts of Che's demise. We soon became caught up in an unusual propaganda tug-of-war, of considerable cunning and viciousness, over how the end of the great revolutionary hero would be interpreted in what bourgeois Marxists refer to in their stuffy fashion as the bourgeois press. The question was whether Che would enter the Hall of Myth as Wrong Way Corrigan, or Sir Lancelot.

In Wrong Way Corrigan's corner there were of course the Americans, and their minions. There were also the Russians, and their minions. Anyone who has seen a Ronald Reagan commercial could guess the American reasons. Moscow's motivations were slightly more complicated, but boiled down to the matter of that simple contradiction that has plagued the ideal of Communism: Granted that there must be the dictatorship of the proletariat, who is to dictate to the dictatorship? Orthodox Marxist-Leninism has lent itself to some great and stimulating debates on this issue, but it has always, to date, been resolved in the favor of the few (the party and the bureaucrats), as opposed to the many (the masses).

The revolutionary theory that Che was attempting to put into practice in Bolivia was a frontal threat to the Moscow brand of Marxist-Leninism, as it advocated the primacy of the people before the party. Che made the cautious Moscow-line Communist parties in Latin America appear conservative and cowardly. "The first duty of a revolutionary is to make revolution," Che said, criticizing Communist parties which called themselves revolutionary but spent their time roasting marshmallows waiting for all the necessary party precepts and preconditions of revolution to be fulfilled. Castro more diplomatically stated the differences between Russia and Cuba, but underneath his polite phraseology there was the streetfighter's challenge to the leadership of the block: "There are those who believe it is necessary for ideas to triumph among the greater part of the masses before initiating action, and there are others who understand that action is one of the most efficient instruments for bringing about the triumph of ideas among the masses."

It was thus in Moscow's strategic interest to see that Che did not make good in Bolivia, as his stated goal of creating many Vietnams in Latin America could only be done at the expense of Moscow's leadership. In any event, the countries that could benefit from Che's success would be Cuba and, to a lesser extent, China, all to the extreme embarrassment of Russian orthodoxy. To Moscow, Che was Dubcek with a gun.

In the corner of Che as Sir Lancelot there was, first, Fidel Castro. If Che could deliver on Castro's oft-repeated promise to ferment Cuban-style revolutions throughout Latin America, his revolutionary leadership would provide Castro with additional bargaining power with Russia, a wedge he dearly needed if Cuba was to maintain any independent course, rudder-stuck as it was between its necessary enemy, America, and its necessary protector, Russia—a position Cuban politicos of my acquaintance privately refer to in the Spanish equivalent of the devil and the deep blue sea. The seriousness of Castro's predicament was illustrated by the fate of his friend Che, whose death was, in large part, due to the dastardly efforts of the Russians and the Americans, through their respective Bolivian stooges.

Ramparts was one of the logs in the American flotsam and jetsam which banged up together in Castro's corner —disenfranchised romantics, Communists who had not soured of the revolutionary vision, antipolitical and non-parliamentary radicals, and all those whirlpool-washer elements of societal change and contradiction which are so carelessly, if conveniently, mashed together as the New Left. My accustomed position in any such political vanguard was an observer's seat in the rear but, with Che dead, the fight was all over but the shouting, which dictated the media as the choice of weapons on both sides. That left most of my allies and enemies in the fashionable revolutionary set to sit it out, since the only tactic the New Left has ever mastered, the non-negotiable demand, was of little use in this to-do.

Although the paper at that point in its development was no bastion of women's liberation, my sense of the division of labor between the sexes was not such that I was averse to fighting from behind a skirt. I happily relied on Michele Ray to do the scut-work in disemboweling the explanation propounded by the opposition for Che's breathing his last in Bolivia—that Che was an adenoidal zealot whose traveling circus of revolution collapsed of its own weight, his death representing the final defeat of his vision. The presumption that Che's vaunted revolutionary theories had backfired on him entailed the assumption that he had lost in a fair fight; he had called his big shot, and blown it; he was not so much a martyr as a fool. Said his killer, General Ovando: "Guevara chose the wrong country, the wrong terrain and the wrong friends. He was a brave man but God was not with him."

That was one way to look at it. Michele went to the Andes to see if she could find another way.

Michele talked President Barrientos into giving her a lift over the Andes in his DC-3 to eastern Bolivia, the territory of Che's last stand. Barrientos himself piloted the plane, pointing out the sights along the way, landing at one city en route so Michele could witness a native *Te Deum* and a military parade. My compliments at this accomplishment were received with a demure smile, and a French so-what; she said she had found the lower echelon members of the Bolivian military even more accommodating. Colonel Reque Teran, commander of the 4th Division of the Bolivian Army, even called out his troops and treated Michele to a reconstruction of the battle in which he had captured Régis Debray. Teran drove her to the staged fight in a gray Toyota that had belonged to a pretty girl known as Tania, besides Che the only Argentine in his band, and the only female guerrilla in the group, said by some leftist cranks to have been a Russian double agent. Tania was killed in an ambush—although not by him, Colonel Teran hastened to inform Michele; he was a gentleman who didn't shoot ladies, guerrillas or no. The fates had not been kind to Colonel Teran, as the battle in which he captured Debray had prompted Che and the remaining guerrillas to move south into the territory of Teran's archrival, Colonel Joaquin Zenteno, the commander of the 8th Division, into whose hands had fallen the plum of capturing Che Guevara.

A fancy, mustached man, Colonel Zenteno proved equally friendly to Michele; like Tristram Shandy's Uncle Toby, he was given to the zestful re-creation of his military adventures. Colonel Zenteno had amusing stories of the efforts of the American Green Berets to fire-drill his soldiers in the ABC's of antiguerrilla warfare. He recounted one incident of Dale Carnegie extremism in which the Americans, fearing a lack of pluck and gumption on the part of their South American charges, had passed entire days at the training camp leading the soldiers in shouting, "I'm the strongest! I'm the best!" The Colonel, however, was uncharacteristically vague about Che's death.

Michele rented a jeep and drove to the American Special Forces camp in the eastern slopes of the Andes. Her arrival was a tribute to the small world of American imperialism, as several of the Green Berets knew Michele from Vietnam. She said she withstood a heavy rush of déjà vu—again the Americans, in the familiar fatigues, again "advising" the natives, again the stacks of comic books and empty beer bottles and *Playboy* foldouts on the walls. "Counterinsurgency," she said, "looks the same all over the world."

The Special Forces team had been in Bolivia for five months to hand-pick and train a battalion of Bolivian Rangers to track and kill Che Guevara. Michele knew the Green Beret intelligence officer from Vietnam. He told her, with a lack of discretion that the best-trained soldiers at times exhibit when bitching about interference from the higher-ups, that the CIA had "lorded it over" the entire operation, trusting the Bolivians to do nothing by themselves but tie their boots. The Green Beret took racist umbrage that the CIA operatives giving him orders were Cubans, members of a CIA "Che team" operating out of Washington and Miami. (One of the CIA Cuban operatives was, in normal working hours, a Chevrolet salesman in Miami.) The CIA, he said, coordinated all intelligence and military planning for the Bolivians, from the original judgment that the elusive Che was, indeed, in Bolivia, down to the final kill—even supervising the embalming of Che's body.

Michele's forward progress up the Andes foothills was ended by an army roadblock on the only road to La Higuera, the tiny mountain village where the wounded Che Guevara had died. No one could go any more to La Higuera, she was told. The village was "quarantined." She drove instead to the larger hamlet of Vallegrande, where Che's body, strapped to the runner of a helicopter, had been flown, embalmed, then put on display nude from the waist up, a look of Mona Lisa repose on Che's face. The Reuters' correspondent who had been in Vallegrande that mortuarial day told Michele that a

CIA agent had directed the Bolivian soldiers in transporting the body, a man the soldiers knew as Eduardo Gonzales. Confirming the bizarre scuttlebutt Michele had heard in the Special Forces camp, he said the CIA man had actually supervised the embalming process. The portions of his dispatch mentioning the presence of the CIA had not been transmitted, said the Reuters' man.

Although this is not primarily a book of record, it would seem niggardly not to relate here what Miss Ray discovered about the details of Che Guevara's death. Like a lady Maigret, she pieced together an account of Che's murder that has been confirmed in its essential aspects by all subsequent accounts save those of the murderers and their sponsors.

Michele met a priest, a Dominican, Father Roger Schiller, a French Swiss who was delighted to find someone who spoke his language. A traveling missionary to the *campesinos* of the Andes, the priest had been the only foreigner to enter the village of La Higuera before Bolivia put it out of bounds to the outside world. (In 1970 the village was still closed to travelers.) Father Schiller arrived there just one hour after Che Guevara had died. The villagers were milling about in front of the schoolhouse where Che and the other captured guerrillas had been held. Father Schiller rushed inside the schoolhouse; he found the floors wet with puddles of blood, and the adobe walls cheesy with bullet holes. The Dominican found a bullet on the classroom floor, which he took from his Friar's robe and showed to Michele. "Look," he said, "I have a souvenir."

Father Schiller had talked to the only villager to see Che alive—the 22-year-old schoolmistress, Julia Cortez. Che, prisoner in a classroom, had asked to see the *maestra* on the morning of his death. She said she was afraid, but went. Che had a bandage on his leg but was otherwise well. He pointed to a drawing on the classroom wall and asked the teacher why she had an accent on the "*se*" of *ya se leer*; there should be no accent, he said. The guerrilla told the teacher that her school was "antipedagogical." In Cuba, he said, the schools were better than this; in Cuba they would call her school a prison. She said that her country was poor; Che replied that the generals and officials had Mercedes cars and other luxuries, that was why her school was poor, and that was what he was fighting against. Che asked her to return in an hour to talk some more, but she did not come back. She said Che's eyes had frightened her; his gaze was at once soft and strong, unbearable; she had to look down when she talked to him. Two hours later, the schoolteacher heard the clatter of gunfire and ran to the classroom. She found Che on the floor; he seemed to her almost to be floating in his own blood.

The other villagers gave Father Schiller corroborating accounts: of the arrival of the soldiers and the prisoners the night before, helicopters the next morning bringing generals to see Che Guevara, the shooting in the schoolhouse, the removal of the bodies on stretchers. Che's body rated a helicopter ride, his compatriots' corpses the back of the truck. The natives said that a *gringo* had been in the village that morning, directing the soldiers where to carry the bodies; the priest did not know who he was; the soldiers had called him Gonzales.

That was the way it was from outside the schoolhouse, looking in. Michele got an account of what it had been like on the inside from the one other person—other than soldiers, peasants and representatives of the CIA—who had been in La Higuera on the day of Che's execution. He was Jorge Torrico, a young journalist for a Bolivian military magazine who had been traveling with the soldiers, in hot pursuit of the guerrillas, to record their heroics for military posterity. He had spent four days in La Higuera interviewing the men who were accomplices before, during and after the fact in the murder of Che Guevara. It was a great story but one he knew could never be told in Bolivia. The military journalist offered it to Michele for that most traditional of motives, the promise of safe passage; the young Bolivian journalist yearned for the green pastures of Paris, and Michele got him a plane ticket and a meal ticket good for milk and honey with a French magazine.

The soldiers debriefed by Torrico told a story as consistent as it was opposite to the account given by their superior officers. Only slightly wounded in the battle, Che was brought to the village suffering more from his chronic asthma than from the bullet in his leg. He was dumped on a classroom bench with his hands tied behind his back, a position in which he received a steady file of ogling officers through the night unto the dawn, when helicopters brought the plumed serpents of Bolivian brass, including General Ovando and Rear Admiral Urgatche—the chief naval officer of that landlocked nation. The Rangers lined up to greet the rear admiral, as his function was to hand out money to each man, a bonus for capturing the prize booty. The admiral left La Higuera in a flutter, because Che spat in his face when he came to advise the prisoner to repent of his sins.

The soldiers received another lagniappe in grab bag form that morning when the few possessions in Che's knapsack were tossed out to the men bunched together in the village square, burly bridesmaids elbowing one another for the bouquets. There was a wrist watch, fountain pen, dagger, belt, compass, a beret with bullet holes in it—the El Dorado relics of a warrior saint. The soldiers began swapping their prizes, squabbling, arguing relative values the way children fight over bubble-gum trading cards. A pair of cuff links in a tiny box puzzled them; what would a guerrilla leader be doing with cuff links? A soldier asked Che if they were his; Che nodded, the cuff links were from the disguise, that of an Argentine businessman, under which he had entered Bolivia the previous year. Che asked that the cuff links be given to his son; the soldier said nothing. An officer, arriving late, wanted a pipe; the pipe in Che's knapsack was gone, but the prisoner was smoking another one, which had been filled and lit for him by some good Samaritan soldier. The officer yanked Che by the hair and snatched the pipe from his mouth; Che kicked him in the stomach with his wounded leg.

Meanwhile, word had come down from the ruling council of elder statesmen and petit larceners of Bolivia, assembled that morning in La Paz, to murder the man. There was no death penalty in Bolivia, so as to maintain a high profile of civilization it would be announced that Che had been killed in battle. If the deed was to be done it was best it be done quickly; those rubbernecks of higher rank in the Bolivian armed forces who had flown in to peek left La Higuera, and those junior officers remaining drew straws for the honor of doing in Che. The short straw went to Sergeant Jaime Teran, a man of no relation to the aforementioned Colonel of that surname. He was, also, apparently a man of some sensitivity if not qualms, as he came out of the schoolhouse less than a minute after he had gone in. His carbine was unfired, his hands shaking. The other officers stared him back through the door. Che told the trembling sergeant that he wished to stand; he said he knew that he was going to kill him. Teran, protesting too much, said no, just relax, it is nothing, only routine inspection; he made as if to walk out the door again, and then whirled around, firing his carbine first into the adobe wall and then into the still-seated Che Guevara. Che, squirming in the agony of several bullets in his legs and chest, was on the floor, still alive, when several of Teran's comrades burst in the door, demanding seconds. The sergeant stood aside as his friends began firing away, shouting that they could tell their grandchildren that they, too, had shot this man who was the king of the guerrillas. At the same time, other soldiers, unable to get in line to shoot at the dead or dying Che, rushed into the next classroom and killed those guerrillas who had been captured with him.

Che came to La Higuera with a superficial bullet wound in his left leg; he left with nine bullet wounds, five in the legs, one in the chest, one in the right shoulder, one in the right arm, one in the neck. And that, in the tradition of zap, was the end of the line for Che Guevara.

BIG HEAT PRINT IS WATCHING

Back in journalistic dry dock in San Francisco, an unexpected flaw developed in rushing Michele Ray's scoop to press. The flaw was in her nylons. Michele wore a funny kind of French stockings which looked nice in broad daylight, but in the Kodachrome cover photographs we hurriedly took of her, posed in a simulated jungle, her hose came out looking as if carmel syrup had been sprayed on her legs.

To beat the engraver's clock, Stermer had a photographer

steer Michele out to Golden Gate Park and fake a jungle picture against the local flora and fauna; the traveling mini-skirt she had on that day had to pass for jungle fatigues, but such are the desperate ways of magazines at deadline. When her stockings came out looking like they were a brass band marching off her legs, we made do with what we had, substituting a black-and-white cover of Che Guevara's death mask with a small color photo of Michele—snapshot size from the waist up, so as to avoid the stockings—cut into his face where his left eyeball and forehead would have been. Printed in large letters above the ferns surrounding Michele's head was her by-line and a gratuitous declaratory statement about the CIA doing in Che, topped off with the words, in red capital letters, IN COLD BLOOD.

Although it did not look anywhere near as frightful as it might sound, as a cover it was not the high point of subtlety. But I found it suitably rotten and direct for the mean story we had to tell inside, and thought cutting a serviceable hole in Che's face a fine way to set the paper apart from the indiscriminate efforts towards hagiography then prevailing in the New Left county fairs and wax museums of the larger culture. The cover brought forth bat shrieks of protest from the staff. The majority considered it a sacrilege. There were mutterings of reprisals, from resignations to assault and battery, should I let this hideous thing come to life. Stermer and I stood our ground, but afforded Scheer, who sided with the shriekers, an honorable way out by stating that it would cost too much money at that point to change the cover—an untruth most members of the staff, who lived in daily fear of their pay checks bouncing, accepted with the fatalism of miners hearing the canary had died.

So *Ramparts* again gave the old ultraviolence to the CIA, Red-baiting its calloused hands with Che's blood. My modest aim was not even to put the CIA Agent-Chevy salesman or whatever he was in the dock, but to make people aware of the massive American string-pulling, finger-pointing, quarter-mastering and quarterbacking in the elimination of Che Guevara.

To anyone who might raise a dime-store set of William

Buckley eyebrows at such a ready assertion of statutory bias, I should repeat that *Ramparts* never made any pretense to neutrality. The commercial press all too often operates under the assumption, to my mind perilous, that the government should be reported innocent until it proves itself guilty. I think the opposite. *Ramparts* was out to hang the government's highwaymen at every turn; our approach, outrageous to many, was, in a barnyard sort of fashion, fair: If we couldn't get the goods on them, we simply washed out the story; if we could, it was their fault for getting caught.

In the matter of Che Guevara, it was not so much a question of making a case against the CIA that would satisfy a coroner's jury in Iowa as it was of propaganda gamesmanship. To do away with Che's attraction as a symbol of man against the system, the CIA wished it thought that he had failed as a man, and not that the system had unfairly done him in. Although the CIA's version of Che's end was not altogether without merit, its postulate, that there had been a fair fight in Bolivia, was acceptable only if one ignored the massive American involvement. It was like maintaining that the Indians lost to the cowboys, without mentioning the frontier spoiler's role of the U.S. Army.

I learned later, from a reliable spook, that the CIA had tracked Che down not only on land, but by air as well. "If the *yanquis* are so anxious to find Che, why don't they send up a U-2 to take a picture of him?" Fidel Castro had once taunted. That was just about what they did, according to Hill, the reform-minded mercenary and CIA contract pilot with the neon blue eyes.

Hill surfaced a few weeks after we published Michele's story, with a high-altitude kicker for it. While hanging around a pilots' hamburger heaven near the Santa Barbara airport, he overheard some local flyboys talk of an aerial photography firm nearby which had "had a piece" of the Che Guevara action. An aerial survey company had an AID contract to take aerial photographs of Bolivia for some neo-geographic function. Those pictures were taken by day. At night, the same planes photographed Bolivia, flying in grid patterns over the area where Che's guerrillas were expected to be, exposing rolls of special infrared film so sensitive that it could register heat patterns given off in the dark jungle below—the type of heat generated by a guerrilla band in motion. The planes the Santa Barbara men flew out of remote Bolivian airstrips during the Che hunt were twin-engined Beechcrafts, once used for bombardier training, cameras now replacing the bomb bays. The film was exported to Santa Barbara for processing, where the developed rolls were hung on a giant pasteboard on a screened-off wall in one of the company's hangars. Hill said the technical name for the pictures was "heat prints"; a completed paste-up of a given land area was known as a "mosaic." Once Che's band was located, its forward progress, direction, even miles-per-hour, could be calculated on the mosaic hangar walls of Santa Barbara. Big Heat Print Is Watching.

The CIA had ample ground-level information to pinpoint Che Guevara, most of it from the Bolivian peasantry, who seemed as receptive to Che's attempt at whistle-stop revolution as Benedict Canyon hill dwellers in Los Angeles would be to a knock at the door from Charlie Manson, so this infrared espionage was probably as unnecessary as most of the other expensive toys cranked up by the military and spy boys to keep up with the Joneses. I read once in a John Birch Society pamphlet that the federal dispensary sequestered in Washington, D.C., spends some $480,000,000 each 24 hours on the Brobdingnagian requirements of government. If the Birchers be right, and for all I know they may be conservative on this, too, it is a dizzying prospect, even multiplying by one's fingers and toes, to figure where it all goes. But this brief accounting of the extraordinary item of the CIA's making heat prints in Santa Barbara of Che Guevara in Bolivia gives some idea of how all the little things we never hear about add up.

The intelligence about nocturnal overflights reinforced *Ramparts'* primary devil theory, the CIA wearing the horns. But to view Che's death only as a thinly-veiled triumph of American technology, as we did then, was a mistake. That was only half the story. The other half was revealed later that year in *Ramparts,* although not on our authority, but that of Guevara himself. The irony of the paper's surprise publication of Che's Diary was that it contained some big surprises for the adherents of the solitary American devil theory, among whose foremost proponents were the editors of *Ramparts*.

First, by Che's own account, his theory of revolution, or at the least his practice of his theory in Bolivia, looked to be a loser, even if his enemies on both sides of the Iron Curtain had not moved in to leave nothing to chance. Che violated his own commandments in Bolivia. He had written that guerrillas must be of the people and as one with the people, yet the guerrilla team he fielded was more visiting firemen than recruits from the hills; over half his small band consisted of foreigners, the majority of those Cubans. Bolivia is a nation of tongues, yet his men did not speak the most common native dialect; even the Bolivians with him did not know the regional tongue dominant in the area in which they were operating. Che had written that to be successful a rural guerrilla operation must be in close contact with the cities for money, volunteers and propaganda, yet Che was isolated—his wayfaring guerrillas connected with the cities the way a skunk railroad in Arkansas is to Grand Central Station. Che had written that where even some hope of peaceful change exists among people, the time is not right for guerrilla warfare; yet Bolivia, while no model-city of a nation, had experienced a successful revolution in 1952, entailing land reform and some redistribution of wealth, and had popular elections and other fixtures of democracy; Che found himself bucking the widespread belief of Bolivia's peasant citizenry, that while their country was no Nirvana, it was no Haiti, either.

Che Guevara's dream had been to transform "the Andes Mountains into the Sierra Maestra of Latin America." But the Bolivian Andes made a molehill of the Sierra Maestra, and his Diary revealed that most other parallels to the Cuban revolutionary experience—the model that Che held to be so vital to future successful revolutions —were similarly out of proportion, or nonexistent, in Bolivia.

The biggest surprise in Che's Diary was that his own mistakes, primary though they may have been, were as venial sins compared to the treacherous facts of Moscow's entrapment,

betrayal and sabotage of his revolutionary experiment. Indeed, Che's fundamental error, the assumption that Bolivia
was a nation ripe for revolutionary picking, was significantly
the product of phony intelligence and lies on the part of the
Moscow-line Communist Party of Bolivia. In their efforts to
insure that Dr. Guevara be reduced to ketchup, the Russians,
through their Bolivian chimney sweeps, employed most every
exercise and feint in the masterbook of knavery. Red Iagos to
the Moor, they suckered Che into a life-or-death situation in
the hills, and then left him high and dry. The Communists
told Che that they were recruiting arms and men for him in
the cities, but they did no such thing; instead they were telling
those few volunteers who raised their hands that the
guerrillas—who were in as good shape as squirrels trapped in
a washing machine approaching the rinse cycle—neither
needed nor wanted any help. At the same time the C.P. was
turning off Che's friends, it was, by some accounts not too
strenuously denied, informing on him, providing Bolivian
intelligence, but a surrogate for the CIA, with information on
the whereabouts and disposition of the guerrillas.

All the while sabotaging the only potential support and
lifelines for Che, and cooperating with his executioners, the
Bolivian C.P. put on a happy face at Latin American revolutionary congresses, proclaiming itself to be the best friend
and supporter of the guerrillas. When, close to the end of the
line, the guerrillas' plight at last became public knowledge, the
C.P. stopped the more militant of its members from going to
Che's aid, taking the position that, after all, there was no good
in sacrificing money and men on a hopelessly lost cause.

Such exercises of principle on the part of the Communist
Party were why so many of the kids on the New Left block
during the sixties laughed when people called *them* Communists.

A CHRISTMAS PACKAGE IN JUNE

Midday of an April Saturday in 1968, Scheer called me
from a pay phone in the customs lockup at the Los Angeles

airport. He had just arrived from Mexico City, en route home from Cuba, and had accordingly been subjected to the usual harassment and hassling that the customs gents inflict upon travelers who journey to those countries out of passport favor. Scheer had been in Cuba for a month, give or take a few days, and I had just about given him up for lost. He said that something was up. He asked me to meet him in ninety minutes at the San Francisco airport. "Come alone," he said. This had been Scheer's second, or third, trip to Cuba in as many months, all to land an interview Castro had been promising us with the regularity of someone telling Avon Calling to come back again next week. But the interview had always been put off, at the last minute, to *mañana*—for that legion of reasons of scattered and conflicting priorities endemic to an underdeveloped country under blockade by the United States. From the tone of Scheer's voice, I figured Fidel had finally showed up at the appointed street corner.

The afternoon was blustery and sullen with the threat of rain, but the first thing Scheer did when he got in the car was ask me to put down the top. He turned on the radio about as loud as it would go to an Oakland hard rock station, and didn't say another word until we were out on the freeway, fighting head winds and poking along at seventy to a roaring and clanking chorus of buses and gravel trucks.

"No one can hear what we're saying out here even if they've put a bug in your car," Scheer said, more by way of reassurance than declamation. I told him to yell a little because I couldn't hear.

"I saw Fidel," Scheer shouted into the wind. "He said he has something more important than an interview for us. He's got Che's Diary. He said he's going to give it to us. Che's Diary. He said we could print it. It's ours! He wants us to scoop everybody."

If the Lord had parted the clouds and asked for a match I could not have been more open-mouthed. "You're shitting me," I said, not really believing that he was, but incapable that moment of registering any reaction but awestruck vulgarity. Scheer shook his head; no, no kidding: Castro was going to give Che's Diary to us, the journalistic bad boys, the neo-

Capitalistic Black Barts of the New Left. I had that instant a hot flash that burned down to my socks: What if Castro hadn't yet seen our Che cover? Scheer said, relax. Castro had already seen the issue, and liked Michele's story.

Scheer shouted more good news. Castro was giving *Ramparts* the Diary because he actually *liked* the magazine. He found it amusing that we shocked so many people on the American left. He understood fighting slick with slick. He knew about guerrilla journalism. And he was betting *Ramparts* would slam Che's Diary into the United States in a way that would pull the rug from under the CIA's own publishing plans. Castro seemed keen on the technical details. He, himself, was writing an introduction to the Diary. That should run in front. He would write in English. And there would be pictures. And photostats of the original pages, which were at that moment being translated into English in Havana, so we would not have to risk a security leak by trusting Berlitz. . . .

Secrets—supersecrets we called them—were the staff of life at *Ramparts*. We were as security conscious as the builders of the Maginot Line, although somehow our roof always seemed made of cheesecloth and our walls had see-through cracks. *Ramparts'* big supersecret of 1967, the exposé of the National Students Association sharing a sleeping bag with the CIA, remained about as confidential as Rockefeller's credit rating. . . . It was the torrential leaks that finally led me to that decision of legend, to scoop ourselves in newspaper advertisements rather than let our political or journalistic competition do it for us.

It is thus no exaggeration to say that the Che Guevara Diary was the only secret we ever kept at *Ramparts*; it was, literally. Scheer and I maintained that radio silence by a simple, if for us radical, expediency: We actually didn't tell anyone. Invoking the need-to know rule I remembered from a James Cagney war movie, I didn't even tell Stermer, the third member of the paper's triumvirate, until the thing was almost upon us—a caution that he, of course, resented. There was reason other than our own pathology to play it close. As a literary property, Che's Diary had by then become as volatile and explosive as the Hindenburg at mooring in Lakehurst. The rate of desire is always in some proportion to the availability of that desired, and the months of delays, frustration, collapsed big deals, and continuing plots to acquire the Diary had left publishers staggering and inebriated with the wine of rumor; a considerable plum in 1967, by the spring of 1968 Che's Diary had assumed aspects of the Holy Grail. As one publisher-gunslinger fell or backed away, another stepped up to try his luck, his holsters stuffed with contracts. Industrious as always, Andrew St. George, according to the latest rumor, was tempting Barney Rosset at Grove Press, suggesting that Rosset use his Third World connections to arrange an understanding with Che's widow so the Diary could be published without any copyright problems arising; then St. George would try to arrange, *quid pro quo,* to spring Régis Debray from his Bolivian jail. However, Havana responded only with scoffing, punctuated by growls.

The copyright minefield was the one area that even the most reckless of publishers was loath to enter, and there Castro had the Bolivian generals at what might be referred to as a Mexican standoff. Under international publishing agreements, and by that distillation of Anglo-Saxon common sense known as the common law, the rights to a literary property belong to the estate of the author—and Che's wife and children were in Cuba, comfortable under Fidel's wing. Lawyers for competing publishers, Talmudists studying the books, tried to find a way around this principle, but the high priests of legal scholarship all tended to agree, dourly, that if Mrs. Guevara did not consent to the publication of her husband's Diary, she would be able to send a lawyer into any court in the United States and stop publication. There were of course complications that gave hope to the plunderers: Cuba did not honor the conventions of copyright; Che was but a naturalized Cuban, and had other family, who would have a claim to his estate, in his native Argentina; Bolivia had passed legislation making the Diary a war prize and the property of the state, a claim that might be able to be tested at The Hague against the author's survivors. . . . The Talmudists had points to count on both fingers. But the generals insisted on their

pieces of silver up front, and the perils of loss remained as
great as the temptations of profit, so publishers kept ventur-
ing to the edge of the lagoon, staring down through the shark
fins to the treasure chest at the bottom.

That was the situation with the generals in sole possession of
the Diary. But what no one knew, except for Fidel and those
Cubans under seal of confession, and now Scheer and me, was
that Castro had secretly acquired a copy of the Diary and was
preparing to publish it in its raw form, so to cheat the generals
of their honor, and their profit.

That sounded, at first, hunky-dory. But upon sufficient
reflection a bit of the bloom came off the rose proferred to
Ramparts. Cuba notoriously refused to honor the capitalistic
concept of copyright; it published everything in the public
domain, freely pirating books from Hemingway to Harry
Truman's memoirs without paying a cent of tribute. So once
Fidel published Che's Diary, it meant that anyone with a
mimeograph machine could grab it up and reprint it. We were
going to have to sing for our supper. Our royal flush had to be
played as a straight, our sure thing was really but an inside
track to get there first. *Ramparts* would have to catch everyone,
including the CIA, with their publishing pants down. It was an
engagingly difficult proposition, and I often caught myself
skipping down the street at the joy of the prospect, which I was
certain we could pull off—somehow. My euphoria rested
somewhat in being continually high on Havana cigars,
walnut-paneled humidors of which the Cubans kept hand
delivering, with Castro's compliments, and which I took to
chain-smoking, so as not to appear nervous while waiting for
Fidel.

The source of the cigars, and otherwise our pipeline to
Havana, was the Cuban Mission to the United Nations, an
emaciated gray townhouse on East 67th Street within spitting
distance of Central Park. The novelist Earl Shorris insists the
Cuban building is John Kenneth Galbraith, it is so skinny and
gaunt amid its plumper fellows. In theory the townhouse was
the official residence for members of Cuba's delegation to the
UN. In practice it was the rump embassy, intelligence anten-

nae and all-around fallout shelter for the necessary activities
of the island nation, which has had no relations with the
United States since the good old days of the Eisenhower
Administration. The business of maintaining a bad-neighbor
policy tends to be depressing; and inside, the Cuban Mission
was grim and gray, with only a frayed red rug to brighten the
décor. But if a bit shabby, it was a folksy place, and in the days I
used to punch the broken doorbell at East 67th Street there
were always a dozen or so children, presumably of diplomatic
issue, playing happily in the foyer.

Our man in this little Havana on 67th Street I called the
Great Gálvez, a rotund career officer in the Cuban foreign
service who was refreshingly free of the canker sores and
polished warts of professional diplomats. Other foreign officials I have met on American soil appeared wary or harried,
but Gálvez was more like a wide-eyed cop assigned to a Community Relations detail. His attitude was that good will would
eventually come to all men. His brown eyes purred rather
than twinkled, and his charm was not unlike that of a part-
time Santa Claus.

Little Havana's communications with the outside world left
something to be desired even by standards prevailing during
the Spanish-American War. The Cubans regarded using the
telephone in the same light as holding an asp to the ear, and
little wonder, since their phones were tapped as discreetly as
beer kegs at a fraternity party. When you dialed the Cuban
Mission you heard first a series of strange clicks and electronic
gurgles; then there was ringing, and the ringing had echoes;
when finally a distorted voice answered, it sounded as if you
had been plugged into a public convenience at the bottom of
the Grand Canyon. This was laughably more intimidation
than effective surveillance, but it had its psychological effect.
The Cuban who answered the phone at the mission usually
asked who was calling at least several times; often another
voice would come on the line, to ask again who was calling,
before you got your party, if, indeed, you did. Speaking into
that echo chamber somehow carried with it an unwarranted
patina of guilt, like that associated with taking the Fifth
Amendment. Gálvez disliked answering the telephone at the

Mission, and many times I would be told he was not in, to have
my phone ring a few minutes later, Gálvez on the line, puffing, calling from a pay booth down the street.

Long-distance use of the blower was circumscribed by prudence in any event, so Scheer and I took jet turns on the San
Francisco to New York merry-go-round, going about our
normal marketing chores in Gotham, but at some point sneaking off for a clandestine meeting with Gálvez to see if he had
any news from home. In lieu of news, we kept getting boxes of
cigars.

The prevailing uncertainty was compounded by Little
Havana's methods of communicating with the main island,
which were decidedly pre-Sputnik, limited to the teeth-
pulling process of elaborately coded messages via cable, radio,
or telephone—which were time-consuming, subject to ambiguity, and of course, breakable. Safer, but slower, was the
diplomatic pouch, which had to go via Canada, and whereby
most sensitive questions, answers, arguments and fiats were
passed between Little and Big Havana. There was, in addition, the problem of Fidel, who carried the government in his
cap and the cabinet in his jeep, and was as fiercely overextended as a hurricane with two coasts to blow. Fidel was the
only man who could say when and where we would get the
Diary, which I was convinced he had stuffed in the glove
compartment of his jeep. But Fidel was forever off in the
boonies, scouring up an emergency shipload of tractor parts,
or purging the grain ministry of fifth columnists, or putting
out some one of a hundred daily brush fires.

"I expect we will have news soon," Gálvez would say, offering a cigar.

Gálvez's idea of a good place for a confidential conversation
was to take a walk in Central Park, an art form that I thought
had gone out with hiding microfilm in pumpkins. One day,
while strolling, Gálvez said, "I have a question for you from
Fidel. He has decided to coordinate publication of the Diary in
Havana and America. How many days will it take you to
publish, once you have it?"

I shuddered at the word "coordination." "Why don't we do
it first, and *then* you publish it in Havana," I suggested, cheer-

ily. Gálvez said he did not think Fidel would cotton to that too well.

I sat the diplomat down on a pigeon-stained park bench for a little talk about the facts of life of fucking over the capitalist system of publishing. What did he think would happen when Fidel published the Diary in Havana without copyright? Gálvez said the people would be pleased that Fidel had given such a book to them. No, I said, Cuba's enemies, the generals, not to mention a score of pirate publishers, would rush into print in the United States with their version of Che's Diary. The CIA-edited version would be right there on the bookshelves next to Fidel's, the generals would make money, and Cuba would have blown its chance to pull the rug out from under Che's killers. Gálvez nodded, glumly. But, I said, there was a way. No reputable publisher would pay a dime for the general's version if *Ramparts* were to flood the country with the authentic Diary, tying it to Fidel's surprise announcement that he possessed it and was giving it to the people. Gálvez nodded, happier.

However, I said, to make that happen he must explain some things to Fidel. American publishing is a congress of delaying tactics. Nothing happens fast, the workers are not mobilized, as in Cuba, and the printers!—the only way printers are mobilized is to drive to work, and a lot of them in Cadillacs. I could bribe them to keep a secret, but not to stay up all night. Things took *weeks* to get printed—but, I would work a miracle, I would beat and kick workers, give them pills, kidnap their children, cheat and grovel, and would get the Diary printed in less than a week. But the Diary had then to get to newsstands and cigar stores all over America, a tortuous process that took several weeks by truck, the normal way magazines are delivered. At great expense I could airfreight it overnight to the big cities—a publishing excess that *Ramparts* committed with Portnoy-like regularity, anyway. The Cuban, caught up in the scenario, beamed appreciatively. No, not yet, I said—after the airlift we had to hack and claw our way through the jungles of distribution, fighting the monsters of monopoly who controlled magazine deliveries in big towns, who were more inclined to rush out *TV Guide* than Che Guevara.

Gálvez took copious notes. What message, he asked, did I wish to send to Fidel. "Tell Fidel that until you guys replace the capitalist system with something that works better we need a two-week head start, at the minimum. OK?"

"OK," said the Cuban.

May Day came and went, and the month of May, without word from Fidel. The heebie-jeebies gradually took hold of Scheer and me. We wore ruts in familiar paths on our strolls in Central Park. "One must have patience," said Gálvez, taking refuge in aphorism, "the revolution was not made in a day." The publishing rumor circuit grew overloaded with stories of who was planning to do what with the Guevara Diary. One such private revelation made me play a rotter's role. *Ramparts* then had a book publishing program with McGraw-Hill. One day that May, Frank Taylor, McGraw's editor in chief in the golden years before Clifford Irving, told me a secret. "This is extremely confidential, but we're getting the Che Diary. I've got a man in Cuba right now, and a man in Bolivia, too, and it's all set. It's the publishing coup of the year, and I think I may be able to work it so you can print some excerpts." Frank was a friend, in addition to being then a provider of bread to *Ramparts* through our book contracts; he was one of the few flamboyant accomplishers in the dark cellar of New York who had lost neither his humor nor his humanity, and I yearned for a way to warn him without telling what I could not tell. I said I hoped one of his men abroad wasn't a chap by the name of Andrew St. George. Frank said yes, in surprise, one was. "Well, you know, Frank, I think the Cubans think that guy's really a CIA agent," I said. It was a pale warning that, had I been Taylor, I would have dismissed as New Left sour grapes, as I believe he did.

June was yo-yo month. I was jerked back and forth between San Francisco and New York a half dozen or more times to deal with financial embolisms in our corporate shell, and a pending criminal indictment before a New York Federal Grand Jury. (The pending indictment was for the peculiar crime of four undraftable *Ramparts* editors—Sol Stern [asthma], Stermer [four kids], Scheer [avowed revolutionary] and me [eyepatched]—burning our draft cards on the cover of the paper. Naturally we were not about to put the torch to the things out there on a street corner with the rabble; so four models were hired, at least their hands were, and the cards were burned—while the registered owners were 3,000 miles away—under the proper technical conditions in the studio of ace *Esquire* cover photographer Carl Fischer, who was suprised when the FBI some weeks later burst into his darkroom to inquire about this unusual cover setup. The complications inherent in such a procedure so confused the prosecutors that the indictment never came down, although for a while there the Grand Jury hassled us something severe.) Late in the last week of June, the town was beginning the silent evacuation for the overextended holiday that summer New Yorkers attempt to make of the Fourth of July. I had to be present when the cock crowed on a Thursday morning in Foley Square Courthouse to curtsy before the Grand Jury and read off, from the words typed on little recipe cards, provided me by the great Edward Bennett Williams, who successfully represented me in this pickle, the First, Fifth, and Sixth Amendments relative to my traveling across the country so I could refuse on those constitutional grounds to say anything more than Good Morning to the group that had brought me there. That charade over, I went uptown to the less sepulchral surroundings of the St. Regis, where I had taken refuge from the process servers who had learned my habits and begun to collect like flies around the familiar tent of the Algonquin.

There were telephone messages; Mr. Gálvez had been calling, and would call again at three that afternoon. I went off to a Eugene McCarthy fund-raising luncheon, to see if I could sandbag any rich Democrats from his cause to ours, and returned about three to catch the telephone ringing. It was Gálvez, with un-Latin punctuality. He acceded to my suggestion that we have a drink, instead of another walk in that accursed park. The Cuban was not usually so ready to meet in public rooms, but I figured perhaps it was his tail's day off.

The St. Regis bar is large enough for the staging of Camelot. Gálvez was sitting at the table which appeared upon random calculation to be at the geometrically farthest point from the few other tables occupied at that early afternoon hour. He was eating peanuts and sipping a drink and seemed immensely pleased with himself. "Sit down. Have a drink. I am having Chivas Regal," he said, gaily. He asked me about the Grand Jury that morning, if Scheer had received the last box of Havanas he mailed to him all right, if the rooms in the St. Regis were nicer than the Algonquin, and kept on chattering through one drink into another.

When the waiter had gone away, Gálvez leaned forward with a happy face, and tried to focus his two brown eyes on my one blue eye.

"I have a present for you," he said. "It is the thing that you have been waiting for."

I started a question, but the Cuban's eyes cautioned me not to use any forbidden words aloud. I began again. "You mean *the* thing I've been waiting for?"

Gálvez wagged his head yes as fast as an excited puppy his tail, and I said my first Hail Mary in a decade.

"When?" I asked. "Where?"

"Now," Gálvez said. "Tonight. It is here. It arrived this morning, unexpectedly. It is being wrapped. I will give it to you." We could have been two brassiere salesmen discussing a new product sample.

Gálvez talked on, but I heard him only on a two-second delay. I was submerged in a split-second henna rinse of unreality—awash with lightbright images of Castro as Merlin, and some faceless Cuban, one of those tin voices which answered the echo-phone, getting glue all over his thumbs while wrapping up Excalibur.

Gálvez was still talking ". . . Fidel made his decision suddenly, and he is going to publish the Diary in Havana on the first of July."

I was never very good at calendars. I asked Gálvez, just to be sure that I had heard what I thought I had heard, when the first of July was.

"Monday," he said.

I distinctly recall that moment thinking that Merlin was a motherfucker. "Gálvez, this is crazy. Fidel just can't do that!

This is Thursday night! There's a weekend coming up. And a holiday. If you publish that on Monday we're screwed. It's impossible. We could never get it out. Once they hear what's going on in Havana, the Bolivians will get their Diary published before us. They've already had six months to get their shit together, and we haven't even seen ours yet. What happened to the two weeks you promised me? What's with Castro? This is madness."

Gálvez sat calmly across the table from me, smiling, a Cuban Cheshire cat. "I told Fidel this was very short notice, but he said you would improvise—like the way you did that time to the CIA with the newspaper ads."

I thought of telling him what to tell Fidel, but then thought better of it. "Tell Fidel thanks a lot," I said.

There was no possibility of delay. Gálvez volunteered, a bit glumly, that Fidel had already ordered 100,000 people to be in the stadium Monday night in Havana to acclaim the publication of the Diary. When Fidel decided things, he decided things.

Gálvez asked me to meet him at the United Nations, in the Delegates' Lounge, at 6 o'clock. "I will have your present for you there," he said. I was in no mood to go to the UN, or anywhere else; I asked the Cuban just to drop his present off at the hotel; I would wait in the bar until he came back.

No, Gálvez said—it had to be done at the United Nations. That was international territory. It was not part of the United States. He must hand it to me on international grounds. If anything went "wrong" on American soil, his diplomatic immunity would not protect him.

I asked what about me. I didn't have any diplomatic immunity.

The Cuban smiled a Dr. No smile, and got up to leave, leaving me with the bill.

I was late meeting Gálvez. I suffer from the recurring belief that it only takes ten minutes to get anywhere in any city, refusing to bow to the track record of tardiness that fair screams it can't be done. . . . I left the St. Regis at four minutes before the witching hour of six. There were of course no cabs, a light rain was falling, and the East Side streets of Manhattan were as sardine cans filled with cars caught darting for the escape hatches of bridges and tunnels to flee the beast for the weekend. I elected to run the whole way, in expiation for the sin of standing up Excalibur. A wheezing Roger Bannister of the sedentary New Left, I jogged into the UN in the shadow of seven, entertaining thoughts of frightened Cubans taking my alarming tardiness as a signal that something had gone wrong (Tom Hayden had always told them they could never trust *Ramparts,* anyway), preparing to flush the evidence down toilets somewhere in that great glass Tower of Babel on the East River.

The Delegates' Lounge looks like an airport terminal. UN subconsuls and diplomats meet there to rub noses when there isn't a red-hot reception going on for free somewhere else. I arrived a burned-out case but Gálvez was cool, more ebullient than ever, looking as comfortable as a male model in a Grant's Scotch ad, the soul of relaxed protocol on his own turf. He sat me down on a couch that appeared to have been made of a crocodile's large intestine and came back in a wink with glasses of Scotch, Chivas Regal, he said, which he noted a poor country like his could not afford at the prices charged in the surrounding continental United States. "I am late," Gálvez said of himself, ignoring the fact that I was late, "and I must leave for a reception. But first let me get you your present." He reached behind the couch and handed me a package the size of a baseball glove. It was wrapped in Christmas paper —crawling with Santa Clauses, holly berries and bells with Noel printed on them, and held together by a fat red ribbon tied in a clumsy bow.

"This was the only wrapping paper we had in the Mission," Gálvez said, with a straight face, but I believe to this day that the bastard went out and bought it on purpose.

"I hope you enjoy it," he said. "I must go now, but we will of course be in contact soon." Before I could say thanks, the diplomat skipped away from the scene of the crime, a halo of diplomatic immunity glowing about his head.

Outside the UN, clutching my package in both hands, I looked around with the ease of an Arab leaving the Gaza Strip, trying to decide if I dare step off the internationalized sidewalk onto the American-held asphalt. I damned myself for not having told anyone where I was going, I thought about how store dicks never grab a shoplifter until he's outside the door. After several bad moments standing there like a tight-rope walker unsure of his next step, the thought came to me that there was hardly anything more conspicuous than a guy with an eye patch hanging around in front of the United Nations at seven o'clock on a June night holding a Christmas package. I hailed a taxi, and talked all the way back to the St. Regis about matters before the General Assembly, so the driver might think I was a person with diplomatic immunity.

Enthroned on a Louis XIV coffee table, the rain-stained, Santa Claus package looked every inch a joke amid the hired elegance of a St. Regis living room. I walked a circle around it, thinking about opening it. I ordered a drink from room service, but then remembered noticing that many of the waiters were exiled Cubans, refugees to butter patties from Fidel. I called back and canceled the drink. I tried to raise Scheer in California, but he was off somewhere soaking in a bathtub without a phone. There being no further excuses for ceremony, I undid the thing.

I was fascinated by the way unknown hands in Havana had packed the remains of Che Guevara very much like a box lunch. There was on top the watercress of photostats of the pages of the Diary, which appeared to have been written for the most part in an odd datebook, apparently an advertising giveaway of some German pharmaceutical company. The hen-scratching on the pages was of the variety familiar to anyone who has had a prescription filled; a doctor who turns revolutionary does not thereby improve his penmanship. Under the photostats was a stash of photographs of Che and his men in the jungle, typical candid campfire snapshots. The next level down was a fat sheaf of pages of Che's text in the original Spanish, which the Cubans had typed on a 1930's all-script typewriter that was almost as hard to decipher as the original handwriting. After that came an English translation. Last, but not meant to be least, was Fidel Castro's essay, which had the heading "A Necessary Introduction"; it was unclear whether that was supposed to be the title, or a little love note from the Cubans to make sure we ran it in front, the way newspaper city desks mark "must go" on stories about the publisher's favorite charity.

The biggest surprise was that the Diary itself was readable. One entry began: "May 13: Day of belching, farting, vomiting and diarrhea; a real organ concert. We stayed absolutely motionless, trying to digest the pig. We have two tins of water. I was very ill until I vomited and felt better. . . ." I had feared the Diary would read like tea leaves from the central committee, but it was instead the raw stuff of literature, the intensity and conciseness of detail at times near poetry, salted with irony, and an occasional pinch of the pepper of scatology.

In the parapsychology of publishing, there is a dynamic known as the Event. That is a work so notoriously sought after that the very act of publishing it becomes the Event itself, without regard to how disappointing or boring the actual book might be; the memoirs of Stalin's daughter are typical —if she got laid or farted, or did anything in any way human or interesting in the entire book, I missed it. So I took my hat off to St. Che—he had produced that rare thing, a readable relic.

I stuffed Che back in his Christmas wrapping to protect against the elements while I figured how best to field the time curve that Castro had thrown us—an underdeveloped country giving the old shaft to an underdeveloped magazine.

AN ELEGANT SOLUTION

The next seventy-two, or ninety-six, or one hundred and twenty hours were all as one blurred moment, midnight on the ocean, made up of grotesque situations out of an Al Capp wet dream, a no-sleep, non-stop roller derby of publishing madness, the Chicken Littles versus the Boxcar Berthas. I think our side won.

I had scarcely got the Diary back in its bag when I realized I was an hour late for dinner with a rich fellow at his Gramercy

Park digs. I hoped to borrow $25,000 amid postprandial pleasantries, to keep the mag's payroll and other checks for sundries from bouncing up there with the Fourth of July fireworks the next week.

I ran about the St. Regis suite looking for a place to hide the Diary. On an inspiration, I took the pillows from under the bedspread and tossed them in the closet, cleverly substituting the package under the bedspread and smoothing things over so it looked very much like a pillow. At that moment the maid came in to turn down the bed. I grabbed the package and took it with me. I apologized to my host for being so tardy, explaining that I had had the devil's own time getting the Christmas present in my arms wrapped on June 27th in Manhattan, which I had to bring the next day to a child breathing its last in Ohio, the fatally diseased son of a political prisoner. The boy would not live to see another Christmas, so he would have Christmas in June.

Although that lie got me a lot of points at the dinner table, I didn't get the $25 grand.

The dregs of the night passed like gallstones. I had not raised a breadcrumb to put in the chirping New Left mouths of the hungry *Ramparts* multitude back in San Francisco. I had at the moment no clue what to do about the Cuban pickle I was in. A creature of bar habit no matter what, I went lamely about my routine ministrations to East Side watering holes, my package shielded from the rain like a portable pregnancy carried under my trench coat. The evening ended toward the dawn at Elaine's in useless debate with an ex-priest with one brain cell about whether Dreiser was hallucinating when he saw John Cowper Powys materialize before him; I defended Dreiser's honor.

In other moments of crisis I have behaved in equally dilatory fashion, heeding the little-known sixty-fifth hexagram of the I Ching: Indecision; when you really do not know what to do, do nothing; something will happen.

One of the good things about a round, full disaster is that the halfway house of rationality is of no avail. Nothing will save the day except the elegant solution. Elegant solutions come at right angles, or from left field, or from most any

direction except that in which you have been proceeding; they
come in a flash, but you do not conjure them; like social
diseases, you know them when you have them. One must trust
the vague metaphysics of osmosis and inspiration to put something in the pot, and then take pot luck.

The day came on like an Excedrin commercial, but somewhere in the sawdust filling my sinuses was the spoor of an
elegant solution. I met Gálvez in a dim corner of the morning
to explain what now had to be done to beat the Bolivians. The
capriciousness of Havana's decision-making had ruined my
plans to sneak up on the country with half a million copies of
the Diary while the generals slept. To achieve the same end,
we had now the more difficult task of bringing Birnam Wood
to Dunsinane. The paper would attempt to rush out a perfunctory World War II-type magazine extra over the
weekend; that would at least get the Diary on the streets, but
would have little prohibitive effect on the competition.

The elegant solution was to no longer publish it ourselves,
but have someone bigger sandbag the generals for us. I told
Gálvez I was going to sell reprint rights to the *Ramparts* edition
of the Diary to a mass paperback publisher who could flood
the nation with a million Che paperbacks. That was the only
way we could win it for the Gipper. Surprise was all we had
left, and Fidel had left us with precious little of that.

Gálvez stared at me as if I had just suggested we hijack the
St. Regis and fly it to Havana.

"You want to *sell* Che's Diary to someone?"

I said Fidel had given it to us, it was ours, so we could sell it if
we wanted to, that was the law about gifts, and he had to
understand the psychology of capitalism, for Chrissakes, if we
tried to *give* it to a commercial publisher they'd be so suspicious they'd call the cops . . . and besides, *Ramparts* could use the
money.

Gálvez said that he would have to tell Fidel. Fine, I said.
While he was talking to him, ask Fidel to come up with a
copyright from Mrs. Guevara. I was going to try and talk a
paperback house into printing without copyright, but if they
insisted, and we couldn't deliver, we would all be in the soup.

"The Cuban position is that it would degrade the purity of the author's words to put the corruption of a capitalist copyright on them," said Gálvez, reciting.

"Never mind that stuff," I said. "Trust me. Just try and get us a copyright. Tell Fidel what the score is, OK?"

"OK," said the Cuban.

"This disaster is the best thing that's ever happened to us," I am fond of saying, perhaps too readily, to some soul standing next to me staring into the jaws of ruin. The odd thing is that I mean it. There is always lemonade to be made. I saw the possibility of finessing two disasters with one blow; paperback power could avert the Cuban shipwreck, and might also put some unexpected cash in *Ramparts'* empty sugar bowl.

I took my disaster to the funny eagle's-nest office, a round-windowed cubbyhole high atop the Scribner's bookstore on Fifth Avenue, of our literary agent, Cyrilly Abels. Cyrilly is a terrific lady with a rye-crisp sense of humor. Cyrilly had been managing editor of *Mademoiselle* for fifteen years, and then associate editor of *The Reporter* before leaving one side of the publishing fence to straddle it as an agent, a position she has maintained gracefully, for clients from Katherine Anne Porter to Eldridge Cleaver, by expanding the traditional function of agent into that of combination editor and ombudswoman.

Cyrilly has always brought art and joy to what I consider the dreary task of wrenching money from the tight fists of publishers—those princes of movable type who annually slay millions of innocent trees in that Hundred Years' War upon one another that is known as the book industry.

Next perhaps to white slavery itself, there is no meaner and more dispiriting business than publishing, entailing as it does the trafficking in ideas and marketing of people's souls and psyches. The average publisher's commitment to higher purpose would make Benedictine scholars of the television network programmers. The industry is technologically antiquated and must face each season knowing that the majority of its new entries will die. It is therefore beset with a frenetic outpouring of energy and self-doubt, a slave to trendiness and rumor, a consumptive victim of the crap-shoot psychology of the best seller it must have to even out the odds against itself. Cyrilly is one of the few people I know in that beseiged and insecure industry who knows how to accommodate the necessities of commerce with the sensibilities of art. When she negotiates with a publisher it is like a symphony—beginning with the orchestration of minor points and legalisms, building among the watersheds of Handel, the mountains of Bach, and occasionally the thunder of Wagner towards a crescendo involving money. The money finale is important for other than pecuniary reasons. Cyrilly knows that the better a money deal made with a publisher, the better chance a book has of surviving the infant mortality rate of publishing—a horrifying statistic consistent with that of a maternity ward where the equipment is limited to tweezers and war-surplus iodine. . . . But that is a horror story that will keep until Halloween.

Cyrilly immediately knew what to do about Che Guevara. Within an hour we were sitting in the inner tabernacle of Bantam Books, the paperback people. The Christmas package was resting innocently on the couch beside us. Bantam had the reputation of being able to produce books in a flash. Its stockholders had done well by overnight editions of various fat and controversial reports in the quasipublic domain, issued by public commissions mandated to make exhaustive inquiries into such matters as assassination, violence and sex.

With the Christmas package resting securely on the couch beside me, I made a little speech, in the tones of childlike arrogance of a sixth-grader who had just memorized "The Cremation of Sam Magee," about how as everyone knew, the Che Guevara Diary was the most sought-after publishing prize of the year, that so many had tried and failed to get it, blah, blah, but now I could reveal that Fidel Castro had secretly acquired the Diary, which had been authenticated by Che's widow herself, and that Fidel had given it to *Ramparts* to publish. We would be out on the newsstands on Tuesday. I chattered on until I noticed that the publishing executives sitting across the room were reacting as if in a state of deep shock. I couldn't figure why. The Bantam people did not have that lean and hungry look that is the normal happy face of

New York publishers. They were sophisticated veterans of a thousand big deals, so why the stares? The Che Diary was a coup, but hardly a matter that should provoke paralysis. I looked my query.

Oscar Dystel, Bantam's president, wiped the fog off the windshield. He explained that Bantam, but a few hours before, had said, more or less, yes to my friend Frank Taylor —who had offered them the paperback rights to a McGraw-Hill edition of Che's Diary. After months of dealings with Andrew St. George, and the expenditure of many tens of thousands of dollars in various attempts to get Mrs. Guevara's permission to publish, McGraw-Hill had elected to plunge ahead. It planned the ingenious stratagem of setting up a trust fund into which the Guevara family's royalties would be paid, on the gamble that such a precaution would sufficiently impress an American court that it would not grant an injunction against publication to Che's widow, should she seek one on copyright violation grounds.

Dystel was one of the brightest men I have met in that business, and he evidenced an instant understanding of the commercial consequences of Castro's sleight of hand—those book buyers who wanted to read Che Guevara would of course not buy a CIA-tainted edition sanctioned by his killers when there was one with the imprimatur of Fidel.

"You realize," Dystel said, "that what you have just told us puts us in a very awkward situation." I said I understood it was awkward for Bantam, but what he had just told me made it awkward, in spades, for *Ramparts,* since we had a book publishing program with McGraw-Hill, and by contract would have brought a hard cover edition of the Diary to them—but the Cubans, when I had raised the question, had blackballed McGraw because it had been dealing with Andrew St. George, about whom the Cubans thought many unkind thoughts. Dystel said, ouch. St. George was the man who had originally approached Bantam to bid on the Diary, but they had wisely declined his invitation to get involved, suggesting that he take his proposal to a publisher such as McGraw-Hill, which he had done. McGraw was but returning what they thought was a favor by offering Bantam the paperback rights. "I appreciate this information," Dystel said. "If we had gone ahead with McGraw-Hill, which we obviously cannot do now, it would have been disastrous."

"But Oscar," Cyrilly said, "we didn't come just to tell you this. We came to sell you the paperback rights to the *Ramparts* edition." Oscar looked up. "But who," he said, in the manner of someone asking who was going to break the news to the new widow, "is going to tell Frank?" I volunteered to take the short straw. *Ramparts'* knife was stuck the deepest into McGraw-Hill's back. I said I would do the deed before the weekend was out.

"Now," said Cyrilly, "I think we should talk about money."

Under conditions approaching normality, Che's Diary would have had a price tag of $100,000 plus to a publisher. But with the vexing question of copyright blowing in the wind, the price was up for grabs and dependent on many variables, not least the speed with which Bantam could rush out its edition to preempt the competition, if any. Dystel asked what figure we had in mind.

Cyrilly folded her hands in her lap and looked thoughtful. Finally she said in the *sotto* but very firm voice she always used for money, "Well, Oscar, all things considered, I think we should get at least forty thousand." That seemed a nice round sum. As I watched the ebb and flow of executives in and out of Dystel's office during the next hour to argue the merits of the dare, I perceived that Cyrilly had made an excellent stab; Bantam was of course not quick to say yes to $40,000, but it became apparent they would have been quick to say yes to, say, $25,000, and no to $50,000. They wanted to see the Diary, but I said it was all wrapped up at the moment—a quite literal statement, as it was.

I all but sang the Cuban national anthem to calm their quite legitimate concerns about the copyright, parroting the Cuban position that a copyright would be degrading to the author. I suggested this was a harmless political idiosyncrasy, which could have no real effect on our publication of the Diary —based as it was on Jack-be-nimble elements of surprise and speed. After all, Bantam had successfully published U.S. Government documents, such as the Warren Report, without copyright protection, and now it was a Cuban government document they were getting. Why discriminate? My arguments sounded, to me at least, a little better than the Cubans deserved, but we ended up leaving Bantam that afternoon with an agreement to go ahead, an appointment to come back Monday with the Diary and sign a contract for our $40,000, and as testimony to the stability of the situation, sheets full of the scribble of telephone numbers where key people were going to be over the weekend—so everybody could keep in touch—in case.

I had no idea there was such an animal as a liberal typesetter until Marc Stone, the resourceful PR man, pulled one out of his hat. Stone's address book was a yellow pages of serviceable leftists, a fount of information for which he had paid dearly over the years in attending thousands of cocktail parties and fund-raising dinners for lost causes, peopled by rich Long Island socialists and pinko dentists from the Bronx, at such citadels of plasticity as the Americana—in the 60's the most favored hotel of the New York middle-class left, which was its upward mobility thing from the ragamuffin 50's tatty décor of the Hotel Diplomat. I told Marc I desperately needed a typesetter who would keep our secret, work all weekend on credit—and had nine point Times Roman on his machines. He knew a place in the West Twenties that filled such arcane specifications, even unto the type face. One of the partners was a friendly fellow named Jerry Zinn, the younger brother of Howard Zinn, the abolitionist-historian, and Jerry was willing to mobilize his plant to give it the old college try for Che Guevara. That night the Diary shed its Christmas cocoon, and the next day began to emerge, at caterpillar speed, in curly galley proofs from six wheezing linotypes, one of which collapsed and died under the nonstop schedule of the weekend.

I recruited proofreaders from the ranks of the deaf and dumb, so as to minimize the possibility of loose talk, and set up secret production quarters in the Algonquin, figuring it a safer place to assemble the nuts and bolts of the Diary than the St. Regis, where refugee Cuban waiters lurked behind every monogrammed pie plate. Unluckily for her, *Ramparts'* copy editor, Leslie Timan, was vacationing on Fire Island, and was brought in her bathing suit to Manhattan, supplied with nitrous oxide and a Spanish dictionary, and left to her own devices to render the Diary readable and printable by Monday. Norm Eisner, our printer, had squealed a printer's crybaby squeal when I told him, with some relish, that the edition of *Ramparts* all set to go to press at 6 A.M. that Monday had to be junked. He was to hold the presses, let the men play dominoes, charge us for the idle time, I didn't care—we would arrive sometime that day with the stuffing for a special edition which must roll through the night; no, I couldn't tell him what it was he was going to be printing in such an all-fired rush; no, it wasn't anything illegal, just scurrilous.

The printer's squawks were as the warm breath of baby chicks compared to the noise from Scheer and Stermer when I sent urgent orders for them to catch the next air rattler to New York, refusing to explain why on the phone. By this point in our relationship they had grown cranky about what they considered to be my penchant for yanking them back to New York from San Francisco, or vice versa, on various journalistic impulses susceptible to the metaphor of craving pickles and ice cream.

However, they came, arriving in thunder and sitting down in awe to champagne and hosannas. Our orgy of self-congratulation was short-lived, overshadowed by the logistics of our fourth-down situation. Stermer and I occupied ourselves with the not inconsiderable technical problems of fashioning the extra momentarily to go to press into a finished product that would look sharply other than the overnight handout that it was. I wanted to run a photograph on the inside front cover of the Christmas paper the Cubans had used to wrap the Diary, but Scheer said that would be politically incorrect.

Scheer threw himself into intense and lengthy conversations with Gálvez, the significance of which I never quite fathomed, except that it was doubtless the fitting and proper way to normalize the relations between Cuba and *Ramparts*, Scheer as the magazine's ambassador to the revolution, exercising his mandate to engage in sophisticated political discus-

sions about the *fait accompli*—providing a balance to my rant-
ing and cursing to the Cuban representative about typesetters
and distributors and Fidel screwing us up. There remained
some diplomatic points to be resolved. Although Havana was
enamored of the idea of giving Che's Diary free to the world,
and so to us, I insisted, for a variety of legal and propaganda
reasons, that we announce that we had bought it from Cuba's
state publishing house. I ended that discussion by grandilo-
quently handing Gálvez the contractually nominal dollar as he
got into a taxi. Scheer was particularly concerned that we
follow to the letter Havana's stipulation that the Diary be
published as we had received it, without editorial revisions or
supplement. The careful observance of such a bridlesome
condition was a trust not best left to the likes of Stermer and
me. Marc Libarle found a trustworthy high school Spanish
teacher to improve upon the English translation, and Stermer
engaged in some cookie cutting during production, leaving
out a few of the illustrations supplied by Havana that did not
fit, or did not fit his art director's fancy. This omission Scheer
discovered only as the magazine was coming off the press,
which provoked in him a most bloodcurdling reaction, replete
with cries of treachery and stop the presses. The art director
stared back daggers and stomped off in a blaze of Van Gogh
purple. To mollify the inconsolable Scheer, I had four extra
pages printed, Pages 34a to 34d, with the left-out tiny pictures
of Che Guevara scattered incomprehensibly thereon, which
were stapled into the center of the issues not yet bound, so
Scheer could keep his word to the Cubans.

Gálvez had bad news for me late Saturday night. Cuba
could not provide a copyright. It no longer belonged to the
International Copyright Convention. Things must stay as
they were. Gálvez had, by now, become caught up in the
mechanics of strategy, and he hastened to point out to me
what Havana had pointed out to him—that we would not need
a copyright, anyway, as no publisher could dare compete with
the edition of Che's Diary that carried an introduction written
by Fidel himself. I asked how much he wanted to bet.

Sunday, in remembrance of Pearl Harbor, I phoned Frank Taylor. He said he was taking the call in the kitchen of his house in Connecticut. "You'll never guess what I'm doing right now," the editor in chief of McGraw-Hill said, his usual cheery self. "My barber has just come over, and he's giving me a haircut, right here in my kitchen, while I'm speaking to you."

"Well, Frank," I said, "I'm glad you're sitting down."

There was only the sound of clippers on the other end of the wire as I told Frank my story. I ended by saying that had it been the other way around, I would have expected him to do unto me what I had done unto him.

Frank said he would have. He took being stabbed in the back with a grace beyond Caesar, the pro who appreciated the game's being played the way it should be, even if it had to be at his expense. Men of Taylor's mettle are as rare in the New York publishing pack as dancing pumps in a street gang. Rumbles of a more typically tatterdemalion reaction from the ranks of his fellow publishers soon disturbed the Sabbath calm.

Over in the corner the radio was playing, and I heard to my horror that some bigmouth in Havana had announced, a day ahead of schedule, the news that couldn't wait, that Fidel had got his hands on Che's captured Diary, and would publish it in Cuba on the Monday. To say that the news came as a blow would be to traffic in understatement. I had been counting on that remaining day of cloud-cover the way a leper counts his last toes. We had hauled Birnam Wood but half way to Dunsinane Hill in secret, and now would have to brazen it out in the open, exposed to snipers and demolitionists alike.

Oscar Dystel called. He had heard the news from Havana, and knew that it was bad news for us. He had reports of other inauspicious rustlings in the bushes. Sol Stein, of the publishing firm of Stein and Day, had all morning been on the blower trying to reach Marc Jaffe, Bantam's editorial director. Stein wanted to put out a rush paperback edition of Che's Diary, which he said he was getting the official right to publish from the Bolivian government. Jaffe was getting a stiff neck ducking Stein's phone calls. That was, indeed, bad news. Once

Stein knew that Bantam was planning to publish the Cuban edition, and with *Ramparts* no less, there would be no appealing to the logic of profit and loss with the man. Politically an Archdeacon of the Cold War, Stein was the former executive director of the American Committee for Cultural Freedom, one of the CIA's dirty little secrets of the fifties. The publisher still had fond words for another former employer, the Voice of America. Oscar said he'd call back on a conference call; he wanted to plug in a few of his people. With that, I knew we were in trouble; only federal prosecutors or very worried businessmen hold conference calls on Sunday morning.

Scheer was at the door, looking nervous, surrounded by room service carts in the tow of two bright-eyed Cuban waiters. Scheer in moments of the greatest peril will hunt and peck about to see what there is to eat and he complained that there was no cantaloupe. I headed for the bathroom, to get out of the towel I was wearing, and told Scheer to order cantaloupes, lots of cantaloupes. Order drinks, too. Screwdrivers and Bloody Marys. And salty dogs. Order a dozen of everything, what the hell. People liked to eat and drink at wakes, and we seemed destined to convene a rouser of the species.

Scheer's dozen cantaloupes arrived, three to a white linen-covered cart, floating in a china shop of plates and cups, each lonely melon set off with silver service and embroidered napkins. The lot of it was hauled in, elephant-train fashion, by a committee of two waiters and two bus boys whom Scheer detained in the hallway while I dashed about the living room snatching up telltale proofs of Che Guevara from the floor.

A panache more suited to a grander time, this improvident flotilla of produce had an especially enervating effect on Scheer, as he had to forge my name to the check while I was attempting to hold up my end of the Bantam conference call. The discussion generated much gloom and little light at the end of our tunnel. Sol Stein had been busy the last hour—on one phone line to Bolivia, on another making various threatening calls to Bantam. He had somehow divined what Bantam was planning, and was insisting that when the official papers arrived in a few days from Bolivia he would serve writs on everyone, and seek an injunction against Bantam's publication of *Ramparts'* hot copy of the Diary that he said the Cubans had stolen from its rightful owner, the generals.

The indefatigable Stein was next reported forging a politically unexpected axis with another publisher spurned and left on the junk heap in the Diary race, Barney Rosset's Grove Press. Grove published a hodgepodge of trendy Marxism and erotic French novels about dim-witted girls who ride motorcycles nude under their black leather jackets and are flogged with roses in the climax. It did not seem exactly up Stein's Voice of America alley. The Stein and Day-Grove Press pact was, allegedly, that Grove, which had facilities to distribute paperbacks that Stein did not, would do a quickie paperback edition of Stein's "authorized" text of the Diary to come out contemporaneously with Bantam's Cuban edition. Half the people on the line were starting to speak at once, the way it happens on conference calls. Someone had just talked to Barney Rosset, who had voiced hurt and chagrin that the Cubans would give the Diary to the wretched *Ramparts* instead of him, Barney Rosset, the publisher of Régis Debray! Rosset was reported as being in a real high-left pique, desirous of vengeance at any price.

Bantam's lawyer suggested unkindly that maybe they should forget the whole idea. They might be paying $40,000 to walk into an ambush. Another of the conference voices said that even if Bantam proceeded under these drastically changed conditions, the right to get shot at certainly wasn't worth the $40,000 that it had been on Friday. Optimism was not the order of the hour. Groping about the bottom of the ingenuity barrel for any idea that would avoid a total collapse then and there, I suggested that we treat the $40,000 as sort of reverse hazard pay—*Ramparts* would keep it, or pay portions of it back on a sliding scale, according to the hazards Bantam encountered in publication. The top of the scale would be the full $40,000, should we by some miracle find a workable copyright or should our stratagem succeed and no competing edition emerge from the thicket of threats heard that morning—all the way down to zero if Stein was granted a permanent injunction against Bantam's publishing the Diary.

That way, I suggested cautiously, no one could possibly get hurt.

That confused matters sufficiently, and it was agreed to let everything rest until Monday, when we were due to sign our contract. The lawyer's voice trailed off with something about hazard pay clauses not being in the standard publishing contract. . . .

I summoned whatever authority can attend a person dressed only in a bath towel and eye patch and standing in the middle of a hotel suite surrounded by uneaten cantaloupes. "Tell the Cubans that if they don't get us that copyright, they're sponsoring a publishing Bay of Pigs!" I told Scheer.

Scheer went down to the lobby to lie in wait for Gálvez. The waiters arrived in a wave once again with the several dozens of drinks ordered in an earlier hour's impetuosity. Not wishing to waste, I called up a number of derelicts and likable freeloaders of my New York acquaintance and asked them over for drinks and cantaloupe. The secrecy lamp blown out, I also called Henry Ramont. Henry was one of my favorite journalists because he reported the news of publishing for the New York *Times* with the delightfully patrician ways of a bored butterfly collector, shooing some stories off because they were too common, popping others into his net with an air of absent-minded expertise. He was engagingly pompous in a spontaneous, distracted sort of way, not so much disdainful as oblivious about the self-importance of New York publishing and literary cliques, and maintaining a regnant attitude in all things.

The Che Guevara Diary command post was filled with wretches by the time Henry Ramont arrived to be fed his scoop for the next day's *Times*. My freeloading friends, a dozen Henry VIII's of Charles Laughton mannerisms, were swilling and clowning and stuffing their faces with melon instead of mutton. All that was missing was a turkey flying around the room as in the cinema *Room Service* of the Marx Brothers. Henry was oblivious to the madness and sat cheerfully leafing through proofs of the Diary and sipping a Bloody

Mary. He had written many stories over the past year about the six-figure negotiations for the Diary, and he asked how much I had paid the Cubans. I said it was "an undisclosed sum." Henry then asked about the copyright. I was in the midst of reciting how we were publishing Che's work without copyright, because to do otherwise would tend to dishonor the author, when I was interrupted by an excited Scheer, who hauled me out to the hallway where a mute Gálvez leaned against the wall under a Fire Exit sign, looking every inch a house dick.

"You tell him," Scheer said to Gálvez.

The diplomat shuffled one foot to the other, smiling slightly. "The Government of Cuba," he said, "is prepared to grant you the copyright to the Diary of Che Guevara."

I caught myself screaming at Gálvez; how could Cuba do that? What about the International Copyright Convention, which he himself had told me Cuba no longer belonged to?

Gálvez said "belonged" had been the wrong choice of word. His English was not perfect. Cuba was no longer active in the copyright association, and did not recognize its prescriptions, but had never actually resigned; in fact, its dues were paid up. This sudden right-turn in policy, Gálvez said, was to avert a larger evil: "Mrs. Guevara is granting a copyright because she does not wish the dignity of her husband's work to be violated by his murderers seeking to profit from it," said Gálvez.

I marveled at this very neat shift in the Cuban line; it was largely the same words and sentiment, but a light year of difference in effect. I also saluted Scheer's power of persuasive panic, as he had somehow convinced the Cubans, who obviously were prepared to do this before today, but had been holding out lest it not be necessary, that it was.

The Cuban expertise in the devices of capitalism, when they had to stoop so low as to use them, was considerable. They had worked out the copyright mechanics in a way that would do justice to a Wall Street lawyer, and for all I know there were a pair of those aboard the Cuban Ark. Che's widow had granted all rights to his Diary to the Cuban state publishing house, Instituto Nacional del Libro, which, in turn, was granting with all the formulism, talismans and sign language of international copyright law the license to *Ramparts* to publish the Diary in America. The documents would arrive via diplomatic pouch Tuesday night.

It was all as swift as a Bingo on the eleventh number. I was back in the room before I realized that I had forgotten to say thanks.

Henry was impatient to get to his office. I told him there was one more thing—Mrs. Guevara had granted *Ramparts* the exclusive copyright to publish her husband's Diary in the United States.

"I thought you said," Henry said, looking at his notes, "that you were publishing the work without a copyright because a copyright would tend to dishonor the author."

"Well, if I said that, I certainly didn't mean *that*." I expunged the record with a song and dance about how the leg bone of *Ramparts* was connected to the shin bone of the Instituto Nacional del Libro, which was connected to the ankle bone of Aleida March de Guevara. It was kind of fun, this business of shifting the official line, in the way high school debating used to be fun.

"Very well," said Henry, revising his notes.

RAMPARTS TO PUBLISH MANUSCRIPT SAID TO BE GUEVARA'S DIARY, read the five-column headline, couched in the grammar of *Times'* supercaution, on Henry's story in Monday's editions. The story put Sol Stein on notice that we had the copyright, and once we had it, we flaunted it. The *Times* on Tuesday ran a front-page story and a half page of photographs and excerpts from the Diary, which I had given to Henry with the stipulation that every picture the *Times* used must carry a *Ramparts'* copyright line. This was a method of photo credit not routine at the *Times*, although after considerable discussion, they agreed to print our copyright notices.

The technical provisions of publishing copyright law represent a kabala unique unto itself. One such stipulation is that the copyright notice might be no good at all if it is not printed within the first four pages of a publication; it is additionally uncertain whether the cover and inside front cover count as pages one and two, or not. There also exists actual authority and wisdom for the argument that the farther up in those first four pages that the notice is printed, the more potent it may be. There was no sense in arguing about herbs with witches, so I printed copyright lines in *Ramparts'* Diary edition on several pages, in a type size suited to a Rosser Reeves advertisement, with a giant © symbol staring out at the reader like an anemic CBS eye.

I convened another conference call Sunday night to the Bantam people to tell them about the manna from copyright heaven. They received that news with an enthusiasm that was dimmed only by my suggesting that perhaps the sliding scale should work both ways—now that we had the copyright maybe the price should go up above $40,000 in relation to the hazards they would *not* encounter. I thought that a sporting suggestion, but they seemed to consider it closer to banditry, so to keep peace in the family, I did not pursue the point.

Gálvez materialized again later that night. "We have taken care of Mr. Rosset," he said.

He and two hefty fellow diplomats from the Cuban Mission had shown up without warning at Rosset's Greenwich Village townhouse and asked the Grove Press publisher out for a short drive, as they had a matter of most urgent confidence to impart. During the drive the Cubans suggested to Rosset what some of the "consequences" might be if he persisted with his plan to publish a spite edition of the Diary. Gálvez diplomatically did not enumerate for me all the consequences that were put to him, but one, embodying mere financial harm, was that Grove Press would be put on the shit list of the Third World, and would never again be commercially successful in publishing works of the revolution. Rosset apparently got the idea early, as their trip, Gálvez reported, was short and sweet.

"You mean you guys took Barney Rosset for a ride!" I shouted.

"That is a gangsterism which is not suited to the pursuit of diplomacy," said Gálvez. "We merely took him for a drive."

I have for some time been searching for a cheery little tune to put music behind the words, so that I can sing them in the shower, of Dick the Butcher in Part Two of *Henry VI*, "The first thing to do, let's kill all the lawyers." I find those agreeable sentiments. In most every big fight that I have been in, I have had more unnecessary trouble and aggravation from lawyers, including the ones on my side, than from the enemy. The denouement of the Che Diary battle proved no exception. Sol Stein had lawyers, and his lawyers got other lawyers: experts. Bantam had lawyers; and their lawyer, and the lawyers who were *his* lawyers, wanted me to hire yet other lawyers, to help the lawyers Bantam's lawyer had hired fight the lawyers that Stein's lawyer had hired. I kid thee not.

In a moment of weakness, brought on by my fever to get the $40,000 and publish the Diary and get the hell out of New York, I went along with this drunken sailor's weekend of lawyer-hiring. It had its amusing aspects, mostly because it involved, on a revolving-door basis, Ted Sorensen, the ghost writer of Camelot, wearing his lawyer's cap. But, as is usual with lawyers, I could not afford the laugh.

I will explain. But first I should explain, so I will not be accused of objectivity, what I think about lawyers. Most fall into one of two categories. They are plumbers; you tell them where the leak is and then must watch to make sure they fix it right and do not overcharge you. Or they are obstructionists, who get in the way of efficiency and common sense and make everything more complicated than it need be, thereby rendering necessary their own existence, which is to sort out the problems they make. There is alas little middle ground between the two. The fiction that there is something sacred about the legal profession is one propagated by lawyers, so to powder over their profane and pedestrian contribution to the human race, a copper penny in the collection plate of just causes. Lawyers are by definition the scientists and technicians of right and wrong, but as a class they have, past and present, exhibited no more social conscience than tinkers. The profession is in hock to humbug and a slave to roll call, and the notion that it is a competent or rational calling is largely a delusion. If justice is blind, it is because the legal profession has grown and prospered as cataracts over its eyes. As John Clancy, a barrister of my acquaintance, once told me—if you find a lawyer who has no respect for other lawyers, hire him; he knows something you don't know.

That said, I should modify it by saying that some of my best friends are lawyers. And that was approximately the spirit in which I sat down to reason with the lawyers the day we were shoo-flying the Diary to press. Cyrilly and I had arrived at Bantam's offices at the appointed hour Monday afternoon with a bag to take away the money. It was just as well we did not have a cab waiting outside. We had raised the copyright from the bottom of the deep, and subdued Barney Rosset with Cuban cold towels, so I thought we were in pretty good shape, considering the shape that we were in. But lawyers as optimists make obstetricians of hangmen, and while the rest of the people around the Bantam table were hot to get to work on the paperback, their lawyer, Victor Temkin, kept waving a legal pad full of provisions he wanted to write into the contract. He demanded that *Ramparts* insure against every conceivable disaster. I responded as the bull to the red flag, as there is no sport I enjoy more than beating up on lawyers. It was difficult for others to fathom what all the table banging was about, as his friends and co-workers around the conference table knew this fellow Temkin as a simple and kind human being, and did not know that I saw any lawyer with whom I might be arguing as a poisonous horny toad croaking *fee-faw-fum.* Oscar Dystel was a prince during all this; obviously itching to get on with the hard work of getting out a book, he assumed a referee's position in the war of words between his man and me, on occasion ruling that there was no need to cut a particular paper doily—but he could hardly be expected to tell his own lawyer that he was being too protective of his own company's interests.

Lawyers love a good delay, taking nourishment in temporizing. But we had to saddle the horse that afternoon, so I gave Temkin two of his points. Both of them of course came back to haunt me almost immediately. I agreed to hire yet another high-priced New York law firm, on top of the ant farm of lawyers already involved, lest Sol Stein's copyright challenge our copyright to arm wrestling. I also agreed to limit the number of copies *Ramparts* would print of the Diary. I had said I wasn't sure, which at that point I wasn't, how many we would put out—probably somewhere between 200,000 and 300,000. I was thinking about newsstand copies, which would be out there bumping up against the paperback editions. I finally settled on 250,000, a concession which made Temkin as happy as a whore in heat.

I went next to the newsstand distributors and announced that I could lay a quarter-million copies on them. Magazine distributors are an altogether unusual breed of human animal, made of the stuff of Ford dealers in Dearborn, Michigan, or candy store concessionaires in a prisoner of war camp. They sharpened pencils and clipped cigars, and came up with the magic number of 230,000 copies for the newsies of the land.

I told the printer, what the hell, run 250,000, anyway. Later that night, I asked Stermer what he thought we should do with the extra 20,000, short of giving them to disabled veterans in hospitals. What about the subscribers, he asked. Oh, shit, the subscribers; I had forgotten about the subscribers! All 120,000 of them. Stermer painfully reminded me how I was always shafting the subscribers one way or another—they were forever reading about some big *Ramparts* story in the newspaper, and then watching people whistle down the street with a red-hot *Ramparts* off the newsstand where I had air-freighted them, while the subs stewed for two weeks before their copies arrived stale and ragged in the mail.

"You can't screw the subscribers like that," Stermer said, in the tone of voice of the good laboratory technician telling Vincent Price he can't transplant the gorilla's brain into the young girl's body. I supposed I couldn't. I phoned the printing plant and told them damn the torpedoes, to keep running till they hit 350,000 copies.

The next day we held a high-noon joint press conference with the Bantam brass at the Overseas Press Club to announce the simultaneous magazine and paperback publication of the *Ramparts* edition of Che's Diary. It was consistent with the political background of the previous year's maneuvering that the loaded questions came both from representatives of Hearst's flagship *Journal-American,* then in its last gasps, and the *Daily Worker.* The otherwise melodious occasion was marred only by a hallway shouting match between Temkin and me, the lawyer refusing to surrender a $20,000 check in his pocket, the publisher's down payment to *Ramparts,* to me until I gave him a letter agreeing to retain outside legal counsel.

The afternoon brought a new flurry of escalades from an enraged Sol Stein, who was dispatching threatening telegrams at a furious rate asserting his connubial rights under his marriage to Che's killers. But the eye of the hurricane seemed to have settled in by the dusk. The first copies of the *Ramparts* extra were off the presses, and I organized a modest cocktail party at the Algonquin so the champion bowlers and pinsetters of New York's publishing alley could feel up the pages of our scoop. The many *Ramparts* and Bantam types in attendance seemed in a deservedly triumphant mood; even the Cubans were all smiles. It was hail fellow and well met, so I thought I had best fess up about that matter of the subscribers, lest it surface later and the lawyers, in their fashion, claim I had been trying to pull a fast one. I told Marc Jaffe, the Bantam editorial director whose cool I had come to admire during the previous five days of crisis orientation, that in our talks about the press run I had been thinking only of newsstands, and had completely forgotten about our subscribers—which I of course assumed that Bantam assumed we would naturally send copies to; no matter what, I had left them out, and had to print for them.

Jaffe began to say that he had not thought about the *Ramparts* subscribers, either, but as a goodly number of them would also likely buy the paperback edition. . . . Temkin, who was standing nearby, proved to have the ears of Rubber Man, and was suddenly between Jaffe and me. He was making menacing gestures with a copy of the contract and demanding to know exactly how many copies I had printed.

I said, three hundred and fifty thousand.

The lawyer reacted to that number as a pinball machine registering Tilt. He made a rather impressive speech pointing out that by my own admission I had breached the contract, that in his opinion this had been a project fraught with peril from the start, that the legal battle might cost them more than the book could make, that he had no choice but to call a meeting in the morning and lay the facts of my perfidy on the line, that thank God it was not too late for his company to withdraw—and in that likely event *Ramparts* would be liable for the legal costs they had incurred prior to my violating the agreement.

Before I could say as much as pooh to all that, another county was heard from. "Now you've done it; you've really done it this time!" It was Marc Stone, the assistant publisher, also publicity man, also advertising salesman, also loan-finder, and general worrier of *Ramparts*. The lovable quality that characterized Marc's unflagging energy in these pursuits was that, in Wordsworth's phrase, his apprehensions came in crowds. A battle-scarred but amazingly unweary veteran of losing leftist newspapers, Marc had been aboard the business side as the great *PM,* and then its short-lived successors, the *Graphic* and the *Compass,* went under the financial waves. Such sinkings had taught him the importance of caution, moderation and survival, instincts that were as alien to me as Mars. Stone was in constant dismay at my all-or-nothing approach to publishing matters, which he considered to be both improvident and reckless in the extreme; but he always pitched in to help rescue me from some burning building or falling wall, and each time that I, somehow, blithely escaped, he would lecture me, the good Jewish uncle, about even cats only having nine lives.

But at that moment of the lawyer pulling the plug, Marc saw the end happening before his eyes; I had finally tripped up from running too fast, the whole house of cards was tumbling down—as he poured forth such general lamentations, I could not help thinking that, this time, he might be right. For the Grand Strategy to work, we desperately needed Bantam, but they hardly needed us. Jaffe and Dystel were reasonable men, but corporations were not reasonable beasts. Corporations

332   *If You Have a Lemon, Make Lemonade*

have a dynamic of their own, and when the lawyer sounded a general-quarters alarm among the executive ranks the next day, we might very well come out the loser: And the lawyer, with a broken contract in his hand, held the high cards.

The four of us stood staring at one another, in partial shock from the admissions and outbursts we had just partaken of. All I could think of was a similiar, horrible incident that a friend had once described to me. He was living a combination-plate AC-DC life in San Francisco, having an affair with a very social girl, and at the same time having a homosexual affair with someone else. An afterhours spot on the waterfront, the Broken Drum, then featured mixed dancing—in San Francisco parlance, "mixed" does not mean boys and girls like high school—but boys and girls, boys and boys, and girls and girls. One night at the Broken Drum he was dancing with his boyfriend, when he whirled around in a waltz step and came face to face with his girlfriend, dancing with another man. I said, "My God, what did you do?" He shrugged. "What could I do?" he said. "I just waved and waltzed on!"

I was going to tell that story to Temkin, to ease the tension a bit, but suddenly I thought of an elegant solution. I grabbed up the contract.

"Now this contract says we can only print 250,000 copies, right? And I had to print 350,000, so I owe you 100,000 copies, right?"

"Uhh . . . Right," said Temkin.

"All right," I said, "I'll buy 100,000 from you to make it even."

Marc Stone gasped.

I wasn't really sure what I was saying until I had said it, and then I found it a wonderful idea. "We can easily use 100,000 of them over the next year or so. We're always printing little things to give away as bonuses to get new subscribers. We'll just give them the paperback. You sell them to us at the price you would receive if you'd sold them in a bookstore. Fair enough?"

Temkin stared. Jaffe, smiling, volunteered that it sounded fair enough to him.

Stone came out of his shock enough to begin sputtering that we couldn't afford it, but I hushed him; that was tomorrow's problem, which we would worry about tomorrow. As for today, I grabbed up the contract and scribbled down the side my intent to buy 100,000 paperbacks and then initialed it, the way lawyers tell you to. I handed it to Temkin, to make sure everything was legal.

If more be told, *Ramparts* actually bought most of the damned things, although it went bankrupt before it could use them.

The law firm Temkin had his heart set on my hiring was Paul Weiss, Goldberg, Rifkind, Wharton and Garrison, an exemplary set of wigs even by New York High Druid standards. Goldberg was Arthur Goldberg, ex of the Supreme Court, and Rifkind was Jackie Kennedy's lawyer in the William Manchester whoopee, which gives some idea of the polish of the brass.

I arrived at their Madison Avenue offices, which had the look of an anteroom to Fort Knox, Wednesday morning —hung over and twenty-five minutes late for an ungodly early ten o'clock appointment. I hoped for the money that I would at least get Arthur Goldberg, but I had not realized that the place was a complete refugee camp for Camelot. An officious secretary, who looked as if she had posed for WAC recruiting ads in World War II, ushered me into the presence of Ted Sorensen. He explained, rather giddily, that as the most famous junior partner, he had the duty desk on the day before the Fourth of July.

Sorensen had the sweet accommodating attitude of a superior Houyhnhnm bureaucrat. But I had trouble explaining all the problems to him, because what felt like a very large rat, propelled by the bilge in my stomach from the evening previous, was attempting to climb up my throat, its hot black nose tickling in the vicinity of my Adam's apple as I tried to speak. I fought back the presence, and Sorensen finally got enough notes down on his legal pad to say that he would have to get immediately to work and consult with some other lawyers about this. He then mentioned a retainer, in

334 *If You Have a Lemon, Make Lemonade*

some ferocious amount, to which I nodded and pretended I was writing down, but didn't; I figured that once we got past the immediate crisis I could always say his check must have gotten lost in the mail. I left to attend to the serious matter in my throat.

The *Ramparts* gang were all sprawled about the Algonquin lobby late in the afternoon. They asked what had gone on during the day, and I told how I had to hire none other than Ted Sorensen because Bantam wanted *Ramparts* to have a fancy lawyer.

"But he's a murderer!" Scheer began shouting. Scheer delivered a twenty-minute New Left diatribe about how Sorensen was a Kennedy gunsel, a war criminal, a person who probably had a direct hand in the American role in killing Che Guevara, politically a wholly disreputable character with whom *Ramparts* could not possibly be associated. Scheer's remarks were met with a chorus of applause for him and hisses at me for being so corrupt and stupid. The crescendo reached considerable proportions, and I said all right, I didn't give a damn, I had just hired Sorensen, so I'd fire him.

I drafted a telegram, which Marc Stone went to a phone booth to dictate:

I REGRET THAT I WILL NOT RETAIN YOU RE CHE GUEVARA DIARY AS YOUR ASSOCIATION WOULD TEND TO DISHONOR THE AUTHOR.

I fled the big town to avoid Sorensen's Fourth of July fireworks. I was exhausted but the elegant solution was successful—the Diary was on the stands, the paperback edition on the presses, and Sol Stein was squashed (his lawsuits proved bluster, and a month after the Cuban edition went unchallenged everywhere through the land, he published a Dog Show edition of the Bolivian version of the Diary, complete with the mandatory cream puffs for the generals, which was received with the thud it deserved).

Marc Stone was the only *Ramparts* type in Manhattan on the Friday after the holiday. He received a curious phone call at the *Ramparts* New York office. The caller was Ted Sorensen, who was most puzzled by a telegram he had received signed with my name.

He read it to Marc: "I regret that I will retain you re Che Guevara Diary as your association would tend to dishonor the author."

It was left to the public relations man to explain about Western Union having left out one little word.

8.

Curtains for the Sixties

It had become the *Ramparts* way to start off each new year with a new millionaire. The sugar daddy for the wooden-nickel year of 1968 was an American mineral king living in Mexico City, Stanley Weiss, a mainstream jet-setter, a big plunger, gambler and charmer, a fellow lucky in money and sought out by honey, an importer of Russian vodka and an exporter of rare metals who, approaching 40, was desirous of buying some meaning for his life. Stanley promised me the world, and like Joan Crawford in *The Damned Don't Cry*, I said I had to have it.

Indeed, I needed it. The paper had gone off the gold standard after the Arab Israeli War of 1967. Marty Peretz and Dick Russell, the two liberal Jews who had filled *Ramparts'* kitty to overflowing after our exposés of the CIA, had rather abruptly withdrawn one million of their dollars, which we sorely needed to live on, because they objected to the paper's editorial on the Six Day War, which, although pro-Israel, was not pro-Israel enough. Thus sank the Good Ship Lollipop. *Ramparts* for five years had been a remarkably robust terminal case, but to loose a million under those circumstances was a blow even its moonshine-laced financial nervous system could not survive; at least it was an honest way to go. Marty Peretz some years later bought the *New Republic*, which *was* for sale.

337

Thereafter the great iron bird that was *Ramparts*, lopsided and gasping for money, attempted for a while to fly on one wing with no prayer in its Sisyphean climb toward publishing's cruising altitude, while I scanned the bare horizon for a rainbow of finance capital.

At the moment when we needed him most, along came Stanley Weiss, as if sent by God—a millionaire from Allah, I assumed, since Jesus and Jehovah had indicated a strictly hands-off attitude. The rainmaker for this miracle was Gossage's sidekick, Gerry Feigen, that practitioner and master of many trades, who knew Weiss professionally, one of Gerry's professions being that of proctologist, in which capacity Weiss came to him, patient to doctor, as so many rich and poor men come to Dr. Feigen to undergo the equalizing experience of having their behinds picked at. Gerry cured his body and then went to work on the millionaire's soul, which was in thirst of redeeming social importance. "You've been middle-aged since puberty," Feigen told him, in characteristic Feigenese. "You're standing still running uphill. Just making money is no way for a grown man to behave. Throw the bull over the fence." The millionaire asked Dr. Feigen what he should do to make his life more meaningful. "You've got to be willing to stick your finger into an electric light socket," Feigen said, and, by way of direction, introduced Stanley Weiss to me.

My experience with prospective angels has been uneven; some are lambs who want to be petted, others, out-of-sorts chiropractors in need of flesh to pound. But Stanley Weiss was all platinum and velvet. He even told me, repeatedly, to keep the meter running while we talked—he would invest a "token" $50,000 in *Ramparts* no matter what, just for the hell of it, to buy the boys a beer, should our protracted negotiations about really big money not pan out.

Before January was far along I was three-stepping through a great waltz of negotiations with Weiss and his accountants, tax advisers and attorneys—the ever-present footmen to the contemporary rich. I liked Stanley because he was as willing and able to talk business in bars and restaurants as in an office. He exhibited a prehensile ability to remain relatively sober through evenings ending at the dawn, drinking cognac and discussing money and politics, two subjects joined as Siamese twins at *Ramparts*. That agenda consumed a dozen nights of talks at floating conference tables from the mini-Louvre home of Stanley's art collector father-in-law in San Francisco to the walled-in fortress homes of his jet-set friends in Mexico City, to which I began to commute, a conquistador in reverse, to break bread and talk turkey.

Stanley's Mexico City friends were mostly Rudolph Valentino types with annelid eyelids, some skinny with diamond walking sticks, others fat and wearing fezzes, but not a beret or a pair of Levis in the lot. They were mostly Greeks, Turks and Mexicans, either sons of the idle rich or the idle rich *père,* but not so idle that they weren't constantly on the move, skiing in Gstaad, sailing in Greece, making money in Rio, making whoopee in New York; some of them clipped coupons and others owned the coupon factories. Their one common allegiance, aside from fun, was money, which they played with in an insouciant manner that could be mistaken for abandon. During their frequent evenings of poker and other games Stanley was, most of the time, king of the mountain. I watched him dump $20 grand at poker one night in Mexico City, a sum he brushed off as if it were dandruff, explaining, cheerfully, that he had won $30 grand the week before.

If Stanley played harder, he also seemed more industrious than his gambling companions; he got up early every morning and made a good deal of money, and seemed destined to go on making a good deal more. He had started by beating a jinx. He was a kid from the wrong side of the Philadelphia tracks—and Philadelphia, as some dice-players will tell you, is a bad roll. But Stanley managed. He wandered somehow to Mexico, a prospector in search of a vein, and succeeded, after various hair-raising setbacks in the *Treasure of Sierra Madre* tradition, in getting his foot solidly implanted on the slippery corner of the magnesium market. He went on to deal in other of the rarer elements, the names and valuable virtues of which he enumerated to me but which I slovenly forgot; he established an import-export company in Mexico, compiled a smallish to middling fortune, married a beautiful girl whose family also had a lot of money, and took up the high life of the rich

American expatriate businessman, world traveler, and quasi-international socialite. Somewhere along the way, he shed his Philadelphia twang in favor of a higher mobility tea-and-crumpets accent; he was engagingly frank and not in the least bit dissembling about how he had acquired his cultured tone. Successful at the counting and gaming tables, Stanley became a culture vulture, succeeding, at first swoop, in lending a hand in bringing the Russian film version of *War and Peace* into the United States. That slight experience gave him a taste for the extracurricular, which he pursued via financial flirtations including importing Russian vodka and helping finance a Jean-Luc Godard movie.

Ramparts, said Stanley, as the January of negotiations grew into a February of financial desperation for the magazine, was his ideal vehicle—a commercial enterprise exuding political principle and plugged into the with-it forces which were creating change in the world; the magazine could continue to tell the truth in America and he would use his European contacts to spin off other profitable properties, even movies, from it. The millionaire's commitment to *Ramparts* increased in almost direct proportion to my anticipation of the grim reaper. *Ramparts* was then strangling without cash in one of those magazine doomsday rocket rides of circulation growth, like the one that nearly did in Henry Luce's young *Life* some thirty years before its time; but at least Luce had friends in High Protestant places and could walk into banks without the security guards being alerted, as was the case with *Ramparts.* There was alas nowhere to go but forward as the paper owed so much money, and so much of that to hostile investors, that to retrench would have brought the roof down. But to go forward, or even down, required capital, and we had lost our Israeli War Bonds.

Stanley stopped talking communications empires long enough to talk cash. It was not cheap talk—for starters half a million dollars. The deal involved some complicated financial arrangements—tax-loss carry-forwards, the creation of a holding company, exchanges of old stock for new, and more money in the shape of debentures down the line that would put Weiss in the position of owning half the *Ramparts* act.

There was considerable trepidation in the ranks at the prospect of giving up half ownership in the paper to a comparative stranger. But it was midnight on the ocean and not a streetcar in sight; I observed that Stanley didn't strike me as the type who would be hanging around the office looking at galley proofs. We sorely needed an angel, and here was one right from central casting—fun loving, lean without a lean look, liberal and libertine, well-tanned, rich, and above all highly desirable in that he desired us.

We were at the stage of "drawing up the papers," as they say in the real world of money, when Stanley extended a generous invitation. He asked the *Ramparts* editors to fly to Mexico for a few days, so all the star players and their new owner could get to know one another better. He would pick up the tab. For a special treat, he had arranged that we all get together for some intellectual give and take, an exchange of disciplines, with the world-famous author and psychoanalyst, Erich Fromm. "You guys are all working too hard," Stanley said. "You deserve a few days off."

It was, of course, an invitation we couldn't refuse. The *Ramparts* crew queued up at the San Francisco airport midday of a gray February Sunday for our free trip to Mexico, exhibiting all the gratitude of conscripted laborers. To our surprise, Weiss's lawyer was waiting for us. He was a pleasant, frail man named Bernard Petrie, a San Franciscan of a quiet, compassionate nature and watchful hawk eyes, who seemed always about to catch a cold, and had brought a topcoat along with him in case Mexico wasn't warm enough. He said Stanley had invited him down "for the ride." I asked if he was along to act as a Fair Witness; "No, no," the lawyer said, "I'm going for the fun of it, just like you."

Scheer and I boarded the jet late, after dallying in the airport bar, to make a discovery that was to cause consternation and bitching the rest of the journey: Stanley had bought our seats in tourist. All of us seemed on the lookout for something to become upset about, and the cramped accommodations served to upset everyone mightily. Feigen was particularly incensed. "What kind of a millionaire is your client anyway?" he said to the lawyer. "Sending us tourist, when he's got all that money. What's he trying to prove?" Fred Mitchell, the history professor who by that point had put $300,000 in *Ramparts* and given up academia to assume a $12,000-a-year senior editor's job to be nearer to the funnel from which his money poured, was journeying to Mexico to take the measure of a man who was going to put in even more money than he. Mitchell took our accommodations as an omen. "It would seem," Mitchell said, figuring quickly on his fingers that it would have cost Weiss something in excess of an additional thousand dollars to send the lot of us first class, "that the new owner is trying to tell us something." It was the first time I had been in steerage in an airliner since I discovered credit cards, and Scheer and Stermer had long ago become corrupted by my insistence on traveling only first class. But, since the lawyer was watching, we elected to remain crammed in the rear, despite Feigen's strong declarations of intent to change his ticket to first class when the plane stopped in Los Angeles before the long leg of the flight to Mexico City. Feigen, displaying admirable obstinacy and independence, did just that, leaving us chickens packed in the rear with the lawyer, who, skinny fellow that he was, seemed the only one comfortably seated during the next three hours of low moans and slow burns from our company.

"How long are we going to have to stay in Mexico City?" the art director, in a prosecutor's voice, asked the lawyer.

The lawyer said, "Oh, I thought you knew. We're not staying in Mexico City. We're going to Cuernavaca. Dr. Fromm lives in Cuernavaca, and he doesn't like to travel."

Cuernavaca is an asphodel city of hardly 20,000 souls, yet the place is overpopulated by displaced mandarins. A resort town an hour's drive by race car from Mexico City, ideally pretty in the Hallmark Card rendition of quaint, a Mexican Bethlehem, ornamented with cantinas, churches, gardens and some superior hostelry, it has been a fashionable place for the élite to meet since the days when Carlota would drag Maximilian there by the ear; but this century, as with other excesses, would appear to have overdone the tradition. Cuernavaca has become something of a landlocked Elba for freelance gurus, well-to-do geomancers, and artists with and without causes—there Malcolm Lowry, the American novelist, studied dipsomania, and David Siqueiros, the Mexican painter, read Karl Marx. More recent decades have rendered it institute-heavy, a sort of south-of-the-border Cambridge without a Harvard, where behind scores of heavy oaken doors fronting on the twisting city streets purr the genteel intellects who have made Cuernavaca their corporate headquarters for tax-deductible thinking, safe from New York cocktail parties, the atomic bomb, and undesirable graduate students who say "far out."

Radical Catholic experimental farms have captured the hills which side the city: on one height, a monastery of Benedictine monks, where the mandatory psychoanalysis of novitiates was the rule until the Vatican cut them off; on another height, the antipedagogical Christian think tank of Ivan Illich, a modern *grand seigneur* and former Jesuit who also was fair to boiled in holy oil in Rome for his nonconforming views. The city proper holds a bewildering disarray of political and apolitical residences, including that of Cedric Belfrage, the aging Communist-in-exile, whose home is a sort of wayward hotel for devotional leftists who can afford to help maintain the upkeep by paying day rates to sit around the swimming pool and talk about the old days with the master of the house.

On another hill, which would have to stand on tiptoes to qualify as a mountain but was high enough to afford a splendid pastoral vista of the peasants toiling in the fields below, was the villa of Cuernavaca's most distinguished intellectual taxpayer, Erich Fromm. There the *Ramparts* editors arrived tardy and grumpy in the noonday sun.

Erich Fromm was a short man, pale and Metrecal-stocky, with neutral, unobtrusive mannerisms and eyes that stared heavy with wisdom but were weary and information-satiated, like the eyes of a prisoner in a Telenews Theater. The analogy is, properly, from the fifties—of those news-and-short-subjects-only movie houses that flourished and died in the few years between the decline of movie newsreels and the ascendancy of television network newscasting. The fifties were

Fromm's golden years, when he was to psychology what Edward R. Murrow was to broadcasting. Kids then climbing the beanstalk of ideas about soul and psyche read Erich Fromm the way kids now read R. D. Laing, but with more universality, as there was less competition and fewer distractions in the fifties; acid was still something used only in chemistry classes, and Fromm's popular Freudian revisionism was new and voguish. In the sixties, heavily-respected but less-heavily read, Fromm kept his finger in the intellectual pie from the remote lectern of his spacious house in Cuernavaca, where he revised his famous old books, tinkered with new ones, and occasionally traveled to lecture in the American heartland. One activity that occupied a good deal of the doctor's time, but also contributed to the maintenance of his standard of living, was the use of his home for private intellectual seminars, at which the very rich paid to rub brains with the very great. The *Ramparts* people unfortunately fit neither of those categories.

"I always believe it is wonderful to sit around a table so we can all see each other," said Dr. Fromm, as we sat down around a dining room table large enough to hold the cast of the Last Supper. The psychoanalyst sized us up as if one among our number were singlehandedly guilty of the primal crime. Stanley Weiss lounged at a far corner of the table, smiling expectantly. The lawyer inspected his fingernails. Everyone else looked bewildered. Dr. Fromm removed three thin gold pencils from his suit pocket, lined them up in precise, soldierly rank on the table in front of him and turned over an hourglass, which apparently signified the opening of the intellectual starting gates.

"Let us begin," he said, "by discussing the distinctions between biophilia and necrophilia."

We sat through the ensuing one-sided discussion with the polite restiveness of kids kept in school during recess —prisoners in a theory factory, Mitchell analogized later —and the unpleasant feeling dawned among us that there was more to this than met the eye, that we had not been brought to Cuernavaca simply to have intellectual greatness thrust upon us. We were there to be tested, to run some sort of an intellectual gauntlet, and that famous little man emitting heavy Germanic vibrations from the head of the table was going to prod and poke and plumb the shallow depths of the boy storm troopers of the New Left to see what neuroses we were made of—it was a goddamn intellectual rabbit shoot, and Stanley Weiss, the man who was buying us, was going to sit back and watch the hunt, his lawyer a Fair Witness at his side, to see who came out on top, his old liberal friend, or his recent New Left acquisitions.

Dr. Fromm changed the subject. He wished to talk about social progress and education, in particular the achievements of his friend Professor Paulo Freire, who was making great if gradual leaps forward in raising the literacy levels of the Latin American masses. In one experimental slum, said Dr. Fromm, the professor had achieved astounding success, by working with familiar objects, in getting the children to symbolize and concretize words. Within a matter of months, for example, the slum children had come to recognize the symbol for a garbage can and transfer the word value to it.

Cautiously, as there was money watching, Scheer asked, so what?

That was the thrust the psychoanalyst appeared to have been waiting for the opportunity to parry. He asked Scheer if he had another way to improve the world without endangering the species, and the conversation shattered into the polite but frosty prism of that eternal debate about the arbitrary either-or proposition of gradual progress versus revolution. Dr. Fromm preferred to formulate it as Reason versus the Apocalypse.

Fromm's political style was suggestive of what some students of European politics would call the social democratic tradition, a political posture which demands of its adherents the ability continually to tread water while looking out over their right shoulder for the tidal wave of fascism, and over the left for the equally dangerous whirlpool of the disorderly spontaneous revolt of the masses.

The psychoanalyst was known for his crusade for the "spontaneous self," but interrogatories during the course of the day indicated that his definition of the "spontaneous self"

did not include the forging of violent revolution and a
number of other radical things of which the psychoanalyst did
not approve. Dr. Fromm's predilections about order and
political progress on the one hand were balanced on the other
hand by an oft-repeated fear of the atomic bomb. His distaste
for revolutionary activity was grounded in his belief that it was
ineffective and unreasonable, in part because it could provoke
war, ultimately the final war, with the atomic bomb going off,
thereby ending all progress and hope of progress.

Fromm's courtly if cautious politics fit the New Left proclivities of the men of *Ramparts* as a jock strap Abelard; though
itching to get into a scrap, we minded the money, and bit our
tongues and smiled, and tried to think nice thoughts. We took
out our aggressions when Fromm passed around a box of his
obviously expensive cigars. Each *Ramparts* lout grabbed up
two or three cigars. Fromm seemed more taken aback by this
piggishness than by the Stalinist excesses he imagined to be
our politics. He appeared unhappy when we returned for the
afternoon session of intellectual darts following a swim in his
expensively-tiled pool and a siesta in the formal gardens
which sloped part-way down the hill to a forbidding barrier
that fenced off the peasants.

It was cold and gloomy in the shadowy corner of the dining
room, where the psychoanalyst sat at his great table awaiting
our return. I suggested that the weather was so nice perhaps
we might gather outside, on the patio.

Seminars, Dr. Fromm said, icily, are conducted indoors, at
tables; this seminar, at *this* table.

The afternoon skidded downhill. Stanley Weiss kept smiling, but not with his whole mouth. Dr. Fromm perked up only
once, when he recalled, with obvious pride, a study he had
conducted in Germany in the mid-thirties which elucidated
those psychological characteristics of the German lower-
middle classes which led them to so readily accept Nazism.
The psychoanalyst did not respond favorably to my query as
to what he was doing going around asking questions at a time
like that when he could have been stashing away guns and
organizing resistance activities. "You are obviously politically
unsophisticated," he said.

Scheer, who had successfully restrained his usual aggressiveness, slipped as the afternoon lengthened. "If I knew we were going to be *schlepped* down here for this . . ." Scheer blurted out, and then caught himself.

Fromm's head snapped to attention. He glared, instinctively restating Scheer's garment-district Yiddish in the more proper German.

"You were not *geschlepped* here, Mr. Scheer," he said in a tutorial manner, "you came here of your own free will. People do not come to my home against their volition."

"Well, I feel like I was *schlepped*, anyway," Scheer said.

Stanley Weiss spoke up from the other end of the table. "What is this *schlepp* they're talking about?" he asked, the world's most assimilated Jew speaking.

The psychoanalyst asked Scheer just exactly what he meant; Scheer said that if he knew what *schlepp* meant, that was what he meant.

"What is going on?" Stanley Weiss demanded. He kept asking, "What is all this about?" shrugging his shoulders, making magnificent psuedo-Jewish gestures of bewilderment, asking everyone around the table in turn what was *schlepp,* but no one could answer him, because they were laughing too hard; everyone, that is, except the lawyer.

The hostility index at dinner was sufficiently high to keep conversation safely on the Edwardian novel. Fromm retired early, without offering anyone after-dinner cigars. The psychoanalyst safely in bed, we drank his cognac and indulged in a giant release of guilt and venom, much of it directed against our benefactor, our Jewish Jay Gatsby, Stanley Weiss, for spending his hard-earned money to force us to walk such an intellectual tightrope.

There was a new actor in our psychodrama, who made of it a group therapy session. He was Michael Macoby, a follower and colleague of Fromm's, a young fellow with Irish features, who later proved himself to be his master's intellectual henchman. Macoby played the devil's advocate, asking questions, drawing us out, seeking to unravel the unstated concerns that had twisted the day into such a pretzel of suspicion and anxiety. Gradually, our resentments surfaced. Scheer told Stanley, in more than so many words, what *schlepp* meant. Feigen asked the millionaire who he thought he was, anyway, locking us up with this famous old fart who wouldn't let anyone get a word in edgewise. Stermer, an angry art director, demanded to know if our continued attendance at this seminar was mandatory if we were to get the half-million dollars.

Weiss seemed distraught and apologetic. He said he hadn't intended that our meeting with Fromm be anything but a nice get-together, and he was sorry that things had gotten off to such a bad start. As to our suspicions that this visit was in any way a string tied to his investment in the magazine—why, forget it, Stanley said. He had already said he was putting in $50,000, no matter what, and, as a matter of fact, he already had made up his mind to invest the whole half-million—the accountants were working out the details right now.

"Look here," Stanley said, smiling, attempting to cheer us up, bending over slightly and holding his hands in front of him as if he were pushing an imaginary wheelbarrow, "here's the money, right in this wheelbarrow, it's all yours, I'm giving it to you, here, take it!"

That was just the therapy we needed. The evening ended in a hyperventilated state of euphoria and relief, clapping good old Macoby on the shoulder, marching around the dining table with Stanley Weiss, looking for rooftops to shout from.

The next morning, hung over but happy, everyone showed up on time for the seminar, eager to please as puppydogs. The psychoanalyst, sensing the change in our emotional metabolism, looked curiously around the table for some clue. The *Ramparts* men beamed back, truants sitting attentively in class. Fromm's curiosity hardened into suspicion as his guests became openly solicitous of his opinions, which they had all but given the raspberry to the day before.

"Why are you all being so nice?" he asked, and received in answer a row of Cheshire smiles.

Stanley took advantage of the unexpected display of good feeling to bring up something that had obviously been on his mind all along. He asked Fromm to tell us about a major new theory the Doctor had been developing these last few years, but had not yet publicly unveiled. Fromm, whose normal body warmth seemed that of an iceberg, appeared to heat up by a few degrees. He said that he wasn't sure if he should go into it at that time. Upon considerable coaxing, he relented to the extent of discussing his theory "in a minimum way, generically," with the caveat that it would be of course impossible to go into many details with the uninitiated.

He called his theory the "New Synthesis." He delivered a preamble of an hour's duration about the significance of the New Synthesis, which would occupy a position in the intellectual big leagues somewhat analogous to the Super Bowl. If Fromm's dissertation was calculated to leave the uninitiated in the dark, it succeeded to that extent. As we prepared to break for lunch, he leaked it that the New Synthesis had to do with, but was not only about, the reconciliation of Marx and Freud. I earned a glare from the great man by asking if that wasn't the same thing that Wilhelm Reich had tried before he got into orgone boxes.

Perhaps, Stanley said, we could continue this discussion after lunch; perhaps we could raise with Dr. Fromm the possibility that he might consider publishing his New Synthesis in *Ramparts,* which would surely be a great scoop for the magazine—a proposition to which the editors assented with a series of grunts.

Outside, in the sun, Feigen was cracking jokes at a furious pace. Among the surgeon's resources was an almost inexhaustible routine of jokes—as he had once analyzed and categorized every joke in the lexicon of humor, from the vaudeville to bordello genres. Feigen had us all rolling on the grass holding our sides from the pain of excess hilarity. Many of our belly laughs were at the expense of Dr. Fromm's Germanic mannerisms. Feigen at this juncture was in high dudgeon after a day-and-a-half of listening, the iron rules of the seminar ordaining against topics being raised from the floor. Gerry was highly irreverent, if highly hilarious, about the "New Synthesis," which we had to worship without being told what it was, slaves to the shadow in Plato's cave.

I began to worry that we were laughing over par, and looked up to realize, too late, that we had been sitting directly under the balcony off Fromm's second-floor bedroom. He had retired to take his siesta, although I thought I had spied the curtains moving.

As we were straggling back toward the chilly dining room for our last scheduled meeting, Scheer, his face saffron-tinged, pulled me aside to inform me that we were in the soup.

Scheer had just had a disastrous experience. Having drunk too deeply of the local waters, and inconvenienced by diarrhea, he had spent the better part of the luncheon hours stranded in a bathroom off Dr. Fromm's private study.

While thus occupied, Scheer said he had been surprised to hear his name taken in vain directly outside the bathroom door. The psychoanalyst and Stanley Weiss were having a heated discussion about the *Ramparts* people. Dr. Fromm did not like them. The discussion boiled into an argument. Scheer attempted to extricate himself from the bathroom as rapidly as possible. This was complicated by the annoying fact that the flushing mechanism in Dr. Fromm's toilet was broken. Scheer had to fish around inside the tank to engage the flushing apparatus manually.

The argument meanwhile had become a shouting match. Macoby had apparently just related to his boss the content of the previous evening's rump session of group therapy, and the psychoanalyst was furious. He accused the millionaire of using their friendship for gross purposes, and of plotting to bring such degenerates and dangerous fanatics as Robert Scheer into his home to spy on him.

At that, Scheer opened the bathroom door and sauntered into the study, mumbling something incoherent about feeling a little under the weather and trying to find some aspirin. The famous psychoanalyst turned snow-white at the specter of the bearded New Left Polonius surfacing from behind his bathroom door, obviously having overheard him losing his cool. He ordered him to leave the room. Scheer, shrugging, complied, mumbling that maybe he could find some aspirin in the kitchen. . . .

Dr. Fromm convened the seminar with a medium hello. He took longer than usual to line up the gold pencils in front of him. Weiss was slumped off in a corner, looking as if he would have liked to press his wrist and disappear.

Feigen spoke up. Before we got back to that business about the "New Synthesis," he wanted to raise a subject that might be a bit "more contemporary." Crisply, Fromm inquired what subject could possibly be of more relevance.

Feigen took this as an invitation, and brought a copy of *Encounter* magazine onto the table, opened to an article that he had been underlining with a yellow filter-tip pen. It was, he said, an article on the "New Technocracy." Oh, asked Fromm, in almost a whisper, just who had written so interestingly on this "New Technocracy"? Feigen read the name of the author: Zbigniew Brzezinski. A shudder passed around the table. Brzezinski—a high priest of the technocratic society, a pocket calculator for the State Department, a defender of the Vietnam war at campus teach-ins.

Fromm, empurpled, began to shout. "Do you know who that man is, Dr. Feigen, whose ideas you want to bring to my table? He is a monster, a man of the Cold War, a man who wants to replace people's souls with computers! I will not have that man's name uttered in my house!"

Feigen said, "Well if that's the way you're going to behave, then I won't read it!" He stood up, took the magazine off the table, put it down on his chair, and sat on it. A magnificent gesture, he said later, for a proctologist.

Fromm's attitude suddenly changed. It was now part hunter stalking the fox, part that peculiar condition that Lewis Carroll once tried to describe as "uffish," which he said was that state of mind when the voice is gruffish, the manner roughish, and the temper huffish.

"On second thought, Dr. Feigen, I would be most interested in discussing what you people really think. Yes, I am very interested in discussing this. I think it would be instructive for Mr. Weiss to hear how the people of this magazine in which he has expressed such an interest think more of a monster than the 'New Synthesis,' " Fromm said.

Feigen began to protest that he only wanted to discuss technocracy, not get into bed with it. Scheer, sensing an entrapment, jumped into the breach. Very carefully skirting all the fine intellectual edges, he suggested that Fromm might be subconsciously harboring totalitarian feelings against those with whom he did not agree.

It was a double whammy that scored. The psychoanalyst brought his palm down flat on the table, *smack,* like the sound of a dueler's slap in an Errol Flynn movie. He measured each syllable as he spoke:

"Gentlemen, I can no longer carry on this charade. I have long been suspicious of the real purpose of this gathering and of the real motives of the parties here, and my darkest suspicions were confirmed by a disgraceful incident which occurred during the lunch hour."

There was a good deal of coughing and shuffling of feet. Weiss and his lawyer were fidgeting like crossword puzzle fans without pencils.

Scheer raised his hand. "Just what incident are you referring to, Doctor?"

Fromm glowed with pique. "You know very well what I am referring to, Mr. Scheer. It was a private incident involving yourself and myself and I do not wish to discuss it before the entire gathering."

Scheer maintained an insufferable innocence. "But Dr. Fromm, shouldn't we get this out on the table? I mean, I've read all your books and you're always talking about how it's bad to repress unpleasant experiences and everything."

Fromm hit the table again, this time with his fist clenched, with the sound of a grapefruit hitting wood.

"You know damn well what I'm talking about, Scheer! It was when I caught you spying on my private professional conversation with Mr. Weiss!"

Scheer leaped to his feet, talking stream-of-consciousness fashion:

"Now just a goddamn minute Fromm. I was in that bathroom *first.* I was there before you guys came in. And I wouldn't have been there in the first place if your goddamn water hadn't given me goddamn diarrhea. And you guys were only talking about skiing in Gstaad or something and if there'd be enough bedrooms in Weiss's house, so considering the condition I was in I decided to stay on the john. When you started getting personal, I *tried* to get out of there, and at *great personal inconvenience,* and if it weren't for your fucking toilet I would have got out of there sooner. . . ."

Rolling up his sleeve to demonstrate, Scheer began to grope around in an imaginary toilet tank at his feet: "For Chrissakes, I had to roll up my sleeve and get it all wet trying to pull up the bulb so it would flush, because a guy can't have diarrhea and *just walk away,* for Chrissakes!"

The seminar ended as a shoe-banging summit meeting. Fromm was standing, shaking a gold pen at Scheer. Mrs. Fromm, a pleasant lady with yellow teeth who was a foot taller than her husband, was at his side, trying to give him a glass of water and a tiny white pill. The art director, a former lifeguard at Southern California beaches, was on his feet, saying that for two cents he'd bust this psychiatrist right in the mouth. Weiss remained crouched in a monkey-see-no-evil position in the corner. The lawyer was whistling without any tune coming from his lips. Mitchell, looking philosophical, puffed on his pipe. Feigen, ignoring the whole show, continued calmly underlining his magazine.

That was the scene where we lost the sauces of Dives for the sores of Lazarus. I remember it very clearly. It is not every day half-a-million dollars goes down the toilet.

"DEPEND UPON IT, SIR, WHEN A MAN KNOWS HE IS TO BE HANGED IN A FORTNIGHT, IT CONCENTRATES HIS MIND WONDERFULLY."
—DR. JOHNSON

Dying, wrote Gossage, is viewed as being in questionable taste by our society despite the fact that ten out of ten still do it.

Gossage was dying when he wrote that. He received his death sentence on Valentine's Day, 1968. He was given six months to live, but stretched it out to a year and a half. In that time he adopted the Caribbean island of Anguilla and helped the natives declare a Quixotic independence, organized a publishing company, launched an environmental organization, developed the theory and structure of a new science for the middle-aged he christened "Mediatrics," agitated to make San Francisco a city-state, wrote a brilliant advertising campaign against the Anti-Ballistic Missile in which he likened the ABM to the fallout shelters of the fifties, planned an academic seminar on the subject of Hell, to be held in Dublin and opened with a Mariachi Mass, coined the phrase "Ear Pollution" for the problem of noise, which he had plans for solving, began compiling a massive "Dictionary of First and Last Lines" of appropriate books and plays, discovered an obscure professor named Leopold Kohr whose recondite wisdoms about the dynamic of bigness in society were such that Gossage handicapped him as the McLuhan of the seventies, worked out a plan to render unnecessary the remaindering and destruction of unsold books, gave dozens of speeches warning advertising men to repent before it was too late for him to save them, got one of his kids out of jail on a marijuana charge, went to Europe several times, arranged for Jessica Mitford to handle his funeral so the undertakers wouldn't dare to gouge, and wrote an essay about dying which he titled, "Tell Me, Doctor, Will I Be Active Right Up to the Last?"

Howard had leukemia, and throughout this fantastic expenditure of energy he needed constant blood transfusions to keep going. He would often call up around 11 of an evening and say, "Come on over to the hospital and talk to me while I'm getting this fucking blood."

The way Gossage went about dying changed many things, including my own relationship with *Ramparts.* When a man like that tells you he has only six months to go and asks you to help him save the world in that time, you don't say you're too busy.

Of the passing examples in this book of the application of the Lemonade Principle—if you are stuck with a lemon, make lemonade—the most extraordinary is the story of how Gossage dealt with the fact of his own imminent death. His only reaction was to make lemonade out of it. It was instantaneous. He didn't even blink when they told him. He jumped out of bed and shook the hand of his doctor, Sandor Burstein, and said, "Congratulations, you son of a gun, you've been taking

care of me for ten years and this is the first time you've been
able to find something wrong with me!"

Besides being Gossage's doctor, Burstein was his friend,
and he and Gerry Feigen together steeled themselves to give
the bad news to their buddy. They had just come from the
laboratory where they looked at Gossage's leukemia profile
under a microscope. It was about as bad as it could be. "It
looked like a mob of people come to a lynching—the entire
field was occupied by those dark-stained cannibal cells," said
Feigen.

"It must be pretty bad if it takes two of you to tell me," the
patient said, before his physician pals could get a word out.
Their faces were guilty with their knowledge. Feigen, when he
is feeling dour or gloomy, has the countenance of a basset
hound and an air about him of the *da-da-da-dum* of
Beethoven's Fifth. Burstein is a Rabbi's son who looks like a
Head Rabbi himself, a handsome devil with an admiral's hat
of curly hair and a big white beard and X-ray blue eyes, who
has a pleasantly disarming fatality about everything except
fatal illnesses. Gossage accused the pair of putting on their
best graveside manners. They told Howard there was a
"gray-zone" hope he might live two to three years. "Oh, you
mean it's fatal—but not serious," he said.

But the best prognosis was that he had six months left.
Gossage reacted to that as if they had given him a license to
shoot ducks out of season. "Who-who-who do you think I
should tell first," he stammered at Feigen. "Boy, will this make
a lot of donkeys toe the line!" Feigen said he didn't think
Howard should tell anyone. "People will treat you differently
if they know," he said. Of course, said Gossage—that would be
the only way he could squeeze something out of the grand-
slam lemon of leukemia; he had made his living making
lemonade out of lemons, and he didn't see why he should
treat dying any differently. "Just think," he said, "now nobody
can tell me, wait till next year."

The sensation of knowing you are going to die is "not
unpleasant and even a little heady," Gossage reported. His
was the rarest breed of one-upmanship, life laughing literally

in death's face, a gut instinct beyond bravery, a final act played with great style but without bravado—he simply refused to accept death's own unimaginative terms, and made of the experience a love song to the innocent merriment of existence.

Howard made great sport of telling his friends, a performance which was part Shinto ceremony, part Miracle Play, part barroom hijinks. "Hey, no shit, I'm really going to die," he would insist, somewhat impatiently, to those who failed or refused to accept his technicolor announcement of his own doom. He told his thirty or so best friends in San Francisco —usually in a Last Supper setting of a private lunch or dinner, sometimes at a command performance high tea with Irish whiskey in his Firehouse office—and then he went to New York to tell some more. Gossage treasured the stories of his friends' reactions. His favorite was John Steinbeck's. Gossage broke the news during a visit to the hospital room where Steinbeck was recovering from one round of a losing fight with a bad heart. Steinbeck looked at Gossage gravely and said, "If you tell your friends you're going to die in six months, you'd better do it or they'll be pissed off at you."

He used his fatal disease as a club to get what he wanted. He organized his advertising agency for a six-month dash to perfection to get his associates in condition for the lonely mile ahead. If someone objected to a particular point of order, Gossage would glower, and say, "You don't have leukemia —who the hell are you!" And then he would laugh, a triumphant, cock-a-hoop laughter that filled the room and seemed to echo from the sky, a laughter that suggested what fools these mortals be, that life was but one good joke and the man laughing alone knew the punch line.

Gossage never completely approved of *Ramparts*. He felt about the magazine the way he did about Sally Stanford—he didn't want to sleep with her but he thought it important that she be around. He always told me that *Ramparts* read like it was edited by the Grimm Brothers; I would agree, New Leftishly challenging him to find something to be un-grim about. He forgave *Ramparts* its saturnine splendor because it was making things happen, and causing trouble, which was dear to his heart; if not always on his terms, it was at least doing it on his turf—in a miniblock of San Francisco between Pacific and Broadway, which contained Gossage's elegant Firehouse and *Ramparts'* tier of discalced offices and a semi-naked girl in a glass cage high above a topless joint—it was an article of faith to Gossage that everything worthwhile that happened in San Francisco during the golden years of the sixties (except the hippies, which he did not find interesting) originated or was propelled by the nucleus of hyperbolic energy in that little block; it is not saying much for the San Francisco of legend to observe that, in his grandiloquent assertion about where the action was, he was largely correct.

In addition to sharing the block, Gossage and I shared some faults of character which I found splendid in him but desultory in me, and he vice versa. Howard loved to make events happen but wasn't much interested in carrying them out thereafter. If a job excited him, he tended to take on all the responsibilities and do everything himself until it was the way he wanted, and then expected his associates thereafter to do it exactly as he had done, and became impatient when they did not. He was restless. He believed in the diversification of effective madness. Beating the Establishment at their own game was his Nicene Creed, and he was beset with a Pauline fervor to see it practiced by the multitude, or at least a greater number of the few among them. This same Pauline sensibility made him tire easily of accomplishments that most people would be satisfied to go on repeating all their lives; he was, accordingly, a loner in his profession and an enigma to his equals, since he was, half-asleep, better than they and more often brilliant at the advertising business, but shared few of their values and none of their career goals. The better he was at the game, the more he wanted to quit and go on to something else—a restless attribute he also claimed to see in me, because I was unaccountably bored with the *succès d'estime* of the magazine and was continually launching newspapers and other costly diversions to take up the slack.

My adventures with Gossage were all endless summers, complete with bottles of Château Peyraguey and baskets of strawberries. That was the Marx Brothers side of *Ramparts,* competing with the grim reaper New Left Marxism, which was the other half of the editorial schizophrenia it was my strange function to keep in balance. Gossage described *Ramparts'* editorial posture as "filling a teacup with a fire hose"; its finances he called a twenty-four-hour crap game that went on year after year. He liked to tease me about getting *Ramparts* organized enough, or just rich enough, so I could get out of the magazine, just the way he was going to get out of his advertising agency, and we could go off to do some creative strip-mining in the Elysian fields.

"You and I have got the same prob-prob-problem," Gossage stammered, delighted at the thought, "both of us are basically unemployable. We always end up hiring our-selves—but the trouble with hiring yourself is finding a way to fire yourself."

Part of Howard's bemusement at his fatal disease was the idea that after all those years of talking about it, he was finally going to get out of advertising. "Leukie"—as he nicknamed his cancer—was going to fire him. When he told me about it, he said "Leukie" was going to fire me, too—"at least for the duration"—if he had his way, and ought not a dying man have his way?

Howard assumed a Popish demeanor and announced a thirty-second sermon. It was about as easy to turn a deaf ear to one of Gossage's sermons as to eight million Chinese stomping their feet in unison atop the Great Wall.

He was brief: He had a lifetime of earth shaking to accom-plish in the next six months and he needed some help. I was drafted. Besides, he said, presciently, *Ramparts* had done everything it was going to do except repeat itself. Howard said that I had burned out the magazine, and probably its welcome—as no one likes a prophet hanging around—by somehow packing the intensity of a decade or two of journalis-tic change and rejuvenation into the space of several years; it was enough already of this turning water into wine. He dipped his fingers into the glass of Paddy's in front of him and sprinkled me with an expansive sign of the cross; "You've been about the Father's business long enough now, Hinckle,

and it's time to stop, or else sure as hell by the time you turn
thirty-three you're going to be crucified. I absolve you of
further obligations to perform miracles. Let those donkeys do
it themselves. You come with me."

I asked Gossage where we were going.

"To Germany," he said.

Three days later on a snowy, slushy dawn I was screeching
southward along the Autobahn from the Frankfurt airport.
Herr Apple was driving. Herr Apple looked like a prison
guard and drove like a meteorite. The tires on the black
Mercedes were smoking as if from the wear of atmospheric
reentry. Herr Apple worked for Senator Herr Franz Burda. I
took Herr Apple's grim haste for an expression of silent
Germanic rebuke that I was two days late for Herr Burda's
sixty-fifth birthday party, to which I had not been invited.

Gossage, who had been there for the festivities, had been on
the transatlantic blower from Baden-Baden the day previous.
The German operator finally tracked me down in Cookie's,
which she pronounced *Kook-vie's*. "You're supposed to be
here!" Gossage screamed over the bad connection. "Old man
Burda wants to see you right away. He wants to talk business.
It has something to do with *Ramparts*."

Burda owned approximately half the printing plants in
Germany. He was to that country's huge graphic arts industry
what Carnegie was to steel in America in the good old robber
baron days. "What's he want with *Ramparts*?" I yelled over the
static of the connection and the pounding and clatter of two
cops playing bull dice at the bar. "Beats the hell out of me,"
Gossage shouted. "Get your ass on a plane tonight and we'll
find out. Bring a tuxedo; everybody's fancy here." Gossage
said he would call again in four hours to make sure I was on
the plane, as he guessed that I was not hot to trot to Germany.

What Herr Apple lacked by way of fancy he made up in
speed and silence. We were halfway along the 100-mile-drive
to Baden-Baden before I dared to ask if we could stop to pee.
He consented without enthusiasm, and without peeing. He
smiled the smile of a *Popular Mechanics* instructor when I
fumblingly failed to find the correct Nazi coins to put in a

monstrous automatic beer dispenser in some super-automated *hofbrau* along the superhighway. His may have been a benign smile, and I may have been short with Herr Apple, who was the first real-life, native-soil German I had met, as I have always been short with his countrymen. I remain unable to consider it as another regretful statistic that they executed six million Jews within my lifetime and for all intents and purposes got away with it. Germany became a nation of collective amnesiacs. The Germans weren't responsible. Somebody else was. Nobody was. It all rings sour, and the hearty German confidence and smugness is no sweetener. It may be because I grew up, mostly Irish, with a German name, and disliking what it stood for, that I feel that way; but until that cold morning I had made my way, when in Europe, around instead of through the Fatherland.

"Herr Hinckle?" Herr Apple spoke up, the first sound that morning inside the newish leather-smelling Mercedes other than the racing groan and wail of the tires, "you are by any chance of the family of our famous Hinkle fighter plane?"

I leaned over and whispered in his ear, "I'm Jewish." The Mercedes accelerated.

 *Epilogue*

ONE BLUSH FOR THE SEVENTIES

> " 'Begin at the beginning,' the King
> said, gravely, 'and go on till you
> come to the end: then stop.' "
> —*Alice's Adventures in Wonderland*

Gossage died on July 9, 1969, which seems a date sufficient as any to hang up on the sixties.

Before he died, enough happened to make another book about eccentric conduct over money. On our trip to Germany Howard and I became strategic chess pieces—pawns, that is—in a feud between Herr Burda and Axel Springer, the Neanderthal Hamburg newspaper baron. Before that intrigue could be resolved, I had to rush back to the United States in response to an S.O.S. from the financially sinking *Ramparts*, but the only person I found who was willing to invest was K.O. Konigsberg, a notorious mobster whom I hit up in the forbidding Federal Medical Center in Springfield, Missouri, where the much-feared K.O. was under heavy lock. I was cheerfully planning a press conference at Wall Street's stuffy Bankers Club to make the shocking disclosure that *Ramparts* had once again beat the devil with a poor box contribution from a noted killer. However, the old ladies of the New Left found such a survival prank too distasteful, and I had to tell K.O. thanks, but no thanks. With disaster imminent, I put on a happy face and announced that things had never been better, and upped the ante by publishing the dying *Ramparts* twice a month.

My relationship with what was left of the New Left declined with my ability to take the wrinkles out of their bellies. Things

came to a hilarious falling-out during the Democratic Convention & Riot in Chicago, where *Ramparts* published a daily
newspaper that it could ill afford. Tom Hayden wanted an
"analytical tabloid," but I made it a giant sheet "wallposter"
instead, and appropriated the front page for news as I saw it,
leaving room for the New Left analysis on the back of the
wallposter, where the glue went.

In February of 1969 *Ramparts* took refuge in the bankruptcy courts, from which a more ideological *Ramparts fils*
emerged, while I plotted with Gossage and my New York
Times buddy Sidney Zion to start a new *Ramparts*, impishly to
be called *Barricades*. To our great surprise, Charles Plohn, a
New York underwriter, bought the proposition. I made Howard the Chairman of the Board, and after he died the
SEC-approved stock prospectus listed the chief executive officer of our public company as "The Late Howard Gossage."

Like a toy soldier running down, I went through the motions of launching a new venture for the seventies, but the
spirit wasn't there, even if the money was. The stock issue for
the new *Barricades,* then *Scanlan's (née Ramparts)* squeaked out
in the bear market of late 1969; the day I got the money from
Charlie Plohn I didn't have enough scratch in my pocket to
pay for a celebratory drink in the bar in the Pan Am Building
and almost had to resort to the old game of asking the bartender if he could make change for the $675,000 check in my
hand.

Scanlan's began publishing in a burst of hyperpromotional
glory early in 1970. It stopped dead in its tracks under cumu-
lous clouds of confusion in 1971. Don Goddard, who was one
of its managing editors, called it "the *ignis fatuus* of liberal
journalism." It was an impossible proposition from the start
without Gossage around to be father goddamn. The chemistry that made my friendship with Zion did not serve to make a
magazine. *Scanlan's* became an East Coast-West Coast tug of
war, with Sidney ensconced in an old ballroom next to a porno
movie on West 44th Street off Times Square, dealing with
police lawyers and informants and revisionist Israeli historians, trying to produce an editorial atmosphere that would
rehabilitate the reputation of his beloved Stern Gang, and

re-create the secular toughness of his hero, Ben Hecht. I battled back from Gossage's old Firehouse in San Francisco, with the likes of Hunter Thompson and Robert Crumb and a painted wagon full of counterculture freaks and left-wing bombers who drove Zion berserk. It was a crosscountry clash of generations between two journalists and friends of roughly the same age and the same generally liberal politics.

During the short-lived *Scanlan's* carnival I became engaged in ridiculous battle with Spiro Agnew over the alleged pirating of a suspect memorandum from his office; was censored in Ireland; upbraided by the Bank of America for instructing love children how to counterfeit its credit cards; sued for one million dollars by the Chief of Police of Los Angeles; threatened by Lufthansa Airlines for an innocent editorial prank which they claimed cost them dearly, and also some other things happened. Finally, the entire press run of *Scanlan's*—an issue about guerrilla warfare in America—was confiscated by the Royal Canadian Mounted Police and left to rot in the snow north of the Canadian border, an absurd if outrageous act which the Montreal newspapers reported had been done at Washington's behest, but some of my critics said admiringly I had arranged for the publicity. That issue of *Scanlan's* never reached the readers, and there was never another one. The seizure was financial as well as political, and corporate guerrilla warfare ensued within the *Scanlan's* organization, Sidney and I ambushing one another in horrendous board-room-type showdowns, he wanting to sell the valuable carcass of the magazine to some other company and walk away from the wreckage with something approaching dignity, I plotting to keep the magazine going at any cost. In the end, we both lost. I went off to write a book about guerrilla war in the United States which was, suitably, published only in Germany. Zion went on to perform the journalistically enigmatic act of fingering Daniel Ellsberg as the man who gave the Pentagon Papers to the New York *Times*.

But all that is another story, and of another decade, which I may, or may not, get around to putting down someday. It is too early to tell about the seventies.

Index

Abels, Cyrilly, 313-14, 316, 328
Agnew, Spiro, 132, 163, 363
Ally, Carl, 127
Alpert, Richard, 140
Ansara, Mike, 177
Antoninus, Brother, 46
Apple, Herr, 359-60
Arguedas Mendieta, Antonio, 279
Arnold, Marty, 194, 195
Artzybasheff, 131
Ascoli, Max, 121
Aubry, Leon, 69, 69, 70, 71-73
Austin, Jan, 177
Avakian, Robert, 177
Aymé, Marcel, 217

Barrientos, René Ortuño, 272, 279, 286
Barrymore, John, 211
Beardsley, Aubrey, 46
Behn, Noel, 236
Belli, Melvin, 200
Benavides, Edward, 224
Ben Barka, Mehdi, 261
Ben Bella, Ahmed, 228
Bennett, John C., 63
Bensky, Larry, 258-60, 264, 267
Berrigan, Daniel, xiv, 45
Berrigan, Philip, 45
Bess, Donovan, 189
Bigart, Homer, 161
Black, Shirley Temple, 37, 123, 184
Bogart, Humphrey, 201
Boorstin, Daniel, 126
Bosch, Hieronymus, 131
Boswell, James, 104, 126
Bowen, Robert O., 41, 43, 49, 50
Boxley, Bill, 234
Boyd, Bud, 23-24
Bozell, L. Brent, 79
Brackman, Jacob, 227
Brammer, Bill, 220

Brown, Barbara, 98, 185
Brown, Helen Gurley, 227
Bruce, Lenny, 39
Brzezinski, Zbigniew, 351
Bucklcy, William, 292-93
Burda, Franz, 359, 361
Burdick, Eugene "Bud," 165
Burnstein, Mal, 192
Burstein, Sandor, 354-55

Caen, Herb, 106, 188
Cagney, James, 298
Capp, Al, 310
Carlton, Dean, 230
Carnegie, Andrew, 68
Carnegie, Dale, 286
Carroll, Lewis, 135, 351
Cassady, Neal, 142, 143
Castro, Fidel, 84, 237, 271, 273, 274-75,
    278, 284, 285, 293, 297-98, 299, 300,
    302-3, 306-7, 309-10, 312-13, 314,
    319, 320, 324
Celler, Emmanuel, 152
Chain, Steve, 177
Chambers, Whittaker, 9
Chaplin, Charlie, 10
Chermi, Rose, 221-22
Chesterton, G. K., 46
Chrisney, Judson, 96, 109, 110
Churchill, Winston, 261
Clancy, John, 328
Clark, Ramsey, 241
Cleaver, Eldridge, 25-26, 81, 100, 115,
    313
Clifford, Jim, 6-7
Cohan, George M., 119
Cohen, Arthur, 95
Cohen, H. Indian, 177
Cohn, Roy, 254, 262
Colaianni, Jim, 38, 101, 187
Collier. Peter. 156

Condon, Gene Ann, 82
Connally, John, 205, 206, 229
Conniff, Frank, 55
Conrad, Barnaby, 108-9
Contino, Dick, 97
Cook, A. G., 23
Cortez, Julia, 288-89
Corvo, Frederick B., 46
Cosby, Bill, 164
Cowles, Gardiner, 54
Crane, Hart, 36
Crawford, Joan, 337
Cronkite, Walter, 220, 226
Crowley, Walter, 28
Crumb, Robert, 250, 363
Culkin, John, 129

D'Angolo, Hymie, 143
Daniel, Clifton, 194
Davalos, Gerry, 5
Davis, Ronnie, 142
Day, Doris, xii, 16, 44
Dayan, Moshe, 182
Debray, Jules Régis, 271-75, 286, 299, 322
De Gaulle, Charles, 105, 257, 267
Degnan, June, 195
De Onis, Juan, 282
Del Valle, Eladio, 238, 239
DePugh, Robert, 231, 232-35
Diem, Ngo Dinh, 146, 147-48, 151, 152-53, 154, 166, 168, 170
Dillinger, John, 283
Donovan, William, 151, 152
Dooley, Tom, 147, 153
Dougery, Ed, 28
Draper, George, 22
Dreiser, Theodore, 311
Du Bay, William, 73-78
Ducret, André, 257
Duke, Angier Biddle, 152, 153
Duncan, Donald W., 154-57, 159-60
Duvalier, François, 247-48
Dylan, Bob, 101
Dystel, Oscar, 315-16, 320, 328, 331

East, P. D., 86
Ehrlich, Jake, 17
Ehrlich, Reese, 177
Eisenhower, Dwight David, 146, 147, 153
Eliot, T. S., 45
Ellsberg, Daniel, 363
Epstein, Edward J., 211-12
Erikson, George, 29-30

Falk, John Henry, 86
Feeley, Raymond T., S.J., 9
Feigen, Gerry, 105-7, 109, 121, 124, 128, 180, 186, 338, 348, 349, 351, 355
Ferlinghetti, Lawrence, 142, 143
Ferrie, David, 237-38
Field, Maggie, 213
Firbank, Ronald, 46, 175
Fischer, Carl, 305
Fishel, Wesley, 165-66, 167, 170
Flynn, Errol, 352
Ford, Ford Madox, 45
Fowler, Gene, 211
Freberg, Stan, 127
Freire, Paulo, 345
Freud, Sigmund, 26, 349
Fromm, Erich, 341-53
Fromm, Mrs. Erich, 353
Fulbright, J. William, 232
Fuller, Buckminster, 105

Galbraith, John Kenneth, 300
Gálvez, the Great, 301-4, 305-8, 312-13, 318, 319, 323, 324, 326
Gam, Rita, 41
Gambella, George, 110-11
Gandhi, Mohandos K., xiv
Garmise, Bert, 158
Garrison, Jim, 197-204, 212, 213, 234, 235, 238, 241-45, 249, 252, 253, 254, 257
Gaynor, Mitzi, 155
Geismar, Anne, 80, 81
Geismar, Max, 64, 79-80, 81
Gibbons, Archbishop James, 53
Ginsberg, Allen, 20, 139, 142, 143, 145
Gleason, Ralph, 101, 144, 188, 189, 190
Godard, Jean-Luc, 340
Goddard, Don, 362
Gogol, Nikolai, 11
Gold, Mike, 225
Goldberg, Arthur, 333
Goldstein, David, 177
Goldwater, Barry, xii, 97, 171
Goldwyn, Sam, 199
Gonzales, Eduardo, 288
Gordon, Ruth, 213
Gossage, Howard, xv, 15, 105, 106-9, 123-38, 157, 158, 181, 188, 195, 269, 338, 353-63
Graham, Billy, 234
Greenburg, Dan, 197
Greenstreet, Sidney, 276
Gregory, Dick, 87

Griffin, John Howard, 64, 81, 84-87, 217-18, 219
Grogan, Emmet, 145
Gromyko, Andrei, 265
Guevara, Ernesto "Che," 269-301, 303 ff.
Guevara, Mrs. Ernesto "Che," 299, 312, 315, 324, 325

Halberstam, David, 162-63
Halliburton, Richard, 180
Hamilton, George, 228 Hand, Learned, 84
Harris, Jones, 213
Harris, Phil, 53
Harris, Richard, 163
Hawkes, Monsignor, 75
Hawley, Cameron, 93
Hayden, Tom, xii, 308, 362
Hearst, William Randolph, 19
Hecht, Ben, 60, 363
Hefner, Hugh, 113-14, 185
Hegel, G.W.F., 160
Hemingway, Ernest, 300
Hepburn, James, 252, 253, 256, 262-63
Heschel, Abraham, 64
Heywood, John, 27
Higgins, Marguerite, 275
"Hill," 247-51, 266, 268, 293-94
Hinckle, Denise, 122
Hinckle, Marianne (Vampira), 37, 228
Hitler, Adolf, 54-55, 56, 58
Hochhuth, Rolf, 53, 54, 55-57, 59, 63, 67
Ho Chi Minh, 97, 151, 152
Hoffa, Jimmy, 263
Honig, Bill, 121, 123, 183, 195
Hoover, Herbert, 163
Hoover, J. Edgar, 9, 97, 206, 207, 231, 240
Hopkins, Gerard Manley, 46
Hoppe, Art, 22
Howard, Tom, 223
Hughes, Sarah T., 230
Humphrey, Hubert, 170
Hunt, H. L., 263
Hunter, Bill, 223
Hutchins, Robert, 120
Huxley, Aldous, 228

Illich, Ivan, 343
Ippolito, Joe, 110-11, 113, 114, 122
Irving, Clifford, 304

Jacobs, Paul, 100, 188, 189, 190
Jaffe, Marc, 320, 330, 331

Jaffee, Steve, 255-58, 266
James, Henry, 80
Jaspers, Karl, 183
John XXIII, 39, 108
Johnson, Lyndon Baines, xii-xiv, 115, 149, 171, 182, 206, 215, 220-21, 230, 241
Johnson, Samuel, 104, 353
Jones, Leroi, 126
Jones, Penn, Jr., 217-19, 221-23, 224, 226
Joyce, James, 2, 45
Justinian, 8

Kaiser, Robert Blair, 75
Kaldenbach, Robert, 182
Kaplan, J. M., 176-77
Kaplan, Joel David, 177
Keating, Edward, 35-38, 39, 40, 41-44, 47-50, 54, 56, 63, 64-65, 66-68, 79, 87, 89-101, 103, 107, 109, 110, 111, 118, 123-24, 147, 181, 184-87, 189-93, 194, 195, 198
Keating, Helen, 40, 187
Keep, Peter, 99
Kelly, Edna, 152
Kennedy, Alfred, 41
Kennedy, John F., xiii, xv, 14, 55, 149, 152, 198, 199, 203-4, 210 ff., 233 ff., 255 ff., 265, 267
Kennedy, Joseph, 60
Kennedy, Lawton, 41-43
Kennedy, Robert F., 150, 204, 207, 263, 264, 265
Kerouac, Jack, 142, 143
Kerr, Clark, 165, 178
Kesey, Ken, 142-43
Khrushchev, Nikita, 105
Kierkegaard, Soren, 160
Kilgallen, Dorothy, 224, 226
Killam, Hank, 224
King, Martin Luther, 182, 204
Kipling, Rudyard, 153
Kissinger, Henry, 148
Klein, Herb, 140
Koethe, Jim, 223
Kohr, Leopold, 354
Kolodney, David, 177
Konigsberg, K. O., 361

Laing, R. D., 344
Lamantia, Phil, 142, 143
Lane, Mark, 209-10, 212, 213, 215
Latham, Carl, 32
Laucks, Irving, 120-21, 123

Leary, Timothy, 138-43
Le Carré, John, 236
Lee, J. Bracken, 152
Lenin, V. I., 9
Lerner, Max, 152
Levine, Faye, 227
Levinson, Sandy, 112, 113
Lewis, Wyndham, 45-46
Lewy, Guenther, 55
Libarle, Mark, 177
Lichten, Dr., 57
Liebling, A. J., 126-27
Lifton, David, 214, 227
Lind, Jakov, 81
Lindsay, John, 239
Lippman, Walter, 172
Lipset, Hal, 99
Locker, Michael, 177
London, Jack, 27, 91
Louis XV, 8
Lowell, Robert, 46
Lowenstein, Al, 209
Lowry, Malcolm, 343
Luce, Henry, 340
Lumumba, Patrice, 271
Luther, Martin, 38
Lynn, Conrad, 81-84

Macoby, Michael, 347-48, 350
Maggard, Jane, 20
Manchester, William, 333
Mann, Thomas, 60
Mansfield, Mike, 151
Manson, Charles, 294
Marchman, Hank, 186, 187
Marco, Count, 21, 22
Marcus, Stanley, 220, 232
Martin, Shirley Harris, 212-13
Marx, Groucho, 254
Marx, Karl, 343, 349
Masferrer, Rolando, 278
Mattei, Enrico, 261
Maxwell, Elsa, 12
McCabe, Charles, 42-43
McCabe, Joseph, xi, 5
McCarthy, Michael, 142
McCone, John, 253, 254
McIntyre, James Francis, Cardinal, 69-70, 72-77, 78
McKean, William A., 155
McLuhan, Marshall, 107, 128-29, 270, 354
McNamara, Robert, 155
McPherson, Aimee Semple, 139
Meagher, Sylvia, 214, 229

Mellinkoff, Abe, 21, 32, 190
Mencken, H. L., 58
Mercer, Julia Ann, 221
Mercouri, Melina, 168
Meredith, Burgess, 219
Merrill, Charles, 177
Merton, Thomas, xiv
"Michel," 256-60, 261-64, 265-66, 267, 268
Miller, Henry, 40
Mindszenty, Jozsef, Cardinal, 5
Mitchell, Frederick, 121-23, 342, 353
Mitchell, John, 243
Mitford, Jessica, 104, 185, 188-93, 194, 208, 354
Monroe, Marilyn, 217, 228
Montgomery, Ed, 23-26
Mooney, Nancy Jane, 223
Moore, Francis A., S. J., 10-11, 12, 13-14, 16
Mosk, Stanley, 23
Moynihan, Daniel P., 254-55, 263, 264
Mundelein, George Cardinal, 70
Murray, Justin, 97
Murrow, Edward R., 344
Mursl, Shig, 159

Nelson, Truman, 81
Neuberger, Richard, 152
Newhall, Scott, 21-24, 31
Newson, Brennan, 11
Newton, Huey, 24
Nhu, Madame, 162, 166
Nietzsche, Frederick, 194
Nixon, Richard, 14, 140, 148, 149, 161, 162, 245
Nolte, Carl, 13
Nunes, Brother, 7

O'Connor, Frank, 145
O'Connor, John, 38-39
O'Daniel, Michael, 152
O'Donnell, Kenny, 254
Onassis, Jacqueline Kennedy, 252, 333
O'Neill, Dan, 7
Oram, Harold, 152
Orwell, Sonia, 104
Orwell, George, 47
Oswald, Lee Harvey, 199, 202, 205, 209, 210, 212, 213, 218, 233, 235, 238, 250, 257
Oswald, Mrs. Lee Harvey, 215
Ovando Candaná, Alfredo, 281, 282, 286, 290

Passman, Arnold, 101
Patman, Wright, 175-76
Patton, George, 14
Paul VI, 74, 108
Pauvert, Jean Jacques, 280, 281
Pearson, Drew, 79, 147
Pegler, Westbrook, Sr., 22
Peretz, Marty, 337
Perez, Leander, 90
Petrie, Bernard, 341-42
"Phillipe," 258
Picetti, Cookie, 25, 209
Piel, Eleanor Jackson, 173
Piel, Jerry, 118
Pius XII, 54-55, 56-57
Plohn, Charles, 362
Pompadour, Madame de, 8
Popp, Bob, 27
Porter, Katherine Anne, 313
Powell, Adam Clayton, 83
Powys, John Cowper, 311
Pynchon, Thomas, 245

Ramont, Henry, 323-25
Rand, Ayn, 202
Raskin, Marcus, 173
Ray, Ellen, 214
Ray, Michele, 275-82, 285, 286-89,
    291-92, 298
Reagan, Ronald, 284
Reich, Wilhelm, 349
Reston, James, 162
Rexroth, Kenneth, 142
Reynolds, Malvina, 33
Reynolds, Ruth, 81
Ridgeway, Jim, 183
Roberts, Earlene, 221
Rockwell, George Lincoln, 56, 58, 231
Roosevelt, Eleanor, 57
Roosevelt, Franklin D., 60
Roosevelt, Kermit, 254
Roquemore, Dallas, 234
Rosset, Barney, 299, 322, 326, 328
Rothenberg, Don, 187, 190, 191-92
Rougemont, Denis de, 110
Rubin, Sam, 115
Ruby, Jack, 200, 209, 218, 220, 221-22,
    224
Russell, Bertrand, 161, 211, 274
Russell, Dick, 184-86, 191, 337

Sahl, Mort, 43
St. George, Andrew, 277-79, 282, 299,
    304, 315
Sairanen, Augy, 27-28

Salandria, Vincent, 213
Salinger, J. D., 40-41, 43, 46
Samstag, Nick, 127
Sanders, Ed, 223
Sartre, Jean Paul, 211
Saussy, Tupper, 256
Savonarola, Girolamo, 2
Schanche, Don, 282
Schechter, Dan, 177
Scheer, Anne, 101, 103
Scheer, Robert, 25, 101-3, 108, 111-12,
    113-14, 147, 156, 169, 178, 179, 184,
    185, 186-87, 188, 189, 190-91, 195,
    215, 228, 275, 277, 292, 296-98, 300,
    302, 304, 306, 309, 318, 319, 321, 323,
    334, 341, 342, 345, 347, 348, 350,
    351-53
Schiller, Roger, 288-89
Schlesinger, Arthur, Jr., 152, 173
Schoenman, Ralph, 210-12
Schopenhauer, Arthur, 62
Schwartz, Ed, 177
Shaw, Clay, 242, 243
Sheehan, Neil, 210
Sheinbaum, Stanley, 167-69, 218
Shorris, Earl, 124, 300
Shumlin, Herman, 58-60, 61, 62, 63, 67
Silverstein, Shel, 113
Siqueiros, David, 343
Sitton, Claude, 194
Smith, Paul, 19
Snelling, Walter, 199
Snyder, Gary, 142, 143, 145
Sorensen, Ted, 327, 333-35
Spectorsky, A. C., 113
Spellman, Francis Cardinal, 56, 65,
    145-49, 153
Spinelli, Henry, 21
Spitzer, John, 177
Springer, Axel, 256, 258, 361
Stalin, Joseph, 9
Stassen, Harold, 165
Stein, Jean, 150
Stein, Jules, 150
Stein, Sol, 320-22, 325, 327, 329, 330
Steinbeck, John, 356
Stermer, Dougald, 107-8, 124, 158, 184,
    225, 292, 304, 318, 329, 342, 348
Stern, George, 362
Stern, Sol, 169-70, 178, 304
Stetler, Russell, 274
Stevenson, Adlai, 67, 228, 265
Stiehl, Harry, 36, 44, 46, 99
Stilson, Bruce, 230
Stimson, Henry, 163-64, 165

Stock, Maureen, 157
Stone, I. F., 54
Stone, Judy, 54, 55
Stone, Marc, 158, 183-84, 317, 331, 332-33, 334-35
Stringfellow, William, 95
Sulzberger, C. L., 274
Swift, Lou, 159

Tate, Allen, 46
Taylor, Frank, 304, 315-16, 320
Temkin, Victor, 328-29, 330, 331, 333
Teran, Jaime, 291
Teran, Reque, 286
Theriot, Charles de Young, 20
Thomas, Norman, 152
Thomas, Terry, 106
Thompson, Hunter, 363
Timan, Leslie, 100, 318
Tippit, Jefferson Davis, 221, 223, 224
Tomlinson, Darrell, 229-30
Torrico, Jorge, 289
Toynbee, Arnold, 185, 186
Tracy, Spencer, 119
Treuhaft, Bob, 185, 193, 208
Truman, Harry, 300
Turner, Bill, 199, 206-8, 218, 231, 234, 235, 245-46, 247, 266, 267
Turner, Wally, 194
Twain, Mark, 68
Twiggy, 43

Urgatche, Admiral, 290
Urusov, 9

Vanden Heuvel, William, 150-52

Wagner, Robert, 57, 153
Walker, Edwin A., 49, 220, 223
Warner, Betty, 168
Warren, Earl, 208
Wayne, John, 4
Webb, Lee, 177
Weills, Anne. *See* Scheer, Anne
Weills, Kit, 177
Weills, Tuck, 177
Weisberg, Harold, 214
Weiss, Cora, 115
Weiss, Stanley, 337-42, 343-45, 346-53
Welk, Lawrence, 136
Welles, Orson, 228
Welsh, David, 218, 224, 226
Wenner, Jan, 144
Westmoreland, William, 155
Whalen, Philip, 142
Whaley, William, 224
White, William Allen, 220
Wicker, Tom, 176
Wilde, Oscar, 46
Williams, Edward Bennett, 207, 305
Williams, Robert F., 81
Williams, Tennessee, 40, 46
Wills, Gary, 165
Wolfe, Tom, 106
Wood, Michael, 172-73, 175
Woolley, Monty, 28

Zahn, Gordon, 64
Zapruder, Abraham, 206, 266-67
Zenteno, Joaquin, 286-87
Zinn, Howard, 317
Zinn, Jerry, 317
Zion, Sidney, 242-43, 362, 363